THE
SUCCESSOR

THE
SUCCESSOR

THE HIGH-STAKES LIFE OF LACHLAN MURDOCH

PADDY MANNING

SUTHERLAND HOUSE

TORONTO, 2022

Sutherland House
416 Moore Ave., Suite 205
Toronto, ON M4G 1C9

Sutherland House and logo are registered
trademarks of The Sutherland House Inc.

First edition, November 2022

If you are interested in inviting one of our authors to a live event or
media appearance, please contact sranasinghe@sutherlandhousebooks.com
and visit our website at sutherlandhousebooks.com for more
information about our authors and their schedules.

We acknowledge the support of the Government of Canada.

Manufactured in United States of America
Front cover designed by Tristan Main
Back cover and spine designed by Lena Yang
Cover photograph © Mike Cohen
Book composed by Karl Hunt

Library and Archives Canada Cataloguing in Publication
Title: The successor : the high-stakes life of Lachlan Murdoch / Paddy Manning.
Names: Manning, Paddy, author.
Identifiers: Canadiana 20220391580 | ISBN 9781989555996 (softcover)
Subjects: LCSH: Murdoch, Lachlan, 1971- | LCSH: Businesspeople—Australia—
Biography. | LCSH: Businesspeople—United States—Biography. |
LCSH: Mass media—Australia—Biography. | LCSH: Mass media—
United States—Biography. | LCSH: Publishers and publishing—
Australia—Biography. | LCSH: Publishers and publishing—
United States—Biography. | LCGFT: Biographies.
Classification: LCC P92.5.M875 M36 2022 | DDC 070.92—dc23

ISBN 978-1-989555-99-6

Contents

Prologue

Istros

I
T HAD A BEEN A remarkably chilly start to winter and there was a stiff breeze on Sydney Harbour when Lachlan Murdoch and his wife, Sarah, took a few friends out for a spin in their new $30-million motor yacht, *Istros*—a present for her fiftieth birthday. On a Wednesday afternoon in early June, when most of America was fast asleep, Lachlan could afford to take time off from his day job overseeing Fox Corporation, parent of the world's most controversial cable television outfit, Fox News. Paparazzo Jayden Seyfarth watched through his long lens as Lachlan and Sarah helped their rugged-up guests aboard, settled in for drinks, and took in the sunset.

At 43 meters long, *Istros* was modest by today's standards, when megayachts and gigayachts two or three times the size may cost upwards of half a billion dollars. Oozing old-world charm, the ship was built in Holland in 1954 and originally owned by Greek shipping tycoons the Pappadakis family. In 2001, it won the grand prize for the best restored vessel at Monaco's Classic Yacht Show but then fell into disrepair, sitting idle in Malta until it was bought for a song, gutted, and completely refitted by van Geest Design, Dutch builders of super yachts for moguls, oligarchs, and kleptocrats the world over. Lachlan had bought the *Istros* in February 2022 and had it delivered down under, where it would entertain family and friends, a few lucky contacts from business and politics, and faithful toilers from across the Murdoch media empire, which had been founded in Australia by his grandfather, Sir Keith, and turned into the first global news conglomerate by his swashbuckling father, Rupert.

Nowhere did the Murdoch's wield such concentrated power as in Australia, where the family had controlled two-thirds of newspaper circulation for nearly four decades and had an outright monopoly over pay-TV. Lachlan was a third-generation media mogul, living it up in his adoptive hometown—his older sister Prue had good reason to call him the "king of Sydney." *Istros* took months to arrive, and on Lachlan and Sarah's first outing the *Daily Mail* reported the couple looked as "happy as ever." The next week, they took their teenage daughter Aerin and her friends around the harbor to see the Vivid festival, when Sydney's world-famous Opera House, Harbour Bridge, and Circular Quay were bathed in illuminated works by visual artists from all over the globe. Papped by Seyfarth again, Lachlan stood by the gunnels of *Istros* and directly faced the cameraman, throwing his arms out wide as though surprised or annoyed at the attention. After spending his entire adult life in the spotlight, the man who probably employed as many journalists as anyone else in the world still bristled when he was the subject of their inquiries.

Beautiful as *Istros* might be, she was only a stop-gap runabout: Lachlan was awaiting delivery of the boat of his dreams, a 60-meter, $175 million, ultra-modern sloop under construction at another Dutch shipyard, Royal Huisman. The largest carbon-fibre yacht ever built in Holland, Murdoch's new purchase was known only by the codename "MM597" and would accommodate twelve guests and ten crew. According to the manufacturer's website, distinguishing features included "a huge transom opening which . . . will give access to an expansive, lavish beach club." Lachlan and Sarah had paid a stunning $37 million for a boatshed and jetty at Point Piper, a few minutes' drive from their $100 million Bellevue Hill mansion, Le Manoir. In the meantime, *Istros* would have to do.

While the Murdochs were relaxing on Sydney Harbour that Wednesday evening, it seemed America was going to hell. The following night, US time, in a throwback to the Watergate era, the House Select Committee investigating the attack on the Capitol on January 6, 2021 would conduct its first televised hearings, revealing damning new evidence of an unprecedented attempt by a sitting president, Donald Trump, to stop the peaceful transfer of power after the 2020 election. Fox News Channel had announced earlier that week that it would not carry the hearing live at primetime, unlike every other network in America, opting instead to broadcast commentary on the hearing, even as it was underway, from its anchors Tucker Carlson, Sean Hannity and Laura Ingraham. Fox went so far as to make this programming ad-free to avoid shedding audience to other channels during commercials. Millions of Fox viewers watching that evening would not have seen the opening statements of Democratic committee chair Bennie Thompson and Republican deputy chair Liz Cheney, the testimony of former attorney general Bill Barr and Ivanka Trump, the fresh video footage of the Proud Boys and Oathkeepers who led the attack, or the evidence of Capitol police officer Caroline Edwards who was knocked unconscious and pepper-sprayed. Instead, they heard Carlson, Hannity, and Ingraham undermine the committee and downplay the hearings. Carlson had previously called the committee "wholly illegitimate" and now told his viewers, "They're lying, and we're not going to help them do it."

As CEO of Fox, Lachlan had undoubtedly okayed the extraordinary decision, which once again called into question whether Fox was in the business of news or propaganda. Watching Fox's coverage that night, it was hard to imagine how Americans would ever bridge the deepening divides over guns, abortion, the pandemic response, immigration, climate change, Black Lives Matter, gender and sexuality—and even over whether or not these disagreements could be resolved through democracy and the rule of law rather than through violence and authoritarianism. If Americans could not even agree that Trump had lost the 2020 election, much less that he had then mounted an unprecedented and dangerous attempt to overturn the result, what could they possibly agree on? Fox News thrived on controversy and of its primetime anchors none was more controversial than Carlson, one of Lachlan's personal favorites and the highest-rated host in the history of cable television. Carlson had proved many times that he could make or break the careers of conservative politicians. His program, *Tucker Carlson Tonight*, had been described as "the most racist show in the history of cable news."[1]

As Bloomberg journalist Tim O'Brien told MSNBC anchor Nicole Wallace, it was important not to focus too much on the Fox anchors, who were ultimately just the hired help: "You're leaving the most important actor out: Lachlan Murdoch. Rupert Murdoch's son runs that network. The family controls the company. If they wanted that network to do something other than engage in propaganda and to delude people and to serve other goals, he could put anybody he wants in that anchor seat. Tucker Carlson exists because Lachlan Murdoch wants him to exist."[2]

Reports indicated the House committee believed it had enough evidence to indict Trump for sedition. His former campaign strategist Steve Bannon warned on his infamous *War Room* podcast: "We Dare You." As a "red wave" of Republican victories loomed in November's midterm elections—bigger than 1994 or even 2010, former House speaker Newt Gingrich told Laura Ingraham on Fox—Trump Republicans vowed to impeach Joe Biden over the alleged chaos at the Mexican border, the disastrous withdrawal from Afghanistan, or the influence-peddling of the President's son, Hunter. Credible voices feared America, lurching from crisis to crisis, was spiralling into civil war.

Lachlan knew things were not getting better in America any time soon. Raised in the US from the age of three, Lachlan felt like an Australian and had divided his adult life between the two countries. Both his parents had grown up in Australia, and Australia was where he met Sarah, and founded his own successful private investment firm after falling out with his father and turning his back on a career at News Corp in 2005. In 2015, he had returned to the family business at Rupert's express request, but after six years in Los Angeles, as the coronavirus ravaged America, Lachlan and Sarah decided they'd had enough and moved back to Sydney with their three kids . . . perhaps for good. Lachlan might not say so publicly, but in his bones he believed Australians had a better way of life. Although Tucker reckoned Australia had turned into a "COVID dictatorship," the country had come through the pandemic with a death rate one tenth that of the United States and a vaccination rate of 95 per cent. Schools were safe from gun violence. The politics of hate and polarization had not yet split the lucky country down the middle.

Curiously, those things that made Australia a cocoon for Lachlan and Sarah, and a better place to raise their family, like tougher public health restrictions and gun control, were the very things that Fox News railed against in America, on a nightly basis. Running Fox from Australia suggested a fundamental disconnect: he was hardly practicing what his network's primetime anchors preached. At work, Lachlan was a ruthless five-star general in the culture wars, overseeing the Fox News juggernaut, pumping "America First," and driving earnings growth in the family business—what Senator Elizabeth Warren famously called a "hate-for-profit racket." At home, or on one of his many fabulous holidays, Lachlan was a laid-back Australian and all-round smooth operator: spectacularly rich, impeccably mannered, handsome, open-minded, adventurous, savvy, fun.

* * *

Lachlan's move to Sydney also spoke of a fundamental ambivalence: he had never wanted to be CEO of the family business, or, if it came down to it, the CEO of anything. As the oldest son, he was the presumptive "first among equals" of his siblings and had always aspired to be chairman, like his father—preferably non-executive, that ultimate position of power without day-to-day responsibility. Never your eighty-hours-a-week, chained-to-the-desk kind of manager, Lachlan was happiest in the elements, mountain climbing or sailing. Now, having racked up three years' service as CEO of Fox Corp, and with Rupert at ninety-one taking a back seat, Lachlan could look forward to ascending to the role of non-executive chairman and owner of a controlling stake in the most powerful news business in the world.

What could go wrong? After years of jockeying over the succession his brother, James, and sister, Liz, were out of contention—it seemed for good. If Tucker or any other host got too controversial, they could always be fired or redeployed – it was an iron law of the Murdoch empire that none of the talent was indispensable. If Fox or News shares slid, the family business could always be taken private or sold. Whatever happened to either company, the bulk of his fortune lay elsewhere: he owned a ton of Disney shares; his investment firm, Illyria, had made him a billionaire in his own right; there were mega-mansions in LA and Sydney, and more bikes, cars, and yachts than he knew what to do with.

As *Istros* lumbered around a blustery harbor, Lachlan knew it was only a matter of time before the succession was behind him and he could do as he liked.

PART 1

Lachie

1

A Son Is Born

L ONDON, 1971. The centuries-old newspaper industry was in
crisis. Reporters and copy editors had imposed rolling strikes
in response to a new minimum pay deal struck by the national
journalists' union, and a shutdown loomed. The cost of newsprint and
wages was spiralling and circulation and advertizing were falling. The
venerable *Times* was losing a million pounds a year and the *Daily Mail*
twice that.

While the lords of the British press—Thomson, Beaverbrook, Rothermere
—racked up losses on their flagging mastheads, there was a bright spot.
A brash new contender from down under, Rupert Murdoch, had taken
over both the *News of the World*, the highest-selling English-language
newspaper in the world, and *The Sun*. Alone among the national dailies,
The Sun was enjoying a spectacular rise in sales. Murdoch turned the staid
broadsheet into a raucous tabloid full of nudes and sports news. Newly
arrived in England with his young Australian family in tow, he pushed into
television and reported surging profits as *The Sun*'s circulation jumped to
two million copies a day, forcing the other tabloids to play catch-up.

On September 8, a crisp Wednesday in autumn, Murdoch had another
reason to be proud: his wife, Anna, gave birth to their second child,
Lachlan Keith Murdoch, at the Merton hospital in Wimbledon. A decade
younger than Rupert, Anna was born in Scotland but emigrated with her

family to Sydney, where she endured a tough childhood, looking after her siblings after their father's business went broke and their mother left home. Anna had met Rupert while she was a cadet reporter on one of his tabloid newspapers and they married in 1967. The couple's daughter, Elisabeth, named after Rupert's mother, was born in Sydney in 1968. They were also raising Prudence, Rupert's daughter from his first marriage, who had just turned thirteen. Lachlan's younger brother, James, would be born fifteen months after him. Lachlan's middle name was a nod to Rupert's father, the late Sir Keith, a pioneering journalist who had towered over Australian politics for decades as editor of the powerful Melbourne *Herald* and as chairman of the Herald and Weekly Times, where he forged the country's first national media chain.

Keith was not rich, however, and when he died of a heart attack in 1952 at the age of sixty-seven, all that was left for Rupert was control of a company, News Ltd., which held stakes in two small newspapers in Adelaide, the *News* and the *Sunday Mail*. From that modest base, Rupert expanded into Perth, then Sydney, then New Zealand and now the UK. As the first son, Lachlan shouldered the weight of Rupert's expectations that the Murdoch dynasty would carry on into a third generation of newspapermen.

* * *

Although Rupert boasted that News' business was making "good progress," there was trouble on the home front. A pall was cast over the Murdoch family's life in London after a terrifying attempt to kidnap Anna went tragically wrong. On December 29, 1969, two brothers from Trinidad, Arthur and Nizamodeen Hosein, sons of a Muslim cleric, abducted Muriel McKay, the wife of Rupert's second-in-charge in London, Alick. Alick had been using the Murdochs' Rolls-Royce while Rupert was in Australia and the Hosein brothers followed the car to the Murdoch home in Wimbledon. Breaking in one afternoon, they kidnapped Muriel, believing she was Anna, and demanded a million-pound ransom. The saga dragged on for weeks— the *News of the World* covered it in detail—until undercover police found and arrested the Hosein brothers. Muriel's body was never found, and the men were convicted of murder. Even fifty years later, Anna was loath to discuss the kidnapping, telling *Forbes* magazine it was a "really, really terrible time."[1] The episode put Anna off London; the feeling got worse after another tragedy, when she knocked down and killed an old woman while driving. Anna wanted to move the whole family to America, later admitting she "couldn't wait to leave." Lachlan would hardly remember his early childhood in Britain and would joke as an adult he was embarrassed to have been born there, although he retained his UK citizenship.

The family's opportunity to move came in 1973, when Rupert bought his first American newspaper, the *San Antonio Express*, in the fast-growing sunbelt state of Texas. Applying the proven Murdoch formula, he juiced up the morning broadsheet; one edition carried the famous headline "KILLER BEES MOVE NORTH." The following year, the family moved to Manhattan when Rupert launched the *National Star*, a tabloid rival to the *National Enquirer*. His private meetings with Dolly Schiff, the ageing proprietor of the *New York Post*, culminated in him buying the paper in 1976. He followed up with controversial acquisitions of *New York Magazine* and *The Village Voice* in quick succession.

In 1977, *Time* magazine put Rupert on the cover, with his head on the body of King Kong above the strapline: "EXTRA!!! AUSSIE PRESS LORD TERRIFIES GOTHAM." Lachlan, then five years old, later recalled seeing his father "on top of the World Trade Center with little planes trying to shoot him down"; he would come to realize that no one else's dad was publicly portrayed as such a monster.[2]

The Murdoch children lived an enchanted life, spread across luxury apartments in New York and London, mansions in Los Angeles and Sydney, a ranch in northern California, a ski lodge at Aspen with a pool in the living room, and the historic Cavan cattle station near Canberra. For Liz, Lachlan, and James, their home base for most of their childhood was a fabulous 1930s penthouse on the corner of Fifth Avenue and East 88th Street on Manhattan's Upper East Side, overlooking Central Park. Across the road from the Guggenheim Museum, the apartment was described by the *Washington Post* as having "an understated elegance, a country feel of browns, beiges and peach tones, with mostly period furniture":

> There are 18th-century Chippendale bookcases from Rupert Murdoch's father, Sir Keith Murdoch, filled with 17th-century china; two brown velvet couches flanking a mantel; and a French baroque couch covered in green and peach silk . . . A terrace surrounds the penthouse offering a glorious view of Central Park, its reservoir, and New York's skyline. The elevator opens into their apartment, its door tended by the butler, George.

Anna told the *Post*: "It's just like being in a house once you're inside. We like it."[3]

From a very young age, the Murdoch kids understood they were in the media business. As Lachlan recalled in a 2001 interview with the Australian Broadcasting Corporation's *Dynasties* program:

> Liz, James, and I would come up for breakfast before we had to get the bus to school and all the papers would come out and we'd have the *New York Post*, *The New York Times*, the *Daily News*, and the *Wall Street Journal*, and as we read the papers my dad would be handing out the stories and saying, "Read that" or he'd say, "Look at the headline, that's a shocking headline."

A similar ritual would play out in the evening; if the Murdoch children wanted their father's attention, they needed to enter his orbit and talk media and politics. "We always had staff serving us," Lachlan told the ABC. "My father would come home; we'd have to get dressed to see him. We would have half an hour with him alone before the guests came over."[4] Rupert was affectionate, always ready for a big bear hug, but he was not a "wrestly daddy," as Anna said once, for fear the kids might rumple his tie. He was often distracted. "Is Daddy going deaf?" young James once asked his mum. "No," said Anna, "he's just not listening."[5]

"We could never take our family life out of business," Anna once said. "They were so intermingled."[6] In the same vein, Lachlan told Geraldine Brooks in a *New York Times* interview: "We're a private family. We don't talk about our personal affairs. But we can talk about business forever."[7]

From his grandfather's bookshelves to his father's business deals, Lachlan was constantly surrounded by the history of his family, the closest thing Australia has to royalty. The Murdochs' spiritual home was Cruden Farm, the charming property south-east of Melbourne which Sir Keith had bought for Dame Elisabeth when they married, where Rupert and his three sisters had grown up, and where the whole extended family sometimes gathered for Christmas. Lachlan liked to trace the family's history back further, to the two great-grandfathers on his father's side. Sir Keith's father, the Reverend Patrick Murdoch, was a strict Presbyterian minister with a powerful work ethic who had emigrated to Australia from the Scottish village of Rosehearty. Dame Elisabeth's father, Rupert Greene, was a hard-drinking raconteur with a chronic gambling streak, who gave his namesake grandson his legendary appetite for risk. In a 2001 interview, Lachlan saw the genetic mix of Patrick Murdoch and Rupert Greene "playing itself out in all our lives every day. Everything from the fact we all tend to work too-long hours and sacrifice a lot for it, but at the same time we all enjoy . . . taking risks and making quick decisions."[8]

As Lachlan got older, summers were often spent getting work experience in the family business. One year he was sent to work at Boonoke-Wanganella, a century-old sheep stud in the NSW Riverina, where he earned his first pay cheque from News Corp. Lachlan loved the raw, rugged Australian bush. Bob Sefton, the manager, reported that "Lachie" was just like his father, even as a teenager. "He was always asking questions. He wanted to know how everything worked. We paid him a jackaroo's wage of $150 a week, which he was saving towards buying a motorbike back in the States. Every night he'd want to know the latest exchange rate, and was dismayed to find it was falling."[9] Another year, Lachlan cleaned the printing presses for Sydney's *Daily Mirror*—he even joined the printers union—and worked as a cub reporter for the *San*

Antonio Express-News. These brief immersions reinforced the sense that the young Murdoch was destined to follow his father and grandfather into the media, although not necessarily at News Corp; Anna's plan was that her kids would work for other companies, at least initially.

Family holidays could be anywhere in the world, sailing the Mediterranean, skiing in Aspen, or relaxing on the family farm at Cavan. One year, the family reportedly went on a guided trek high into the Rockies and Lachlan was told that, according to legend, young native American braves had to scale a mountain to get their eagle feather. He climbed a nearby peak and on returning to camp was presented with the feather of a hawk. He would become an avid rock climber. Lachlan loved getting out into the wilderness: when a reporter cornered Rupert and the boys at a gala event in Los Angeles in 1984, he asked Lachlan the best thing about his dad. The teenager paused before deciding to play it safe, saying cheerfully: "Um, well, he always likes to go camping with us!" James showed a bit more spark, describing his dad as "different to what the newspapers say and the TV shows. Well, I think the papers and the shows about him and stuff make him look too mean and dark and sinister and really he's a really nice person, a fun person."[10]

Close in age, Lachlan and James were ultra-competitive. Family Monopoly games were intense and everybody was prepared to cheat.[11] According to one story, possibly apocryphal, the two boys would use the beams in the lodge at Aspen for chin-up competitions that went on until their hands bled.[12] Like most brothers, they sometimes fought; as an adult, Lachlan would brag that he usually won.

Anna was a devout Catholic and more conservative than Rupert in many ways: she didn't like *The Simpsons*, voted Republican, and thought abortion should be illegal. With Rupert so often at work, the discipline was left to Anna. James described his mother as "tough as nails."[13] Although the kids were raised Catholic, they were not sent to Catholic schools and Lachlan describes his own faith as Christian, rather than Catholic, atheist, or agnostic. Anna's strong influence on Lachlan is often overlooked and underestimated. According to a source close to him, Lachlan identified strongly with his mother's Scottish heritage and felt "a strong pull towards the values of the Scottish people . . . that frugality [and] sort of being outsiders within Great Britain." Despite their wealth and influence, Lachlan felt he grew up in an ordinary family with ordinary family issues, albeit in extraordinary circumstances. "We were never badly spoiled," he would say, adding that his parents "never let us think that we were at all special or different in any way." Part of it was growing up in New York, which had a grounding effect on Lachlan, "because everyone moves around on the street level, and you can be sharing a bus or getting on a subway, and you don't really see other people's families or their homes, or no one has fancy cars or anything like that."

For elementary school the Murdoch kids were nonetheless sent to Dalton, an elite, co-educational private school on Manhattan's Upper East Side, and then to exorbitantly expensive Ivy League preparatory schools. Lachlan went to the all-boys Allen-Stevenson School in his middle years and then to the co-educational high school, Trinity, nearby. Lachlan was an average kid at school, happy to try his hand at anything. As he later recalled, he was not an athlete, or focussed on sport, but was "good enough to sort of spend time with those groups. Neither was I the best student ever, but I was good enough to hang out with studious types, and [nor] was I a totally social animal, but social enough that I got along with everyone in a sense." At high school there was plenty of chopping and changing. Biographies of Rupert contain varying accounts of their childhoods. Thomas Kiernan wrote that Rupert complained that the bad press he received in New York was affecting his kids, with the two boys showing behavioral problems and Elisabeth expelled from her Connecticut boarding school.[14] According to Neil Chenoweth, she had smuggled in a bottle of rum.[15] One year, when the Murdochs were considering a move to Australia, Elisabeth was sent to Geelong Grammar, Rupert's old boarding school, while Lachlan and James remained in New York. The move never happened, and Liz returned to America.[16]

From his early days at Trinity, Lachlan showed signs of leaning to the right, politically. In 1987, at the age of sixteen, he was one of five boys who formed the Trinity Conservative Society, believing that there was a "definite imbalance of political ideology in the school community." The group's statement in the school yearbook, alongside a photo of the boys, all with jackets and most with ties, explained:

> Our school is based on the premise that one's opinions should be based on a full understanding of all the facts. The Trinity Conservative Society was formed in an attempt to create a healthy balance between all points of view so that none can be given more attention or clout. T.C.S. is an organization with no budget, no activities, and few meetings. It is open to all those who share in our belief of equal representation of political views (Right or wrong!), and those with a clear conservative conscience.[17]

"Few meetings" turned out to be the guiding principle of the T.C.S., and there was no activity at all so far as Lachlan can recall. In the fall of 1988, as he was turning seventeen, Lachlan was sent to board at the Phillips Academy at Andover, Massachusetts, one of the top ten schools in the country. Phillips alumni include six presidents over more than two centuries, but Lachlan hated his time at Andover, a small town an hour north of Boston, where the winters are bitterly cold. Like his father, Lachlan was a middling student, albeit smart enough to get into the selective Phillips Academy, and now he found himself competing with the best and brightest kids from around the world. The discipline was strict and the academic demands relentless. But the opportunities were also boundless, with overseas exchanges, internship opportunities in Washington, and a storied student newspaper, *The Phillippian*, which has produced many senior journalists.

Lachlan arrived at Andover in 1988, during an unprecedented debate about the school's culture, including high expectations, stress, and a lack of diversity. In his first year, a student attempted suicide and a thousand students signed a petition calling for a "moratorium day" without classes and a "light week" to ease the pressure. The school responded by embracing multiculturalism, overhauling the timetable to free up afternoons, and giving students a greater say in decision-making. But Lachlan did not get involved, either through the student paper or through any of the representative bodies. In fact, his only appearance in *The Phillippian* was a good-natured comment he gave for a story in mid-1988 about the school's new martial arts club. Described as a devoted member of the club, Lachlan said he hoped to see more structure the following year, "bowing your head when you enter, that sort of stuff."[18] But there would be no following year: Lachlan left Phillips Academy after the fall. Attending Andover is a privilege; very few students turn their back on it. As a teenager, Lachlan showed he was prepared to defy expectations and walk away, even from the most extraordinary opportunities. Decades later, he would do so again.

Anna moved Lachlan to the small, unpretentious Aspen Country Day School in Colorado, where he was a boarder and where the focus was on outdoor learning. He was one of just eight students in the class of 1990; the school stopped teaching to year twelve the following year. The fact that Prue, Elisabeth, and James all graduated from prestigious Ivy League feeder schools while Lachlan went to Aspen no doubt contributed to the perception inside and outside the family that he was less academically gifted than his siblings. Anna herself touted James as the smartest of her children in a profile for *The New York Times*, in which she pointed out that "[James] has his father's powers of memory and intellect."[19]

Growing up, young Elisabeth was more interested in the television side of the business. In a 2012 *New Yorker* profile, she told Ken Auletta that she watched television voraciously, especially reruns of *I Love Lucy*, *The Brady Bunch*, and *The Partridge Family*.[20] For work experience as a school student, she interned at Sky News.

James did a stint on Sydney's *Daily Mirror* as a teenager, but it turned into a nightmare when a photo of the young intern asleep at a press conference wound up on the front page of a rival paper, *The Sydney Morning Herald*. "Everybody knew who I was," James recalled. "I wouldn't do it again."[21]

Lachlan, by contrast, had always had a genuine passion for newspapers. He fondly remembered standing in the loading dock of the *New York Post* as a six-year-old, among the trucks and stacks of papers, which he loved "not for the business but for the craft of journalism that they represented."[22] Straight after graduating from Aspen, he did a short stint as a junior reporter with the London *Times*. Asked to take care of Lachlan, one *Times* journalist took him to the pub and got a call from the news desk within ten minutes: "For God's sake, whatever you do, don't get him pissed!" They need not have worried: Lachlan drank orange juice.[23] He also worked as a subeditor on *The Sun*, where he was slugged "MURDO" in the computerized copy management system. He showed some flair for a headline—he got a few page ones—and earned the respect of the editors and subs. On the high-pressure, no-bullshit news floor of Britain's highest-selling tabloid, Lachlan held his own. As one editor observed, "He loved them, and they loved him."[24]

For all his fondness for the craft of journalism, however, Lachlan's time as a working journalist was short, and he never had a by-line. Reflecting later, he had no doubt that his newspaper jobs helped him to get a handle on the print side of the business: "I understand that I'm not the best subeditor in the world, but I certainly can appreciate good subediting."[25]

In 1990, Lachlan was thrilled to be accepted into his first preference, and enrolled in an arts degree at Princeton University in New Jersey; he would get his Ivy League education, after all. Established in 1746 on empty paddocks halfway between New York and Washington, Princeton's main buildings are built from dark stone in the beautiful "collegiate Gothic" architectural style, a delight to walk through. Lachlan chose Princeton partly because it was near New York, so he could get back and see his parents regularly, although as it happened Rupert and Anna started spending more time in Los Angeles in those years. Although he was the son of a media mogul, Lachlan found he could blend in at Princeton and was by no means the wealthiest guy there. He lived on campus for the first two years before moving into a rented attic unit in the cheerful little adjacent township, full of bookshops and cafes. Lachlan was a relatively straight arrow at college: he kept a low profile, with zero presence in the *Daily Princetonian* and no youthful hi-jinks to speak of. At Harvard, by contrast, James bleached his hair, pierced his eyebrow and penned an edgy cartoon series for the *Harvard Lampoon* before ultimately dropping out.

Lachlan started dating a history student from Atlanta, Kate Harbin, who had graduated from the elite Christian school Westminister and got into Princeton on a scholarship. Harbin was a go-getter: student chair of her residential college and heavily involved with the *Daily Princetonian*, where she was a junior editor. Lachlan and Kate were soon getting pretty serious about each other.

Lachlan also got serious about rock climbing, training eight hours a day, racing his friend Peter Hunt, a classics scholar ten years older than Lachlan, up a gym wall wearing weighted backpacks, and enjoying weekends climbing in national parks. In his first two years of university, Lachlan later admitted, he didn't open many books and hardly had a typical university experience at all. "I wasn't drinking. I was very, very, very focused, and wrote down everything I had to eat that day. People considered me odd [because of all] the training I was doing . . . you know, I always had chalk on my hands." Lachlan was soon a climbing instructor, competing regularly, and considered going professional. He realized he could not keep climbing at a competitive level, and complete his degree. A turning point came when he read Desmond Zwar's authorized biography of his grandfather, *In Search of Keith Murdoch*. Looking back, Lachlan told the ABC: "I thought about his life and about the ability to really change a community for the better and play an active role in a community. It comes down to how you define being a human being, is it just a selfish thing? Or is there something that's broader that has to do with relationships with the rest of humanity? And I remember specifically one night really thinking about this. And I never, never put on a pair of rock climbing shoes again afterwards." When he retired from climbing, and apparently in line with tradition in the sport, Lachlan got a tattoo – a gecko, on his right bicep – as a mark of his years of dedication to the sport. "You've got to understand, this is a guy who could've been a world champion climber," says one old friend, Joe Cross. Years later, in a foreword for a book by legendary Australian mountaineer Lincoln Hall,

Lachlan pondered why "some of us climb mountains while others are happy with a comfortable job and a decent retirement plan," concluding that the answer could not be taught or learned but "must be felt." Denying the sport was for people who had a death wish, Lachlan acknowledged that a number of the great climbers he'd met over the years "prematurely met their end."[26] Climbing would remain part of who Lachlan was, and he dedicated his Princeton thesis to Hunt, for setting an example "which led to the two most happy and fulfilled years of my adult life."

Lachlan described himself as a decent student, getting mostly Bs and B-plusses, and it wasn't until his final year that he really hit the books. Like a journalist, Lachlan tended to push his deadlines. "I tended to leave everything to the last minute," he recalled. "So I'd be finishing up my essays until, you know, the last second, the morning they had to be done."

Arts students at Princeton must write a final-year thesis of more than ten thousand words, the culmination of their study. Lachlan majored in philosophy, and his thesis wrestled with Immanuel Kant's categorical imperative. In an earnest paper, Lachlan rejected Kant's narrow view that only autonomous actions, motivated by a sense of duty, are morally virtuous. Instead of such black-and-white extremes—autonomous and heteronomous, moral and non-moral—Lachlan argued there should be room for shades of grey:

> . . . for example, if I refuse to allow someone to steal from my family, or if I refuse to lie to my girlfriend, these actions are motivated by a healthy respect for the moral law . . . and also, at least in part, I am motived out of love. Because my love plays some role in my choice of maxim, my will would not be autonomous in Kant's vocabulary, but it would be free, if we could succeed in loosening Kant's notion of freedom to include heteronomy, and as free it would be a morally responsible and meretricious action.

Lachlan wrote that his aim was to "ratify" the teaching of the Bhagavad Gita that discipline is more important than renunciation of action. He quoted Lord Krishna: while the man of eternal renunciation is one who neither hates nor desires, the man of discipline "has joy, delight, and light within; becoming the infinite spirit, he finds the pure calm of infinity."[27]

The journalist Peter Maass interviewed some of Lachlan's friends and teachers at Princeton, including his advisor, Professor Beatrice Longuenesse, who agreed to re-read a copy of the Kant thesis as they talked. "I had forgotten how good this is," she told Maass. "It's a young man struggling with questions that are clearly his own questions, but working on them through major issues in philosophy." Longuenesse remembered Lachlan as a poetic character, because of his interest in the outdoors. "It was quite clear that he wanted to be a decent person," she recalled, "and he was a decent person." At the same time, Longuenesse felt Lachlan was clearly not about to rock the boat. As Maass observed:

. . . his devotion to German philosophy and the spiritual questions of the Bhagavad Gita did not dominate the next phase of his life. Princeton, like other top universities, tends to function as an incubator of the status quo. After four years of apparently sincere immersion in history, philosophy, or literature, a large number of students from Princeton and other elite universities glide to the highest reaches of the business world, which they do not tend to disrupt with the lofty ideas they explored as undergraduates.[28]

Longuenesse agrees: she says now that while she has happy memories of supervising Lachlan, she believes Fox News and the Murdoch machine have a "detestable" responsibility for the increasing polarization of the United States. Lachlan's story, she says sadly, "has become very dark and gets darker by the day.

2

"Why Not?"

WHILE LACHLAN FINISHED his degree, Rupert Murdoch was staking the future of News on television, which he saw as the dominant medium of the twentieth century, and with an increasingly conservative bent. Through the 1970s, as Lachlan was growing up, Rupert Murdoch's politics had turned sharply to the right. At the start of the decade, when he bought UK tabloid *The Sun*, he had promised unions that the paper would retain its left-wing leanings. *The Sun* was against apartheid, against capital punishment, against the war in Vietnam and, most of all, against the establishment. *The Sun* backed Labour in Britain's national election in 1970, although the conservative Edward Heath became prime minister in an upset.

In 1972, Murdoch's flagship broadsheet down under, *The Australian*, strongly backed Gough Whitlam's campaign to become prime minister; his famous "It's Time!" campaign ushered in the first Labor government in twenty-three years. Whitlam would prove the country's most progressive prime minister, introducing far-reaching reforms including free public healthcare and university education, Aboriginal land rights, no-fault divorce, and a complete withdrawal of troops from Vietnam. However, by 1975, as the oil shock set in and Whitlam's chaotic style and sweeping agenda culminated in the dismissal of his government, Murdoch's editorial line had turned 180 degrees. News Ltd.'s papers were so stridently opposed to Whitlam's re-election that journalists at *The Australian* walked out amid claims that news stories were being rewritten and skewed. Murdoch was unrepentant and Labor was defeated. By the end of the 1970s, Rupert's newspapers were strongly backing Tory leader Margaret Thatcher in the UK and Republican Ronald Reagan in the US.

Murdoch's expansion did not let up through the boom years of the 1980s. A new parent entity, News Corporation, listed on the Australian Stock Exchange, was set up in 1980 to consolidate the international operations in the UK, US, and Asia while becoming sole owner of the original News Ltd., which continued to run the Australian businesses. The following year, in one of his proudest moments, Rupert bought the London *Times*. Newspaper acquisitions continued: in the US, the *Boston Herald* and Chicago's *Sun-Times*, among others; in Hong Kong, the *South China Morning Post*; in Australia, Murdoch succeeded in buying back the company his father Keith had once run, the Herald and Weekly Times. This purchase, which Murdoch admitted was emotional, gave him control of his father's old paper, the Melbourne *Herald*, as well as the Brisbane *Courier-Mail* and Adelaide *Advertiser*, which had virtual monopolies in their home cities and came with substantial classified advertizing revenues.

Murdoch's main rival for control of the Australian media landscape, Frank Packer, had sold Murdoch his Sydney tabloid, the *Telegraph*, which was later amalgamated with the *Daily Mirror*. The Packer and Murdoch dynasties competed for most of the twentieth century: Frank vied with Keith, as would their sons Kerry and Rupert, and later their grandsons James and Lachlan. While the Packers' powerhouse asset was the leading free-to-air television network, Channel Nine, after the Herald and Weekly Times deal Rupert's News Ltd accounted for 70 per cent of newspaper circulation in Australia, helping to make it the world's most concentrated media market. News had gone from challenging the Australian media establishment to being the dominant player.

Murdoch had expanded into magazines, including *New York*, *New Woman*, and *Elle* in the US, and *New Idea* and *TV Guide* in Australia, as well as book publishing, snapping up Harper & Row and William Collins

& Sons in the UK, and later merging the two to form an international giant, HarperCollins. By the late 1980s, News Corp was also invested in the music industry, information services, printing and paper, airlines, oil and gas exploration and agriculture. With some 250 subsidiaries, the Murdoch empire was sprawling.

Most importantly, as Murdoch was expanding into film and television, Ted Turner's CNN, launched in 1980, was reinventing television news, delivering rolling 24/7 coverage of breaking US and international stories. In Australia, Murdoch owned a minority stake in the Channel Ten free-to-air television network, but he could not expand his holding under the country's media ownership laws and ultimately sold out. Over the course of the 1980s, however, he took a growing interest in satellite TV, including the Sky Network in continental Europe. He based his satellite service in Luxembourg, from where his signal could reach the UK without being subject to British cross-media restrictions.

Murdoch was also interested in buying content, and after taking an unsuccessful stab at Warner Brothers, he succeeded in 1985 in acquiring a half-interest in the Hollywood studio 20th Century Fox. Within weeks, he followed up with the opportunistic purchase of a half-dozen regional TV stations from Metromedia, covering the major markets of New York, Los Angeles, Chicago, Washington DC, Houston, and Dallas, in what was then the second-largest media deal in US history. Murdoch created Fox Broadcasting and set about creating a fourth TV network to compete with ABC, NBC and CBS. Fox slowly carved out its own identity, with edgy programming including *Married . . . with Children*, *America's Most Wanted*, and *The Simpsons*.

Rupert was now butting up against US laws restricting "aliens" from ownership of TV networks and realized that there was no alternative but to renounce his Australian citizenship. At a ceremony in New York in September 1985, in front of Anna and their three kids, Rupert swore to support and defend the constitution and laws of the United States. Anna was shocked, but for Rupert, it was just business. For Lachlan, the point was moot: America had been his only home since he left the UK as an infant. He became a US citizen in 1993, and later a dual citizen of America and Australia.

By the end of the 1980s, the Murdoch empire was making money, but there was one huge cash drain. Backing away from its investment in Sky in Europe, News had resolved to launch its service to the British market, in head-to-head competition with British Satellite Broadcasting. Both sides lost out in the expensive war that followed: Sky was first to broadcast, but it severely overestimated the number of viewers who would install satellite dishes, and therefore the amount of advertizing revenue it could generate. The two rivals bid up the price of programming and by 1990 both were in dire financial straits. They would ultimately merge that year to form BSkyB, albeit with Murdoch firmly in control.

Throughout the expansion of his media empire, from the 1950s to the 1980s, Rupert had accumulated debt rather than sell down the family's controlling share of News Corp. He might have been a swashbuckling media mogul, but he was always extremely careful to meet his obligations to the banks. Newspapers were the ultimate cash cow, and a good track record meant lenders were always prepared to fund his next venture. Increasingly, through the 1980s, the effective lenders were purchasers of bonds on the global financial markets, including junk bonds issued by Michael Milken's Drexel Burnham Lambert bank. In the aftermath of the 1987 stock-market crash, the heavily leveraged News Corporation was suddenly vulnerable, and the share price started to tank. The inevitable crisis came when a critical refinancing of more than a billion dollars of News Corp debt loomed in late 1990. Famously, a single bank in Pittsburgh that was owed $10 million simply refused to roll over its loan: it wanted its money back.

Suddenly, News faced an existential threat. If it could not refinance, it would be forced into liquidation, triggering a worldwide fire sale of assets. After almost four decades of expansion, this was Murdoch's darkest hour. The consequences of a collapse would be significant. As one Murdoch editor, Chris Mitchell, would later write, inside the Australian government there were secret talks about the possibility of a corporate collapse big enough to risk the national financial system: "No one would say it at the time, but the fear was about News Corporation."[1] A banker with Citi, Ann Lane, who had just restructured the empire of developer Donald Trump, took on News' plight and came up with two principles: "We are where we are" and "Nobody gets out." Lane and Murdoch had to personally reassure hundreds of lenders across the globe.

Lachlan, aged nineteen, was summoned to London to support Rupert during the talks. As they walked home from a meeting along a deserted Fleet Street at one o'clock in the morning, Lachlan recalled, Rupert was stressed and dispirited. "I wanted to put my arms around him and hold him up," Lachlan said.[2]

After a lot of arm-twisting, the fraught negotiations culminated in a final life-or-death phone call from Rupert to the banker in Pittsburgh, who grudgingly assured him of support. As a young man, Lachlan may not have understood every detail of how News had been brought to the brink but seeing his father so suddenly vulnerable must have been a formative experience, reinforcing the sense that it was his family against the world. It would later be said of Lachlan that he was extremely protective of Rupert and that he remembered everyone who had ever said anything critical of his father: "He would always remember their name. Always."[3] It would not be the last time Lachlan rushed to London to support Rupert through a crisis.

* * *

After News Corporation suffered this near-death experience, there was pressure on Rupert to free up the fortunes he had made for the extended Murdoch clan. In 1992, after selling off assets and restructuring his borrowings, Rupert engineered a $650 million buyout of his three sisters' holdings in Cruden Investments, the private vehicle that owned the family's share of News Corp, setting all three of them up for life and endowing each of his nieces and nephews with $20 million. Rupert now had complete control of the Murdoch stake in News, ensuring his own children's inheritance.

While Lachlan finished his degree, Elisabeth and James were charting their own courses. After graduating with a BA from Vassar College in upstate New York, Liz went to work for the Packer family's Channel Nine TV station in Sydney, first in promotions and then as a researcher for

A Current Affair. She then returned to Los Angeles to work as a programming executive at Fox TV, before asking Rupert to guarantee a $20 million loan so that she could buy a couple of Californian television stations. After a brutal but effective restructure, she sold them for a $12 million profit. James meanwhile enrolled in classics at Harvard but dropped out in his senior year as he was drawn into the music industry, co-founding the hip-hop label Rawkus Records. He would sell Rawkus to News Corp for an undisclosed sum a few years later.

Only Lachlan decided to learn the ropes in the old-fashioned print side of the business and to better understand the Australian roots of the family company, partly inspired by Sir Keith's biography. "I had a unique opportunity, in many ways, that is not open to many people, to play an integral role in the broader community," Lachlan said. "So I thought that, you know, how could you not take up that opportunity . . . which, hopefully, you can bring a lot of good to?"[4] By one account, Lachlan's move down under came at Rupert's suggestion, in a conversation with his kids about their future at the family's Aspen ski lodge in early 1994. Lachlan wasn't sure of his plans, so Rupert asked if he wanted to work in Australia for a while. "Sure," answered Lachlan. "Why not?"[5]

The family's original plan, worked on for some months, was that Lachlan would go to work at the *Townsville Bulletin* in north Queensland. But when News Ltd. decided to install color presses for the *Courier-Mail*, Rupert believed it would be a good opportunity for Lachlan to learn first-hand how such a significant capital expenditure project could change the value proposition of a newspaper and sent him to Brisbane instead. "That decision was very well thought through," says one source close to Lachlan. "[In] the early nineties, the newspapers were still making a hell of a lot of money, and Australia was a source of talent for the rest of the News Corp empire—people from Australia were taking the cultural DNA of the company to the UK and the US. [The company] was still headquartered [in Australia]. Coming to Australia may now seem counterintuitive, because of the way the businesses evolved over twenty-five years, but at the time, it absolutely made sense."

So, at the age of twenty-two, Lachlan got his first real job in the empire: general manager of Queensland Press Ltd, reporting to John Cowley, brother of News Corporation's chief executive Ken and a company veteran. John was tough—he'd made his name as the "mayor of Wapping" during the London union-busting operation a decade earlier— and was now given the task of "blooding" the young Murdoch. Lachlan was the same age as Rupert had been when he inherited control of the Adelaide *News* after the death of Sir Keith.

Because Queensland Press Ltd. was majority-owned by Cruden Investments, not by News Ltd., which held a minority stake, Rupert could do whatever he liked. But Murdoch-watchers immediately perceived the shameless nepotism as a succession strategy. With Rupert approaching sixty-five, there was speculation Lachlan was already on the "inside track." The popular theory was that Murdoch senior had sent his eldest son to Queensland to toughen him up. On the first day, John apparently mistook Lachlan for a copy boy and left him waiting in an outer office before realizing he'd just given the cold shoulder to the boss's son.

Lachlan rented a luxury Queenslander by the river in exclusive inner-city Hamilton. Costing a reported $1,000 a week, it was one of the most expensive rentals in Brisbane. He threw himself into the job, trying to make *The Courier-Mail* more appealing to young readers. His approach was bold: notwithstanding that it might ruffle the feathers of then editor Des Houghton, Lachlan asked the young journalists on staff what they didn't like about their newspaper. One later told *The Age*: "It was the first time we'd been asked what we'd do with the paper." Lachlan won over his team by inviting them over for dinner. He hadn't yet found time to buy furniture or install an oven, so they warmed their meals up plate by plate in the microwave and sat on the floor. "That really sort of established him in our eyes," said the reporter, "because he was very, very normal. It was amazing how down-to-earth and natural he was." What came out of it all was a "youth project," a weekly entertainment lift-out like the free gig guides found in pubs and cafes, but with more than music content.[6]

Within months of Lachlan arriving, Chris Mitchell took over from Des Houghton as editor of *The Courier-Mail* and set up a serious investigative journalism unit. Mitchell was appointed by Ken Cowley, but veterans of the paper have no doubt that Lachlan had a hand in his selection. Mitchell cultivated a bunch of young guns, including Paul Whittaker, Rory Callinan, and Michael Ware, the last of whom went on to enjoy success as an international correspondent at CNN, covering the war in Iraq. Under Mitchell that year, *The Courier-Mail* won three Walkley national press awards. The paper had not won a Walkley in almost a decade, and Mitchell later wrote that Lachlan's support was critical to the paper's investment in investigative journalism and helped to fend off John Cowley, who was the more commercially minded Cowley.

Quite suddenly, as he stepped into the family business, Lachlan was subjected to media scrutiny. Giving interviews, he chose his words carefully. Asked straight up whether he would like to run News Corp one day, he answered that the top job should go to the "best" person for the company, "from inside or outside the family."[7] He said there was no grand career path mapped out for him, except to "work very hard" for a few years in Australia under the supervision of Ken Cowley, adding "it's what Mr Cowley and my dad want me to do and where I'm the best use." Lachlan paid tribute to his father:

> One of the reasons [he] is successful . . . is the amount of energy he has. He works incredibly hard and it's that kind of energy, which is awesome and which, I think to do well today, you have to have. It's not just that you have a higher IQ than the next guy, but it's the energy to look at all these different things.[8]

To most observers, however, Lachlan seemed surprisingly normal. He did not appear to have the legendary workaholism of either his father or grandfather. Many of the relationships Lachlan forged in Brisbane—as much over drinks or a game of football as in the office—would endure throughout his career. Chris Mitchell, Paul Whittaker, and a string of reporters and editors with whom Lachlan worked in Brisbane would rise to the top inside News Ltd., including John Lehmann, later at the *New York Post*, and Christopher Dore, later editor of *The Australian*. They formed a Queensland cohort that stamped an outsize influence on the Murdoch business down under. As for his politics, Lachlan described himself at this time as economically conservative but "socially more liberal."[9] One corporate type who worked with the young Murdoch in the late 1990s described him as "soft left, with a touchy-feely view of the world that doesn't really fit with his role."[10]

Lachlan was feted as Australia's most eligible bachelor, but that came with unwanted attention to his personal life. He was handsome as a young man, with piercing brown eyes and his mother's strong features. "Hopefully I've got my mother's looks," Lachlan joked in one interview, although he added: "I've got my dad's skin, so maybe I'll get some wrinkles later on!" At *The Courier-Mail*, according to one report, he was regarded as a spunk, and the young female staff bantered that "his dad married a journo."[11] Almost every party appearance or night out with a companion found its way into the social pages. An early casualty was his relationship with Kate Harbin, who had been snapped up by consultancy McKinsey straight out of college and to whom Lachlan was engaged in early 1995. They were often pictured together: *The Courier-Mail* ran photos of the couple at a Brisbane fashion parade; the ABC's *Four Corners* caught them stepping off the company jet, lugging their bags to attend a 1995 News Corp shindig on Hayman Island, where Prime Minister Paul Keating and British Labour leader Tony Blair famously shored up the support of the Murdoch empire.[12] Lachlan and Kate's engagement did not survive much longer. When they broke up, Lachlan bought himself a Ducati Monster— he'd promised Kate's mother he'd get rid of his motorbike when they got engaged. Lachlan attributed the breakup to his workload but also complained about the strange media interest in his relationships. "It's not a natural position to be in, nor is it a position I want to be in, in terms of that much publicity," said Lachlan, "because I think at heart, I see myself as an ordinary young person with ambitions."[13]

3

The Big League

AT NINE O'CLOCK ON a Saturday morning, Lachlan Murdoch, twenty-three, and Super League chief executive John Ribot stood in the carpark outside Brisbane's empty ANZ Stadium, waiting for the city's exalted Broncos rugby league team to turn up. It was April fool's day, 1995, and the Broncos were reportedly about to sign lucrative contracts to enter a new international competition owned by News Ltd., effectively poaching the team from the long-established Australian Rugby League. It was all supposed to be top-secret, but Broncos coach Wayne Bennett read about the imminent signing of his players, and the role he'd played, in that morning's newspapers. Appalled at the leak, Bennett called off the meeting and left Murdoch and Ribot cooling their heels.

"Where are they, John?" Murdoch asked Ribot, who had to admit he didn't know.[1] "That was a bit of a crossroads moment," says Ribot, "because everybody made the assumption that we had the Broncos tied up, and we didn't at that stage." Just one player ignored his coach and turned up anyway: winger Willie Carne, one of the Broncos' leading try-scorers. Carne, twenty-six, grew up on a farm near Roma in outback Queensland and was as tough as they come, "his own man," as Ribot remembers. Willie was about the same height as Lachlan, who stood at 5'10," but twice as wide, and though the tough Aussie footballer and the American college kid in shirtsleeves and slacks had very little in common, they struck up a friendship. News Ltd. was the major sponsor and part-owner of the Broncos, and Lachlan had been going to games since arriving in Brisbane seven months earlier. He told Willie he knew hardly anyone in town and the pair went out for a drink. They got along well and started to hang out socially. On one occasion, Willie was impressed when, heading off to a weekend barbecue with a few blokes from the team, Lachlan was happy to park his lime-green Kawasaki motorcycle and jump in the back of a car with the kids. Willie describes Lachlan as humble but admits that hanging out with him was a bit surreal. "He was like a king," says Carne. "You get to see how the other half lives."

If Lachlan thought his new mate would be a pushover when it came to negotiating a contract, however, he got a surprise. Willie put the young Murdoch through his paces, asking question after question in a robust discussion that went for almost two hours, before finally agreeing to sign on the dotted line. "That was hard work," Murdoch confided to Ribot afterwards. It would get much harder, as Lachlan was thrust into the middle of Australia's Super League war, the most bitter conflict in the near hundred-year history of the game.

Rugby league is not widely played internationally, but it has a dedicated following down under. The game was invented in northern England in the late nineteenth century as a professional spinoff of rugby union, with simpler rules and faster play. League is brutal, tribal, and thoroughly working class. As the saying goes, union is a thug's game played by gentlemen; league is a gentleman's game played by thugs. In sports-mad Australia, where four football codes compete for players and spectators, rugby league had long been on the back foot as Aussie rules, the one truly indigenous game, managed by the Australian Football League (AFL), expanded from its base in Victoria. In the 1980s, Rugby league responded by trying to expand, forming the Australian Rugby League (ARL). A decade later, however, a dozen Sydney teams still dominated the ARL and resentment seethed, especially among highly successful teams in Brisbane and Canberra, whose best talent was constantly being picked off by richer clubs from Sydney.

Super League was the brainchild of the Broncos, then the only privately owned club in the competition and the only ARL club in Brisbane, League's second-biggest market. When the ARL proposed a second Brisbane club, the Broncos came up with a plan for a new competition. Broncos chief Ribot pitched it quietly to News Ltd., the club's major sponsor, in 1994, first to the Australian chief executive, Ken Cowley, and then to Rupert Murdoch, who gave it the green light. News had been negotiating separately to become the ARL's major sponsor and knew the league was vulnerable. In a confidential document dated August 12, 1994, Ribot proposed that rather than sponsoring the ARL, News should instead fund an elite Super League, which could be marketed internationally. Lachlan arrived in Brisbane the following week. According to one senior sports journalist, Cowley used Lachlan as a "strategic strike weapon" with players and coaches. Ribot himself says the players liked dealing with the budding mogul, hearing about Super League plans from the horse's mouth, and some signed their contracts at Lachlan's house in Hamilton. "Lachlan had a lot of credibility with the players," Ribot says, "because he's talking to guys that are a similar age, so they're talking in similar language, and I remember several times he'd say [to them]: 'You've got to understand, my family want this to happen, and the buck stops with us. Everything we say we're going to do, will happen.'" It didn't hurt that Lachlan could hold his own when it came to having a few beers. "I don't think he drinks every day," says Ribot, "but he could sit down and have a good session with you, and you'd know you'd had a drink . . . he'd be a good mate to have. He liked having fun when the business was done."

Why was News Corp interested in Super League? By now the company was recovering from the debt crisis of 1990 and was paying over-the-odds for football rights to underpin its new subscription television networks. As British journalist Nick Davies has observed, Murdoch employed a triangulation strategy in the US, UK, and Australia, buying premier sporting rights and using them to underpin pay-TV networks that were cross-promoted and cross-subsidized by his tabloids, while his broadsheets wielded influence.[2]

Ironically, it may have been Murdoch's Australian rival, Kerry Packer, who sowed the seeds of this strategy. "You know everything about newspapers," Kerry reportedly told Rupert. "You thumb through the world's leading papers every day. I don't read them, but I do watch TV. The one thing which works on TV is sport. If you want to get out of trouble, you've got to tie up a sport and convert it to pay-TV."[3]

In the UK, Murdoch hired ex-Packer executive Sam Chisholm to save the newly merged BSkyB by paying a fortune for the rights to English Premier League soccer; the network gave away satellite dishes so that punters could watch it and forced advertizers to pay through the nose. In the US, Murdoch paid an unprecedented half-billion dollars for the rights to the National Football League, luring millions of subscribers to his new Fox television network. Super League fitted well into this global picture, although it would once again bring the Murdochs into conflict with the Packers, who owned the free-to-air broadcast rights for the ARL.

Pay-TV was the only option for Murdoch to expand in Australian broadcasting because, as a newspaper publisher, he was constrained by cross-media laws from buying a free-to-air television network. News launched Foxtel, a 50:50 joint venture with telecommunications provider Telstra. Meanwhile, the Packers partnered with Optus, which held the pay-TV rights to both the AFL and ARL, so Murdoch had to create an entirely new football competition. News saw Super League as absolutely critical to the commercial success not only of Foxtel in Australia but also of BSkyB in Europe. A war room was created just across the road from the News Holt Street headquarters in Sydney to plan and execute a hostile takeover of rugby league, an operation as detailed and secret as Rupert's successful move to Wapping in 1986.

The Murdochs had no affinity with rugby league. Rupert grew up in Melbourne, the home of Australian rules, and played tennis. Lachlan grew up in the US, had never played football, and was keen on climbing. But News Ltd.'s Ken Cowley, a country kid from a poor family who had played rugby league as a junior in western Sydney's Bankstown, loved the game.[4] So when Ribot outlined his vision for a Super League to be broadcast not just in Australia and New Zealand but throughout the Pacific Islands and Europe, Cowley got it. Through the second half of 1994, speculation about the new league continued to build. At the beginning of 1995, the ARL held a meeting with the clubs and persuaded them all to sign five-year loyalty agreements and the 1995 season got underway.

News' next move was described in internal strategy documents as "blitzkrieg." The ARL called it "Pearl Harbor": the Friday night on March 31, 1995 when Super League launched secret raids on the teams most likely to join a new competition. The Canberra Raiders, playing in Townsville, signed *en masse*; they had already heard a pitch from Lachlan himself. The Cronulla Sharks, from Sydney's Sutherland Shire, signed up the same night after a game in Perth. Each team had some of the biggest stars in the game.

The Broncos were supposed to be in the bag. After all, the competition was their idea to begin with. So when the coach and players didn't turn up to the meeting in Brisbane the next morning, it was a bad omen. Within days, however, the rest of the Broncos followed Carne's lead and signed up. The Auckland Warriors followed, along with the Canterbury Bulldogs (Cowley's old club), Penrith Panthers, North Queensland Cowboys, and Perth Reds.

The ARL fought back hard over the next week, handing out bonus cheques to hundreds of players put on long-term contracts in what was becoming an expensive free-for-all. The ARL was backed by Kerry Packer, who warned the clubs and News Ltd. in no uncertain terms that he had paid handsomely for the broadcast rights to rugby league and would sue any defectors. Most Sydney clubs stuck with the ARL. Crucially, the Newcastle Knights, who had no love for Sydney and were led by Andrew Johns, one of the game's greatest players, remained loyal. To this day, Ribot believes that if he and Lachlan hadn't been delayed in Brisbane but had been able to get straight down to Newcastle, the Super League war might have ended very differently. News Ltd. took the ARL to the federal court, arguing that the loyalty agreements were anti-competitive. Meanwhile, News quickly snared commitments from the administrators of rugby league in England and New Zealand.

Super League versus the ARL had become a titanic struggle, not only about a point of principle—the privatization of a whole sport—but also about the future of television in Australia. The competition for talent was ferocious, particularly when it came to signing the game's superstars. Lachlan Murdoch and James Packer represented the warring dynasties, handing out enormous cheques. As Mike Colman chronicled in his book *Super League*, one up-and-coming Cronulla star, Adam Ritson, found himself doing a handshake deal at James' luxury apartment in Bondi, only for Lachlan to phone his agent Steve Gillis as they were preparing to leave. "Steve, this is Lachlan Murdoch speaking, how do you do? I understand there is a problem with Adam Ritson. We would really like to sign him. Now, how can we work this out? What can we do to make it happen?" Gillis apologized that Ritson had just come to terms with the ARL.[5] On other occasions Lachlan was more successful: his personal intervention clinched the signatures of stars Matthew Ridge and Ian Roberts, the first "out" gay player in league, who defected from Manly to Super League. Both would remain friends of Murdoch.

By mid-1995, after less than a year in Brisbane, Lachlan had relocated to Sydney, becoming publisher of *The Australian* and soon deputy chief executive of News Ltd., reporting directly to Cowley. He bought a $7 million property on Sydney Harbour, "Berthong" in Billyard Avenue, Elizabeth Bay, a duplex, with Lachlan's home upstairs and a separate residence downstairs for when his parents were in Sydney. Lachlan installed his own fibreglass-and-plywood climbing wall in the garage, which also soon housed a BMW, his Ducati, and a huge Harley-Davidson crated in from the US.[6]

Lachlan was a man-about-town, seen at glamorous openings and the best restaurants. When the Museum of Contemporary Art needed to raise money to fund a new wing, Lachlan donated heavily; in the tradition of his grandparents Sir Keith and Dame Elisabeth, he was simultaneously high-brow and populist. He became one of the museum's young patrons, a group that would deliver invaluable business connections down the track. He struck up a close friendship with a young futures broker,

Joe Cross. Both preferred to watch a game of footy than go to a gallery. Cross didn't have a university education, but he was street-smart. "I think that Lachlan and I hit it off because we were on a board with a bunch of people that were pretty artsy," says Cross, "and that really wasn't his world, either." Another member of the group was an up-and-coming prestige real estate agent, John McGrath, who would later bring Lachlan the deal of a lifetime.

The media scrutiny intensified. Lachlan (or, more often, just Lachie) was now fair game, especially for editors at rival publishers Fairfax. When he went out racing in an eighteen-foot skiff, he was grabbed for a short interview for Channel Ten's *World of Water* program —the camera zoomed in on his cool tattoo"It's a great one, isn't it?" Lachlan asked the interviewer, coyly.

It was deemed newsworthy when he was seen out with Fiona Argyle, a model and researcher from Channel Nine. When he went to the Sydney premiere of the latest James Bond film, *GoldenEye*, with marketing executive Manon Youdale on his arm, that, too, was reported. When his former fiancée Kate Harbin resurfaced by his side at Berthong for the News Ltd. Christmas party, that also made the papers. Their separation had clearly been amicable: six months later, Kate was back in Sydney for a huge twenty-fourth birthday bash at the Danish Design Centre, thrown for her by Lachlan, with food by star chef Neil Perry, crates of Veuve Clicquot, and a private performance by the Aussie rocker Diesel, flown in specially from the US. One gossip columnist reported that the party for Lachlan's "on-off-on amour Kate Harbin has shocked the eastern suburbs social set: none has been asked." The party's PR operative pointed out that it was "not a celebrity event: it's just friends."[7] Sadly, wrote another column, the 130-strong party "was also something of a farewell from Lachlan to Kate, who will shortly return to New York." It is not clear what caused their final breakup, but a well-placed source says they had a semi-public row at the Grand Pacific Blue Room nightclub in Surry Hills, during which Kate tipped a glass of wine over Lachlan before storming out. Cross knows nothing about that one, but says that after Lachlan broke up with

Kate he was literally "the single most eligible bachelor in the whole damn country—he's young, he's fit, he's good looking, he's educated, and he's in a position of enormous power. What's not to like?" Yet Lachlan sought quality relationships rather than quantity, says Cross. "Every single date he went on, the parents loved him, because he's so well mannered, and can sit down and have a conversation, and he paid them a great deal of respect." Lachlan did not leave a trail of destruction behind him.

During this period there were persistent rumors that Lachlan was gay, fuelled perhaps by nothing more than his being seen clubbing around Oxford Street, Sydney's gay strip, or by his well-known friendship with Super League star Ian Roberts. Whether any of the gossip, published and unpublished, was accurate is impossible to say, and it is nobody's business, of course. For his part, Cross says that if Lachlan was gay, he would certainly have known. "I can tell you that all those rumors are completely unfounded and false," he says, adding: "Quite the contrary." Having grown up in New York, Lachlan was open-minded and tolerant, Cross says, and was often miscast. "You know, Lachlan on a Thursday night is having dinner with the prime minister, and then on a Friday night, he's out in the Blue Room having drinks with a group of 22-year-olds." Lachlan never indulged in recreational drugs, according to Cross. "I would bet everything I have, that Lachlan has never done an illicit drug in his life," he says. "A hundred per cent. Drugs were not our thing . . . we would be out and we'd see people doing drugs, and we'd just look at each other and shake our heads." While everyone else around them was indulging, Lachlan and Joe were happy to stick to the beers and vodkas. "Honestly, I don't think he's even smoked a joint," says Cross. Certainly, Lachlan was finding himself in Australia, and told his friends he felt more at home than he ever had in America. "When Lachlan lands in Australia," says Cross:

> . . . he really feels that, 'this is where I belong. I am an Australian.
> I might have an American accent, but I am Australian'. He has
> a deep sense of connection and realizes that this is going to be

his home, even at a young age. He decides, 'I'm planting my flag here. I'm just coming into my own now. I've been under the US system – the well-trodden path of going to middle school, high school, college, and you know, next is a bride and a white picket fence . . . well, I think Lachlan put the brakes on all that. He was 100 per cent Australian, and he was home and he wanted to explore his Australian roots.

Lachlan lamented that, growing up in the US, he had "picked up this bloody accent, which I wish I could get rid of, but I can't."

* * *

In February 1996, Federal Court judge James Burchett handed down a verdict that seemed to crush Super League once and for all. The ARL won on every point it claimed. Murdoch had attempted to paint News as the underdog challenging a bloated monopoly. Burchett rejected that argument, finding that the ARL competed with other sporting codes for players, sponsors, viewers, and ticket sales and could hardly be called a monopolist.

Noting that the ARL was a non-profit organization that had built up enormous goodwill over nearly a century—something which Super League was now trying to take for nought—Burchett accused the Broncos of a "deliberate exercise in deception." He also slammed the dishonest conduct of News Ltd. in what he described as a "meticulously planned operation, involving secrecy, suddenness and deception." The judge found Ribot to be an unreliable witness and questioned the honesty of News executives, including Ken Cowley, who had failed to appear. "I made a judgement that we were not being listened to by the judge," Cowley told journalist Pamela Williams a couple of years later. "I have read the evidence of the previous witnesses and I believe that no matter what I had said or how I conducted myself in court, both myself and the company would be very badly damaged."

Lachlan did not appear, either, and Williams asked Cowley whether he had taken the rap for young Murdoch. "People thought I was shielding Lachlan," Cowley said. "But I was the chief executive and it was my responsibility to defend the company. So I wasn't defending Lachlan, I was defending the company. And if that did take the heat away [from Lachlan], then it wasn't by design."[8] Ribot wasn't happy to be the only person from News to give evidence in court while everyone else—Rupert, Lachlan, Ken—was unavailable. "I was stuck in the box for a week," says Ribot, "but that's part of the deal. I didn't really expect it any other way, but it wasn't a pleasant experience. I guess that's the small print of the contract I had."

News was floored by the judge's decision, but Ribot says Lachlan showed some leadership immediately after the verdict was handed down: "When Justice Burchett handed down his decision, I must admit I was thinking, 'How the hell are we going to respond to this?' I didn't have many answers. When we all got together, Lachlan came into the meeting and he gave everyone confidence: 'This thing's not over with yet. We're going to challenge this.'" On the way out of the courtroom, Lachlan told the News executives to hold their heads high. In brief comments to the media pack, he tried to strike an optimistic note, but the TV networks showed footage of the young mogul, stony-faced, getting jostled and heckled. Lachlan had certainly been thrown in the deep end. The following Monday, Lachlan made sure to walk through the newsrooms of *The Daily Telegraph* and *The Australian*, so that staff did not feel he was hiding upstairs in his office.

A few days later, when Justice Burchett handed down orders prohibiting Super League and its clubs from engaging in any sports or marketing activity whatsoever, even from training in their jerseys, Lachlan called James Packer to propose a peace deal, which was quickly rejected.[9] News had no option but to appeal to the full Federal Court and wait. There was a bout of speculation as to whether Lachlan was up to it, in contrast to the then well-regarded James Packer. Ten months later, Cowley's view was vindicated: the bench set aside Burchett's ruling on the core anti-competitive claim, finding the ARL's loyalty agreements were void.

The stage was set for the Super League competition to finally begin the following year. At a press conference alongside Cowley and Ribot, Lachlan was grinning from ear to ear, admitting "We're rapt . . . no, we're very happy." Rupert had sent his congratulations from LA, Lachlan added, and "He's rapt as well."

By the end of 1996, however, as the costs of Super League piled up, the Murdochs and the Packers were both searching for a compromise, and it was the younger generation who did the groundwork. They had not grown up together, but Lachlan and James had gone out of their way to cultivate a friendship. They had been seen dining together and relaxing at Packer's luxurious weekender at Palm Beach, fifty kilometers north of Sydney. Super League had strained their relationship, but now James reached out to Lachlan, saying that Kerry had loaned him his 88-meter yacht, the *Arctic P*. Would Lachlan and a few mates like to join him for four nights' cruising off Fiji? It was an offer too good to refuse.

With his younger brother James and friend Joe Cross, Lachlan joined Packer and a few of Packer's close buddies on two private jets bound for Nadi airport. The trip became exactly the kind of extended party you might expect of a bunch of twenty-somethings on a well-crewed yacht designed to cater to their every whim. "It's basically a drinkathon, you know, it's a dead-set 24/7 party," recalls Cross:

> I remember the first night, we had this team Lachlan vs team James, and the competition was called The Snorkel. The rules were quite simple—you stand in your Speedos on the back deck of the yacht with a facemask and a snorkel on your head. Just like you would if you were actually going snorkelling . . . but this game is a little different. With this one, your buddy would stand on a chair behind you and pour cans of VB beer down the snorkel . . . you had to make sure you didn't spill a drop . . . and one can of beer was just for starters! The winner of course was defined by how many and how fast! I forget who won but that wasn't really the point. This is what you do when you're twenty-four, twenty-five.

I think if everybody looks back at the mid-twenties, when you feel unbeatable, and you can do anything in life and you've got no fear, and you've got the resilience to be able to drink ten beers and wake up the next morning and go for a two-mile swim. We're jet skiing, we're on kayaks, we're windsurfing, we're jumping off the front of *Arctic P* and it's twenty feet high, we had the time of our lives. We played a lot of backgammon and chess and all for money . . . not big stakes, but enough to make you focus . . . on the *Arctic P* you could press a button, kind of like a remote control for a garage door, and order a cheeseburger or a club sandwich at three in the morning. I guess that was because Kerry liked the idea of the kitchen running in shifts over a 24-hour cycle. Lachlan and I kept the 3 a.m. shift rather busy . . . it was good times, good laughs.

Business was barely discussed, although everyone on board knew the high-stakes game being played out back in the real world. The guests kept their opinions to themselves— you could get yourself in trouble giving unsolicited advice to the sons of billionaires. "When you're that close to the flame, you don't want to get burned, so everyone knows when to keep their mouth shut,' Cross says. "If you speak out of line, you learn pretty quick that you don't do that . . . it's not your place, and fair enough, because most of the time the friends are operating on only half the story and don't know the facts or the history."

The trip served its purpose. James Packer remembers the dynamic well. "It wasn't up to us to make peace," he says. "That was up to our fathers." But he agrees the trip helped to make peace possible; after their time away together, he and Lachlan advised Kerry and Rupert that it was time to end the Super League war, saying it had been "going too long and it's expensive, people have got their egos caught up in it."

As it happened, love bloomed on board as well: Joe Cross's girlfriend had been a late scratch so he brought along his flatmate, Kathryn Hufschmid. When Kathryn met James Murdoch, the two fell for each other straightaway. Within a few years they were married and they are still together more than twenty-five years later.

* * *

The future of Super League was inextricably tied up with the painful birth of pay-TV in Australia in the mid to late nineties, just as the internet was beginning to disrupt everything. When the first pay-TV licenses were auctioned in 1993, Albert Hadid, an opportunistic computer dealer with no background in broadcasting, succeeded in a bid for the first license (aided by future prime minister Malcolm Turnbull, who was then a merchant banker). Within days, Hadid made a windfall of more than $30 million by selling the rights to a syndicate of foreign investors, Australis Media, who grabbed rights to programming from four Hollywood studios, including Murdoch's own 20th Century Fox, and launched the country's first pay-TV service, Galaxy. Foxtel was left high and dry, with no content to sell, and had to strike a humiliating and expensive deal with Australis to buy back programming worth $4.5 billion over the next twenty-five years. This multi-billion-dollar liability hurt the profitability of Foxtel from the start and Rupert Murdoch vowed to be rid of it. All up, the nascent pay-TV industry was losing something like a billion dollars a year.

The politics were also treacherous. The election of John Howard's conservative government in early 1996 brought the possibility of the abolition of cross-media restrictions and a relaxation of foreign ownership limits. Lachlan was drawn into a furious round of lobbying, in an introduction to Australia's cosy political scene. He had the luxury of starting at the top. A fortnight after the election, John Howard hosted a private dinner in his Sydney office with Rupert Murdoch and Ken Cowley. Lachlan, twenty-four, had a seat at the table. The next day, Howard's communications minister Richard Alston announced a sweeping inquiry into media laws. Up for grabs was the Fairfax newspaper stable, which had recently emerged from receivership; both Murdoch and Packer were interested. But the new Howard government soon realized that media law reform was a political quagmire: pleasing one mogul would only infuriate another. After a less-than-transparent inquiry, the reforms were shelved.

Building on the goodwill between James and Lachlan, the Murdochs and Packers proceeded to carve up the pay-TV industry between themselves. In early 1997, within weeks of their sons' Fiji sojourn on the *Arctic P*, Rupert and Kerry struck a peace deal that resolved all the issues between them, reportedly ticking it off on a yacht in New Zealand's Bay of Islands. The Murdochs took northern hemisphere broadcast rights to rugby league, while the Packers kept southern hemisphere rights and agreed to show Super League games as well as the ARL. In addition, the Packers took half of News' stake in Foxtel for some $250 million, or a fraction of the enormous sunk cost. It was said that the compromise involved some give-and-take in which Murdoch gave and Packer took.

Following the deal, the first item on the agenda for both dynasties was to get rid of the pesky interloper, Australis Media, which had the smallest subscriber base and was struggling with technology costs. Unable to buy Australis out, News resolved to play hard-ball. At the end of December 1997, at a secret meeting in Vancouver between Rupert and Lachlan and the Hollywood studios, a deal was done to cut Australis off from its supply of programming, which would be switched to Foxtel. Within months, Australis drifted inevitably into bankruptcy and Foxtel picked up a swag of subscribers, entrenching its leadership over Optus. Australis's US lenders eventually took News Ltd. to the New York Supreme Court, accusing the company of a "nefarious campaign" employing "a multitude of predatory practices" to eliminate a rival. The case was unsuccessful.

Foxtel's next challenge was to win the pay-TV rights to the AFL's Australian rules games, outbidding Optus, and when the landmark deal was finally done at the end of 2000, it was clear to all and sundry that there would be only one major player in subscription television in Australia. That deal led to the biggest media lawsuit in Australian corporate history, the so-called C7 mega-litigation, in which junior mogul Kerry Stokes, who had taken control of Channel Seven but found himself frozen out, launched proceedings against the Murdoch and Packer companies, the

AFL, the NRL, and others, alleging a conspiracy to kill off Seven's hopes of entering pay-TV. The case dragged on for almost a decade and was ultimately thrown out, with estimated costs of $200 million awarded against Channel Seven in what judge Sackville described as a "scandalous" waste of court time. More than half a million pages of documents were tendered and the transcripts of the hearing ran to almost 10,000 pages. Neither Rupert nor Lachlan Murdoch appeared.

By the end of 1997, a fraught, divided season in which the Brisbane Broncos won the rebel competition, and the Newcastle Knights won their first ARL grand final, the Super League had folded its cards and formed the National Rugby League (NRL) as a 50:50 joint venture with the Australian Rugby League. All told, News lost some AUD$560 million on the rebel competition but emerged with a controlling stakes in two key monopoly franchises, the Broncos and outright ownership of the Melbourne Storm, both strong teams and monopoly franchises that would generate millions in earnings. Ironically, for all the loyalty the Packers claimed towards the ARL in the nineties, two decades later it is the Murdoch empire which has stuck with the game. Lachlan remains attached to the Broncos and has intervened to fend off outsider attempts to take control of the team. "It's [still] controlled by News," says Ribot, "and I think the big influence on that is Lachlan. News Corporation don't need the Brisbane Broncos— it's one apple in an orchard—but it's Lachlan's baby, and he's got his people running it, and when he's in town he's still very loyal to them."

At a personal level, the only winners in the Super League war were the legion of players who took home much bigger salaries than they had ever hoped for. In early 1997, Ribot and the ARL chairman, Ken Arthurson, both stepped down as the two sides sought compromise. In April 1997, Rupert's loyal lieutenant Ken Cowley retired as executive chairman of News after thirty-three-years service. According to a piece later that year by Pamela Williams, there was little doubt Lachlan's arrival in Sydney had contributed to Cowley's decision. Some former News Ltd. executives have no doubt the young Murdoch elbowed the loyal Cowley out of the way. Williams wrote:

With Murdoch overseas and Lachlan positioned directly beneath Cowley, it was inevitable that Murdoch and his son would be on the phone nearly every day, discussing the business and a range of matters that would have been the purview of Cowley as chairman and chief executive. By early this year it was obvious to those around Cowley that he was not always in the loop. And further, that he was not going to sit on his hands in such a situation. 'Ken wasn't prepared to wear it anymore,' one insider commented. 'He has great loyalty to Rupert and to Lachlan but it wasn't working.'[10]

Only Lachlan had emerged unscathed, stepping up to become executive chairman of News Ltd. as Cowley stepped down and taking full responsibility for the Australian operations, which accounted for roughly 15 per cent of News Corporation's global earnings. Only months earlier he had become the first of the Murdoch children to join Rupert and Anna on the News Corp board, putting him in pole position for the succession.

Lachlan's appointment to run the family's Australian business made news around the world. Murdoch senior was reportedly worried Lachlan was rising too fast, but after two years mentoring him, Cowley told Rupert his son was "as ready as he can be" to take over at News Ltd. Talking to Williams, Cowley said Lachlan had been tested "and probably will be tested all his life. But being in Australia during Super League and pay-TV, he has learned things he wouldn't otherwise have learned in twenty years."

By this time, his sister Elisabeth was working for BSkyB in England, under the direct supervision of Sam Chisholm. Lachlan took Williams' question about nepotism head-on:

> Anyone in this position, and I think my brother and sister and I would be the first to admit we have taken over responsibility at an early age, but once we're in, judge us by the same standards as anyone else—on how we manage. Not because we're called Lachlan or Elisabeth Murdoch. Take the name away and say, 'Is that executive doing the right things?' There will always be a

debate about nepotism, but what's already happened internally in the company, although not externally, is you are judged by results.

It would take another two decades for Cowley to give his own frank assessment of Lachlan, in an offhand remark to another *Australian Financial Review* journalist, Anne Hyland. In 2014, after a long interview about bootmaking company R.M. Williams, which the octogenarian Cowley part-owned and chaired, Hyland asked him about his time at News Ltd. Cowley said, in what he thought were off-the-record comments, that "Elisabeth, not Lachlan, is the smart Murdoch." "I like Lachlan," he added. "He's a nice man, but he's not a great businessman. He's not a big and good decision-maker in my opinion." The comments caused a minor furore. Hyland insisted the whole thing was on the record and had a tape to prove it, but there were worries about Cowley's advancing years and whether he had been taken advantage of. Lachlan was said to be furious, as for weeks before Cowley had been trying to get him to invest in an R.M. Williams agricultural holding company that was struggling to create the world's largest carbon farm in the Northern Territory, and to join the board. Lachlan declined on both counts and he saw Cowley's subsequent public barb as nothing more than sour grapes. The business went broke.

The bitterness from the Super League war would last for years, as was revealed in Bruce Guthrie's memoir, *Man Bites Murdoch*. The book recounted a 2005 conversation between Guthrie, then editor of the *Weekend Australian Magazine*, and his boss Chris Mitchell, who queried why he had run a puff piece about ABC television host Andrew Denton, who was persona non grata at News Ltd.—apparently a member of a secret blacklist. Denton was a passionate supporter of the South Sydney Rabbitohs, a foundation club kicked out of the new NRL competition at the behest of News Ltd., only to win a stunning upset victory on an appeal to the Federal Court in 2001. Denton had said at the time, "I wish I could take Lachlan Murdoch [and] Ken Cowley by their smug little jowls and sit them down for a while and explain something to them . . . Tradition in sport is a very, very powerful thing." When Guthrie tried to justify the Denton piece, Mitchell pulled him up: "I've just had Lachlan on the phone from New York and he's not happy. In fact, he's very pissed off."[11] Lachlan did not forget a slight.

Rupert had wanted his son "blooded" in the family business. The Super League battle was as hard a fight as they come and still divides the sport two decades later. It had also become a proxy war between the Murdochs and the Packers, and between Telstra and Optus, fighting over the future of pay-TV in Australia. The lesson, for all concerned, was that the working man's sport was not the plaything of media moguls or corporations. Rugby league belonged to the people, the fans, and woe betide anybody who tried to take it from them. Super League was not Lachlan's idea, and nor in his early twenties could he be fairly held responsible for the execution of News Corp's strategy. But as the face of the Murdoch empire, Lachlan had skin in the game, and he had certainly lost some of it.

4

First among Equals

AFTER THREE YEARS IN Australia, things were looking up for Lachlan. He had been promoted almost every six months. As *The Australian* duly reported, he was not so much climbing the career ladder as ascending in the career elevator.[1] He was chairman of News Ltd., atop the entire Australian operation, and on the company's main board. Lachlan was free to exert his influence on the newspapers and he revelled in it. At *The Australian*, Lachlan clashed with the editor-in-chief, Paul Kelly, forcing the closure of the dry-but-worthy Asia Business supplement as a cost-cutting measure. For decades Kelly had been one of the country's most highly regarded political journalists—he had quit *The Australian* in 1975 over its anti-Whitlam campaign but returned to the fold in the 1990s, helping to restore the paper's credibility. Lachlan demoted Kelly, or at best shoved him sideways, giving him the position of international editor after five years at the helm. Kelly's second-in-command, editor Malcolm Schmidtke, was sacked with a single phone call from Lachlan, showing the young publisher had a ruthless streak. Lachlan later told the *Financial Times* that as editor of *The Australian*, "Paul Kelly did a fantastic job of making it the paper of record, and absolutely trusted. However, nobody wanted to read it."[2]

There was speculation Kelly was removed because Murdoch believed he was too closely identified with the totemic issues of the former Keating government, particularly the debate over whether Australia should cut its remaining ties with the English monarchy and become a republic, and the landmark Indigenous land rights case, *Mabo*, in which the High Court recognized a limited form of native title. Showing off changes to the design of "The Oz," Lachlan explained: "We had to broaden the paper's interests, and say that politics is not the only interesting thing. A lot of the old readers, the bureaucrats and politicians, will probably be a bit uncomfortable with what we are doing with the paper." The new editor-in-chief, David Armstrong, was a company veteran—there was nothing radical about his appointment—but Lachlan also brought younger journalists onto the paper, at one point launching a raid on the newsroom of rival Fairfax. Lachlan and legendary Murdoch editor Col Allan sat in a pub across the road from *The Sydney Morning Herald*, ringing favored journalists, asking them over for a chat, and making a generous offer on the spot if it went well. "I think it was the start of my understanding of how fiercely competitive Lachlan was," Allan recalls. "He understood that the only thing that really counts is talent. And that businesses are about people . . . they're not just structures."

Thanks to some forward thinking, the national broadsheet had cornered the information technology sector with its Tuesday computer section, a weekly lift-out filled with indispensable job ads. As the internet took off with the launch of the Mosaic web browser and Microsoft's blockbuster Windows 95, Lachlan was determined that *The Australian* would hang on to that young audience. He roped in his childhood friend Zeb Rice, whom he'd known in Los Angeles and who now came out to work alongside him at News and share his house at Elizabeth Bay. Rice led News' digital push, aggressively targeting rival Fairfax. News had missed out on the news.com domain name in the US amid a frenzy of cyber-squatting but pounced on news.com.au in 1996. The company slowly got behind the site, uploading ads for jobs, cars, and real estate from 100-odd mastheads and promoting the URL through stories in the computer section of *The Australian*.

Lachlan was also closely associated with the launch of a new weekly media section in *The Australian*, modelled on that of *The Guardian* in

Britain. Initially there was scepticism that a Murdoch newspaper could cover the tight Australian media industry with any independence, but the supplement played a useful role and in 2009 Lachlan wished it a happy birthday on its tenth anniversary, albeit while admitting, "I wish there was more advertizing in it!"[3] Lachlan and Zeb had fun, too, setting up a short-lived company called the Moose Corporation, which ran a discounted book and video mail-order service through *The Sunday Telegraph*, called the Mooseline. Each week Dr. Moose, who turned out to be mostly Lachlan, would pen light-hearted reviews of a handful of books and films, and readers could phone in 24/7 for their 35 per cent discount (plus postage). From fiction to cookbooks to motivational tomes, the titles were all international best-sellers, Tom Clancy, Stephen King, Ben Elton, Anthony Robbins, Stephen Covey, except for *Getting Your Message Across* by James Hooke and Jeremy Philips, a mate of Lachlan's who had joined Moose Corp. "Two world-champion debaters explain the seven elements of effective communication," read the review. "Worth reading if you've found that imagining the audience naked just doesn't work anymore." The Mooseline lasted four months.

Lachie and Zeb, who were so close they even had the same crewcut, were seen as progressives and both believed that only the young had the digital vision to see how the internet would change the world.[4] At the same time, Lachlan was determined to cut costs and insisted for years that journalists did not need their own individual internet access, until finally his editors revolted at a group conference in Sydney in August 1999. The deputy editor of *The Australian* at the time, Peter Wilson, told the gathering, "Just because we work for a Luddite company doesn't mean we have to go without the internet and email." Lachlan took it personally and strode to the podium, jaw clenched, peeved that "Peter has just called me a Luddite." It would be too expensive to connect every journalist, he insisted; they should instead get out there and talk to people, rather than searching online.[5] Days later, Lachlan was big enough to realize he'd made the wrong call and in an internal memo begrudgingly announced: "The News Ltd. editors conference today approved email access for all editorial staff and internet access for all reporters, graphic artists, and others who require it to carry out their duties." It was classic News Ltd. stinginess, typical of the Murdochs, whom *The Australian Financial Review* had once described as the "best known scrooges in journalism."[6] Lachlan gave an insight into the family's parsimony, telling the *Financial Times* that while he used to think the company's culture was Australian, "now I think our culture, believe it or not, comes from the Adelaide *News* in the 1950s, when my father came back from Oxford and started running the place. It was a paper going broke, in an incredibly competitive environment, that had to fight its guts out to survive." The *Adelaide News* was the number two paper to the *Advertiser*, and Lachlan would continue to believe that News Corp operated best when it was the underdog, "when we're uncomfortable and when we're really striving."

Lachlan brought change to the powerful tabloids, too, and showed the company was willing to invest in print by splurging a billion dollars on four big new color presses, working in tandem with former *Daily Mirror* journalist and long-time editor of Sydney's *Daily Telegraph* John Hartigan, whom he made News Ltd.'s group editorial director in 1997. Then approaching fifty, Harto was a generation older than Lachie, but the two blokes were thick as thieves, working hard and playing hard with a crop of up-and-comers from all over the News stable, including David Penberthy from Adelaide and Joe Hildebrand from Melbourne. Lachlan wanted to make News Ltd. a more exciting place to work, splurging tens of millions to tart up the old headquarters at grungy Holt Street, where the presses no longer rumbled in the basement, and in the process saving much more by avoiding relocating to a prestigious CBD office tower, as did Fairfax. Rupert and Ken Cowley had been in favor of such a move, but Lachlan pushed for the company to stay in Surry Hills. "I said [the CBD] is too expensive," Lachlan told the *Financial Times*, "and it gives us a great address and nothing else. Whereas around here, this area is very young, and it is changing rapidly." He was proved right. Surry Hills progressively gentrified, while Fairfax would later move into campus-style digs on the city fringes at Pyrmont, and even later across the harbor to bland North Sydney.

Showing his touchy-feely side, Lachlan hoped News would be an employer of choice. In Christmas 1995 he hand-delivered to every staffer at *The Australian* a personalized diary, the recipient's name embossed on the cover. According to *The Sydney Morning Herald*, there was a kerfuffle in the ladies' lavatory when he did the rounds: make-up hastily applied and hair vigorously brushed. Lachlan walked the building often, chatting with staff of all levels in the cafeteria. He made a point of closing the lifts to the carpark so that the senior brass would have to walk through the front door like the rest of their staff.

Lachie's charm did sometimes fail him. One day he was talking to a bunch of News Ltd. cadets about the future of newspapers and the advantages of being a journalist at a global organization. When it came time for questions, one young journo asked if he thought Australia should be a republic or a monarchy. Lachlan reportedly said that the problem with monarchies is that they are full of people who inherit money and power from their parents. "Isn't that what you've done?" asked one cheeky cadet. Another asked what Lachlan's job as publisher entailed. Lachlan gave a brief job description, including meetings with sales executives. "Yeah, but what do you actually *do*?" came the follow-up. Lachlan left the meeting soon after, visibly upset.[7]

One of the major projects Lachlan was tangentially involved with was the Fox Studios development in Sydney, led by formidable executive Kim Williams. The $150 million project, involving the construction of new film, television and advertizing studios at Moore Park in Sydney's inner east, was controversial from the get-go. News Corporation would have access to the historic Showgrounds site, home to the Royal Easter Show, an annual fair popular with families since 1882, almost as a fait accompli, and well before NSW planning approval had been given. News gained access to the sixty-acre site on a forty-year lease at a heavily discounted rent without any competitive tender process. The Fox Studios proposal drew immediate fire from residents concerned about the loss of the local amenity and about the effective transfer of public land to a private business. Years of litigation followed, and although the courts found against the

Save the Showground group, the NSW auditor-general slammed the state government for failing to justify not only why normal tender processes had been suspended to give advantage to a single company, but also why this was in the state's best interests; he estimated the uncompetitive lease could cost state taxpayers more than $100 million.

Lachlan attacked suggestions that inappropriate political advantage had played a part, calling them an "outrageous attack on the integrity of those who had brought the project to life." Kim Williams fought a successful rear-guard lobbying effort, impressing Lachlan, and it was the beginning of an important relationship between the two men. The new studios opened with a spectacular party in early 1998—Keanu Reeves was there, along with a bevy of other Hollywood stars—and it was announced that celebrated director Baz Luhrmann (Lachlan's friend and near neighbor) would shoot two movies there, including *Moulin Rouge*. The studios quickly became a mainstay of the Australian film industry, home to the production of hits such as *Babe* and the *Star Wars* prequels. "As a boy I remember growing up on the *Star Wars* trilogy and adopting its heroes and villains as my own," Lachlan said, describing the decision to shoot the films in Sydney as a dream come true.[8]

Notwithstanding his responsibilities at News, Lachlan made sure he got away as much as possible, often with Joe Cross. Cross recalls one trip to Far North Queensland that was particularly adventurous, after Lachlan was tipped off by someone at *The Cairns Post* about a legendary tour guide who flew three-day helicopter trips out of Cairns.

> So, Lachlan and I arrive at Cairns Airport for this trip of a lifetime and we are met by this bloke called Brazakka. He's standing next to his Robinson 4x4 helicopter and strapped to the outside are fishing rods, spear guns, an axe, three shotguns and a rifle. It was like something out of the movies. The plan was to head north, where it's mostly uninhabited, and this bloke had organized fuel stops in the most remote parts of the globe I've ever been to. We hop, skip and jump our way north for about four hours and the

next thing I know Lachlan is hanging out of the chopper at about a hundred feet, shooting at a wild boar the size of a VW Beetle, with the rifle. He nailed it first shot. When you're flying in this part of Australia you get *sick* of seeing crocodiles . . . you see thousands of [them], right, they're all sunbaking the whole way up these beautiful beaches. We needed to catch our dinner for the first night and so we landed on this beach that must have had twenty or more big-ass crocodiles. And as we land, we see them all darting off into the mangrove estuaries, and they move fast if they want to. I'm looking at Lachlan going, 'Are we out of our mind here?' Brazakka loaded the double-barrel shotgun and said, 'Don't worry, boys, I'll be right next to you if any of those crocs try something.' So Lachlan and I followed the footprints of the crocs down to the sand, walking along with fishing rods, and we're going to stand on the edge where we've just seen sixteen-foot crocodiles go into the estuary and we're standing there for an hour and a half fishing, and we've got Brazakka with the shotgun pointed at the water. Then he realizes it's going to be better fishing on the other side, and so then the three of us are wading through two foot of water, while Brazakka has passed the shot gun to Lachlan while he pulls out a Magnum .45 to face the other way. I look back and would say without doubt that's the most risk I've taken, but hey, Lachlan climbs rocks for fun so maybe it wasn't for him. I will say the meal we had that night was one of the best I've had and we really felt like we earned it. The next day we land out on Haggerston Island and we go out on the boat, and the fellow who runs it there is like the real Crocodile Dundee, and we go fishing for lobbies, crays . . . and there are tiger sharks in the water, there are other reef sharks, but Lachlan wants to go diving with the tigers. At this point, I am like, 'Man, get me back to Sydney, back to the city please' . . . but Lachlan was in his element.

* * *

In mid-1998, Lachlan made his debut appearance before News Corp's top 300-odd executives, editors, and producers at the management conference in Sun Valley, Idaho. Peter Chernin delivered an opening address, described by Rupert as "brilliant," which old hands saw as extremely significant. In it, Chernin explained that the explosion of consumer choice through the rise of digital media meant the death of blandness. Previously, mass media sought to produce the least objectionable programs to appeal to the largest possible audience, the biggest chunk of the mainstream. Instead of this commodified content, he argued, creative media companies now had to "seize the edge." Savvy media consumers would now be asking themselves, "Am I a Fox viewer or a PBS viewer?" Chernin said, dismissing the "drivel-in-the-middle."

Chernin was providing the philosophical underpinnings for a proposal, recently announced to investors, to spin a new Fox Corporation out of News Corp in a $3.6 billion float, so that the growth assets in the US, Fox's film and television channels, including Fox News and Fox Broadcasting, would be freed from the legacy print business. The plan faltered during the dot-com crash in 2000, but the Murdochs would return to it much later.

By contrast with Chernin's sweeping address, Lachlan's speech was more prosaic, opening with a labored invocation of JFK's famous 1961 Moon Shot speech, urging News Corp's 50,000 employees to pull together to "achieve our one singular goal: to be the most creative company in the world." Expressing what he felt was, but shouldn't be, a controversial opinion within News, Lachlan called for lateral collaboration between the various departments: marketing, editorial, finance, IT, printers and machinists, and digital engineers. "The missing element in our creative management, I believe, is an informal but structured communication system, deep within the company." It was a reasonable suggestion, but at a major conference focused on the opportunities and threats of digital media, it may have seemed a little off-point when Lachlan talked in nitty-gritty detail about a workshop held for printers and engineers in Sydney and waxed lyrical about new cost-saving methods of repairing ribbons on the Ferag presses.

Partway through his speech he cut to a pre-recorded video message from Tony Nelson, editor of *The Centralian Advocate* in Alice Springs:

Lachlan, Rupert, we've got a great team at the *Advocate*. But I reckon we could do even better if we could tap into all the people and creativity within News worldwide. Who knows? We might even be able to pass on a few good ideas of our own. Anyway, you guys might be able to sit around for a couple of days having a chinwag, but the rest of us have got work to do. It's edition day today, and I've got a paper to get out. So thanks again, and Lachlan, don't forget to buy everyone a beer tonight for me. So long!

After the clip, Lachlan joked, "He'll get a shock when I send him the bar tab tonight."

As he was being groomed for higher things within News Corp, Lachlan got serious about taking up his father's old pursuit of sailing, buying a yacht, *Tall Cotton*, with *Daily Telegraph* columnist Piers Akerman. Once a week he took sailing lessons with an instructor and he soon upgraded to a Swan 51, which he called *Karakorum* after the Pakistani mountain range. In 1997, Lachlan declared to Joe Cross that they were going to enter the Sydney to Hobart yacht race, along with Zeb Rice, Baz Luhrmann, and ad-man George Betsis, who had handled the Super League account and would become a long-time friend. *Karakorum* had a professional skipper and crew, as well as the four newbies, but when they all started arguing about which sails to put up in a nasty squall on day one, Lachlan put his foot down and captained the boat the rest of the way to Tasmania. Rupert and Anna met them in Hobart on *Morning Glory*, Rupert telling a local reporter he'd like to see his son sailing something bigger and faster, and together they went for a holiday, cruising around the island.

The next year, Lachlan ditched his mates and took up an invitation to join Oracle founder Larry Ellison on the 79-foot maxi *Sayonara*, which was the favorite to take out line honors. The day before the race, on the night of Christmas Eve, thieves broke into Lachlan's Elizabeth Bay garage and stole his $200,000 BMW sedan while he was sleeping. Nobody was disturbed or saw anything at all (police dusted for fingerprints) but Lachlan would soon start looking for a new home.

Signs were bad on the weather front, too, with the Sydney to Hobart fleet prepared for heavy storms. Tragically that year, six sailors died, and five yachts sank in the roughest seas ever to hit the race. *Sayonara* was a frontrunner and beat the worst of the storm, but Ellison said that, facing eighteen-meter waves and winds topping 140 kilometers per hour, he thought he was going to die, especially as sections of the fibreglass hull began to delaminate as they were launched off the mountainous waves and crashed into the canyons below. Afterwards, Ellison swore off ocean racing.

Like most of the crew, Lachlan was heavily seasick—at one point he spewed into the wind, which blew the vomit into the face of helmsman Robbie Naismith, a veteran sailor who had helped New Zealand win two America's Cups. "Ah, Lachlan," Naismith said, "I think I'm going to have a sympathy chuck." Lachlan held up—he only missed one watch—but feared the boat could capsize. When below decks, he lay near the stairway so that he could make a quick escape if necessary.

Sayonara took out both line honors and the handicap that year, but the celebrations were cancelled given the lives lost; most of the fleet was still at sea, and Australia's largest peacetime search-and-rescue operation was underway. Lachlan described the experience as harrowing and admitted to a fellow sailor, "If we had conditions like this last year, I would have lost the boat."[9]

Two years later, Lachlan and Joe Cross joined *News Corporation,* a professionally skippered Volvo 60 that was doing a practice leg for the Whitbread around-the-world race. When another fierce southerly storm hit in the middle of Bass Strait, the skipper sent Lachlan and Cross down under. Volvo 60s are fast but lightweight, and there are no bunks to speak of. Lachlan and Joe tried and failed to sleep on the sail-bags, feeling the hull shudder as it bashed the waves, praying that the boat would hold together. The yacht suffered rudder damage, most likely after hitting a sunfish. They were fifth over the line, but Lachlan and Joe agreed it would be their last Hobart race. "I said to him, 'Promise me, mate, you never bring me on another race again,'" Joe recalls, "and he said, 'I won't be doing one either.'"

* * *

By the end of the nineties, Lachlan could reasonably expect he was on track for the top job. Elisabeth was staking her claim, having taken over as head of BSkyB from Sam Chisholm, and James had been made head of News Ltd.'s new music division and was taking charge of digital media from his base at Fox Studios in Los Angeles. But Lachlan, clearly, was the most deeply immersed in the core business of News. In a 1997 interview, Rupert told Matthew Horsman, author of the book *Sky High: The Amazing Story of BSkyB*, that the succession at News Corp would depend on how long he remained "compos mentis," and that his three children had agreed that Lachlan "will take over . . . he will be first among equals, but they have to prove themselves first."[10] (Rupert's oldest child, Prudence, hit the roof at being forgotten and obtained a grovelling apology from her father, accompanied by what she described as the biggest bouquet of flowers she'd ever seen.)

Pressed to clarify the timing of any succession, Rupert clarified that he did not intend on dying any time soon: "I said that when mortality asserts itself, that my four children will be the inheritors of the shares and it's their decision, but that currently I thought there was a consensus between them that Lachlan should be the one."[11] Shortly after, Rupert backed up this sentiment by appointing Lachlan to the Office of the Chairman, a six-member committee of his most trusted advisers, responsible for the network of private trusts that allowed Murdoch to run News Corp with an iron fist despite holding only a minority economic interest. By late 1998, Lachlan felt comfortable enough to canvass his bright future with the *Financial Times'* John Gapper. Describing speculation over the succession as "a pain in the ass," Lachlan said: "If you had constant speculation over the three deputies to a chief executive in another company, you would say, 'Look, this is not good,' and you would find a way to put an end to it. But it is difficult. It's a juicy story, and I can't think of a way of doing it."

With some foresight, however, Lachlan stressed that any decision on the succession was far from imminent. "Have you met my dad?" he asked Gapper. "Two or three years is not a realistic timescale. We are talking thirty years' time, forty years' time. I would not want to step into that role any time soon." Then Lachlan brought the interview back down to earth: "I don't know if I would be a good chief executive for News Corp or not. What I do know, however—and I hope this doesn't sound too arrogant— is that I am the best chief executive for Australia. I can confidently say these operations are being run extremely well. Looking around, I don't think anyone could do it better."[12]

Investors were not so sure. At the end of 1999, Fairfax's *Business Review Weekly* magazine ran a three-part series on Lachlan, Elisabeth, and James, beginning with a cover story on Lachlan headlined "Murdoch's Boy Fails." The magazine had surveyed fifty fund managers around the world on the performance to date of each of the Murdoch children working for News Corp. It was a highly subjective straw poll, nothing more, but the results were interesting. James scored highest, with 51 out of 100, while Lachlan scored 48 and Liz 28. Leading analyst Jessica Reif Cohen, from Merrill Lynch, told *BRW* James was "an incredibly smart guy. I think he's being trained by the absolute best in the world and it's not just Rupert. He's absolutely light years ahead of where most people are." Lachlan bristled at being asked about the Super League wars, snapping at *BRW* journalist Ali Cromie: "I had nothing to do with that!"[13]

* * *

In his twenties, Lachlan was no conservative culture warrior, describing himself as having "a pretty open mind" on social matters. When redneck Queensland politician Pauline Hanson formed the anti-immigrant and explicitly racist One Nation party in 1997, the young Murdoch was aghast. Lachlan had joined the board of Star TV, the Murdochs' Asian satellite television network, and was sensitive to perceptions in the region that the White Australia Policy remained popular, especially outside the major capitals, twenty-five years after it had been dumped by the federal government. Prime minister John Howard refused to condemn Hanson and Lachlan argued that no political party had been firm enough in challenging One Nation. Lachlan lauded Victorian premier Jeff Kennett, a Liberal leader who was economically conservative but socially progressive, saying he was "the only person to stand up and say he understands why people on farms and stations might be disenchanted, but we cannot have this country racially divided." Door-stopped at the AFL Grand Final breakfast in Melbourne, on the eve of the 1998 federal election, Lachlan declined to endorse Howard as Kerry Packer had done earlier that week: "I don't think media companies should really come out and support one opponent or the other in an election, so close to the actual poll."

In 1999, Australia held a referendum to decide whether the country should become a republic and replace the Queen of England as head of state. *The Australian* favored a 'yes' vote, and so did Lachlan, telling a gathering of Asian business leaders ahead of the referendum that Australia was "yet to have our revolution":

> In just over a month, Australians will have an historic opportunity to take the courageous step to break from our colonial past without bloodshed or loss of life. I can think of no more unremarkable proposition [than] that an Australian should sit at the apex of the Australian system of government. The most remarkable aspect of the 'resident for president' push in Australia is that it has taken a century to happen.[14]

The defeat of the republican proposal—due in no small part to smart campaigning by arch-conservative Howard government minister Tony Abbott, the former director of Australians for a Constitutional Monarchy—was perhaps a lesson in overreach for the young Murdoch. *The Australian* conducted some self-examination of its support for the campaign, which had extended to printing pro-republican bumper stickers and running a front-page editorial for the first time in the paper's history. *The Australian*'s older, conservative-leaning readership was not impressed, nor was Prime Minister Howard, a staunch monarchist. In a clumsy intervention, Lachlan rather prematurely endorsed the leadership credentials of federal treasurer Peter Costello, who was already aspiring to the country's top job. "Perhaps, not surprisingly, the most senior government minister to support the republic has been the treasurer, Peter Costello," said Lachlan, then twenty-eight. "That's the same individual who had the courage to drive through economic reform [and] has also found courage on this issue, and in doing so has again laid his leadership credentials in front of the Australian electorate." Howard would successfully fend off Costello's ambitions for the better part of a decade.

* * *

Lachlan's frustration with Howard was to do partly with the prime minister's social conservatism, but also with the federal government's dithering on media reform. Towards the end of the 1990s, the stalemate over cross-media and foreign ownership remained, while the government was forced to deal with the advent of digital technology and the looming convergence of TV screens and the internet.

At the same time, News Corp, globally and in Australia, was itself dithering on the sidelines as the dot-com sector exploded, watching as start-ups with no track record of profitability floated at market valuations that would soon look obscene. Rupert speculated that News could boost its share price substantially if it had a dot-com angle, adding perhaps a billion dollars to the company's market value. James Packer, never much interested in journalism, was thoroughly taken with the potential of new media, helping to set up the "Ninemsn" joint venture (not unlike MSNBC in the States) and floating off its eCorp internet division to huge acclaim. Presciently, Packer snared early minority stakes in three promising Aussie ventures, Carsales.com.au, Realestate.com.au and Seek.com, which would go on to monopolize the three key categories of classified advertizing revenue (cars, homes, and jobs) that had provided the Fairfax empire with its so-called "rivers of gold" for more than a century.

Lachlan remained somewhat sceptical about the internet challenge to print—if anything, he thought television was in more danger[15]—and was almost dismissive of any threat it posed to News' beloved mastheads. At a World Association of Newspapers annual congress in Japan in mid-1998, he said he was "not at all pessimistic about the future of newspapers," predicting that current "screen technology and consumer habits did not lend themselves to really reading a newspaper online" and that the internet was not going to "wipe us out":

> Perhaps it is the failing of youth that makes me unwilling to surrender to the doomsayers. I don't think the Internet or yet-unimagined forms of new media will kill the daily newspaper. In fact, I believe we can bring together the best of technology on the one hand and our long-standing creative skills on the other to ensure the future of our publications and of our businesses.[16]

Taking a swipe at financial analysts who believed newspapers were "more a relic of the past than a vibrant and essential part of a modern multimedia corporation," Murdoch added:

> Most of these people have never run a business, let alone put out a newspaper. It goes without saying, they are 100 per cent wrong. Newspapers are the backbone on which News Corporation, financially and culturally, was founded. I can think of no business that holds the [same] challenges, the opportunities, the excitement and responsibilities as ours.

It was not until mid-1999 that News Corp finally unveiled a private internet investment vehicle, ePartners, seeded with $300 million. Pundits at the time thought this perilously late, but News Corp's hesitation was vindicated in the tech wreck that followed. In 1997, a digital news start-up, PointCast, knocked back a takeover offer pushed by James Murdoch valued at $450 million. Within two years, PointCast sold for a mere $7 million.

One major investment the Murdochs did make, however, was in an upstart Australian telco, One.Tel, which had been started by a schoolfriend of James Packer, Jodee Rich. Rich and his sidekick Brad Keeling were insanely ambitious big-picture types, marketing whizzes who spotted the appeal of mobile telephones to the young and cornered that market segment with their skater-dude mascot and cheap contracts. Rich and Packer were personally tight— Jodee would later he said he had never had a closer relationship than his friendship with James, who believed in the vision and trusted him implicitly. One.Tel was by this stage the third-largest internet service provider in Australia and there was a lot of blue sky.

In early 1999, as One.Tel sought to raise more capital to fund an overseas expansion, James approached Lachlan to see if News would like to invest. Jodee, James, and Lachlan flew to New York to pitch it to Rupert, who gave the green light to a combined $709 million investment, staggered over three years, that would see News and the Packers' PBL emerge with 40 per cent of the upstart telco. Both James and Lachlan would join the One.Tel board. When the announcement was made, market commentators were staggered at the valuations implicit in the purchase price of the One.Tel shares, but it was just the latest example as the dot-com bubble expanded. One.Tel shares rallied afresh on the strength of the Murdoch and Packer surnames, and within days both companies were sitting on handsome paper profits. Lachlan's champions, including *Herald Sun* columnist Terry McCrann, chalked up One.Tel as a "clear win" for the young Murdoch.[17]

5

"The Best Deal Ever"

LACHLAN HAD ANOTHER REASON for confidence. In early 1998, he had met the glamorous New York–based Australian model Sarah O'Hare on an intimate Sydney Harbour cruise organized by fashion designer Collette Dinnigan, another member of the Museum of Contemporary Art's young patrons group. Born and raised on Sydney's sunny northern beaches, Sarah had appeared on the cover of *Sports Illustrated, Traveller,* and other magazines and was the international face of Wonderbra, a gig that secured her a spot on *The Late Show with David Letterman*. Describing herself as a "beach girl at heart," O'Hare's picture was for a while the most downloaded on the internet, and she was considered Australia's most successful modelling export since Elle Macpherson.

Lachlan told his friend Joe Cross about the encounter and was quickly given Sarah's mobile phone number; as it turned out, a woman in Joe's office was one of her best mates. The couple's first reported public outing came after a pro-am golf tournament on the Gold Coast in March 1998, where Lachlan and Sarah were spotted getting "extremely tactile" with each other at a small restaurant gathering of family and friends, including O'Hare's mum. Unluckily for them, the next table was full of journalists. Once Lachlan and Sarah were dating, Cross says, the couple were "solid as," and gradually he began to see less of his good mate:

It was on . . . he's like, hook line and sinker gone. And fair enough! With Sarah, she's the whole package, she's like a completely down-to-earth knockabout Aussie, being a super model didn't hurt, and she loves all the things that Lachlan loved to do, you know, which is going out, doing stuff, exploring, having drinks, having a laugh, she has a great family and she's got a whole group of fabulous friends that now come together with his tight group of mates, and everyone gets on.

The couple were seen out whenever O'Hare was in Sydney, which was not that often as she remained busy in New York. Within months, there were reports that the pair had separated due to the difficulty of maintaining a long-distance relationship—O'Hare was described as Lachlan's "ex," and he was reportedly seen out with other girlfriends. But their separation didn't last. By November, the couple had announced their engagement. Lachlan had popped the question after a meal at a swanky restaurant in Melbourne during the spring horseracing carnival. As Sarah later described it, Lachlan was telling her how wonderful they were together when he got down on one knee and proposed: "What I'm trying to say is, will you marry me?" O'Hare was stunned:

> When he said, 'Will you marry me?' I was like, 'What?' and he goes, 'Will you marry me?' and I was like, 'Are you asking me to marry you?' and he went, 'Yeah, I'm asking you to marry me.' 'Are you sure? What are you doing?' It was so funny. He said, 'Sarah, I've asked you six times.'

Sarah said yes, of course, and Lachlan called her father to ask his permission. They planned their wedding for early 1999.[1] The handsome couple publicly revealed their engagement at the Melbourne Cup, placing a bet on Tie the Knot, which came sixth.

Nineteen ninety-eight had proved an emotional rollercoaster for Lachlan, with Rupert and Anna announcing their shock separation in

April after thirty-two years of marriage. At first the media reports cited difficulties related to Rupert's workload and constant travel and Anna's desire that he slow down and they spend more time together. With their three children all by now working in the empire in the US, UK, and Australia, Anna feared that Rupert was pitting their children against one another. She had taken up writing during her years in New York; her second novel, *Family Business*, published in 1988, chronicled the implosion of a media empire due to the founder's failure to settle the succession. Now just such a scenario was unfolding in front of her.

Within weeks, however, Rupert confirmed that he was seeing someone new: Wendi Deng, a junior executive at Star TV based in Hong Kong. Deng had accompanied Rupert on tours of the Chinese mainland, and the two were now openly dating. Rupert denied there had been any overlap between the two relationships, but Anna was sure he was lying and determined that she would make her former husband pay. Although the company announcement described the separation as "amicable," it was anything but.

Without telling Anna, Rupert inserted an announcement into the notice paper for the News Corp annual general meeting that she would be leaving the board. Years later, Anna gave an account of her last board meeting in New York at which both Rupert and Lachlan were present to Australian journalist David Leser. Anna kept her dignity, expressing optimism about the company and the future of her children in it, then got up and left to go to lunch with her new boyfriend.

Anna still had to turn up and face the shareholders one last time in Adelaide and Lachlan made sure to accompany his mother out of the meeting. At that point, he was said to be appalled at his father's treatment of her, but Lachlan chose his public words carefully, telling the *Financial Times* that his parents' break-up had been a "blow to everyone":

> For a long time, people in this company looked up to them because here was a couple who obviously sacrificed a lot yet had a wonderful marriage, so when it breaks up, they are somewhat disillusioned.[2]

News Corp investors were rattled, too, as it had always been assumed that if Rupert fell under a bus, Anna would take over the chairmanship until their children had enough experience to step into his shoes. Broking analysts questioned whether Lachlan, if he was to step up, could afford to remain in Australia, which generated only 15 per cent of the company's revenue and less than 5 per cent of profits. There was soon talk that Lachlan would need to get across the US businesses, and in 1999 the company appointed him senior executive vice-president of News Corp's global operations, reporting to the new chief executive, Peter Chernin. Lachlan would divide his time equally between the US and Australia, where he would remain in charge, and he would take responsibility for the global printing operations outside the UK, including the *New York Post*, HarperCollins, and the magazine inserts, coupons, and News America Marketing, the in-store promotions business. It was clearly a made-up role, but it gave Lachlan responsibility for a fifth of News Corp's profits.

The bitter separation between Rupert and Anna would have implications for the succession, too, as Anna sued to ensure that any children of her former husband and Wendi would not accede to the Cruden Investments trust, which controlled the family's holding in News Corp. In this Anna naturally had the support of all three of her children, who were both unhappy at the divorce and wary of Wendi, who was herself an ambitious News executive. At a dinner at the Babbo restaurant in Manhattan, Lachlan and James tried and failed to talk their father out of his new marriage.[3] Lachlan had felt caught in the middle and had tried to support each of his parents until Wendi came along. By that stage, according to one friend, "the whole family's against it."

Joe Cross organized Lachlan's buck's night in Sydney in early 1999, staged on Store Beach near Manly, not far from the former quarantine statio inside Sydney's North Head. The theme was Native American, with waiters dressed as chiefs and twenty scantily clad models who'd signed strict non-disclosure agreements. Media were thrown off the scent, having been told the party would be on an island in Queensland. A bar and tables were set up under teepees and about forty guests, including top News executives, had a sit-down meal. There was no stripping or anything else risqué, and it was over by 11 p.m., when a smaller group went back to Lachlan's place to carry on drinking.

Lachlan and Sarah were married at a strictly private ceremony of about 100 guests at the family's historic Cavan Station, near Yass, which Rupert had bought in the 1960s. At the request of Dame Elisabeth, Wendi was not invited. Anna took care of many of the arrangements. A chapel was erected by the banks of the Murrumbidgee River, with a row of mature trees specially planted as a screen. Guests were bussed down the highway from Sydney, the windows blacked out with newspaper. Zeb Rice was Lachlan's best man; James Murdoch and Joe Cross were groomsmen. Baz Luhrmann and Catherine Martin, Collette Dinnigan and Ian Roberts were all there. No reporters or photographers were invited—the couple asked for no helicopters please, and their request was honored—but media were offered official wedding pics via the News Corp website. The night before, Rupert, family and friends celebrated until 3 a.m. at Lachlan's favorite pub in the little country town of Wee Jasper and father and son went back for lunch the next day.

The wedding day itself poured with rain, and a despondent Channel Nine reporter and crew, hanging outside the Cavan gates hoping for shots of the bride and guests as they arrived, had to make do instead with filming Lachlan as he took off for a morning jog; he promptly took off into a paddock. During the ceremony, Lachlan and Sarah danced a waltz— they'd had lessons from the choreographer of *Strictly Ballroom*—and guests partied on to live performances by Kate Ceberano and Skunkhour. The married couple took off overseas for a two-week honeymoon at a secret destination (Sarah told one outlet it was a 'Kathmandu kind of place', which was later revealed to be Bhutan) followed by a week's sailing.[4] On their way to the airport, the entire wedding cavalcade diverted to a drive-through McDonald's so that Lachlan and Sarah could stock up on burgers and fries for the flight.[5]

* * *

The couple saw in the new millennium partying with a strictly A-list crowd on a decommissioned merchant ship that had been towed all the way from Tasmania. The ship was moored in a prime position, right next to the naval base at Sydney's Garden Island, next to Woolloomooloo. The ship had a clear view of the Harbour Bridge, which was set for an over-the-top fireworks display that would culminate in an exploding "Eternity" scrawled across the arch, harking back to the famous graffito by Arthur Stace that dotted Sydney's streets for several decades from the early 1930s.

One of the first big cities to cross the international dateline, Sydney was one of the best places in the world to be that New Year's Eve. The festivities were all part of a global marketing exercise ahead of the 2000 Sydney Olympics. Baz Luhrmann and Catherine Martin's yacht *Wyuna*, carrying Tom Cruise and Nicole Kidman, had picked Lachlan and Sarah up from a private jetty in Point Piper and sailed on to Woolloomooloo alongside Kerry Packer's *Arctic P*. At Woolloomooloo, everyone transferred to the barge. Lavishly decorated with themed rooms by Baz and Catherine, and with acrobats and performers circulating, the party was described as a cross between Cirque du Soleil and *The Love Boat*. Revellers included actors Ewan McGregor, Leonardo DiCaprio, and a who's who of local celebrities and friends. In a nice touch, the Murdochs invited the two coppers who had turned up when Lachlan's BMW was stolen the previous Christmas. The Murdochs had been invited to the King's Cross police station Christmas party and now returned the favor.

The celebrations went all night. James Packer and his wife Jodhi joined from the *Arctic P* at about 11 p.m. Kerry was supposed to be hosting Bill Gates, the world's richest man, but Gates was a no-show. Looking across to the fun on the barge, Kerry reportedly moaned: "I've got the boat, they've got the party." At ten minutes to midnight, Tom Cruise pulled off an impulsive, daring stunt, climbing ten meters up a rope strung over the deck, no harness, no trampoline, no nothing. Everybody gasped and cheered, before Cruise slid back down like a fireman.

The Australian media at the time were comparing Lachlan unfavorably with James. Most concluded that the Murdochs had been comprehensively outplayed by the Packers on rugby league, free-to-air and pay television, the internet, media law reform—just about everything. The Packer empire was wholly focussed on Australia, which represented less than 10 per cent of News Corp's global earnings, so the Murdoch family's attention was constantly elsewhere. *The Australian Financial Review* reported that News was out of favor with the Howard government as a result of strategic blunders and clumsy political interventions. While Kerry Packer had managed the succession to James adroitly, the *AFR*'s most authoritative commentator concluded that "Lachlan Murdoch does not have those political skills nor the political clout James inherits from his father and spends less and less time in Australia anyway."[6] Given suggestions two decades later that News operated as an extension of the Liberal and National parties, it is noteworthy that in 2000 the Howard Liberal government believed the Murdochs were campaigning against them in *The Australian*, *The Herald Sun* and *The Daily Telegraph*.

One of Lachlan's last jobs before he moved to New York was to oversee News Ltd's sale of half of Australia's second-biggest airline, Ansett, to the publicly owned national carrier Air New Zealand. The sale had a long backstory: after Ken Cowley recruited former Cathay Pacific chief Sir Rod Eddington to engineer a two-year overhaul of the airline, News Ltd had decided to get out of the industry altogether. Owning an airline was not core business for a media company and Ansett had a high-cost structure after buying too many different types of aircraft. Its profits took a further hit from the Super League war, not only in sponsorship, but in the exorbitant cost of flying players all over the world for the international competition.

There followed almost a year of on-again, off-again talks as Air New Zealand considered whether to follow through with the purchase. Lachlan told one newspaper he'd "staked [his] career" on the sale, which was finally announced in mid-February 2000. News did well: Air New Zealand agreed to pay an initial AUD$580 million for the half-stake, and staggered possible payments over the next two to four years could lift the purchase price to over $700 million, a third higher than a year earlier.

Air New Zealand would soon bitterly regret the acquisition. Eighteen months later, as the aviation industry reeled from the September 11 attacks, Ansett would close its doors forever, putting thousands out of work overnight, leaving passengers stranded, and gifting a sizeable chunk of the Australian market to Virgin. The lesson? "Never buy a company from News Ltd.," wrote business journalist and shareholder activist Stephen Mayne, arguing that cost-cutting and asset-stripping by Cowley and Eddington had made Ansett exceedingly vulnerable.

* * *

As he prepared to relocate to the US, Lachlan planned to appoint his successor as chief executive of News Ltd. in Australia. Eddington, who had saved the Murdochs a fortune at Ansett, was seen as the most likely candidate. He was already Lachlan's deputy chairman at News and had joined the global board of News Corp (where he remains). Three months after the sale of Ansett, however, Eddington was headhunted for the chief executive role at British Airways and found the offer irresistible. Instead, Lachlan hand-picked a good mate from News, John Hartigan. According to News insiders, Hartigan was taken by surprise—he had never run a P&L before—and was convinced he had been appointed by Lachlan rather than Rupert. In fact, the view at the top of the company was that Murdoch senior had given his son the Australian operations to run almost as a personal fiefdom, and that many of the announcements made in Rupert's name were decisions taken by Lachlan. He was already calling the shots at News Ltd., albeit under his father's tutelage, as a first step towards running the whole show. As chairman and CEO, Lachlan and Hartigan would work especially closely together in coming years, albeit at a distance as the heir was ensconced in New York.

Lachlan was torn about leaving Australia. When it came time to bid farewell his senior staff at News, he surprised everyone by bursting into tears, but at the same time he felt he was missing out on the action in media and technology by languishing in a laggard outpost of the Murdoch empire. He had been down under for almost the entire first phase of the internet, later called Web 1.0. Just after Christmas 1999, Lachlan and Sarah bought a $3.5 million luxury condominium, freshly built on top of an old six-storey building at 285 Lafayette Street in Manhattan's cool Soho district. The 1886 building, once a chocolate factory, backed onto Mulberry Street, a narrow thoroughfare known as the setting for mob killings in the *Godfather* movies but by now designer-grunge. The Murdochs were three floors up from tennis player Patrick McEnroe and just beneath David Bowie and wife Iman Abdulmajid, who occupied the whole floor above and shared their elevator. The Murdochs' co-op had four bedrooms, four baths, a gourmet kitchen, a wood-burning fireplace, twenty-six-foot-high ceilings, ten-foot-high windows and a huge private terrace where the couple installed a koi pond. It was in walking distance of Rupert and Wendi's $6.5 million penthouse on Prince Street and not far from James' $1.3 million town house on Downing Street.

Reporting on the Murdoch invasion of Soho, *The Sydney Morning Herald*'s correspondent Mark Riley spoke to a contractor working on Lachlan's apartment building. "It's another world up there, brother," the guy said. "All windows and polished floors and views . . . another world."[7]

At the same time, the Murdochs moved to sell their Sydney mansion, Berthong at Elizabeth Bay, which was passed on at auction and finally sold to actor Russell Crowe two years later for $9.25 million. After the deal went through, Lachlan ordered the *New York Post*'s extremely influential Page Six column to kill any unflattering coverage of Crowe, in an example of a favor banking system that protected his mates. At least that's what was alleged by a rogue former freelancer, Jared Paul Stern, who made a series of allegations against the *Post* in a letter threatening to sue after he was sacked for trying to extract money from a source. The *Post* simply published his allegations on Page Six, declaring Stern would not get a cent.

Lachlan's relocation to the US took place as the irrational exuberance of investors was reaching its peak. The $350 billion merger of AOL and Time Warner stunned the world in January 2000 and was hailed as a triumph of the new economy over the old. At last, Lachlan would be at the heart of the action. Almost as soon as he and Sarah arrived in New York, however, the market began to look wobbly. By April, the dot-com crash was underway. According to friends, Lachlan felt that by the time he got back to New York, the boom was over. He concentrated on his day job overseeing the print business, getting a feel for the *New York Post*, HarperCollins, and the decidedly "old economy" News America Marketing. But the market carnage threw up some genuine investment opportunities.

It was perhaps not surprising that the best business deal Lachlan ever made came from an Australian contact. In October 2000, during a trip to Sydney, Lachlan got a call from John McGrath, another young patron of Sydney's Museum of Contemporary Art, inviting him out for a beer. McGrath was a director of an online property website, Realestate.com.au, which was the market leader in Australia but running out of cash. Over a drink in a pub in Surry Hills, McGrath proposed that News Ltd. invest. Lachlan agreed to discuss it in the pleasant war room he had built atop News Ltd.'s Holt Street headquarters.

"[We] were desperate, to be frank," recalls McGrath. "Money was running out rapidly and we had only a few months left before the company would be insolvent." At their meeting, Lachlan, accompanied by Simon Baker (who later became CEO of Realestate.com.au), asked a range of questions and was very engaged. He "asked if we could meet back in twenty-four hours, which we did," says McGrath. The next day, "they gave us an offer on the spot." Lachlan laid out the terms of a deal. News would put in only a fraction of the cash Realestate.com.au was after, just AUD$2.25 million, but would assume the company's debts and steadfastly promote the website through its newspapers, providing contra advertizing worth AUD$8.5 million. In exchange for its AUD$10.75 million, News would take a minority stake in the company, whose shares were now trading at bargain-basement levels, with an option to acquire more. "We were surprised and delighted at the pace at which they had moved," recalls McGrath. "Clearly Lachlan was driving it from the top, as no-one else could have moved that quickly."

Lachlan had rung the chief financial officer back in New York, David Devoe, who was sceptical of investing in an Aussie dot-com and worried the website would eat into News' own property advertizing revenue. But, as Pamela Williams recorded much later in her book *Killing Fairfax*, the amount Lachlan was proposing to invest was "peanuts," and Devoe ticked it off.

James Packer, who subsequently sold his own 10 per cent stake in Realestate.com.au to his friend at News Ltd., later described Lachlan's original investment in the website as "the best deal in media in the last twenty years." As its earnings potential became clearer, News Ltd. tried to launch a full takeover in 2005, which Realestate.com.au, renamed the REA Group, rejected as hostile. McGrath, who was still serving as a director, was given no notice of News' intentions, even though he had brought the opportunity to Lachlan in the first place.

Although the News Ltd. investment in REA was wholly opportunistic and involved nothing more than loose change for the Murdoch empire, Lachlan adopted the right strategy to grow the company. He wore the grumbles from inside News' own mastheads, forcing them to promote REA rather than their own online property pages, while allowing REA's management to remain at arm's length, operating from their own company headquarters.

From McGrath's point of view, Lachlan's contribution to REA was critical. "I believe it was the extra support that News provided beyond the initial deal that made REA what it is," McGrath says. "Lachlan directed most of his local real estate print mastheads to switch to include the REA name and logo across the country. There was a small financial compensation for this, but it was negligible compared to the shot in the arm it gave REA across the country . . . REA may not have survived without Lachlan's lightning-fast deal making and his support after the deal was done."

In October 2000, by which time he was spending only one in every six weeks in Australia, Lachlan was promoted again, taking over as the global deputy chief operating officer from Chase Carey. When the appointment was announced, News Corp shares fell five per cent, confirming that investors remained dubious about Lachlan's management ability and wary of nepotism. Lachlan's relentless rise once again sparked a round of commentary about the heir apparent and speculation about the succession, particularly as Elisabeth, pregnant to Matthew Freud, had recently quit her post as head of BSkyB to strike out on her own.

In an expansive interview with *Television Week*, Lachlan said he worked closely with his brother, James, who was then based in Hong Kong as head of Star TV. "That's one of the things about being in a family company," Lachlan said. "You're forced together all the time, and it's great. I probably spend more time with my sibling and my dad than if we were in different industries and different careers. The press likes to read into us like a soap opera because we're a big family company. And if you look at that kind of coverage over the last several years, there really hasn't been anything new." Lachlan said only a third of his time was now devoted to the broader print side of the business—Australia, the *Post*, HarperCollins and the rest—while two-thirds was spent on "cross-company things like cost control and human relations," as part of his work for his father's Office of the Chairman. He was also spending more time on digital and new media, pointing up the potential of Gemstar as the leading producer of interactive electronic TV program guides.

Still, he came over cautious about the internet and the potential for electronic distribution of newspapers: "About one-third of our costs is generally newsprint, and another one-third is overhead. In that, you have circulation and distribution. So, hypothetically, you could get half your costs back. That would allow us to spend more on the creative side of the business. It would be fantastic to have electronic versions of the *New York Post* and *The Times* in London, *The Sun*, and the papers in Australia. But consumers need to understand that even though it is out there on the web and it's free, this is no easy task. Electronic content, no matter what it is, still is content that costs money to produce. If it's going to be high quality and of value, the consumer will have to pay for it." Lachlan's scepticism that media companies could survive by giving everything away for free online would be vindicated in the long term, although a successful paywall model for newspapers was still years off.

Lachlan described the *Post* as one of his (and Rupert's) pet projects: "People ask why we have one newspaper in the US that loses a little bit of money. They say it's more trouble than it's worth. But I think it is ingrained in the company culture, and I think it's very important to have the greatest newspaper in the greatest city in the world."[8]

While Lachlan was hitting the big time in New York, back in Australia things were going off the rails.

6

. . . And the Worst

LIQUIDATOR STEVE SHERMAN would later describe his first One. Tel meeting as "quite surreal." It was 8 a.m. Monday morning on May 28, 2001 and Sherman had been called to the Packer family's head office in Sydney to find Kerry and James, Lachlan Murdoch, One. Tel's other remaining directors, and a group of executives deep in emergency talks about the rapidly deteriorating situation. While the Packers had about twenty advisers with them, Sherman recalls, Lachlan had just two: News Ltd.'s in-house counsel Ian Philip, and deputy chief executive Peter Macourt. Clearly, Lachlan did not feel he or News had a lot on the line. Indeed, although he had been on the board of One. Tel for two years, Lachlan barely participated in the meeting—Sherman remembers him as an observer more than anything else.

Lachlan had flown in from LA with Sarah the day before, planning to head out for the Sydney premiere of his wife's first movie role as a ditzy Australian model in *Head Over Heels*, a romcom starring Monica Potter and Freddie Prinze Jr. The Sydney do was put on to raise money for the National Breast Cancer Foundation, of which Sarah had just become a patron. Walking the red carpet at Sydney's low-rent Village George Street cinema, she told reporters Lachlan was a no-show—"something came up with work," she said—and joked she was "so scared" about how the local audience would react to her debut film.[1] She had good reason to be nervous: as it turned out, the critics were scathing—bravely, even the Murdoch-owned *Sunday Territorian* ran a review titled "Head Over Toilet Bowl" with the opening line: "Every so often you see a film that totally recalibrates your crap-o-meter."[2] Sarah only had a supporting role and could hardly be blamed for the terrible script, but she nonetheless gave up her acting career and never appeared in another movie.

While she was at the premiere, Lachlan was in the kitchen of their Point Piper mansion, listening to James Packer apologize for recommending the Murdochs invest in One.Tel. Lachlan would tell a packed courtroom years later that James was "shocked and very upset . . . saying to me repeatedly words to the effect of 'I'm sorry'. By the end of the conversation, Mr. Packer was in tears."[3]

First thing next morning, James and Lachlan fronted up for crisis talks at the Packers' city headquarters. A last-ditch effort to persuade Lucent Technologies to bail out the company failed, and One.Tel went into administration two days later. News Corp, the largest shareholder, had lost $575 million. The Packers had lost $375 million. One commentator wrote that the collapse was personally disastrous for the so-called "brat pack," a closely connected group of heirs to massive fortunes, well known to Australian investors by their first names (Lachlan, James, Jodee, and Rodney)."[4]

How had it come to this? Astute market watchers had seen the writing on the wall some time before. In March 2000, One.Tel had paid the federal government a stonking half-billion dollars for new mobile phone spectrum in Australia, as part of an overly ambitious strategy to roll out a 2G network of its own in Australia and Europe, built by Lucent Technologies, rather than keep reselling the services of other telcos. Only weeks later, the dot-com bubble burst and, like many tech-related companies, One.Tel's share price headed south.

A deal to sell a third of the company to Finnish telco Sonera collapsed in September. The next month, brokers Merrill Lynch reckoned One.Tel would run out of money by the middle of 2001, spooking the market. By the start of that year, Kerry Packer was decidedly nervous, reminding Rich of the failure of his former computer retailing business: "You ran out of cash with Imagineering, and you're going to do it again." James Packer maintained the faith, however, and Lachlan seemed happy to rely on the advice of his friend. In his affidavits, produced after One.Tel collapsed, Lachlan said that it was not until May 1, 2001 that he first understood the company was in financial trouble. That was when he took a call from James, who told him that the company was going to need to raise $10–15 million to break even. "Are you starting to lose confidence in the business, or is this a timing issue?" Lachlan asked. The latter, James insisted. He was wrong.

Paul Barry's book *Rich Kids* captured the collapse of One.Tel in lurid detail. Jodee Rich, a close friend of James since their days together at elite Sydney private school Cranbrook, was an entrepreneur whose ability to sell a vision was not matched by his ability to run a business. After a dream run from 1995 to 2000, largely based on slick marketing, One. Tel foundered on an atrocious billing system, an accumulation of bad debts from some dubious younger customers without credit histories, and years of dodgy accounting to cover up these flaws. There was also the fundamental problem that, as a reseller, One.Tel was always in competition with its main suppliers and vulnerable to any change in their pricing or terms of service. As Barry's book revealed, an internal whistleblower by the name of "ghostdogperil" warned the Packers that they were being misled by management, who were running a set of shadow accounts, and that there was a massive hole in the company's finances. In late April, James got the bad news: his own experts confirmed One.Tel had bad debts of more than $50 million and the Packers and Murdochs would have to decide whether to put in a whole lot more money.

To put itself on a sustainable footing, One.Tel would need to raise at least $132 million from shareholders including the largest, News Ltd. James flew to France to meet Lachlan, who was at the Cannes Film Festival for the world premiere of Baz Luhrmann's *Moulin Rouge*, to try to persuade the Murdochs to kick in an additional $66 million. According to his affidavit, Lachlan asked James the same question he'd put on the phone a week earlier: "Is there an underlying problem in the business?" James responded that there was not: "It's only a timing issue for the business plan to break even. Jodee doesn't think they need it."

Lachlan agreed to put in the extra funds, but he insisted time was up for Jodee and his sidekick Brad Keeling: "They've told the market so many times they don't need any more funds. Even if you raise $1 they will not have any credibility. They will have to go." Lachlan did not let the drama at One.Tel spoil his evening, however. He and Sarah partied with Baz and Nicole Kidman, who was staying at their compound. Lachlan was snapped on the red carpet with Sarah, Rupert, and a newly pregnant Wendi Deng in what Paul Barry described as "a splendid scene of family harmony."[5]

Over the next week, Jodee Rich called Lachlan repeatedly to plead for his job. When he finally got onto Lachlan, Jodee found him positive and friendly but unwilling to budge. It came to a head at the next One. Tel board meeting on May 17, with Lachlan dialing in from New York. It was agreed that Rich and Keeling would resign. James and Lachlan paid generous tribute to them—Lachlan thanked them for their 'passion and energy'[6]—but then the meeting hit a snag. According to the minutes, Rich said that he and Keeling had not offered to resign. They had a strong management team and believed they should stay but would "do what the board believed was right." The minutes went on:

> Lachlan Murdoch said that he took back everything that he had said. Jodee Rich said that he hoped Lachlan was joking. James Packer expressed surprise at Jodee Rich's comments, given his discussions with Jodee Rich the previous evening. Lachlan Murdoch said that perhaps he had been misinformed, as he had understood that an agreement had been reached.[7]

The meeting took a break, as James called Lachlan on a private line. Jodee was given a stark choice—resign or be sacked—and saw that it was all over. A joint statement from News and PBL said the $132 million recapitalization and management changes would "set the framework for the future direction of the organization to become a full-fledged telecommunications provider." News Ltd. chief John Hartigan, rather than Lachlan himself, said News Ltd. continued to regard One.Tel as "an important strategic investment and remains confident in One.Tel's underlying business case" . . . a statement that strained credulity. Packer sent in forensic accountants who found One.Tel needed much more cash— between $240 million and $332 million—and the scene was set for the final board meeting on May 28. The board pulled the recapitalization and sent the company under. After the meeting, Lachlan arrived late to a birthday party for his friend Joe Cross at a French restaurant near News Ltd. headquarters in Surry Hills. Lachlan coolly made the cut-throat gesture: One.Tel was done for. He joined the party for dinner.

Although News put in more money than PBL, Lachlan was never as emotionally invested in One.Tel as James, who was best friends with Jodee. Lachlan's affidavit claimed he had relied on James to tell him if News' investment in One.Tel was going OK. If that was true, Barry suggested, for a company director Lachlan had an "extraordinary lack of awareness of One.Tel's problems."[8]

Lachlan and James issued a powerful media statement the day One.Tel went under, crafted by counsel Ian Philip: "Like all shareholders we are angry. We have been profoundly misled as to the true financial position of the company. We intend to explore all remedies available to us." James Packer told media he was assisting the Australian Securities and Investments Commission, which raided One.Tel's offices the next day, along with the homes of Rich and Keeling. In response, Rich laid the blame for the collapse of his company squarely at the feet of James and Lachlan, telling reporters that if the $132 million announced by PBL and News had gone into the company, "One.Tel would be trading today, and 2,000 people would still have their jobs and their careers."

It was the beginning of one of Australia's longest-running litigations, as the regulator pursued Rich and Keeling in the Federal Court. Lachlan and James were both called as witnesses in ASIC's case. James was in the box for three days, Lachlan for just one. Lachlan said "I can't recall" some 881 times. When he finally delivered his verdict some years later, the presiding judge, Robert Austin wrote:

> . . . the evidence shows that on the whole, Mr. Murdoch Jnr. operated at a distance from One.Tel, both physically and in terms of engagement. His answers are open to the alternative inference that, rather than having a poor capacity to recollect, Mr. Murdoch Jnr. did not remember matters concerning One. Tel because he never reached the level of understanding of the company's financial circumstances and affairs that would cause him to remember several years afterwards.

Justice Austin considered Lachlan an "unreliable witness."

Unlike James, who suffered a degree of public humiliation after the One.Tel collapse, especially at the hands of his father Kerry, who banished him and said there would be no more such "fuckups," Lachlan emerged unscathed. Rupert Murdoch was protective of his eldest son, taking a share of the blame for himself. At the News Ltd. annual meeting in Adelaide in October, Rupert said, "It's a *mea culpa*. We shouldn't have done it, I guess. Or we should have taken more efforts to protect it once we were in. But, you know, it's part of our learning experience, I guess, and compared to some of the wins we've had this year it's not of great significance."[9]

In the media, Lachlan's subsequent appearance at the liquidator's examinations in the Federal Court was written up as a triumph of sorts, with one *Sydney Morning Herald* columnist describing the pin-stripe-suited mini-mogul as "the picture of confidence, youthful exuberance and good manners," notwithstanding that the nub of his evidence was that he'd relied almost entirely on his fellow directors and advisors.[10] The same columnist drew a sharp contrast between the relaxed testimony of Lachlan and the strung-out and defensive evidence given by James Packer, who by now had lost his first marriage, was going through a serious nervous breakdown, and was falling under the spell of scientology, to which he had been introduced by actor Tom Cruise.

Quite apart from what their fathers thought of their billion-dollar debacle, much less what the media made of it all, both Lachlan and James were now facing the full legal consequences of a major corporate collapse. The painful saga would be drawn out over more than a decade. First came the all-important question: whether the two men had fulfilled their statutory obligations as directors of One.Tel or had allowed it to trade while insolvent, in which case, they could be held personally liable for the company's debts.

Although the regulator had made clear that it held Rich and Keeling responsible for the collapse, it would emerge in later testimony that ASIC believed neither Lachlan nor James had a good understanding of what directors were required to do. The head of compliance, Jan Redfern, was said to be "keen" to launch proceedings against the non-executive directors for breaching their duties, particularly James given the extent of his knowledge. In an email dated October 13, 2001, an ASIC staffer told Redfern that after interviewing Murdoch, he had formed the view that all the directors had been negligent of their duties.[11] In his hands-off fashion, Lachlan had sailed very close to the wind, legally.

Liquidator Steve Sherman had his own job to do. His second report to creditors determined that One.Tel had been insolvent from either March or April 2001, but he did not recommend proceedings be brought against Lachlan and James as non-executive directors. James and Lachlan's standing took a hit in 2009, however, when judge Robert Austin finally handed down his much-delayed judgement in *ASIC v Rich*. While other One.Tel executives such as Brad Keeling had settled with ASIC, Rich had vowed to fight on. Having transferred all his assets to his wife in the dying hours of the business, Rich had the wherewithal to fund his own defense and spent five years turning up to court on his bicycle and dismantling the evidence presented by the regulator, which tried and failed to prove that One.Tel was broke in the months leading up to its collapse. He was totally vindicated, with the judge ruling against ASIC's case on every point.

The defeat of ASIC's case against Rich opened the door to entirely separate proceedings, brought by special purpose liquidator Paul Weston, seeking $244 million in damages from Lachlan and James, claiming that their decision to cancel the $132 million capital raising was responsible for the failure of One.Tel. That case was not settled until 2014, when Lachlan and James agreed to pay out $40 million, one third of which would be paid by News, the other two thirds by PBL, thereby avoiding another stint in the witness box. There was no admission of fault and the presiding judge, Paul Brereton, observed that the case against both men had "very considerable risk." First, he said, there was never a concluded underwriting agreement at One.Tel; second, Murdoch and Packer were misled about One.Tel's financial position; third, they had properly abstained from voting on the rights issue; and fourth, the case was outside the six-year limitation period. A columnist in *The Australian* questioned whether the whole exercise was "greenmail"—was liquidator Weston simply looking for the deepest pockets he could find? According to a spokesman for Lachlan, it was Weston who pushed to settle the case due to mounting costs and the risk that One.Tel creditors would end up with nothing.

The settlement brought the One.Tel litigation to a close, although the final wind-up of the failed telco continued until 2017, making it one of the longest-running corporate sagas Australia has seen. When it was over, Steve Sherman had secured some 28 cents in the dollar for One. Tel creditors, much higher than expected. Looking back, does Sherman believe that Lachlan and James were "profoundly misled" about the financial situation at One.Tel? "No," he says firmly, arguing that directors cannot plead ignorance of the finances of a company whose board they sit on, and that both Lachlan and James could have made further enquiries of management.

"I disagree with Sherman," says Packer, who received daily cash-flow reports from One.Tel management and repeatedly asked Jodee Rich and Brad Keeling whether the company was going to run out of money, only to be told over and over that it did not need more capital. Packer had been assured the cash balance would never go below $40 million, and was aghast when it did. "As a director in Australia you get punished if you ask for more information," Packer says. "There is a real risk of being seen by ASIC as doing something inappropriate. I was getting the cash balance every day. In the last six months it went down from $100 million to zero." In Lachlan's camp, the fact that One.Tel management was having so many difficulties with its financial reporting and communications with the board spoke for itself.

Steve Sherman marvels at the ease with which Lachlan Murdoch moved on from One.Tel, given the company blew $575 million belonging to the shareholders of News. If there is anyone Sherman admires from the failed company, it is Rich who defied not only the Australian corporate regulator but also Australia's two most powerful families—he took them on and won.

Packer, for his part, arguably never got over the One.Tel disaster. He still castigates himself for bringing News Corp into it and is grateful for Lachlan's friendship. As Packer told his biographer Damon Kitney: "I had so much gratitude for the way [Lachlan] treated me after One.Tel that I regarded myself in his debt. I kept on trying to help him generally and actually ended up hurting him. The things I put to Lachlan, none of them ended up being good."[12]

Packer is not quite right about that. When he sold a 10 per cent stake in Realestate.com.au to Murdoch for $10 million in 2002, he was partly hoping that it would make up for the One.Tel debacle. As it turned out, Realestate.com.au had cornered a niche in which the early-adopting Australian property market was some years ahead of those overseas, including the US, and Realestate.com.au would provide a beachhead for international expansion. Through a combination of his connections and his own acuity, Lachlan had delivered to News Corp a controlling stake in a genuine digital growth asset that could underpin the legacy newspaper businesses for years. Depending on the prevailing share price, that 10 per cent stake James sold to Lachlan is now worth about $2 billion. Packer is philosophical about it, readily conceding: "There is no way I ever thought REA would be a $20 billion business."

7

His Own Man

LACHLAN, BY NOW TWENTY-NINE, had seemed a distant figure to the *New York Post*'s journalists since arriving in New York in 2000. He was rarely seen on the newsroom floor, his role was unclear, and there were always questions about whether he or his father was really calling the shots. The paper's publisher, Ken Chandler, was a Rupert Murdoch stalwart who had been at the *Post* since 1974; he had survived Rupert buying the paper, selling it, and buying it back. For most of that time, however, the *Post* had been losing an estimated $20 million a year and Chandler was now pushed aside to make room for Lachlan; he left not long after to join the *Boston Herald*. In 2000, the Murdochs decided to invest in the paper's first new color printing press, located in the Bronx, and cut the cover price to 25 cents to boost readership and take on its main rival, the New York *Daily News*. Lachlan's experience introducing the new presses at Brisbane's *Courier-Mail* would come in handy. But when circulation failed to lift even after an expensive promotional campaign, the Murdochs decided to take tougher action. In April 2001 the serving editor, Xana Antunes, was axed overnight—news reports said she stepped down for personal reasons—and Lachlan announced that she would be replaced by Col Allan, known in Australia as "Col Pot."

Allan was a veteran Murdoch newspaperman who had succeeded John Hartigan as editor and then editor-in-chief of Sydney's *Daily Telegraph*.

Originally from rural Dubbo in western NSW, he had met Hartigan when they were covering a court case in the mining town of Cobar. Allan was working for a small country paper and Harto got him a start at the Sydney *Mirror*. Allan never looked back, and Harto and Col would form a kind of double-act over the years, following Rupert to London to work on *The Sun*, then heading to Queensland to found the short-lived Brisbane-based *Sun* titles, before returning to Sydney to run *The Daily Telegraph*.

When he took over from Harto as editor of the *Telegraph*, Allan showed killer tabloid instincts, pushing for hard news and publishing controversial front pages like "The Class We Failed," a powerful story about the worst-performing high school in the city, which shone a light on the failings of the school system in disadvantaged areas. A court found the *Telegraph* had defamed the kids whose class photo appeared on the front page but Lachlan believed the story was a prime example of how tabloid journalism could have a positive impact, as it triggered an avalanche of N.S.W. government spending on neglected schools. Allan would soon make waves in New York for *Post* headlines like "Axis of Weasel—Germany and France wimp out on Iraq."

Allan was populist rather than ideological or relentlessly conservative: under his editorship, the *Telegraph* backed the Keating Labor government in the 1993 and 1996 elections. Hard-working, hard-drinking, and rough as guts, Allan had a notoriously bad temper and did not care whom he offended. As former business editor of the *Telegraph*, Stephen Mayne, remembered on his independent news site *Crikey*, Allan used to piss in the sink of the kitchenette adjoining his office, rather than walk to the bathroom, whether other editors were present or not. When Allan's appointment at the *Post* was announced, Mayne's yarn was read by the newsroom staff, who wheeled a urinal into his first editorial conference, just to break the ice. According to one seasoned *Post* journo who was there, Allan didn't even crack a smile at the joke, telling the editors to "get that fucking thing out of here." With his fearsome reputation preceding him, the staff were on notice and expecting the worst.

They called it the Friday morning massacre: June 8, 2001, when Allan, hand-picked by Lachlan to remake the *Post*, cut a swathe through the newsroom, summarily dismissing veteran editors and columnists in the biggest bloodletting in the paper's history. Allan had bided his time for the first month or so, but now purged a lot of older editors and commentators, including the paper's one liberal voice, Jack Newfield, and replaced them with juniors who would be both loyal and enthusiastic. One interesting appointment was James Murdoch's New York-born childhood friend Jesse Angelo, who had been languishing on the business desk and was now promoted to become metropolitan editor of the *Post*. Lachlan backed Allan, telling *The New York Times*: "Col has really needed to clear the decks [so he could] bring up younger people who had an open mind to how *The Post* could be creative." Those who had been dismissed, he said, were "in one sense the barriers to taking *The Post* forward."

What followed was an old-fashioned newspaper war between the *Post* and the *News*, which New York had not seen for decades. With a circulation of only half a million compared to the *News*' 715,000, the *Post* trailed "the Snooze" (as *Post* staffers called it). Lachlan relished the battle, soon becoming publisher and telling the *Times* that the *Post*'s new color press would not only please advertizers but would reinforce for staff that "the world's changed." Sitting behind his desk in a short-sleeved shirt that did not conceal the tattoos on both arms, Lachlan said: "This paper has to get to profitability, but we also want it to be the number-one paper in the market."[1]

The shake-up of the *Post* was absolutely in the Murdoch tradition—brighten the paper, cut the price, take it down-market—and was intended to make it more of a British or Australian-style tabloid. It was all too much for one high-ranking editor, Maralyn Matlick, who was dismissed in early 2002 and subsequently filed an $8 million discrimination suit against the *Post*, claiming she was forced out of her job because management wanted an all-male leadership team. Matlick said Lachlan "made no secret" of his plans to install an all-male, entirely Australian and British team to head the paper and that he sometimes even boasted of the initiative. A *Post* spokesperson said the claim was "simply untrue," pointing out that Matlick had been replaced by a woman and insisting that the paper did not tolerate discrimination of any kind.[2]

Even if he was driving the overhaul of the *Post*, Lachlan was not a constant presence on the newsroom floor. If he directly intervened in coverage, it was only through conversations with Allan. Gregg Birnbaum, the *Post*'s political editor for more than a decade, says the young Murdoch rarely attended the paper's evening editorial news conference, which decided the make-up of "the wood," as page one was called. Birnbaum had no impression of Murdoch's political leanings, in fact, he had the distinct impression that Lachlan wasn't interested in American politics at all, "the complete opposite of his father." Lachlan skipped Washington's biggest night, the annual White House Correspondents' Dinner, preferring to leave it to Allan. "I guess at some point you get too big to go," says Birnbaum. "He wasn't too big to go."

If politics wasn't Lachlan's thing, it was hard to say what was, because his presence simply wasn't felt in the newsroom. "If you really have ink in your veins, you come down to the floor, rather than sit in your office, hiding," Birnbaum says. "I never saw him or had a conversation with him." In a way, Lachlan's hands-off approach was benign; there was no pressure to slant stories to suit the owner's son. And the *Post*'s circulation was growing. The journalists concentrated on keeping Allan off their backs and continued to believe that Rupert, rather than Lachlan, was calling the shots.

* * *

While Lachlan was going back to the future in a tabloid war reminiscent of the nineteenth century, the main profit driver for the Murdoch empire was increasingly Fox News, where the powerful Roger Ailes was reinventing cable television. According to the definitive portrait by Gabriel Sherman, whose biography *The Loudest Voice* was subsequently turned into a TV mini-series starring Russell Crowe, Ailes was a brilliant, sexist, power-crazed paranoiac, who did not like gays, did not like blacks, did not like Jews, did not like liberals, and helped to divide America, stoking a ferocious culture war that continues today.

Ailes was a grossly overweight hemophiliac, born in 1940 in small-town America, Warren, Ohio, where the first Packard automobile was built in 1899. He had a tough childhood, insisting on playing sport despite his bleeding—after one accident he had to have a blood transfusion, for which his schoolmates all donated. His violent father told him: "never forget, son, you've got a lot of blue-collar blood in you." Ailes studied hard, graduated and went to college, but found he was much more interested in volunteering at the college radio station than hitting the books. He soon got a job as a junior producer on *The Mike Douglas Show*, a nationally syndicated daytime talk show broadcast from Cleveland, where he learned many of the techniques he would deploy at Fox News.

A remorseless self-promoter, Ailes elbowed his way into becoming executive producer, until he met Richard Nixon on set and persuaded the aspiring 1968 Republican nominee that he needed a media consultant, a job that didn't even exist yet. A devotee of Hitler's propagandist Leni Riefenstahl, Ailes put television at the center of Nixon's campaign and his success that year, as told in Joe McGinniss' best-seller *The Selling of the President*, launched Ailes' career as a political consultant.

Stung by Watergate, Ailes quit working for the Republicans and returned to entertainment, first in theatre and then back in television, as producer of a new show hosted by conservative talk radio pioneer Rush Limbaugh, who would become a firm ally. Soon Ailes was producing a new cable channel, America's Talking, for CNBC—in format a forerunner of Fox News—but he left after being investigated and reprimanded for an anti-Semitic outburst against his rival David Zaslav, whom he allegedly called a "little fucking Jew prick." When he heard that Rupert Murdoch was gearing up to challenge CNN, Ailes called him. Both men yearned for a center-right alternative to CNN, which Ailes called the "Clinton News Network." Gabriel Sherman wrote that it was only after Ailes met Murdoch and they founded Fox News that, "finally, Ailes could be Ailes."

The next five years would prove revolutionary. Ailes blended news and entertainment, using brighter graphics and introducing conservative hosts such as Sean Hannity and Bill O'Reilly, all delivered 24/7 via cable under Fox News' uber-cynical "fair and balanced" slogan. Fox News proceeded to upend US politics, from the Monica Lewinsky scandal and impeachment of President Clinton to the critical 2000 presidential contest between Al Gore and George W. Bush, when the head of the network's election desk, John Prescott Ellis, controversially and prematurely called Florida for Bush, who happened to be his first cousin. With his upstairs "war room" and basement "brain room," where a team of investigators researched his enemies and rivals, Ailes was widely perceived to be building a political operation within a television network.

If Bush's victory over Al Gore was unconvincing, everything changed on September 11, 2001. Lachlan had turned thirty just three days earlier, celebrating on the Saturday night with Sarah, Rupert, and Anna (not Wendi), his grandmother Dame Elisabeth, James Packer, Joe Cross and Sarah's friend, supermodel Heidi Klum. Cross remembers it was a beautiful fall evening: a double-decker London bus took the guests on a tour through downtown Manhattan, stopping at bars, restaurants and clubs in Soho and Tribeca; at random stops along the way, waiters dressed up as rabbits would get on with shots. "It was a picture-perfect evening, so many happy faces on our bus and on the streets," he says. "Little did we know that it would be the last Saturday night that the twin towers stood. In just three days' time, the world would be changed forever."

On the morning of September 11, just before 9 a.m., Lachlan was at home with Sarah when the doorman, delivering a package, told them that a plane had hit the World Trade Center, about a mile to the south. As O'Hare told *Australian Women's Weekly* magazine a year later:

> Lachlan and I ran to the window because our apartment overlooked the site. We stood there stunned, watching the flames and shards of glass falling. When we saw the second plane hit, we knew it was a terrorist attack. It caused an incredible feeling of dread. I didn't know anybody in the towers, thank God, but we had friends who worked in the area and they lost a lot of friends that day.[3]

As the streets were cordoned off and sirens rang out, the couple watched as people ran down Lafayette Street covered in ash. Lachlan jumped on his motorbike, the only way to get uptown, and rode straight to the *New York Post* offices, where he began working a string of eighteen-hour days as publisher, covering the news event of a lifetime.

The *Post* had been an afternoon paper and got an edition out by 1 p.m. that day, the only paper to cover the terrorist attacks that carried a dateline of September 11. The next day, Allan was the only newspaper editor in the country to run a photograph on page one of three firemen raising an American flag from the rubble; the edition sold one million copies, twice the *Post*'s usual circulation. Rupert had been stranded outside Manhattan after a meeting with Australian prime minister John Howard in Washington. When he got back to the city, he asked Allan, who was friends with police commissioner Bernie Kerik, if he and Lachlan could visit Ground Zero. On the Friday, Rupert, Lachlan and Allan spent more than an hour at the site. Allan recalls:

> It was beyond shocking . . . they were using different-colored vegetable sprays—for example, they would spray something orange if it was evidence—and they were spraying body parts yellow, I'll never forget it. We were literally clambering around the site, and you know, just to see and to understand there were all these bits of people everywhere, was shocking. When we finally left, we got in a car and we went to Rupert's apartment, which was on Prince Street, and we sat at his kitchen table and the three of us demolished a bottle of vodka. I mean, you see it on TV, but when you go there . . .

A week after the attack, the *Post* became part of the story when Johanna Huden, who opened letters to the editor, noticed a blister on her finger and was tested for anthrax poisoning. The test came back positive, making her the fourth case in a news media organization (NBC, CBS and ABC also had scares) and the *Post* tightened security and mail-handling procedures. Workers from the Centers for Disease Control and Prevention went through the *Post* office in hazmat suits and more than a dozen News Corp staff were tested, with their results coming back negative.

Lachlan was planning to attend the annual Al Smith Memorial Foundation dinner, a black-tie fundraiser for the Catholic archdiocese of New York at which Vice President Dick Cheney was to deliver the keynote speech, when he found out about the anthrax incident. He and Col Allan met with the FBI and were asked to say nothing until the test results came back. "We understood that responsibility," says Allan, "and I think that we also understood we didn't unnecessarily want to terrify the staff if it turned out that it wasn't anthrax."

Lachlan and the head of human resources at News Corp were thinking through how to make an announcement the following day without causing a panic, and how to make sure staff were safe. Unfortunately, Ailes, who was at the Al Smith dinner, had heard about the incident—Allan suspects deputy mayor Joe Lhota told him—and went straight to the Fox newsroom, declaring "We're under attack! We're under attack!" An anthrax outbreak suited Ailes' narrative perfectly. Of all America's television networks, Fox was the most bellicose in the wake of 9/11, in keeping with the Murdoch tradition, and Ailes had taken personal charge of the programming. As well as dialling up the patriotic fervor at Fox, he had dialled up security, telling a news conference that the country was at war and "I want my people to be safe. I don't want this building hurt or this newsroom harmed." For himself, Ailes sought police protection and countersurveillance and employed a retired detective as a personal escort to and from the Fox building.

Lachlan and Allan were left in a very difficult position. Allan recalls, "it exposed Lachlan and I as uncaring bosses, because we hadn't told our staff, or warned them, but all we did was follow the advice of the FBI." After midnight it was confirmed that the substance was indeed anthrax, and Lachlan was furious that Ailes had appropriated the attack for his own purposes. Feeling ambushed, Lachlan took the lift to the basement and confronted Ailes. It quickly turned into a slanging match. According to a source close to Lachlan, he told Ailes:

'What are you doing? We're actually trying to deal with this in this building, it's a matter of health and safety of our people . . . you are going to be panicking our people . . . that's the wrong thing to do. We are employers of these people. What are you doing?' And Ailes was like, 'No, no, no . . . you know, we're under attack.' And Lachlan says, no doubt loudly in front of everyone, 'No, this is about establishing protocols, this is about the safety of our staff, and you are behaving irresponsibly.'

Ailes was not going to cop a public dressing-down from the Murdoch heir, some thirty years his junior. Staffers watching the confrontation were shocked: here was Ailes openly challenging Rupert's son. By some accounts Lachlan directly threatened Ailes with the sack and Sherman wrote later that "Roger was very scared. No one had had a conflict with the [Murdoch] children and survived."[4] In a pre-emptive strike, Ailes went straight to Rupert and threatened to resign, complaining that his sons were allied against him. It worked: Rupert offered him a new contract. Ailes had outmanoeuvred Lachlan and would do so again.

8

The Walk-Out

I NSIDE NEWS CORP, the young Murdoch was soon fighting on two fronts. In early 2002 Lachlan picked up responsibility for the Fox Television Stations Group, thirty-five broadcast stations around the US that had their own programming, separate from the Fox News cable operation. It generated roughly 30 per cent of News Corp's operating profits. Lachlan was reporting directly to News Corp president and chief operating officer Peter Chernin, twenty years his senior and a talented Hollywood executive well known to investors who saw him as a bulwark against nepotism at News and a safe pair of hands should any mishap befall Rupert.

Lachlan had expected to spend half his time in Los Angeles and had even bought a house there—the move coincided with Sarah's short-lived acting career—but now he found himself isolated. Chernin refused to mollycoddle the heir apparent, believing it was not his role to be Lachlan's private tutor, and was neither consultative nor deferential. The most substantive disagreement between the two men was over the retransmission fees charged by broadcasters to affiliated local cable operators under a loose policy called "no cash, no carry." Lachlan believed these affiliate or retransmission fees could be a giant extra revenue stream for Fox, alongside advertizing and subscriptions. Chernin believed distributors like DirecTV, Comcast, and Time Warner could resist paying and he was backed by

Rupert, who told *Television Week* in 2003, "I don't think for a minute the cable industry will roll over."[1] Lachlan deferred to his father and News Corp had a foot in both camps through its minority stake in DirecTV. But in early 2005, the industry watched on as Nexstar Broadcasting threw down the gauntlet to cable operator Cox Communications and prevailed, just as Lachlan thought Fox should have done, and would have done had Chernin not blocked him. It was a frustrating stalemate.

"Lachlan isn't as good a debater as Chernin, not even close, and Chernin has better command of the business," one News Corp executive would later tell *New York* magazine. "Lachlan had his points. He wasn't wrong. These in the end are legitimate business questions, but each one Lachlan lost."[2] In a largely concocted role as deputy COO, Lachlan was beginning to feel ignored and undervalued. He was sick of being seen as chairman-in-waiting. As he approached a decade in the business, he believed he deserved more respect and had earned the right to a say in how the company was run.

To help escape the News Corp politicking, Lachlan and Sarah took delivery of their dream yacht in July 2002, a $7 million Swan 80 built in Finland. They called it *Ipixuna*, after a small Brazilian town deep in the Amazon rainforest. As would be revealed in the explosive "Paradise Papers" investigation into international tax avoidance some fifteen years later and picked up by Australian journalist Neil Chenoweth, the boat was ordered in early 2000 and initially paid for by Rupert, perhaps as a thirtieth birthday present, before being transferred to Lachlan via a Bermuda entity set up by local firm Appleby. Nothing in the Murdoch world was simple, especially when it came to tax. *Ipixuna* was launched with a big party in Sardinia, and the couple sailed it round Corsica. Sarah talked fondly about the boat in a revealing interview afterwards, remembering how Lachlan had taught her to sail in Sydney and how romantic she found it. "I don't like to go to the same place twice," she said. "I like adventure. We hope to do all the Turkish coast and the Greek Islands, then bring it to Australia. Eventually, we hope to make it around the world." She flagged that kids were "definitely" on the way, saying she'd "love to be a mum." Sarah put paid to gossip back in Australia that she was "paid to marry Lachlan, which is ridiculous . . . people just can't imagine that we have a normal loving relationship."[3] The couple certainly seemed to be loved-up. In one interview around this time, Lachlan joked: "I realize I've married above myself, so you know, the more time I spend with her, the better it is for me."

Planning for a family, in late 2003 Lachlan and Sarah pounced on a new Manhattan home: an 1888 six-story building, once a carriage house and horse stable, on the northeast corner of Elizabeth and Spring streets in the Nolita neighborhood. As Gabriel Sherman wrote in *The New York Observer*, the gothic-style, graffiti-covered building, with flickering electric candles in each of its dozens of windows, had a creepy feel but was much-loved by passers-by who wondered what went on inside. Paying $5.5 million, the Murdochs planned to turn the "Candle building" into a lavish residence and moved into a rented apartment in Tribeca to prepare for construction. Nine months later, they sold their Lafayette Street loft in Soho for $7.5 million, double what Lachlan had paid for it in 1999, to a mystery buyer, Fairway Isle Ltd. When the International Consortium for Investigative Journalists released the Pandora Papers in 2021, Chenoweth again pored over the documents and revealed that the buyer had in fact been Arnon Milchan, an Israeli arms dealer turned Hollywood filmmaker who was a close friend of James Packer. Lachlan's advisers insisted the private sale was at arm's length and at market value and pointed to comparable sales in the Lafayette Street building that showed similar increases over the same five-year period.

Beneath Lachlan's frustrations at News Corp, a deeper grievance was smoldering. The Murdoch family remained bitterly divided over the fallout from Rupert's divorce with Anna, especially following the birth of his two daughters with Wendi, Grace in 2001 and Chloe in 2003. Rupert and Wendi had proposed that all six of his children should share equally in the trust. Lachlan, who had remained loyal to his mother during the split, was incensed, along with the other three children from Rupert's first two marriages, that Rupert had reneged on his agreement with Anna in

1999. Anna had given up her claim to an equal share of Rupert's fortune precisely to ensure that Prudence, Elisabeth, Lachlan, and James would not have to share the control or assets of the Murdoch Family Trust with any children from Rupert's marriage to Wendi.

Family divisions over the trust became intertwined with the proposal to relocate News from its official headquarters in Adelaide, South Australia, to Delaware, a business-friendly jurisdiction where regulation was lax and more than half the US companies listed on the New York Stock Exchange were incorporated. The move, which was announced in 2004 but had been in planning for two to three years, made strategic sense given News Corp generated approximately 70 per cent of its revenue and 80 per cent of its profits in the United States. Moving the company's primary stock exchange listing to Wall Street would give News Corp greater access to the much larger capital markets and boost the company's share price. Behind the scenes, Lachlan was almost a lone voice opposing the transaction, arguing that the company should preserve its connection to Adelaide, where News Corp's annual general meetings had been held since the days of Sir Keith. Lachlan's time down under had convinced him that hanging on to the company's Australian culture was fundamental to its success, and he saw Adelaide almost as the fulcrum of the organization.

In Australia, Lachlan had been king of the castle, Joe Cross explains, but in the US he had to deal with all the personalities at the top of News Corp: the Office of the Chairman, David Devoe, Chase Carey, Peter Chernin, Roger Ailes, "the whole nine yards." Cross explains Lachlan's mindset at the time:

> He's unhappy with the people around his dad and the direction those people are pushing his dad to take the company. Because remember, Lachlan sees this as a family business with deep roots to Australia. Yes, there are shareholders that are investing in them and alongside them, but for him it's family—investors can sell and walk away. And who are these people that are making these calls—they are Americans, that don't connect to the history of

his grandfather's reporting from Gallipoli, on what the English brass did to our young Aussie and Kiwi boys, sending them to the slaughter. Or what Rupert has done in terms of building this global media corporation from one newspaper in Adelaide. That's why returning to Adelaide each year for the AGM was so important to Lachlan. And those guys just dismissed it without even considering the history.

Adding to the sentimental wrench, as part of the transaction the Murdoch family was proposing to sell Cruden Investments' 60 per cent stake in the wildly profitable Queensland Press, which owned Brisbane's *Courier-Mail* along with other monopoly newspapers across the state, to News Corp for $2.5 billion along with assumption of $540 million in accrued debts. The sale was not strictly necessary to get the change of domicile done, but it tidied up the messy structure in which News Corp only held a minority 40 per cent stake in the Queensland papers, which would be unappealing to American investors. The price represented a healthy multiple of about twelve times forecast operating earnings, whereas comparable Australian media companies were valued at around ten times. Lachlan had a particular attachment to the Queensland Press, having started his career there, but the whole family was attracted to the cashflows—margins were said to be 40 per cent—and felt that News Corp was getting the assets too cheaply. Lachlan believed that in selling a profitable private business in which they held a majority stake to a publicly listed business they owned a minority of, Cruden was giving up hundreds of millions of dollars of value for no good reason.

Rupert hinted at the internal family dissension in a friendly interview with one of his favorite journalists, *Herald Sun* business editor Terry McCrann, with Lachlan sitting in. McCrann asked whether News Corp, if it moved to America, would ever consider spinning off the Australian assets, as had been mooted in the financial press.

"So far as Dad and I are concerned, over our dead bodies," Lachlan volunteered. "It's crucially important for us to continue our Australian culture. Otherwise, we just become a bureaucracy like Time Warner or Viacom."

Rupert backed Lachlan up, suggesting that Fairfax had always "hungered after" Queensland Newspapers and would have paid a lot more than News was about to pay, if given the chance. Then he went further, suggesting that if the Murdochs could have bought News Corp out themselves, and taken the whole of Queensland Press private, "we would do it in a flash . . . a lot of people in the family would have said hold out for a higher price."

According to McCrann, at that point Lachlan disagreed with his father, sounding surprised: "I'm not sure we said that. If there's a way not to sell it, we shouldn't sell it. You agree with that? If there's a way not to sell?"

Rupert responded that the deal just had to be done: "Our reputation is more important than the last hundred million dollars."[4] In another interview during the Murdoch roadshow to persuade investors, Lachlan admitted he had mixed emotions and even regret about the deal. "It will be hard to call it a highlight," he told the *Courier-Mail:*

> Had we taken the business out to auction we would have secured a significantly higher price, but in order to do the right thing by our shareholders and to keep the business broadly in family control—and ultimately have the change in domicile occur—we were willing to sell to News at this price. For the first few weeks of this year, we are actually operating ahead of our plan, so it could turn out to be less than a twelve multiple. The Murdoch family we consider is giving up one of the great assets, but it is important for News and our shareholders so we are willing to make that sacrifice.[5]

Lachlan's apparent regret may simply have been an exercise in advanced salesmanship: institutional investors, when they began to pick apart the terms of the deal, were sceptical about the price being paid for Queensland Press. "The valuation is through the roof," said one analyst off the record.

Independent expert valuers Grant Samuel declared the price being paid for Queensland Press was "relatively high but not unreasonable." The Murdochs were pressured to lower the total value of the deal, including equity and debt, by some $95 million, to $2.95 billion.

News Corp's information memorandum, released ahead of the shareholder meeting that would approve the change of domicile, offered a rare snapshot of the Murdoch family's trusts and their assets, leaving plenty of choice tidbits for journalists to pick over. As a privately controlled entity, Queensland Press had been something of a family plaything and many of the assets it held would not belong in News. So Queensland Press sold to Cruden the Cavan station at Yass for some $21 million, as well as a collection of art and paintings hung in Murdoch offices around the world for another $12 million. The Murdochs also paid Cruden almost $19 million for Lachlan's home in Point Piper, bought five years earlier for $12 million. The price was reasonably close to market value: the home was quickly re-sold to mining engineer Gary Zamel for nearly $21 million.

At the same time, Queensland Press was forced to bring to book a bunch of undesirable investment assets, mostly acquired after Lachlan took over as chair of the company in 1999. *AFR* journalist Neil Chenoweth tallied up more than $120 million in previously undisclosed losses which Queensland Press had written off over the past five years from Lachlan's "hobby investments." They included some $50 million invested in struggling voice-over-internet communications businesses Comindico and Open Telecommunications, written down to nil; a $55 million investment in Zurich Capital Markets Australia; a $31.5 million investment in Dialect Solution Holdings, which Queensland Press had taken over for $2 million and, after writing the value down to nil, sold to Joe Cross in June for a $7 million interest-free non-recourse loan; and a $10 million investment in Joe Cross Pty Ltd, a futures trading company linked to Lachlan's friend, which long-serving company secretary Arthur Kirk had described as a "strange fit" for Queensland Press. Kirk had retired, coincidentally, the day the deal was done. Another $30 million committed to two US venture capital funds that were investing in dot-com stocks was also written off.

The total ran to $190 million, Chenoweth wrote, noting that "Queensland Press accounts do not give a full picture of what, if any, of these funds remain."[6] It was a bad look, but there was a story behind each and Joe Cross, who knew the deals intimately, explains that all were personally signed off by Rupert, and aimed to take advantage of the megatrend of convergence between media, telecommunications, and financial services. In most cases, the Murdochs were operating in partnership with the Packers, in a further example of the close relationship between Lachlan and James, and sometimes also alongside major institutions such as JP Morgan, utility AGL, or Zurich Insurance. Lachlan, as heir apparent to the News Corp empire, did not welcome the scrutiny, but at the same time he felt no need to explain the investments.

Through 2004, Lachlan had an internal team look at a possible buyout of the Australian assets of News Corporation. There were a range of alternative scenarios: Lachlan could find a private equity partner or borrow against his share of the family trust if Rupert approved and arranged a guarantee of the loan. Cross, who was on the team, felt the buyout could give Lachlan freedom in the short term, but was not necessarily the best strategic move in the long term:

> Given Lachlan's relationship with most of the US executives, we felt they'd be more than happy to sign off on those assets being sold, if it meant Lachlan going with them. No one would care in America or Europe or Hong Kong, what's going on down in the convict land? But Lachlan is smart. He's not stupid . . . and he realizes that there's a better trade to make, right, to leave options open. Because if you do that trade, you dramatically limit your options and quite possibly you close a door for good. As it turns out, it was a great trade *not* to do.

The proposition was never put to Rupert. After careful consideration, Lachlan concluded that it didn't make much sense for him to borrow the money for a buyout of News' Australian businesses: with the internet eating into print circulation and advertizing revenues, the numbers didn't stack up. "The writing was on the wall about the newspapers," says Cross.

News Corp's shift to the US wasn't only about the dollars. The company's relocation to Delaware brought with it lower governance standards under US law, which meant more opportunity for the Murdochs to entrench family control of News Corp. The whole deal was seen as part of securing Rupert's succession plan. The first of two key advantages to the move was that under Delaware law, the company could issue super-voting shares, for example to the Murdoch family; the second was restrictions on buying stakes higher than 15 per cent except for special deals approved by the board, which meant the Murdoch family could deal with their stake on terms unavailable to other shareholders. "It's a corporate regime which turns [Rupert's] succession plans for Lachlan and James Murdoch into certainties," wrote Neil Chenoweth.[7]

The Murdochs insisted they had no intention of taking advantage of either option, but institutional investors, particularly those with long memories, had no faith that Rupert would keep promises made ahead of a transaction once he got to the other side. Advised by corporate governance experts, the Australian Council of Superannuation Investors teamed up with big pension funds to bring the Murdochs to the negotiating table by threatening to vote against the relocation. For Rupert, no fan of either corporate governance or fund managers at the best of times, this was a moment of exquisite vulnerability. Because the relocation and the family sale of Queensland Press were inextricably tied together, the Murdochs were conflicted and could not vote when the deal was put to shareholders in Adelaide in November 2004. Rupert was over a barrel and forced to negotiate. It was too much for Lachlan, who felt a bad deal was getting worse. In a sort of symbolic protest he voted his own News Corp shares, the small number he held privately as a result of his salary package, rather than his much larger beneficial holding through the family trust, against the move to Delaware.

When the time came, after the QPL price had been lowered and the Murdochs had made concessions on governance, the deal sailed through at the 3.5-hour meeting in Adelaide. Rupert, who knew the result was assured, was in fine form during the company's last official annual general meeting in Australian, joking that the turnout was much bigger than the ten stalwart shareholders who'd turned up to his first News Corp meeting some fifty years earlier. Rupert's mind could now turn to re-investing the proceeds of the relocation and recapitalization, with family control of the company assured. As veteran *AFR* columnist Trevor Sykes observed sharply: "Murdoch has also fire-proofed Lachlan's position on the board. The one concession he never gave away in his negotiations with institutions was on the power to remove directors. In Australia, it can be done by a majority of votes at a meeting of shareholders. Under Delaware law, a director can only be removed by a majority of all the shareholders in a company, making the requirement almost impossible to fulfil."[8]

Any self-congratulation was short-lived: in the wake of the relocation, Rupert was shocked to find that his arch-rival John Malone had taken advantage of the instability on News Corp's share register—as institutions sold out of the Australian entity and bought into the American one—to increase his stake from 9 per cent to 17 per cent. Suddenly, with a holding only 12 per cent below the Murdochs' own 29 per cent, Malone posed a real threat to the family's control. Rupert had been outwitted by the only media mogul he feared. It was an epic error on the part of News and its investment banking advisers. Any lingering corporate governance scruples went straight out the window as the board adopted a new poison pill provision, by way of a new stockholder rights policy, to prevent Malone increasing his stake. Murdoch would spend the next two years in protracted negotiations with Malone, finally concluding with a deal to exchange the company's 38 per cent stake in DirecTV for Malone's News Corp holding.

Although shifting News Corp to the US was a big deal, Lachlan was preoccupied with an even more life-changing event: the birth of his first child, a son, Kalan Alexander Murdoch, the day before the Adelaide shareholder meeting. Sarah had been reported pregnant in April, after she was spotted with a baby bump at the Costume Institute Ball in New York and then pulled out of an appearance at Melbourne Fashion Week ut explanation. Observers quickly put two and two together. Kalan born at the Royal Mater Hospital in North Sydney on the afternoon of November 9, 2004. Named after an ancient Irish warrior, Kalan was Rupert's eighth grandchild and the first boy. Lachlan was there for the whole birth, Sarah told reporters later. "It was wonderful to go through it together," she said. "I wanted to do it naturally."[9]

The couple still planned to bring Kalan up in New York, they told reporters, with Sarah declaring she'd loved her pregnancy and was "ready to have more."[10] However, they were soon spotted inspecting real estate up and down Sydney's beachside suburbs. In April 2005, five months after Kalan was born, they made an unsolicited bid for possibly the best house in Bronte, in Sydney's east, on a street overlooking the beach known as "the cutting." The three-story contemporary home, built by a former president of the Bronte Surf Club, Graham Ford, was on a 416-square-meter block overlooking Bronte beach, and was deemed more suitable for small kids than running up and down all the stairs to the waterfront in the uber-rich enclave of Point Piper, with its tiny patch of grass by the harbor.

* * *

Returning to New York in early 2005, even though he was technically the third-most senior executive in the company, Lachlan found himself increasingly isolated within News Corp. Rupert had a new crush, as his biographer Michael Wolff described it, on Melbourne-born former *Financial Times* managing editor Robert Thomson, then editor of the London *Times*, and the first conversations about the possibility of a Dow Jones buyout were about to take place. Peter Chernin, who had been mooted as the next chief executive of Disney, had just had his contract renewed as News Corp COO and was throwing his weight around. The contract was generous to a fault, worth up to $US44 million, a sum Lachlan would describe as "unbelievable." Rupert could not afford to lose Chernin, a market darling, especially given Lachlan was not yet perceived to be ready to take on the top job.

During negotiations, Chernin cornered Rupert on the question of succession. As Wolff wrote, "he wanted it understood that if, perchance, the company needs a new CEO during the term of his next four-year contract, it will be him." Once secure, Chernin began a campaign of "nearly open disparagement" of Lachlan, whom he regarded as callow and insubstantial.[11] Although they were not allies—politically, they were poles apart—Chernin began ganging up with Roger Ailes against Lachlan. Ailes had made perhaps the most caustic observation of Rupert's son, calling him "un-Murdoch-like." He undermined Lachlan's control over Fox Broadcasting, run by former Fox News finance chief Jack Abernethy, and renewed his attempts to influence programming on the network. Lachlan kept his own counsel, but among his family and closest friends he made no secret of his frustration, speaking to his father, who tried to calm him down, and his older sister Elisabeth, who had quit the empire herself in 2000 after Rupert overlooked her for the top job at BSkyB. She was now going great guns at her own production company, Shine, and her stated view was that it was easier to be a Murdoch outside the family company than in it. At one point, Lachlan called John Hartigan back in Australia, admitting through tears that he was on the point of quitting the company. Hartigan talked him out of it.

It did not help Lachlan's love for his job at News Corp when he was heckled on stage at the Cannes International Advertising Festival in June. Likened to the Oscars for the ad industry, the festival was a big deal, attended by 8,000 people from all over the world. Lachlan had been named Media Person of the Year for lifting the circulation of the *New York Post* by 40 per cent and flying the flag for the next generation of media entrepreneurs. But Lachlan's acceptance speech, which made a serious point about the industry's over-reliance on TV commercials, extended to three pages, and after a while, whistles, known as the "Cannes boo," started coming from the back. Reporters for News Corp's competitors made sure to cover the heckle.

The last straw came over some apparently minor programming decisions. First, Lachlan stalled on giving a new weekly current affairs show on Fox to colorful talk-show host Geraldo Rivera, an Ailes favorite. Ailes wanted Fox TV to pay Fox News $10 million for the syndicated Sunday program, *Geraldo at Large*, but Lachlan flatly refused. He had his own idea, bringing pioneering Australian producer Peter Brennan over to the US to revive *A Current Affair*. Then, with an eye on cost control, Lachlan blocked Ailes' proposal for an expensive new reality TV series, *Crime Line*. Ailes went over Lachlan's head, straight to Rupert. "Do the show," Rupert told Ailes. "Don't listen to Lachlan."[12] Rupert would later describe his support for Ailes at this point as one of the worst decisions in his life.

Lachlan only found out what had happened when he landed in Los Angeles from Sydney, and he immediately rang Joe Cross from the airport. Joe was in Port Douglas. Lachlan told him he was going to resign. It was less about Roger and more about Rupert. "I remember him telling me that, you know, fuck it. I'm out . . . you know, if they're going to go around my back and whatever, then fuck them." The details of what happened next were later published in a tell-all article for *New York Magazine* by Steve Fishman, clearly briefed by Lachlan. "He loved his father," Fishman wrote, "but he felt undercut, maybe humiliated. The feeling mushroomed. Lachlan began to brood not just about *Crime Line* but about his identity, in the company and out." Lachlan now felt his designation as heir apparent was a poisoned chalice; it made him a threat to the top executives in the company, especially Chernin, his nominal boss, who was always eager to find fault. He felt the weight of expectation.

"Every meeting he has every day of his life, it's the same problem," an unnamed observer told Gabriel Sherman. "They go, 'Oh, I'm not sure he's his father.' It's an impossible slide rule to be held up against, particularly when you're learning and growing."

For his part, Lachlan saw Chernin as a self-promoter and political game-player and was sick of jousting with him.

Lachlan called Rupert in LA and organized a lunch for just the two of them. After eleven years at the company, Lachlan complained, he was not getting the respect he was due as deputy COO, and as Rupert's successor and son. It was certainly not the first time Lachlan had raised such grievances with his dad. Rupert would later say that he'd been able to talk Lachlan out of quitting on a couple of occasions before. This time Lachlan was impervious to Rupert's solicitations and offers to redraw the reporting lines at the top of News.

"Look, that's not going to work," Lachlan told him, getting emotional. "I have to do my own thing. I have to be my own man."

Then the thirty-three-year-old heir apparent got up and walked out of the restaurant, and out of the family business, perhaps, he thought, forever.

Lachlan's decision was a bombshell. When he got back to New York he told Col Allan, who "nearly fell off his chair." Then Lachlan called Hartigan, insisting: "I'm not going to listen to you this time, John. I'm quitting." The eldest son, always considered the most dutiful, could not be talked around. The accumulation of differences between Lachlan and his father had become too great: residual anger over the treatment of Anna, disappointment at the relocation of the company to Delaware, fury at being undermined at work, and a sense of missing Australia all boiled over. Both he and Sarah were longing to return to Sydney with Kalan and to make their own family life there. Three days later, News Corp put out an official statement. Lachlan blandly confirmed he was entering the next phase of his career but was excited to be continuing on the company's main board. Rupert was honest: "I am particularly saddened by my son's decision and thank him for his terrific contribution to the company . . . his achievements include driving all of his reporting divisions to record profits and the *New York Post* to its highest-ever circulation."

The statement appended a one-page bio lauding Lachlan's achievements and Rupert told reporters he hoped his son might return to the company within four to five years. Lachlan, indirectly quoted in Fishman's piece, felt his dad was secretly proud he'd walked. "'Proud that you are doing your own thing,' Lachlan thought, 'and you got the balls to do it, the guts to leave, the courage to leave.'"[13] Within hours he was back on the private jet headed for Sydney, perhaps for good.

PART 2

Illyria

9

On the sidelines

I T TOOK LACHLAN MURDOCH just three days to reserve the name of the new business he would set up in Australia: Illyria, an ancient tribal confederation on the eastern Adriatic Sea, once part of the Roman Empire and now of Albania. Illyria was the setting of Shakespeare's *Twelfth Night*, a gender-bending comedy in which shipwrecked twin Viola disguises herself as a man and falls in love with Duke Orsino, only to attract the true object of his affections, Countess Olivia. Like his boat names, Illyria was a curious, romantic choice that prompted some head-scratching among scribes when the paperwork was filed with the corporate regulator and released. What was Lachlan thinking?

It was of passing interest, however, as Illyria was unable to do anything substantial for some time. Lachlan was sole director and secretary of the new company, but he had signed a two-year non-compete clause with News Corp in return for a generous severance package. In total the package was worth some $15 million in salary and bonuses, termination pay and equity, a new source of grievance for some already-peeved shareholders. However, a lot of the compensation was tied up in short- and long-term incentives and he'd had to borrow the money to buy his house in Bronte. Under the two-year non-compete clause, Lachlan was unable to serve as a director, executive, or consultant for any company competing directly or indirectly with News Corporation anywhere in the world. His first move after quitting the empire had been to go sailing around Tahiti with Sarah and Kalan on *Ipixuna*. It was time to start taking things easy.

Amid reports of deep family divisions over their inheritance, the *Financial Times* revealed within days of Lachlan's departure that Rupert's four adult children were pushing to ensure they would not share control of the Murdoch family trust's voting stake in News Corp with their father's two young kids with Wendi. Rupert denied reports of a dispute but was not ready to agree to the demands of his older offspring, telling the *Financial Times*: "All my children will be treated equally."[1]

Despite their falling out, neither Rupert nor Lachlan wanted to cut ties completely. But Lachlan's seat on the main board of News Corp caused problems when he returned to Australia. Illyria was initially based at News Ltd.'s Sydney offices at Holt Street, where Lachlan was soon spending a couple of days each week in an office perched among the executive suites on level five, known as "Mahogany Row." According to former insiders at News Corp, Rupert was furious and called Hartigan almost daily, determined that his son would not continue to enjoy the privileges of the family business—an office, a secretary, a driver. "Don't let him into the fucking building," Murdoch told Hartigan, insisting that "when you're out, you're out," and complaining that Lachlan had a chip on his shoulder. Hartigan tried to steer a middle course, soft-pedalling on Rupert's instructions while limiting Lachlan's presence at Holt Street, but it was impossible to keep both Murdoch men happy. After a few weeks, at a private lunch, Lachlan accused Hartigan of disloyalty and freezing him out of important meetings, including with the prime minister. Hartigan offered his resignation, but Lachlan declined to take up the offer. From that point, the two old friends would barely speak, even though Lachlan remained an Australia-based director of News Corp and Hartigan the chief executive of News Corp in Australia. Chief operating officer Peter Macourt occasionally had to act as a go-between.

Lachlan sped up the search for Illyria's new offices. Over the next year he checked out dozens of premises, even exploring the possibility of a major tenancy at the famous Woolloomooloo "Finger Wharf" on the eastern fringe of the CBD, where he could also moor his yacht. He looked at a city office in the prestigious Governor Phillip Tower and immediately ran into financial types from Goldman Sachs and KKR, later telling colleagues "we could never work there . . . everyone would know what you were doing by who was coming up and down in the lift."

Lachlan kept his oar in at News, attending the Sun Valley conference at Idaho and returning to New York a few months later to put in an awkward appearance at the company's first annual shareholder meeting in America. On stage with the rest of the board, Lachlan started fidgeting when he was asked about his reported criticisms of chief operating officer Peter Chernin's high salary. Chernin, who sat through the meeting with his arms crossed defensively, increasingly looked like the News executive most likely to take over should anything happen to the company's founder. Rupert Murdoch bristled at questions about the succession, sticking to the line that it would be a matter for the board.

"We have a very strong bunch of candidates, if you like, of senior executives of the company that would please and be seen as a good asset in any company," Rupert told reporters after another shareholder meeting, in Adelaide, later that year. "I'm just sick of being told I'm dying," he went on. "I'm feeling great."

Almost as soon as Lachlan and Sarah returned to Sydney, she was pregnant again. The expecting couple lived at a nearby rental property while they renovated their Bronte home in preparation for an expanding family, with Kalan about to turn one. The plans caused a stir among some locals who wanted to protect native banksias that had been disappearing, allegedly due to mysterious fires and poisonings, from a thin strip of bushland blocking the ocean views of the mansions overlooking the beach. Protesters gathered outside the Murdochs' new home. Lachlan was sarcastic, telling *The Sydney Morning Herald* through a spokesman: "Yes, we have asked for all the vegetation to be moved and every tree in all of Bronte be cut down. Oh, and to redevelop the shops into a mall and rezone the beach."[2]

In his first months back in Sydney, Lachlan had to revisit the One.Tel disaster, turning up in court to give mostly forgetful evidence, although he did reveal that James Packer had broken down in tears in his kitchen after the company collapsed in 2001. Lachlan's testimony triggered another spate of embarrassing headlines until on Boxing Day 2005 an even bigger story broke, with the shock death of billionaire Kerry Packer of a massive heart attack at the age of sixty-eight. Lachlan and Sarah attended the state funeral in Sydney as the sole representatives of the Murdoch family and heard James Packer's emotional speech, including how he had raced home from overseas to make peace with his father on his deathbed. Given Rupert was more than a decade older than Kerry, and given Lachlan's relationship with his father was fragile, the speech must have hit home.

News Corp sailed on without him. James was Rupert's only child still in the business, running BSkyB television in Britain and exerting increasing influence across the empire. In July 2005, News had paid $580 million for social media pioneer MySpace, which was enjoying explosive growth. Google had floated the year before and Facebook had only just launched. Few knew what was around the corner. Lachlan was on the sidelines.

One of Lachlan's earliest moves at Illyria, before he even had an office, was to hire a McKinsey consultant, the economist Siobhan McKenna, as his right hand. Over the next fifteen years, she would become his most trusted adviser and one of Australia's most powerful businesswomen, with a string of prestigious board seats to her name. Lachlan had known Siobhan since the 1990s when she had shared a flat with his former girlfriend Kate Harbin, whom she knew from McKinsey. A partner of the firm by the age of twenty-nine— then the second youngest ever—Siobhan was a brilliant economist, trained at the Australian National University, who had written her thesis on native land title and its significance for mining just after the High Court's *Mabo* decision. She had recently returned to Australia after studying international relations at Cambridge University. When Lachlan asked her to help him set up Illyria, she quit a promising career at McKinsey to join him in his new business. For all her undoubted talents, however, Siobhan was not a media person and it would take time for her to get on top of an industry in the middle of historic upheaval and transformation.

Lachlan was seen at plenty of business events, but it was a full year before Illyria did its first deal. In the meantime, he had a bit of fun. He got back into shape, kickboxing early in the morning with a personal trainer. At thirty-four, he was fit, swimming 2.7 kilometers down the coast from glamorous Palm Beach to Whale Beach in under forty-nine minutes—not a bad time. He played tennis and went to the Australian Open in Melbourne. Days later he was off to the Motorcycle Grand Prix at Victoria's Phillip Island and gave Sarah heart palpitations by jumping on the back of a Ducati two-seater piloted by former race champion Randy Mamola, who took Lachlan on a flying lap of the circuit, hitting speeds of more than 300 km/h on the straight, chucking a wheelie and finishing with a "stoppy," jacking the back wheel up and nearly pitching the young media mogul skywards.

Lachlan and Sarah's second son, Aidan, was born in May 2006. Lachlan's twelve months of fun culminated in sailing *Ipixuna*, which had a replica of his lizard tattoo emblazoned across its spinnaker, at Hamilton Island race week, in Queensland's Whitsunday Islands on the Great Barrier Reef. Helmed by experienced skipper Rollo, *Ipixuna* was by far the biggest and most expensive boat on the water, easily snaring line honors but being beaten on handicap by *Wot's Next?*, a much smaller forty-seven-footer owned by Wotif founder and avid environmentalist Graeme Wood, who wound up making one of the largest political donations in Australian political history to the Greens.

Lachlan's own politics seemed to be shifting to the right. All of his political donations, at least, went to Republicans. He was one of eight News Corp executives who donated $2,000 each to President George W. Bush's campaign in 2004, and the following year he donated $1,000 to the Longhorn Political Action Committee (PAC), supporting the re-election of the Texas Republican Lamar Smith, a climate change–denying representative and member of the House science committee with links to the oil and gas industry. A trace of the socially liberal younger Lachlan remained: after attending a fundraiser in early 2006, he joined former Olympic swimming champion Ian Thorpe on the board of the

Asia Pacific Business Coalition on HIV-AIDS, launched by the Clinton Foundation and backed by the Australian government to fight the spread of the disease in PNG. "The business coalition is realizing how do you take businesses and apply their existing resources, not throwing cash at a problem, but using their existing resources to fight a problem," Lachlan told the ABC.[3] Sources close to Lachlan say his political views are "issues-based, and not derived from support for a particular political movement or adherence to any stringent ideology." They also point to his advocacy and support for First Nations Australians, and philanthropic donations to women's community shelters and children's health, including a $5 million endowment to the Murdoch Children's Research Institute, which was founded by Dame Elisabeth and where Sarah had served as a director and ambassador since 2002.

Still, there were definite signs of a new conservatism in Lachlan. In 2006, he turned up to News Corp's huge corporate love-in at Pebble Beach, near Santa Cruz. British prime minister Tony Blair, whom Lachlan had met at Hayman Island in 1995, was a keynote speaker, as were U2 frontman Bono and President Bill Clinton. Vice President Al Gore spoke, too, giving a presentation of his documentary *An Inconvenient Truth*, which sounded an alarm about global warming. Gore had been invited at the request of James, who had taken BSkyB carbon neutral as CEO and whose wife, Kathryn, had worked on climate change for the Clinton Foundation. During questions, Gore was challenged by two of News Ltd.'s top Australian columnists, Andrew Bolt and Piers Akerman, who were both avowed sceptics of human-induced global warming. Gore hit back and the session degenerated into a slanging match, widely reported. Lachlan, according to Chris Mitchell's memoir and others who were present, was cheering on Bolt and Akerman.

James, as it turned out, had been pushing Rupert to get serious about climate change and had a degree of success. In the UK, Lord Stern's landmark report had concluded the long-term costs of climate change would far outweigh the costs of taking action to reduce emissions. But in America, the Bush administration remained in denial. So did Fox News, which had a cosy relationship with the White House, where former anchor Tony Snow was now working as press secretary. Although many of Murdoch's most senior executives and editorial heavyweights were aghast, Rupert gave a speech to the Clinton Foundation, declaring that while he had his own reservations about global warming, if even a third of what climate scientists was saying was true, it was time to "give the planet the benefit of the doubt." Around the empire, with some notable exceptions, Murdoch newspapers and TV networks began to fall into line. There was even speculation that Rupert, whom James had urged to endorse Hillary Clinton for the presidency, was veering to the left.

It would not last long.

In July 2006, Rupert did an expansive interview with the famed PBS host Charlie Rose, revealing that after a year of bitter wrangling over the Murdoch family trust, everything had been resolved "very happily." He did not go into specifics, beyond saying that all six of his children would be "treated equally financially." Murdoch had been forced to give ground to the demands of his four oldest kids. Asked about the succession, Rupert told Rose that if he died, control of the News voting shares held by the trust would pass to his four older children. "If I go under a bus tomorrow, it will be . . . the four of them will have to decide which of the ones should lead them." Grace and Chloe, his children with Wendi, would be looked after financially but would not have a say in the future of News Corp.

At the same time, Murdoch announced the deal to buy out John Malone, selling him DirecTV and a couple of regional stations in exchange for his News Corp stake, finally seeing off a threat to his family's control of the empire. Rupert opened up to Rose about the impact of Lachlan's decision to quit the company, admitting it had "absolutely" caused him great pain. Although he said the succession had never been finally resolved, Rupert confided that his own "romantic" fondness for print meant his oldest son was at the head of the queue.

I would think the betting was on Lachlan, because he had this— still has this—really intense love of newspapers. But he also has a—it's easy to understand, I guess—but very intense love of Australia. He wasn't born there, he wasn't educated there, went on a couple of holidays there, but his first job was there, and his first responsibility. He spent ten years working in Australia, and all his friends were there, and he loved it.

For himself, Rupert said he loved America and felt American "in every way":

> I really feel at home here, I love it. My children are all American [forgetting Prudence again]. And that's it. I mean, I have strong emotional ties and family ties in Australia, and I enjoy going back there, but there's not much difference between the two countries in their attitudes and their people.[4]

It would take six months before the details of the restructure would be revealed, when the Murdoch Family Trust filed notice that it had distributed more than 26 million non-voting class-A News Corp shares, almost half its stake, to the six children. Each kid got $100 million worth of stock, and over the course of the year this was topped up with $50 million in cash. The trust began to pay out dividends, which it had never done before. Paradoxically, although Rupert's children had enjoyed the trappings of serious wealth all their lives, they had never had access to serious amounts of cash, unlike their cousins, who had inherited millions when Rupert engineered a buy-out of his three sisters in the 1990s.

Lachlan, the only one who had to disclose the gift as a director of News Corp, would now have some serious equity he could parlay into a major acquisition, particularly after his sizeable payout from News was included. After moving back to Australia, he had abandoned plans for the Candle building in Nolita, selling it on to developers for $12 million, doubling his money on Manhattan real estate for the second time in the space of a few years. All up, there were estimates Lachlan had some $220 million to invest. The question was how?

10

Deal or No Deal

RESTRICTED BY THE NON-COMPETE clause he had signed, Lachlan initially scoured the market for both media and non-media opportunities, revealing that he had sought the advice of New Zealand's richest person, multi-billionaire Graeme Hart, and together they had looked at more than fifty different companies.[1] At a time when markets worldwide were awash with debt, with private equity buccaneers snapping up everything in sight at sky-high valuations, Lachlan struggled to find anything to buy.

Illyria did a lot of work behind the scenes, but none of it became public. In 2006, Lachlan and Siobhan McKenna spent six months in intense negotiations with Maureen and Tony Wheeler, founders of travel guide powerhouse Lonely Planet, which was then largely paper-based; Lonely Planet had a blog, but not much else online. Media veteran John Singleton had a minority stake in Lonely Planet and had suggested the deal to Lachlan, who loved the brand, which spoke to his adventurous side. He and Siobhan saw huge opportunity in taking it digital and working alongside the founders to expand into audio and TV. They made an offer to buy half of Lonely Planet, but Illyria's vision and enthusiasm turned out to be infectious. The BBC came knocking and the Wheelers eventually sold 75 per cent of the business to the broadcaster for £88 million, at least three times more than Illyria had proposed. Lachlan and Siobhan "were floored."

Illyria's first public investment was a half-million-dollar stake in Quickflix, listed on the Australian stock exchange, which hoped to copy the strategy of US pioneer Netflix. Back in 2006, Netflix was a DVD rental business worth $2 billion. It was just beginning to deliver video on demand over the internet, or streaming. It would be years before Netflix disrupted the TV industry by launching its own original programming. In Australia, broadband was far from ubiquitous and download speeds were much slower than in the US.

There was some bemusement about whether the young Murdoch's investment represented a breach of the non-compete clause: Quickflix was in the same industry as News Corp, after all, and would rent out movies made in Fox Studios. Pretty soon it became clear, however, that the future of home movies lay not in DVDs but in the increasingly popular streaming format. Quickflix subscriber growth was slower than expected; the company continued to report losses and its shares plateaued. When another Australian internet wannabe, Destra, snapped up a 10 per cent stake in Quickflix amid speculation it was the prelude for a full takeover bid, Lachlan quietly converted Illyria's own 10 per cent stake into Destra shares.

Quickflix batted on for years, attempting a belated switch into streaming, and later attracted investment from HBO and Channel Nine. But both Quickflix and Destra would soon go broke, joining a lengthening list of the Murdochs' failed internet sorties. An investment by Illyria in American online ad-buying software company Spot Runner, which was backed by giants CBS and WPP, would also turn sour amid unproven allegations of insider trading and a string of lawsuits. Neither the amount of money Illyria sank into Spot Runner nor the amount it eventually recouped when the company was finally re-sold were ever disclosed.

Meanwhile, in Australia, the Howard government had finally succeeded in overhauling the country's media ownership laws. As Rupert feared, the reforms favored the interests of the free-to-air television moguls, James Packer and Kerry Stokes, lifting cross-media controls but retaining restrictions on foreign and regional media investment. For News, the deal most likely was a return to control of Channel Ten, the TV station which the Murdochs had been forced to offload after the laws were introduced fifteen years earlier. When CanWest, owned by Canada's Asper family, put its majority stake in Ten on the market in 2006, there was speculation that News might bid, but according to one report, John Hartigan got word from New York to leave the network for Lachlan, as Illyria was planning a bid. In the end, it was too big a bite for Lachlan and arguably a breach of his non-compete clause, which would not expire until mid-2007. Murdoch was effectively sidelined as Australia's media sector went through its biggest upheaval in nearly two decades: in October 2006, within hours of the new legislation passing through parliament, James Packer sold half his stake in Channel Nine to private equity giant CVC in a top-of-the-market, $4.5 billion deal. A day later, half of Stokes' Channel Seven was sold to KKR in another multi-billion-dollar transaction. Less than a year after his father had died, James Packer was cashing out of traditional media—within months he would sell another 25 per cent of Nine—to embark on a development spree in the gaming industry, building vast new casinos in Macau and Las Vegas.

Towards the end of 2006, Lachlan finally held a launch party for the business he'd begun a year earlier. In August, Illyria had paid $4.3 million for an old two-storey warehouse in Surry Hills, a short walk from News Ltd.'s headquarters. Rupert himself was guest of honor and was joined by many of the company's bigwigs, including John Hartigan, Foxtel boss Kim Williams and James Packer. Leaving the launch, when asked what Lachlan's business interest was, Hartigan told *The Australian*'s veteran columnist Don McNicoll, "Frankly I've got absolutely no idea."

As Lachlan was formally launching Illyria, Sarah was dipping her toe into television, taking on a temporary role filling in for Channel Nine morning show host Jessica Rowe, who was on maternity leave. Sarah, Lachlan, and family were certainly settling into Sydney life. When Rupert airily claimed in an interview with the *Financial Times* that Lachlan "might come back" to News Corp, Sarah firmly batted away questions about a potential move back to the US. "Both of us are very happy in Australia and our children are very happy here," she told *The Australian*. "It's a wonderful place to live, we pinch ourselves every day. Really, it is fantastic. Australians have the best of both—a fantastic community, a fantastic business center . . . a fantastic lifestyle."

As 2006 came to a close, News Corp was ramping up a drawn-out takeover battle for Dow Jones that would later become a key plotline in the hit series *Succession*. Rupert had long coveted the *Wall Street Journal*, a prestigious global masthead that had succeeded behind a paywall, which he hoped he could use to take the fight up to the liberal-leaning *New York Times*. At the beginning of 2007, Murdoch launched a $5 billion, $60-a-share offer for the *Journal*'s owner, Dow Jones, which represented a hefty premium to the prevailing share price. The Bancroft family, who had controlled Dow Jones since 1902, were split over the takeover, recognizing that the newspaper business was structurally challenged but fearing that editorial standards at the *Journal* would slide under Murdoch. Ultimately the Bancrofts were no match for a determined Murdoch, especially as their attempts to elicit a rival bid failed.

Throughout the Dow Jones bid, Rupert conferred on a daily and sometimes hourly basis with James. As Rupert's biographer Michael Wolff wrote, the younger son "proved his Murdochness" during the negotiations, and Rupert was "wowed by the boy's pure aggression, by his fight, by his fearsomeness . . . the old man figures that, as he chases the *Journal*, it's time to move James up."[2] Rupert promoted James from running BSkyB to the head of News in Europe, Asia, and the Middle East, a move that was widely seen as vaulting Lachlan's younger brother to the front of the succession queue. Commentators contrasted James' climb up the ladder at News with Lachlan's hodgepodge of investments down under.

Lachlan's two-year non-compete clause expired in August 2007 and by then Illyria had a dossier on every media business in Australia, including a perspective on how each outlet's performance could be improved, the quality of the executives running it, and who else was interested in its assets.

The first dark clouds were rumbling in what would become the worst financial storm since the Great Depression. Through the second half of

2007, what started as a "credit crunch" worsened, as the US housing bubble burst and mortgage-backed securities markets worldwide froze over.

Lachlan was undeterred. He finally began work on a multibillion-dollar media deal of his own: the privatization of Consolidated Media Holdings (CMH), which held James Packer's remaining pay-TV and free-to-air interests and his stakes in Carsales.com.au and employment website Seek.com.au. Packer believed the pay-TV and online assets were undervalued and teamed up with Lachlan in a 50:50 partnership to buy out the public investors for $3.3 billion, or $4.80 per share, 20 per cent more than the float price just months earlier, and a whopping premium to the market price.

The fact that the two media scions were prepared to cast their lots in together showed how close Packer and Murdoch remained, despite the failure of One.Tel. Joe Cross, who has been close to both men over the years, says they were "very much like brothers, joined in this together . . . it would have been easy for Lachlan to throw James Packer under the bus with his father, and he didn't, and I think that James Packer respected him enormously for that and that really forged a much closer friendship." As they sized up their joint bid for CMH, James could afford to fund his side of the deal outright. On Illyria's side, Lachlan had support from San Francisco-based hedge fund SPO Partners. SPO had worked with Microsoft founder Bill Gates and Lachlan stressed that the level of debt, $880 million, was manageable notwithstanding the credit crunch. "The majority of this bid is equity," he said. "It's not one of these deals where it's nine parts debt and one part equity."[3]

When the proposed deal was announced in early 2008, Australia's anti-cartel regulator, the Australian Competition and Consumer Commission, declared it would review the acquisition to determine whether Lachlan was truly independent of News Corp. Murdoch welcomed the investigation but told the *Financial Times* the bid did not raise competition issues. "This is probably the most sizeable Australian asset that does not compete with News Corp," he told reporters. CMH did not have a majority stake in anything, so Lachlan, who was slated as chair, would have to be satisfied with having influence over, rather than outright control of, the companies it part-owned. Still, CMH was a sizeable deal, the second-largest media group in the country, and there was speculation as to how Lachlan could afford it. He denied reports that his siblings had invested, adding, "There is none of my dad's money, either." He said work on the deal had begun months ago and that the announcement was made as soon as the financing was in place. "I'm not sure if we picked the perfect time to launch a bid, or the worst time," he joked.[4] It would prove to be the latter.

Lachlan went all-out to land the deal. In the due diligence phase, SPO's founder John Scully flew out to Sydney to meet with the heads of each business, including Foxtel, Nine, Carsales.com.au and the ACP magazines. Illyria lined up the meetings and Lachlan and Sarah hosted Scully and the most senior executives at a dinner at their Bronte home. A few footy stars were there, too, to help Lachlan make an impression on the American financier. Scully seemed enthusiastic and flew back to the US without a hint he was having qualms, but eleven days later he called Lachlan personally with bad news. SPO was rattled by the state of markets in Australia. Highly leveraged companies were toppling like dominos and SPO was not comfortable with either the level of debt inside Nine or the cost of hedging the Australian dollar, which was then soaring against the greenback.

Lachlan was seriously pissed off: "On a scale of 1–10, where 1 is you want to kiss someone and 10 is you want to murder someone, he was an 8," said one source.[5] But he kept his cool with Scully and caught the first Qantas flight to LA to try to find a new private equity partner in what a statement euphemistically called an "abbreviated timeframe." The *Financial Times*' Lex columnist wrote that the "dynamic duo" of Lachlan and James appeared to be "on the brink of another debacle."

When CMH shares resumed trading, they plunged 10 per cent as the takeover premium evaporated and continued to slide. Lachlan was in a race against time, with days or weeks to find a new investor. He was reportedly talking to Hellman & Friedman, whose director Brian Powers was a friend and ally of Kerry Packer, and the hedge fund Providence Equity Partners, where a former Star TV executive, Michelle Guthrie, was now working. Guthrie started work on a bid, taking an urgent trip to Sydney, but Providence wanted even better terms than SPO.

Watching currency, debt, and property markets all turn against his casino developments, particularly in Las Vegas, James Packer baulked at the rising cost of the deal and pulled out. "[CMH] went from being an asset that I could afford to buy, to being an asset I'd like to sell," he says, looking back. Without a partner, there was no way Illyria could afford to buy even half of CMH, and within weeks it was clear the whole deal would be a casualty of the financial crisis. After all the hype about how the CMH deal would "unleash the entrepreneurial Murdoch blood," as *The Australian* wrote, and that it would be followed by an Illyria bid for the whole of the former Packer media empire, as some analysts had tipped, the collapse brought another bout of speculation as to whether Lachlan had what it takes. Before long, however, most pundits reckoned Lachlan had dodged a bullet: as the financial crisis peaked with the collapse of Lehmann Brothers and as the economic downturn bit into CMH's earnings from pay-TV, the value of the company dropped by more than a billion dollars. Rupert himself said Lachlan had "got lucky" with the collapse of the CMH deal, one he never understood or supported.

In the lead-up to Christmas 2008, Illyria bought 14 per cent of toymaker Funtastic, the listed owner of the Australian licenses to Harry Potter, Bob the Builder, Winnie the Pooh, and Thomas the Tank Engine. The shares were going cheap and for an outlay of $2 million Lachlan became the second-largest investor in the company. But Funtastic was cheap for a reason: it was heavily exposed to the recent collapse of Australia's biggest chain of childcare centers, earnings were falling, and within months the CEO was out the door. Year after year, through one capital raising after another, the company proclaimed it had turned the corner, but Funtastic's share price never went anywhere. For Lachlan, who refused to put any more money in and allowed his holding to gradually dilute, it would prove another dud.

Perhaps the one bright spot for Lachlan amid the market turmoil of 2008 was a minority stake in an Indian Premier League (IPL) cricket team, Jaipur's Rajasthan Royals, one of eight franchises sold to found the Twenty-20 competition, which was soon going gangbusters. Illyria had earlier invested in an Indian talent management firm and in 2008 Lachlan partnered with UK sport management company Emerging Media to bid for the Royals, paying $67 million, making them the cheapest team in the competition and the only team which was foreign-owned. The Royals were unfancied but pulled off a spectacular win in the inaugural year of the competition, captain-coached by former Australian test player Shane Warne. The value of the Royals franchise sky-rocketed and Lachlan and his partners at Emerging Media were soon sitting on a handsome profit. Illyria's 8 per cent stake, purchased for a reported $870,000, soon doubled in value as Bollywood star Shilpa Shetty bought in, touting plans for a Royals clothing line and a documentary film. Within a year, the estimated value of the franchise had jumped tenfold and after another year Illyria's stake was worth $28 million, one of Lachlan's best investments.

But in 2010 there was outrage in India as it emerged that one of Lachlan's co-owners in the Royals was the brother-in-law of the IPL's founder, Lalit Modi, and the tax authorities commenced an investigation. Modi was soon charged with corruption. In Delhi's *Mail Today*, Lachlan was described as a "rich brat with a penchant for wasting his father's millions."[6] The Indian investigators accused the Royals owners of "round tripping," bringing black money back through offshore tax havens, and in late 2010, in a shocking move, the IPL terminated the franchise agreement. Illyria's whole stake was now at risk, although the company stressed in a statement that the value of its initial investment had been recouped through dividends. Although Illyria's stake was indeed held through tax havens, there was no suggestion that Lachlan himself was aware of any of Modi's financial irregularities.

The Royals issued a statement saying the team was shocked to be axed without notice, adding that the ownership structure had been transparent since 2008. The dispute went before the Indian Supreme Court, with

Lachlan telling the *Financial Times*: "Our hope is that the actions taken by the BCCI are not indicative of a broader climate for overseas investors in India."[7] The court stayed the termination, finding it was prima facie illegal, and after a successful appeal the Royals were re-admitted under a new ownership structure. For Lachlan, the attraction for Illyria was purely financial: he never attended a single IPL game.

It was not until early 2009 that Illyria finally made its first proper media investment, shelling out $16 million for 9 per cent of Prime Media, which owned the regional TV affiliates of Kerry Stokes' Channel Seven and a network of country radio stations. Saddled with debt, Prime need to raise capital and Lachlan pounced, paying 48 cents a share. The price immediately surged 10 per cent, again partly on the strength of the Murdoch name. Lachlan said he was sitting on a "fair amount of cash" to invest, most likely in companies that were overloaded with debt.[8] If there was more to Murdoch's strategy than opportunistically chasing value, it was not immediately apparent: Prime was a small piece of the Australian media puzzle, and a minority stake came without any management control. But Illyria's investment in Prime was a prelude to bigger media plays. A few months later, Siobhan McKenna joined the Prime board, suggesting Lachlan intended to buy and hold.

In November, more than four turbulent years after quitting News Corp, Lachlan finally got his hands on his own media business and like all of Illyria's moves it came completely out of the blue. The deal was brought to him by an old hand in the merchant banking business, Simon Mordant at Greenhill Caliburn, who had known Rupert since the 1980s and was advising the UK's Daily Mail and General Trust (DMGT) on the sale of their DMG radio business in Australia. DMG owned two languishing commercial FM stations, Nova and Vega, and one talkback radio station in Adelaide. DMGT had invested roughly $700 million dollars in the national network, but it was deemed non-core in the aftermath of the financial crisis.

Mordant knew Lachlan was on the hunt for media assets and that Illyria had made some "pretty ordinary investments." He sounded Lachlan out about DMG Radio, and found he was interested but could not afford to buy the stations outright. "I don't think he had very much cash at all," Mordant remembers, and it was true that to fund the purchase, Lachlan had to sell some of the News Corp shares he had inherited in 2006.

But Lachlan personally knew the chairman of DMGT, Jonathan Harmsworth, a British viscount who had been managing director of the London *Evening Standard* until the death of his father in 1998. Harmsworth was looking to sell without a competitive process for fear that a public bid would expose DMGT's losses and Lachlan now had the inside position. Whenever negotiations looked like they were going off the rails, a phone call from Lachlan to Jonathan could get them back on track.

Under the 50:50 joint venture deal, Illyria paid DMGT some $50 million and took on $60 million in debt while assuming full management control, which valued the whole network at a bargain-basement price of roughly $220 million. "Patience is a virtue," Lachlan said in a media statement, "and after exhaustively searching the market for the right acquisition, we have found in DMG Radio Australia the right business, the right partner and the right brands, which are positioned for exemplary growth." Lachlan became DMG chairman, leaving in place the well-regarded chief executive, Cathy O'Connor, who would remain for a decade. It was largely her strategy, documented before the sale, that was implemented by Illyria. Lachlan saw the ability to reposition the business, says Mordant, and always intended to buy the whole thing as soon as he could afford it.

"It was a brave thing for him to do," says Mordant. "DMG had had an absent landlord and hadn't had a lot of TLC. He engaged with advertizers as if he was the proprietor, and engaged with the team." DMG abolished Nova's promise never to play consecutive advertizements, increasing revenue and pleasing advertizers no end. Lachlan had a hand in nurturing Nova's up-and-coming drivetime stars, "Fitzy and Wippa," a pair of Aussie knockabouts whom he befriended. Vega switched to a classic rock format, non-stop Led Zeppelin, Pink Floyd and Midnight Oil, and when that didn't work went back to square one.

After a get-to-know-you meeting in London, Lachlan hired British radio executive Paul Jackson to become Nova's head of programming. Jackson had a reputation as a turnaround expert—his favored strategy was to play the hits—and he was recommended by O'Connor. At a management retreat at Cavan, attended by Lachlan and Siobhan, Cathy and Paul and a host of executives, they decided to switch Vega to an easy listening format, SmoothFM, playing hits from the 1950s and '60s. A key was to ditch the reliance on talented hosts, explains Cathy O'Connor:

> The whole proposition with Smooth is that it's a station built around a lifestyle and a mentality, not necessarily a demographic or a music genre. [Lachlan] didn't want it to be a sort of dated, easy listening station, he really supported this idea that we could make easy listening appealing and contemporary and aspirational. You know, we came to the table to say, 'How do we build a station that doesn't need big talent, you know, as its DNA, because that's costly, and it's risky. And that model of no big-talent shows is an incredibly profitable model.

Before too long, as the economy rebounded and with the help of a structure that funnelled profits through tax havens and virtually eliminated taxes in Australia, Smooth FM was making money hand over fist. As the profits piled up, Illyria accumulated the capital to buy DMGT out of the other half of Nova at the price previously agreed with Harmsworth, which now looked outrageously cheap.

There had been plenty of wrong turns and dead ends, but with control of Nova and a small stake in Prime Media, Lachlan had a foothold in the media industry. There were other deals in the pipeline. Lachlan's spokesman reckoned Illyria had looked at something like 300 investment opportunities since 2005 and in Nova, Illyria had picked a winner. Lachlan now had his own source of wealth, independent of his family, and he could point to a deal he had got right on his own terms.

Showing his unsentimental side, Lachlan had examined and knocked back some real media treasures through the crisis, including the celebrated weekly news magazine *The Bulletin*, a crucible of Australian journalism and culture that was first published in 1880. By 2007 it had been sold out of the Packer empire and was on the private equity chopping block. Lachlan talked about "the Bully" with his father, leaving Rupert with the impression he was interested. Rupert told biographer Michael Wolff, with evident excitement, that while *The Bulletin* would not make Lachlan rich, it was "a great magazine" that would keep him occupied. Instead, Lachlan declined to invest in the influential masthead and its last issue was published in 2008.

The decision showed that Lachlan was first and foremost interested in making money, but also that he had something of a blind spot when it came to burnishing his political power. FM radio did not generate influence in Canberra; nor, for that matter, did eclectic plays like Funtastic, Quickflix, or the IPL. If the Murdoch genius, passed down from Sir Keith to Rupert, was to "govern by media," Lachlan showed no sign that he had the gene. If he wanted political influence in his own right, he would have to earn it.

11

Trouble Brewing

O N THE OTHER SIDE of the world, James Murdoch's promotion to run News International was turning into a poisoned chalice. Only six months into the role, on a Saturday afternoon in May 2008 while at home in London, James received a forty-seven-word email from Colin Myler, the editor of the company's biggest-selling tabloid, *News of the World*, updating him on a lawsuit against the paper by a former high-ranking English soccer official, Gordon Taylor. Taylor was enraged, having obtained police documents which confirmed the newspaper had hacked his phone. In the second line, Myler wrote ominously: "Unfortunately it is as bad as we feared."

News of the World had investigated false rumors that Taylor was having an affair with his secretary back in 2005, based on intercepted voicemails. Although no story was ever published, Taylor's lawyers had a copy of an email in which transcripts of his voicemail messages were sent to *News of the World* star reporter Neville Thurlbeck. Taylor was demanding a million pounds.

Myler's email drew James' attention to News International's "extremely telling" legal advice, forwarded by in-house counsel Tom Crone, relaying that Taylor wanted to prove that phone hacking was "rife" throughout *News of the World*. Crone's email to Myler warned of a "nightmare scenario" in which Taylor's secretary and solicitor, who had also had their phones hacked, followed up with similar claims based on the same evidence. Crone recommended that News International cough up to settle the Taylor case. He reckoned it would take £700,000.

Despite such dire warnings, James does not appear to have read the whole email. At home with his family on the weekend, he took just two minutes to reply to Myler's request for a meeting with Crone on Tuesday: "No worries . . . if you want to talk before I'll be home tonight after seven and most of the day tomorrow." James would subsequently testify:

> I think Mr Myler sent me this note unilaterally, forwarded me this correspondence, and I don't believe that I read it. I didn't read it at the time. I have responded to it in minutes, and it was a Saturday, I had just come back from a flight to Hong Kong and I was with my young children at the time. And I invited him to give me a call that evening after they went to bed, I assume, and I don't have a record or recollection of any phone call that occurred.

Three years later, however, James' prompt reply to that email would come back to haunt him. Lachlan and other US directors of News Corp would be facing an FBI investigation and Rupert's grip on the company was under its most serious threat since the debt crisis two decades earlier. The Murdoch family business would never be the same again.

The scandal had been building for years. In August 2006, Clive Goodman, the royal editor of *News of the World*, was arrested and charged with the criminal offense of conspiring to intercept communications. Goodman and a private investigator paid by the paper, Glenn Mulcaire, had hacked into the voicemails of Prince William, revealing in a gossipy item that William had pulled a tendon in his knee, but the details were known to almost nobody outside the royal family. Alarmed, Buckingham Palace went straight to the police. Scotland Yard investigated, raiding the *News of the World* newsroom and Mulcaire's office, collecting boxes and boxes of evidence. In January 2007, Goodman and Mulcaire were convicted and given short jail sentences. The paper's editor, Andy

Coulson, resigned while maintaining he knew nothing about the hacking. News International replaced Coulson with Colin Myler, former executive editor of the *New York Post*, who spun the line that Goodman was a "rogue exception." The police backed this up, closing the investigation and concluding there was no evidence that other journalists were involved or that the phones of anyone outside the royal family had been hacked. The UK Information Commissioner's Office and Press Complaints Commission conducted similarly perfunctory reviews. Myler told the Press Complaints Commission that Goodman's case was "an exceptional and unhappy event in the 163-year history of the *News of the World*, involving one journalist."

Phone hacking had taken off in Fleet Street newsrooms in the late 1990s, a symptom of the "whatever it takes" culture of the ultra-competitive British press. The culture had been particularly toxic at Murdoch's *Sun*, which, according to *The Guardian* investigative reporter Nick Davies' authoritative book *Hack Attack*, was the first paper to work out how to intercept voicemail messages, using the trick to chronicle rock star Mick Jagger's 1999 divorce from Jerry Hall.[1] It spread quickly to *News of the World*, where former *Sun* journalist Rebekah Wade, a rising star of the Murdoch empire, was appointed editor in 2000 at the age of thirty-two, extraordinary for a British newspaper, with Coulson her deputy (and lover, as would be revealed years later). As bad as phone hacking was, it was just one of a number of ways *News of the World* obtained information illegally, using an army of private investigators to "blag" or extract information by deception, extending all the way to payments to corrupt police. Wade, who rose to become the first female editor of *The Sun* in 2003, told the UK parliament as much in her testimony to a media inquiry that year, admitting that "we have paid the police for information in the past." She quickly corrected her testimony.

Lachlan knew Rebekah well, perhaps mostly as a favorite of Rupert, who treated her almost as a daughter and spoke with her daily. Lachlan was famously photographed at a London club when actor Russell Crowe came to blows with kiwi financier Eric Watson and Rebekah's then husband, *Eastenders* star Ross Kemp, had to pull them apart. Gossip columns the next day ran pictures showing Lachlan in the background. *The Sun* went so far as to airbrush the Murdoch heir out of the shot, much to the amusement of rival papers. Lachlan also knew Colin Myler from his time at the *Post*. Almost from the beginning of his tenure as Coulson's replacement, Myler was on the back foot, facing an unfair dismissal suit from Goodman, who had done his time behind bars and expected to be re-hired. Goodman did not get his job back, but he got a more generous payout and Mulcaire was also looked after.[2] Myler would spend the next four years managing a phone-hacking crisis that only seemed to get worse. As he later described his time as *News of the World* editor: "I felt that there could have been bombs under the newsroom floor and I didn't know where they were and I didn't know when they were going to go off."

When in-house counsel Crone learned of the email to reporter Neville Thurlbeck, which attached transcripts of Taylor's voicemails and would soon be known as the "for Neville" email, he wrote in a memo that it was "fatal to our case." Soon after, Myler handed the evidence to a prominent media law specialist, Michael Silverleaf QC, who advised him there was a "powerful case" that there was "a culture of illegal information access" at *News of the World*.[3] There were no notes from the meeting attended by Myler, Crone, and James Murdoch on June 10, 2008, but News International agreed subsequently to pay more than a million pounds to Taylor, his secretary, and his lawyer. Nonetheless, James later testified that he continued to have no more than a general understanding that a reporter had illegally intercepted voicemails, that the reporter and private investigator had gone to jail, and that it was all in the past. James said he had himself pondered, "Why wouldn't they just come and tell me? I was a new person coming in. This was an opportunity to actually get through this, and they didn't.' He pointed to a line in a file note made by News' external lawyer, Julian Pike, after a phone conversation with Myler, which read: "James wld say get rid of them—cut out cancer". James continued: "I don't want to conjecture, [but] I think that must be it, that I would say, 'Cut out the cancer,' and there was some desire to not do that." James would continue to plead ignorance and Rupert later testified in th Parliament that neither he nor the directors of the News Corp board were ever told of the payment to Taylor, even though he admitted that such an amount was far in excess of the normal spending authority given to editors.

There was hope within News International from 2008 onwards that it might be possible to put the phone-hacking affair behind the company. Rebekah Wade, who had divorced Ross Kemp and married horse trainer Charlie Brooks, was promoted from editor of *The Sun* to chief at News International, reporting to James. But half a dozen other hacking victims of *News of the World*, advised by the same lawyers that had negotiated Taylor's settlement, were determined to have their day in court. As their legal actions ground through the justice system, a major cover-up got underway, including the deletion of millions of emails. By now, *The Guardian* investigative reporter Nick Davies was on the trail, and on July 9, 2009, a front-page story revealed that News had paid more than a million pounds to settle the Taylor claims. The payments secured secrecy over evidence that Murdoch journalists using private investigators had hacked the phones of numerous public figures, including cabinet ministers, members of parliament, actors, and sports stars, and had gained unlawful access to confidential data, including tax records, social security files, bank statements, and phone bills.[4]

If the Murdoch family were not yet aware of the gravity of the unfolding scandal, they should have been. *The Guardian* story triggered the launch of a new inquiry by the House of Commons culture, media and sports committee. When the committee reported in February 2010, it accused the News executives of "collective amnesia" and concluded that it was "inconceivable" that only one reporter had been involved in the hacking. Meanwhile the *The Guardian*, struggling to find support from other Fleet Street papers, took the unusual step of approaching rival masthead *The New York Times* and offering Davies to brief their reporters. After a months-long investigation, *The New York Times* delivered its own bombshell at the beginning of September, interviewing former *News of the World* journalists who confessed that phone hacking was so rife in the newsroom, even "the office cat knew."[5] James would later testify that it was only after the *Times* piece ran, at the end of 2010, that he realized phone hacking was not an isolated incident and there were more claims to come out.

With Lachlan off doing his own thing in Australia, James believed he had bigger fish to fry. He was preparing to launch the biggest acquisition News Corp had ever undertaken, buying the remaining 61 per cent of BSkyB it did not already own. Defying those critics who said his appointment to run BSkyB at the age of thirty was nepotism, James had set audacious growth targets for the British pay-TV operation, aiming for ten million paying subscribers by 2007, and then set about achieving them by bundling pay-TV and broadband. By the time he was promoted to run News International, against his wishes, given that he had no love for newspapers, BSkyB was generating enormous profits and News Corp was planning to increase its 39 per cent stake.

James was on a roll, building his own powerbase within News Corp, separate from his father. He questioned why News Corp should be run out of New York, when the company's best prospects for future growth lay in Europe and Asia, regions under his responsibility. Perhaps headquarters should be in London? Without challenging Rupert directly, James began asserting his influence, portraying the old man as an obstacle and, according to *The New York Times*, even telling members of the board that he was worried about his father's mental health.[6] A step-change came in mid-2009 when Rupert's right-hand man, Peter Chernin, finally decided to quit after twenty years. Chernin had been no fan of the Dow Jones acquisition at a price he thought was way over-the-top and he knew, with James staking his claim to the top job, that he could rise no further within the Murdoch empire. Chernin negotiated an unprecedented exit package, including rights to use the company jet, obligations on News Corp to buy any television or films he went on to produce, and even a "most favored nation" clause allowing him to top up his package. James saw an opportunity to replace Chernin loyalists with his own people, or his own court. News' long-standing corporate affairs chief Gary Ginsberg was forced out of the company, while James hired Matthew Anderson, based in London.

After much preparation and speculation, in June 2010 News Corp launched its $12 billion bid for the rest of BSkyB, subject to approval from shareholders and the British government. As he worked up the BSkyB bid, James decided unilaterally to appoint advisers based in London, giving the mandate to Deutsche Bank guru Rob Rankin, an Australian who'd worked closely with the Packer family. Rupert realized he could no longer afford to let James set up his own court in London. He wanted to bring his younger son back to New York with a view to confirming him as the eventual successor, but was also furious with him. Lachlan, Prudence, and Elisabeth all got involved and, as *Vanity Fair*'s Sarah Ellison would later sensationally report, things got so dysfunctional that the siblings started attending family counselling. "They told James that if they worked together . . . they could help him and their father have a better relationship . . . and that together the kids could hold Rupert to account to be a mentor to James and not undermine him, as he had done with Lachlan so many years before." They gave James some frank advice, agreeing he was best placed to be heir apparent, but telling him to tone down his aggressive public posturing, exemplified by his defiant appearance at the prestigious McTaggart Lecture at the Edinburgh Television Festival the previous year, where he had launched a broadside at "authoritarian" public broadcaster the BBC and argued provocatively that "the only reliable, durable, and perpetual guarantor of independence is profit."

In early 2011, Rupert gave his younger son a promotion and an ultimatum: James would become deputy chief operating officer, as Lachlan had been years earlier, but reporting to Chase Carey rather than Chernin and based in New York. If he didn't accept, Rupert told James in no uncertain terms, "You are fired."[7]

* * *

Back in Australia, Lachlan was increasingly finding himself on one side of a deepening divide in federal politics. *The Australian* had backed Labor in the 2007 federal election after editor-in-chief Chris Mitchell had convinced Rupert. Lachlan also had a decent relationship with Kevin Rudd's Labor government, attending Rudd's 2020 Summit in Canberra in April 2008. "I think it's hard in a couple of days to do anything more than just have a great airing of ideas," Lachlan said ahead of the elite gathering of a thousand government, business, community and arts leaders, "and I think that's probably the best we can hope for." The summit was quickly forgotten and soon *The Australian* was turning on Kevin Rudd.

Hostility from the News Ltd. papers ratcheted up through 2008, particularly over the multi-billion-dollar stimulus spending announced in the wake of the global financial crisis. In April 2009, Rudd announced the government would build, own, and ultimately privatize a new national broadband network (NBN), rolling out high-speed fibre-optic cable into 93 per cent of Australian homes and businesses at a cost of $43 billion. There were some, including Rudd himself, who reckoned the Murdochs saw the NBN as a fundamental threat to News Corp's Foxtel pay-TV outfit, which was delivered through an existing network of hybrid fibre-optic cable. News Ltd. papers, including *The Australian*, were largely negative in their coverage of the public infrastructure program, in line with the small-government Murdoch ethos. At the end of 2009, perhaps as an olive branch and perhaps in an effort to forestall more hostile reporting, the federal communications minister, Stephen Conroy, announced that Lachlan's partner at Illyria, Siobhan McKenna, would be invited to join the board of the new government-owned NBN.

Even more divisive was climate change. In the lead-up to the 2009 UN climate summit in Copenhagen, the opposition's hard-right faction dug in and knives were sharpening against the moderate Liberal leader Malcolm Turnbull. The leading conservative was Tony Abbott, whom Lachlan and Sarah knew well—he was local MP for Sarah's home turf on Sydney's northern beaches and like Sarah he was a passionate supporter of the Manly Sea Eagles rugby league team. Sarah was a high-profile patron of the National Breast Cancer Foundation when Abbott was health minister in the Howard government and he had announced $40 million funding for new and replacement prostheses. Sarah had followed this up with friendly jousts with Abbott during her stint as a host on the *Today* show in 2007. In July 2009, when Abbott was emerging as a potential rival leader to Turnbull, he asked Sarah to launch his political memoir, *Battlelines*. There was a minor kerfuffle at the Sydney launch when Abbott thanked Lachlan for "allowing" Sarah to launch the book, as though it was not her decision, but the ensuing bad publicity probably helped book sales. Abbott and Lachlan would become increasingly close friends. Looking back, Rudd believes that decision alone speaks volumes about the far-right conservatism which Tony Abbott and Lachlan Murdoch have in common:

> If you become best buds with Abbott, who is—let's call it—on the far right of the Liberal Party in this country, and you take what is a calculated political risk in 2009 to have your wife go out and launch a principal conservative antagonist's personal manifesto, you are saying 'this is a valued relationship and therefore we're placing a priority on it, and we don't care whether there is any mainstream political cost.'

Sarah was matter-of-fact about the event, saying she was pleased to launch it for Tony, "not only because I've known you for some time, but because I have read *Battlelines* and, in fact, I couldn't put it down."[8] Rudd, by contrast, took the launch as a deliberate "screw you" from the Murdoch media to his government and its successful navigation of the financial crisis. Rudd says it is hard to think of a more symbolic act by Lachlan and Sarah, and that Murdoch media outlets around the country would have got that message loud and clear: "News Corp editors have PhDs in nothing except reading the Murdoch family tea leaves. And you don't have to be a Rhodes scholar to work out where that set of tea leaves lined up . . ." Lachlan's friendship with Abbott would prove enduring, as a source close to the young mogul explains:

> Lachlan is right into politics de jure, in whatever jurisdiction he's in, because that's the news business. However, a politician who has read

all the major philosophers and has deep thoughts about the role of the Judeo-Christian ideology on society and can sustain a dinner conversation about that is probably of more interest to Lachlan than a politician who is in it because they're a politician. So, you know, I think that intellectual sort of curiosity is probably something that Lachlan and Tony Abbott like about each other. Also, Tony Abbott was a journalist, and while that means not very much to most people, if you're a journalist, and you believe in journalism, then actually that means a lot. So it's the idea of seeking out the truth, it's the idea of holding people to account, the idea of holding the powerful to account is, I think a part of journalism. And that's what, that's what we believe in. And so I suspect that Tony Abbott having been a journalist was probably part of their friendship.

In December, just days before the Copenhagen summit, the Liberals dumped Turnbull for Abbott, who had recently declared it was "absolute crap" that climate science was settled, and had vowed to oppose any emissions trading scheme, which he labelled "a great big new tax on everything." A decade of toxic climate wars began. After the Copenhagen summit failed to deliver a binding outcome, the Labor government shelved its plans for a carbon price. The political damage was compounded when Rudd's government proposed a new tax on the "super-profits" of the resources industry, only to face a multi-million-dollar industry-funded advertizing campaign, amplified by an unremittingly hostile Murdoch press, which swung firmly behind Abbott as opposition leader. The campaign culminated in a stunning overnight challenge to Rudd's leadership by deputy Julia Gillard, an unprecedented party coup against a first-term prime minister. Eight weeks later, Labor barely clung to power in the August 2010 election, in a minority government propped up by the Greens and independents. *The Australian* went into overdrive, declaring that the Greens were "bad for the nation" and "should be destroyed at the ballot box." The Greens responded that the newspaper, with an openly partisan agenda, was now the Fox News of Australian media.

Some weeks after the election, in a move that stunned the media industry, James Packer pounced on an 18 per cent stake in Channel Ten, the free-to-air network that had been languishing third of the three national networks. The network's share register was wide open after Canada's Canwest had gone into administration and sold off its majority stake a year earlier. Packer's move confounded those pundits who reckoned he'd quit traditional media for good. With hindsight, Packer cannot believe he was persuaded to reinvest in free-to-air television. "I have no idea why I went back into it," Packer says now, while pointing out that in 2010 the rise of streaming was not so clear. Channel Ten had been considered a possible takeover target for Lachlan, and Packer approached his friend, offering him half his stake in Channel Ten at cost. At the time, Packer admits, he was partly motivated by a desire to make up for the One.Tel debacle, but he does not blame himself for the unmitigated disaster that ensued. "I blame myself for One.Tel," Packer says. "With Ten, Lachlan and I share the blame. He walked into it with his eyes open." For his part, Murdoch jumped at the chance to get his teeth into Ten and a few weeks later, it was duly announced that Illyria would join Packer on the register and Lachlan would go on the board.

Soon after the deal was announced, Packer took the podium at the Sydney Opera House, in a heartfelt speech to a 1,000-head lunch celebrating the twenty-five-year career of conservative talkback radio host Alan Jones. Packer spoke emotionally about his old friend, describing him as "without peer." Sitting in the audience was Australia's richest woman, iron-ore magnate Gina Rinehart, who had campaigned vociferously against Labor's mining tax. Rinehart, from Perth in Western Australia, was moved by Packer's speech and told him so in a brief private conversation afterwards. Soon, Rinehart's brokers were quietly amassing her own stake in Ten and she was soon writing to Packer, indicating her intention to join him on the board of the ailing network. With commodity prices soaring, Rinehart might easily have bought the media companies outright, had she wanted to, but she had zero experience and nobody had any idea what her agenda was. Certainly, there was very little money to be made. After one early board meeting, Lachlan was aghast when Rinehart lectured him about how *The Simpsons* was not family-friendly viewing, oblivious to the fact that it was one of the most successful Fox television productions and beloved by Rupert.[9]

Suddenly, the ailing Ten network had four billionaires on its board: Bruce Gordon, owner of the competing WIN regional network, had 17 per cent; Packer's Consolidated Press, and Murdoch's Illyria held 9 per cent each; and Rinehart held 10 per cent. It was a recipe for instability. One of the Ten board's first announcements was that the serving head of television, Grant Blackley, would become chief executive. Ten had always been the edgier, youth-oriented network, partly as a result of Fox TV shows like *The Simpsons*, but only months earlier the board and Blackley had approved a new strategy to focus on an audience of "grown-ups" who would be attracted by investment in serious news and current affairs programming. The hope was that Ten's existing younger audience would migrate to a new digital multi-channel, Eleven. But the billionaires on the board, all staunchly conservative, faced a problem: the network's young audience skewed progressive. James, Lachlan, and Gina wanted to give News Corp's star right-wing *Herald Sun* columnist Andrew Bolt his own show. *The Bolt Report* was duly launched on a Sunday morning to abysmal ratings. The ideologically motivated billionaires were going against the grain.

Soon, Packer, and Murdoch decided Blackley was part of the problem. Packer invited him out on his boat, cruising round Sydney Harbour on a Friday evening. Effectively held captive, Blackley was subjected to a withering tirade from Packer, dressed in his swimming costume, about what was going wrong at Ten. "Why don't you try listening?" Lachlan chimed in, as Blackley attempted a feeble defense of a strategy which had been signed off by the previous board and which he was faithfully implementing. There was nothing he could say to save himself: Blackley was sacked, effective immediately.

Just as surprising, Ten announced that, at the "unanimous request of the board," Lachlan would become interim chief executive while a replacement was sought. To many who knew Lachlan, this was completely out of character: he had always aspired to the role of non-executive chairman, a strategic role that would leave him free to pursue other interests. Now, he would be wholly responsible for the day-to-day operations of a 24/7 television station, including sales, programming, management, the lot. His only previous TV experience was a few years overseeing (but not managing) News Corp's network of Fox-affiliate stations in the United States, a job that mainly involved dealing with the owners, who actually ran the stations.

One of Lachlan's first big public moves at Ten turned out to be a spectacularly bad one. Everyone on the Ten board agreed that James Warburton, sales director of Channel Seven and the natural successor to Seven chief David Leckie, was the most capable media executive in the country, but no-one believed Ten would be able to attract him. Lachlan volunteered that he knew James and offered to sound him out. The meeting went well. Warburton told Murdoch he was interested and the Ten board was thrilled. But as would emerge later in court, Leckie confronted Warburton, asking if he was close to Lachlan. "I've got to know him well," Warburton replied. According to Warburton, Leckie replied: "You know me. If you want to leave to do Ten, no dramas." Kerry Stokes, however, was not so chilled and rang Lachlan, threatening: "I'm going to kill your company. I'm going to fucking kill it."[10] On the day Warburton's appointment was announced, James Packer quit the board of Channel Ten without explanation, only weeks after he'd bought almost a fifth of the company. Business reporters quickly filled in the blanks: Packer was opposed to the Warburton appointment, partly because he wanted to preserve his relationship with Stokes. Lachlan was dismayed; Packer had supported his approach to Warburton but had second thoughts after Stokes hit the roof. Lachlan was left holding the bag and if he and Warburton had hoped that Stokes would accept the inevitable, they were dead wrong: a week later, Seven filed breach of contract proceedings against Warburton in the NSW Supreme Court.

Lachlan ploughed on. One of the first programming deals announced under the new regime was with his sister's production company, Shine, to air the British adaptation of *MasterChef*, which had won millions of viewers in its first two Australian seasons on Ten in 2009 and 2010, for at least the next three years. Elisabeth Murdoch confirmed Shine was delighted to formalize a long-term deal with Ten, for a show which "continues to beat even its own remarkable ratings records." Days later, in February 2011, News Corp confirmed that it would pay a staggering £415 million to buy Shine, in a deal that would see Elisabeth finally join the board of her father's company. The deal was immediately criticized as nepotistic. Disgruntled fund manager Amalgamated Bank, which held a tiny stake in the company, soon filed a lawsuit accusing Rupert of treating News Corp "like a wholly owned family candy store." Amalgamated was followed by other shareholders in suing. Later company filings revealed Elisabeth had personally made some £129 million from the sale, a stunning payout for a company she had founded a decade earlier. In her defense, the value of Shine had been proved by the earlier sale of a 20 per cent stake to Sony and up until the financial crisis there had been no lack of potential buyers for the rest of her stake.

At the same time, *The New York Times* wrote a long profile of James, headlined "The Murdoch in Waiting." It took in the looming $12 billion bid for the rest of BSkyB and the intensifying controversy about phone hacking, but also quoted informed observers who said that James was a "business genius" based on his track record at Sky, who had "got the Rupert genes," with "intensity wrapped around energy." With Rupert about to turn eighty, the *Times* reported, the Murdoch succession had taken on more importance and James was laying a serious claim:

> The perennial speculation is whether James Murdoch, 38, will one day run . . . News Corporation. But the pertinent fact is that as the chairman and chief executive of its businesses in Europe and Asia, he already runs a large and growing part of it. If the Sky transaction is approved, the businesses reporting to James Murdoch would account for roughly half of the News Corporation's annual revenue.[11]

While Lachlan was mucking around with Illyria, picking up stakes in also-ran TV and radio stations in Australia, neither Liz nor James was standing still.

12

The Humblest Day

THE FRONT PAGE OF the *The Guardian* on July 4, 2011 sent the Murdoch empire into meltdown. The report revealed that *News of the World* journalists had hacked into the voicemails of murdered British schoolgirl Milly Dowler and may have impeded the police investigation into her disappearance. While public concern for the privacy of the royal family, politicians, celebrities, and other well-off elites had been limited, there was an outpouring of sympathy for the Dowler family whose suffering had been prolonged by the belief that their teenage daughter was alive, a belief sustained by checking her voicemail; a number of messages now appeared to have been deleted by reporters who were trying to make room for more.

The backlash against News was immediate, visceral, and global. Fuelled by decades of resentment against News Corp's influence, it had enough force to split apart the Murdoch empire, and the family. Rupert himself agreed that the reporters' conduct was "deplorable and unacceptable." While minor details of the story were later corrected, for example, the reporters involved probably listened to messages without deleting them, the effect on the Dowler family was the same and the substance of the story was dreadfully true.

When the Dowler story broke, Lachlan was at the annual retreat known as "summer camp for billionaires," organized by investment firm Allen &

Company at Sun Valley, Idaho, along with his father and chief operating officer Chase Carey. Both James and Elisabeth had been expected to attend but had cancelled as the phone hacking scandal worsened. Rupert and Lachlan spent most of the conference holed up in their rooms on the phone to Liz and James as they thrashed out how to respond. The family was deeply torn and the divisions worsened day by day as the crisis escalated. Should *News of the World* be closed, as James proposed? That happened on day three. The 168-year-old paper, which Rupert had bought back in 1969, shut down with the loss of some 200 jobs, many of whom had nothing to do with phone hacking. News Corp shares crashed, losing $6 billion. After nine days, Prime Minister David Cameron commissioned the independent inquiry by senior judge Lord Brian Leveson, and News deferred its bid for the rest of BSkyB.

The next question was whether Rebekah Brooks, who had been editor at the time of the Dowler hacking, should resign. Rupert flew to London and, when reporters asked him what his top priority was, pointed at Rebekah and simply said "this one." She resigned on day eleven. Hours later, so did Les Hinton, the executive chairman of News International (now CEO of Dow Jones), who had given five decades' loyal service to the Murdochs. All of which brought the family to the most sensitive question of all: should James himself stand down, as some major investors were calling on him to do? While there was no doubt the hacking had gone on long before James had taken the reins, he had handled the crisis badly, opting for a defensive strategy, covering up as much as possible while telling the board that everything was under control. It did not matter to the outside world that James may have had his hands tied, but within the Murdoch family there was a degree of sympathy for James' position. As a London friend told *Vanity Fair* journalist Sarah Ellison, James had found himself "staring at malfeasance that occurred under the nose of his father's best friends."[1] Anna Murdoch flew to London to support her children. Although she could hardly stand talking to Rupert, she pushed him to stand up for their youngest son amid speculation that James might even be arrested.

Elisabeth's position was pretty clear, especially after Rupert's biographer Michael Wolff reported that she had privately made the accusation that Rebekah and James had "fucked the company," a statement she denied. Accounts to date have varied: did Liz push for James to take leave, or for him to be fired and replaced by her? A spokesperson for Liz denied the latter, but her relationship with James was in tatters. Likewise, there have been varying accounts of Rupert's position: did he ask James to take leave or agree that James should go? In either case, what changed his mind? Lachlan's intervention to keep the family together, joining with Anna to stop James getting fired by Liz and Rupert and to turn the guns back outwards, has been under-appreciated.

Lachlan had flown home from Idaho at the end of the conference, as Rupert headed to England. Almost as soon as Lachlan landed in Sydney, James called to ask him to join the rest of the family in London, saying Rupert had asked James to resign. Lachlan flew straight back out, calling Rupert during a Bangkok stopover to try to stay his hand: "No, hang on, let's take our time over this." Lachlan felt he had some distance from the situation, while the rest of the family were caught up in the febrile environment of the UK.

A few days later, Rebekah Brooks was arrested. She would spend the next three years fighting to clear her name. News announced it would cooperate fully with criminal investigations by police and set up a compensation fund for victims. After initially saying they would be unavailable, Rupert and James were summonsed to appear before the House of Commons committee on culture, media and sport, which would be the first time a Murdoch was served up to MPs. Lachlan was a calming presence throughout the crisis, a comfort to father and siblings alike.

"I think Lachlan wants to be above it all," a News Corp executive told *Vanity Fair*. "He's looking at this as purely a family issue. This has nothing to do with him professionally." The whole episode underlined the toxicity of the family business, and Lachlan had told friends he had no interest in returning to News Corp. He was content to "paddle his canoe" in quieter waters back in Australia.[2]

Two weeks after the *The Guardian* story broke, James and Rupert faced the House of Commons inquiry. Looking all of his eighty years, Rupert famously confessed: "This is the most humble day of my life." The proceedings were interrupted by a pie-thrower who tried to attack the elderly mogul, only to get punched in the face by Wendi Deng.

Bad as things were in the UK, it was only the beginning of the fallout. The scandal quickly jumped the Atlantic, as Democratic senators Jay Rockefeller and Barbara Boxer wrote to the US Justice Department and the Securities and Exchange Commission, requesting an investigation into whether News Corp, by paying bribes to police in the UK, may have breached the *Foreign Corrupt Practices Act*, raising the possibility of substantial fines and even jail time if US executives were found responsible. Then London's *Daily Mirror* published explosive allegations that *News of the World* had tried to hack the phones of 9/11 victims. The *Mirror* provided no evidence, but trust in News was so shattered that the allegation itself was enough to spur an inquiry. Rupert firmly denied the allegations when he testified to the House of Commons inquiry in the UK, telling MPs the company had seen no evidence of an attempt to hack the phones of 9/11 victims. Col Allan was interviewed by the FBI and told investigators that US News journalists had not engaged in phone hacking.

The potential legal liabilities continued to multiply. In a move that may have caused Lachlan particular discomfort, New Jersey Democratic senator Frank Lautenberg brought up the time News Corp's junk mail and coupons business, News America Marketing, was sued by a rival firm, Floorgraphics, for hacking into its computer system to gain confidential, commercially sensitive information in 2004 and causing $300 million in damages. Lachlan had been in charge of News America Marketing at the time, although there was no evidence he was aware of the hacking, and the case involved colorful allegations against then-manager Paul Carlucci, who had taken over from Lachlan as publisher of the *New York Post*. The case was only finally closed in 2009, when News America Marketing bought Floorgraphics outright for $29 million. The case was one of a trio of lawsuits brought by competitors of News America Marketing, which held a 90 per cent share of the market, based partly on evidence from a whistle-blower, Robert Emmel, who had worked for the company for seven years until he was dismissed in 2006. News denied all the allegations but employed an army of lawyers to fight the cases and ended up paying a staggering $655 million to settle them. Emmel's Texan lawyer, Philip Hilder, who had previously represented the star whistle-blower against Enron, accused News of using "scorched-earth" litigation tactics to destroy his client. Senator Lautenberg wrote to Robert Mueller at the FBI and to the attorney general, Eric Holder, to make sure they were aware of the historical hacking allegations against News. Was Lachlan implicated, as the Murdoch in charge at the time? The parallels with James' own studied ignorance of UK phone hacking were obvious. The FBI's ongoing investigations in the US formed a dark cloud over News for years.

More costly than Floorgraphics' suit was a new writ, filed in Delaware by the Massachusetts Laborers' Pension & Annuity Funds, which alleged News Corp's directors had breached their fiduciary duties by allowing Rupert Murdoch to engage in nepotism and use the company as his own personal fiefdom. "Plaintiffs allege that at all relevant times the Board (which includes Murdoch's two sons, James Murdoch and Lachlan Murdoch) was conflicted and beholden to Murdoch," the writ stated, "and should be liable for its refusal to investigate and to stop known misconduct at the Company." The legal action was not settled until April 2013, when News paid out $139 million, the largest derivative settlement in the history of Delaware's Court of Chancery. News Corp agreed to sweeping corporate governance changes designed to prevent future misconduct.

The fallout from the UK scandal spread to Australia, where News Ltd. boss John Hartigan appointed two former judges to conduct an internal inquiry, auditing editorial payments to determine whether anything like phone hacking had been going on in the company's newsrooms. Bob Brown, leader of the Greens party, which *The Australian* had vowed to destroy, called for a wide-ranging inquiry into self-regulation of the media industry, particularly print media. The Labor prime minister, Julia Gillard, speaking at the National Press Club, noted she'd "truly been disgusted" at the UK phone hacking revelations and expected that "we will have a discussion amongst parliamentarians about this, about the best review and way of dealing with all of this." A year earlier the communications minister, Stephen Conroy, had announced another review of Australia's media laws, this one branded as a "convergence review," to take account of the explosion of mobile internet use of TV, radio, and print content, to consider the abolition of cross-media restrictions, and to look at relaxing anti-siphoning laws intended to ensure Australia's most popular sports were broadcast free-to-air. Now, Conroy acquiesced to the demands of the Greens, announcing an inquiry headed by former judge Ray Finkelstein, to focus on the business pressures on newspapers in the digital era, the effectiveness of codes of conduct, and ways to improve the Australian Press Council, which was widely seen as a toothless tiger. The Finkelstein review posed a regulatory threat to News Ltd and became an object of scorn for the company's papers. As hostilities between the Murdoch empire and Labor intensified, Conroy accused *The Australian* and *The Daily Telegraph* of waging a "jihad" against the Gillard government, aimed squarely at "regime change." He was not wrong.

* * *

Although Australia was a safe backwater for Lachlan, he was still paddling hard. In May 2011, the federal court had ruled that James Warburton had to serve roughly half of a twelve-month non-compete period before he could take on the top job at Channel Ten. Warburton would start on January 1, which gave Lachlan something to look forward to. He'd never wanted an executive role in the first place. Lachlan was dividing his time between three offices: his Illyria base in Surry Hills, an office at DMG Radio, and another at the nearby Channel Ten building in Pyrmont.

Ten was the biggest headache, by far, and Lachlan was in limbo: on the one hand, the network needed an urgent fix, with costs rising and profits plunging; on the other, he did not want to make major programming or commercial decisions that would tie Warburton's hands when he took over in 2012. Lachlan rolled up his sleeves, drawing on his experience overseeing Fox television in the US, and tried to implement the strategy endorsed by the board, outlined in a nine-page document drawn up when Packer had bought in.

Part of his problem, however, was that the strategy was flawed: it imagined a return to Ten's profitable past when it had a younger audience drawn to low-cost programming like *The Simpsons*. As digital disruption hit the Australian television industry, younger viewers were the first to drift away from free-to-air TV. Ten could not return to the past, any more than newspapers could. Ten was not alone: all three of Australia's commercial television networks had changed hands at handsome prices in the boom years before the financial crisis and were now struggling with heavy debt loads that needed refinancing. Free-to-air TV networks were battling to survive.

Although he was only keeping the seat warm, Lachlan was forced to make some big calls in 2011. The first was to undertake a thorough review of costs, which sounds like management 101 but culminated in a June announcement that more than a hundred jobs would have to go, 12 per cent of the headcount, with the axe falling particularly hard in the expensive news division. Senior managers quit in response. Then, Lachlan decided to pass on bidding for rights to broadcast the AFL from 2012–2016, leaving the sport to Seven. The decision saved tens of millions of dollars but left a big hole in the weekend programming schedule. Third, Lachlan made a fateful decision to lowball Ten's bid for an all-new "shiny floor show," *The Voice*, which Shine was developing for Australia based on a format pioneered in Holland. Nine won the bidding for *The Voice*, paying $20 million and beating Ten by $2 million. Instead, Ten went all-out to launch an entirely new reality series, *The Renovators*, to be produced by Shine as a cross between *MasterChef* and *Grand Designs*, intended to compete with Nine's *The Block*. No expense was spared, including shooting episodes at the biggest studio in the country. Top-flight advertizers were wowed, including a few who defected from *The Block*: Bunnings, Telstra, the Commonwealth Bank—the biggest brands in the country. Lachlan was not responsible for *The Renovators*, which was commissioned before he started at Ten, by Blackley, but hopes for the show had partly informed Ten's decision to bid lower on *The Voice*. Head of programming David Mott, who had dreamed up the all-new concept, was so confident he declared there was "no plan B" if *The Renovators* failed.

At the industry's so-called "upfronts," meetings at which hundreds of media buyers previewed the next year's programming, Lachlan did his first big presentation as acting CEO, announcing a raft of new shows, including a relaunch of the old Australian classic *Young Talent Time* to compete with Nine's blockbuster *The Voice*; a new series based on the 1979 novel *Puberty Blues*; and a push into breakfast television. Although Murdoch held his upfront weeks ahead of rivals Seven and Nine, key advertizers were sceptical about Ten's strategy. It was the breakfast TV push that generated most commentary, especially after Lachlan hand-picked controversial New Zealand broadcaster Paul Henry as host. Henry was a bona fide star on kiwi television but had been sacked by his own station, TVNZ, after he caused a minor diplomatic skirmish by mocking the name of New Delhi's chief minister, Sheila Dikshit, ahead of the 2010 Commonwealth Games. "The dip shit woman," Henry ranted on and on. "God, what's her name? Dick Shit . . . it's just so funny." Not to everyone: Henry's comments sparked a record number of complaints to TVNZ and drew criticism from the country's Race Relations Commissioner, politicians, and ethnic and community organizations. Back in India, New Zealand's High Commissioner was dragged in to explain the slur. So Henry was an odd choice for Murdoch, who rang personally to offer him a million dollars-plus to come to Sydney. For Henry, who had been reduced to afternoon radio, it was too good to refuse.

At the end of October, Ten released a disastrous set of results for 2010–2011, with profit after tax crashing by more than 90 per cent, from $150 million the previous financial year to $14 million. Ten had taken an $85 million hit from Lachlan's restructuring, including the cost of redundancies, written-off sports contracts, and Seven's case against

Warburton. The announcement insisted Ten was now well positioned for 2012, but its shares fell again on the day. In short, Ten was in a world of pain.

Towards the end of the year, Lachlan helped orchestrate his own regime change at News Ltd. After more than a decade at the helm, John Hartigan was flagging, worn down by the years-long impasse with Lachlan and perceived in some quarters as an old-fashioned newspaperman at a time of disruption. "Harto" knew his time was nearing its end and told Rupert he was happy to stand aside. His job went to Foxtel boss Kim Williams, who had spent the past decade turning Foxtel into a profit machine, but who had not one drop of ink in his veins. Williams, who had been close to Lachlan, right back to the launch of Fox Studios, took over in October, determined to wreak a belated digital transformation on News Ltd. That would mean bringing in expensive management consultants and streamlining the company's archaic state-based structure. That was threatening to the publishing fiefdoms established around the metropolitan mastheads of each state capital, and it was not long before an undercurrent of resentment began building against the edicts coming from Holt Street. Almost from day one, Williams unsettled the assembled News Ltd. editors and hacks by declaring that the era of navigating media disruption by gut instinct was over and warning he would not be "grin-fucked," management-speak for getting ignored with an obliging smile.

It had been a dramatic year for Lachlan and his family. Sarah was stepping back from her TV career. After an excruciating blooper during the grand finale at the end of the previous year's season of *Australia's Next Top Model*, when an apparent miscue caused her to crown the wrong winner on live TV, Sarah slogged her way through a final, disappointing season and quit her hosting and EP roles at the end of the year. Lachlan and Sarah wound down by spending the new year in the Caribbean with Rupert, Wendi, and all the kids, sailing their matching forty-meter superyachts off St. Barts. Lachlan was said to be closer than ever to his old man and the family was seen out dining and shopping in the luxury French enclave. Amid heightening media speculation about Lachlan's next move, there is no doubt father and son spent hours discussing the future of the family business after the hacking scandal. Within weeks, *The Australian*'s veteran media columnist Mark Day, who was close to the mogul, wrote that it was "widely understood that Rupert Murdoch would like his son to return to the business."[3] It would not be long before News Corp confirmed to investors it was planning to spin off its newspapers from the Fox news and entertainment business, adding fuel to speculation that Lachlan would run the print side of the empire, possibly from Australia.

13

A Difficult Night

WHILE LACHLAN WAS OFF in the Caribbean, James Warburton finally got his feet under the desk at Channel Ten, turning up for work bright and early on the Monday morning of January 2, 2012. As he later told Mumbrella's founder Tim Burrowes, "You could tell on day one it was going to be a disaster." Looking at the sales numbers for November, he saw the company had missed its target by $65 million. In shock, Warburton said to chief financial officer Paul Anderson, "There must be a typo." There wasn't, of course. One of Warburton's first moves as CEO was to hire a new sales director, Mike Morrison, who was a strategist and had not sold TV advertizing before. "The market revolted pretty much straight away," Warburton told Burrowes. Morrison was gone within months. As Burrowes records in his book *Media Unmade,* Morrison's LinkedIn page has a bitter description of his short-lived role at Ten: "To sell $50M a month in ad sales without any ratings."[1]

After handing the reins over to Warburton, Lachlan was announced as Ten's new chairman. The year at Ten went from bad to worse. The numbers for *Breakfast* with Paul Henry were dire from the start and while management made noises about their long-term commitment to the show, the kiwi shock jock never connected with Australian viewers. Pundits called Henry "the worst hire in twenty years." When Nine aired its first episode of *The Voice*, just after Easter, the ratings were sensational. The show would become a ratings juggernaut. By contrast, *The Renovators* launch on Ten fell just short of a million viewers. Those figures would have looked like a smash hit a decade later, but in 2012 they were a bust. The network decided to air the debut episode partway through the grand finale of the third season of *MasterChef*, leaving viewers in suspense. Hate-watchers of *The Renovators* took to Twitter, still a novelty, to pan everything about the show as they waited for *MasterChef* to come back on. As was increasingly common, audience feedback on social media set the tone for reviewers and *The Renovators* was off to a bad start. Ratings dived and never recovered. The words "no plan B" came back to haunt David Mott, who soon quit Ten altogether after more than a decade. The bodies were piling up.

For News Corp, the scandals were piling up, too. The company had been fair game for critics before the phone-hacking revelations, but now almost no form of corporate skulduggery could be put past the Murdochs. In March 2012, the BBC's *Panorama* program, working with *The Australian Financial Review*'s Neil Chenoweth, came out with allegations that in the late 1990s, a News subsidiary, News Datacom Securities (NDS), had hacked the smartcards of British pay-TV rival ITV Digital and used affiliates to promulgate key codes that allowed pirates to get the signal for free, giving BSkyB an overwhelming commercial advantage. Similar tactics were then used in the US, Italy, and Australia. NDS, which manufactured the smartcards used by Sky, had been run by former UK Metropolitan Police Commander Ray Adams, whose laptop was stolen in 2002 and contained an archive of thousands of emails that included evidence that the company had fostered piracy against its rivals. ITV Digital went out of business that year and sued NDS for huge damages, the first of a string of legal actions which either failed because the evidence from Adams' laptop was inadmissible or were settled by News. Uncomfortably for the Murdochs, NDS had reported to the Office of the Chairman, Rupert himself was on the board, and both Lachlan and James had served on the board. Once again, the Murdoch sons were faced with tough questions about how much they knew about the hacking, and when.

In this case, however, there were mitigating circumstances: first, it was not illegal to work out the secret key codes used in a rival's smartcards, but it would have been illegal to distribute them publicly, and News denied that it had ever done so; second, five previous lawsuits airing the same allegations had failed. In Australia, there were no effective laws against pay-TV piracy at the time of the alleged hacking and the *AFR*'s story conceded that none of the actions that followed would be illegal. NDS issued a comprehensive statement denying any role in promoting piracy or providing competitors' codes for use in piracy. Rupert, who had recently discovered Twitter, posted: "Seems every competitor and enemy piling on with lies and libels. So bad, easy to hit back hard, which preparing."

A report in *The Australian* suggested the BBC and *AFR* had misrepresented the situation, claiming News was hurt by the piracy—it all got rather murky. As for Lachlan, although he had served three years on the NDS board until 2005, there was never any suggestion either he or James was aware of the company's covert activities. "The question is whether they should have been aware," Chenoweth wrote in his book on the scandal, *Murdoch's Pirates*.[2] However, the NDS story did help force James' resignation as chairman of BSkyB: the Murdochs felt that he had become a lightning rod for criticism, and NDS had only become such a big story because the youngest son remained on the board.[3]

News Corp had bigger fish to fry, like investing the cash hoarded up for the aborted BSkyB bid, and there was no shortage of opportunities. In early May 2012, *Herald Sun* columnist Terry McCrann stunned markets with a piece tipping that James Packer was preparing to finally sever his family's century-old ties to Australian media, selling off Consolidated Media Holdings which owned a quarter of Foxtel, and the other half of Fox Sports, to fund his casino interests. Back in 2008, when Packer had left Lachlan in the lurch, Illyria had tried and failed to buy CMH at $4.50 a share. Now, the asking price was just $3.50, and with Kim Williams at the helm of News Ltd. there was no one who knew the value of the assets better. News had first rights of refusal under the peace deal struck fifteen years earlier after the Super League conflict, which had dealt the Packers into Foxtel in the first place, and was really the only logical buyer of CMH. Rupert himself described the deal as a "no brainer," and News offered enough to motivate both Packer and rival Kerry Stokes to sell their stakes. Having just completed the $4 billion acquisition of regional pay-TV provider Austar, giving Foxtel a truly nationwide footprint, Williams knew there was upside in the CMH deal for News, which stood to double gross profits from its pay-TV arm by something like $200 million a year. There were fewer legal obstacles to the CMH acquisition, since News already exercised management control. *Hollywood Reporter* wrote that the Austar and CMH acquisitions would turn News in Australia "from a newspaper company with TV interests to a TV company with a newspaper division."[4] Lachlan was not directly involved in the CMH deal, as he was largely preoccupied with Illyria. But the CMH deal crystallized a billion-dollar profit for James Packer. He had done much better out of the Murdochs, it seemed, than they had done out of him. The careers of the two junior media moguls had been intertwined over the years, through Super League, One.Tel, REA, and Ten, but in business their paths would diverge once the CMH deal was done, although they remained close friends.

A precondition of the CMH acquisition by News, and implicit in the price of CMH was a successful bid for the National Rugby League rights for 2013–2018, which were up for renegotiation in 2012. For the past five years, Nine and Foxtel had split the rights between them, and now mobile, tablet and streaming rights were also up for grabs as viewing habits shifted. Nine and Foxtel also owned extremely valuable 'first and last' rights over the NRL's free and pay-TV games respectively, extending all the way to 2028 (meaning they had the right to negotiate first and the right of last refusal, to match any rival offer). Their position seemed unassailable, but the last rights were extinguished if another party came in with a bid which was 20 per cent higher, and there were expectations that Stokes at Channel Seven was preparing a knock-out bid, partly using cash from his CMH deal. Having sat out the 2011 AFL deal, Channel Ten was also preparing an aggressive bid for the NRL rights. Media reports suggested

Lachlan, a big fan of rugby league, was driving the bid personally. The NRL's chief executive, David Gallop, had made it clear the game was looking for more than a billion dollars for the combined rights.

Foxtel had a pay-TV monopoly in Australia, but in a way News Ltd. was over a barrel: it simply *had* to win the NRL rights to retain its subscriber base in New South Wales and Queensland. The NRL knew it and as the deadline for competing bids approached, it decided to play hardball with Nine and Foxtel. During negotiations, the NRL was ably represented by Graeme Samuel from the merchant bank Greenhills Caliburn. Samuel dangled the possibility the NRL would deal with Seven or Ten and might even allow the subscription rights to lapse for a year, near-unthinkable for all concerned. Crucially, the NRL wrote to Nine and Foxtel, requesting the release of the first and last rights to 2028. Williams was not inclined to call the NRL's bluff, fearing Foxtel could be sidelined. He advised Rupert and Chase Carey that News would have to go all-out and may need to relinquish its first and last rights.

In the Ten camp, Lachlan had more riding on the bid than anyone might have expected. As CEO, James Warburton had made a disappointing start by hiring and firing his head of sales, and it did not help that *MasterChef*, entering its fourth season, was trumped in the ratings by both Nine's *The Voice* and Seven's rival cooking contest, *My Kitchen Rules*. David Leckie, running Seven, crowed in the media that Ten had "literally nothing" to sell to advertizers by way of successful programming. As Tim Burrowes wrote, Ten was becoming known as the "makegoods" network, because of the number of times advertizers had to be compensated with bonus inventory when shows failed to hit their promised ratings targets.[5] Ten's share price by now had slumped by more than two thirds since late 2010, vaporising more than a billion dollars on paper, and the shareholders, including Packer, Murdoch, Rinehart, and Gordon, had to stump up $200 million in a capital raising. Winning the NRL rights had always been part of Lachlan's long-term thinking for Ten—many pundits expected he would use it as leverage to sell the network back to News Ltd. should media laws change—but now it was the critical plank in Ten's turnaround.

Talking to Graeme Samuel, Lachlan hinted that Ten was going to hit Seven and Nine "out of the park."

When it came to the crunch, Seven was uncompetitive, leaving two bidders, Nine/Foxtel versus Ten, who held final meetings with Samuel and the head of the Australian Rugby League Commission, John Grant. At the last minute, Lachlan dropped Ten's bid, offering a lower than expected $1.1 billion.[6] It was a misstep: first, it wasn't 20 per cent above the reported value of the Nine/Foxtel bid, meaning their last rights were still exercisable; secondly, unbeknownst to Murdoch, Nine and Foxtel had raised their joint bid to a thumping $1.2 billion.

Samuel and Grant sat down with Williams and Nine boss David Gyngell and demanded that the last rights be relinquished. Williams emphasized that it was a heavy price to pay: some thought the last rights for the next fifteen years were alone worth a billion dollars. "That's the price," Samuel said. Williams and Gyngell agreed, and they all shook hands.

After the meeting, Samuel and Grant looked at each other. At long last, they'd freed the NRL from the clutches of News, which had relinquished the first and last rights that would have locked the game up for the next decade and a half. Lawyers from both sides worked through the night to ink the deal before a press conference scheduled for 9 a.m. A triumphant Williams emailed Rupert Murdoch and Chase Carey directly with a summary of the deal to be announced the next morning, including explicit mention of the concession over the last rights, which he described as "defective." Rupert replied to Kim and Chase a few hours later: "Great job. Congratulations. You had me worried last night!"

When Lachlan found out the next morning, he was furious. He called Williams in what the News boss would later describe as an "apoplectic" rage, accusing him of being dishonest and deceitful, and of having misled him. Williams recalls that Lachlan rang him three or four times: "He kept on calling back and I'd say, 'No, that's not what happened, this is what happened . . . yes, we got the rights.' He said: 'You stole them from me.' I said: 'By the way, you never even discussed it with me. I'm meant to interpret these things through the ether, am I?'" Williams was profoundly offended but did his best to repair the situation while defending his actions. Lachlan simply did not believe that Ten's offer had been topped by Nine's, so Kim got permission from Nine to show him the actual bid documents which showed he'd been beaten fair and square. Two days later, sensing that the relationship was in tatters and that the young Murdoch was no longer listening to him, Williams wrote a heartfelt letter and walked around the corner from News headquarters at Holt Street to Illyria's Surry Hills offices to hand-deliver it. The letter began with an open plea to Lachlan, and cited their friendship stretching back to the 1990s:

> Your trust is important to me. I really need to win it back. I want to try to explain what happened. I want you to see that I didn't try to hurt you or help anyone else hurt you . . . it is so important that I clear the air with you.

Williams' letter explained in detail that News had not realized that Ten had bid high "until very late," and "we always thought our threat was Seven." Foxtel had stood to lose everything, Williams wrote: "The threat was that if we didn't increase our bid the NRL would use Stokes' upfront payment to carry the game through 2013 without granting us any rights." Kim told Lachlan there had hardly been any contact with anyone from Ten. Lachlan read the letter slowly, and coolly told Williams he accepted the explanation.

Kim knew Lachlan well enough, however, to know he remained angry. That seemed to be confirmed as a drip-feed of articles began to appear in the press, never attributed directly to Murdoch, of course, reporting how disappointed he was at the outcome. "Hell hath no fury like a media mogul scorned," observed one sports journalist later.[7] Williams remained in the freezer, until at one point he snapped: "Lachlan, the last time I looked, the News Corporation had no shareholding in the Ten Network and you as a News Corp director know that a fundamental precondition to acquiring CMH was the obligation to secure the NRL rights on workable terms, no ifs, no buts."

Clearly, there had been a communication breakdown. Defying all expectations, and despite their previously warm relationship, there was no back-channel between Murdoch and Williams. Nor did private conversations happen between Lachlan and Patrick Delaney, then head of Fox Sports, or any other News executive. According to sources close to Lachlan, executives at Channel 10 were asking him:

> 'What's News doing?' And he was genuinely saying, 'I don't know. We just have to play this negotiation out on our own.' And was it incredibly disappointing that we didn't get the rights? Yes, because we'd offered more money, and the NRL chose not to go with more money. But that's okay—that happens in sports rights negotiations. Sometimes incumbency is really valuable, and they stayed with Nine.

Williams was soon to feel the ground shifting beneath him as chief executive, as his relationship with Rupert also began to suffer. Like Hartigan before him, Williams had found himself caught between doing the job that Murdoch senior employed him to do and trying to please Murdoch junior, whose interests were difficult to gauge and, in some cases, directly at odds with those of News. As the *AFR* would later observe, "fiduciary duty crunched up against family connections and Williams found himself on the outer."[8] In October Williams took four weeks off for excruciating back surgery. When he got back to work, the general attitude to his leadership of the company had changed.

There is little doubt Lachlan felt betrayed personally and professionally over the NRL, and years later remained bemused that Kim would not have read the tea leaves, picked up the phone and called him directly, especially once it became clear that News and Ten were on a collision course. Murdoch accepts that Williams had obligations to News shareholders, but questions why Foxtel would deal exclusively with Nine, rather than work on equal terms as pay-TV partner with whichever free-to-air network emerged as the highest bidder, as had happened in the past. It all might have been cleared up with a single phone call, but Lachlan and Kim each blamed the other for the lack of contact. "I was meant to know," Williams says, adding that Lachlan told him during a subsequent conversation: "I would've looked after you."

In fact, Lachlan saw the setback as proof that he remained an outsider to the family empire, almost as though his surname was more of a liability than an asset when dealing with News. The bitter experience reinforced Lachlan's reluctance to return to News except on his own terms.

* * *

At the same time, the pressure on Lachlan to return to Rupert's side was rising. Not only was James' reputation tarnished by the hacking scandal, but Elisabeth by now was almost estranged from her father, waging her own war for integrity inside the company. In late August 2012, delivering her own McTaggart Lecture, Elisabeth finally went public with her criticisms of both her brother James and News Corp.

In what was billed as a *cri de coeur*, Liz opened by confessing that writing the lecture had been a welcome distraction from some of the "nightmares closer to home." She attacked James for his own McTaggart three years earlier, in which he'd argued profit was the best guarantor of editorial independence. "Profit without purpose is a recipe for disaster," Liz cautioned, admitting that News Corp was "asking itself some very significant and difficult questions about how some behaviors fell so far short of its values." In a rhetorical departure from the Murdoch commitment to free enterprise and small government, Liz spoke about the need for commercial *and* public purpose, describing the media as a business of mutuality. The speech won her a standing ovation, with her husband Matthew Freud jumping up first, and laudatory coverage the next day, but Rupert saw Liz's performance as a betrayal of the family and himself. He was so angry he did not speak to her for months. He refused to read the speech, which was perhaps unfortunate, as Liz had concluded with a rousing tribute to him, quoting in glowing terms from his own McTaggart lecture twenty-five years earlier. Rupert was already in a war of attrition with Freud, who in 2010 had slammed Roger Ailes' Fox News in an interview with *The New York Times*. Perceiving Freud's influence in Liz's speech, Rupert grew increasingly wary. As would emerge in a sympathetic *New Yorker* profile of Liz towards the end of the year, "The Heiress," it took Robert Thomson to broker a grudging peace between father and daughter.[9] Even a decade later, within the Murdoch empire, the McTaggart lecture comes up to explain how Liz wrote herself out of the succession.

Lachlan continued to concentrate on Illyria, which was like a tale of two cities: DMG was firing, while Ten was tanking. Smooth FM was launched in May and, after a dip in listeners as rock fans fled, began its inexorable rise to become the number one FM nationally, an easy listening station concentrating on purely commercial fodder. In September, Lachlan doubled down on DMG, agreeing to pay about $120 million for the other half of the company. DMG was turning into a highly profitable cash cow and analysts reckoned it was now worth something like $600 million, or twice what Illyria had invested. There was speculation Lachlan would soon move on the radio assets of rival newspaper publisher Fairfax Media.

By contrast, Channel Ten was going from bad to worse. With hardly any successful programming to sell, Ten was running out of money to keep up its interest payments, putting it at risk of breaching loan covenants, despite raising $200 million in the middle of the year. Ten started to sell off assets, starting with its outdoor advertizing division, and announced another disastrous set of earnings results for 2011–2012 before embarking on another round of cost-cutting, including retrenching a hundred more staff. At the same time as jobs were going, Ten released its annual financial report for the year showing that Lachlan had been paid $1.3 million for four months work as interim CEO, while Illyria had received additional management services fees of $800,000 and, buried in the fine print, a "related party" of Lachlan, whom journalists quickly identified as his wife Sarah, had received $502,373 for hosting services for her short stint on *Everybody Dance Now*, which came in at more than $167,000 per episode. Ten's report noted that the unnamed related party had been "contractually entitled to a significantly higher amount but voluntarily agreed to reduce it to this level," but given Murdoch was lecturing all and sundry about cost control, the optics were poor. In the lead-up to the October AGM, Lachlan spent weeks meeting with grumpy institutional shareholders to shore up proxy votes. Ten had turned into a disaster and Lachlan and James Packer faced the dilemma of whether to throw good money after bad. As they discussed the dire situation, Lachlan was stunned when James offered to buy back his entire stake at the original purchase price, as a make-good gesture. Lachlan refused to entertain the offer—not even slightly.

In mid-2012, Illyria had sold out of Channel Seven affiliate Prime Media for a modest $7 million profit, which only raised more questions about Lachlan's bigger strategy. If he wasn't gradually building up his own Australian media empire, what was he doing? Careful stewardship of an inheritance in the pursuit of unspectacular profits was hardly the Murdoch way. Rupert had made his name with audacious, debt-fuelled bids for control of prized media assets, not trading in and out of passive stakes in second- and third-tier assets for modest gains. Lachlan was not building a media empire, like his father; he was simply looking for returns. "There's a difference between operating assets versus investing assets," says a close associate of his. "The strategy isn't to put them together to make them collaborate to create synergies between them, it's to assess them on their merits and make money from them."

Behind the scenes, Lachlan did not feel at all constrained to invest in media (nor, for that matter, had Rupert before him). He quietly took a $100,000 punt on a new tech company with a killer app, Uber, the ride-sharing pioneer that was set to disrupt the taxi industry worldwide. If Illyria was not quite getting in on the ground floor, it was pretty close: Uber had only incorporated in 2010 and, after offering shares to friends and family in 2011, sought to raise $39 million from venture capitalists in the first half of 2012. Illyria would make a hundredfold return on its small stake.

In October, the word went round the Murdoch family that the matriarch, Dame Elisabeth, who had been hospitalized with a broken leg, was about to be discharged and may not have long to live. As the extended family made plans to travel to Melbourne, Rupert's ex-wife, Anna, even turned up. Wendi raised a few eyebrows by absenting herself, taking off for a weekend with her girlfriends at the Murdoch ranch at Carmel, California. Dame Elisabeth had had an astonishing life, marking her centenary in 2009 at a party for 560 people, with tenor José Carreras singing and tributes flowing from all and sundry. Prime Minister Kevin Rudd was there, describing Dame Elisabeth as an "extraordinary woman" whose contributions to academia, the arts, children and research would "benefit generations of Australians." In 2012, when she turned 103, she was honored with a birthday recital at a concert hall renamed in her honor, and was named the first "Freewoman of the City of Melbourne." Even as a centenarian, she was physically active, sharp, and engaged. In the past year, Dame Elisabeth had ventured her opinion on the phone hacking scandal, gently pointing out she'd never supported her son's purchase of *News of the World*, and signed an open letter of Australian dignitaries calling for a price on carbon. But Dame Elisabeth had never fully recovered from her fall, and on December 5, the great-great-grandmother died peacefully at Cruden Farm, surrounded by family.

For Lachlan, perhaps closest of Rupert's six kids to Dame Elisabeth, the next day was rough. Having had just a few hours' sleep, he had to chair the annual general meeting of Channel Ten in Melbourne, on the same day the company announced another profit downgrade along with a deeply discounted and dilutive rights offer to existing shareholders in an emergency capital raising of $230 million. Given James Warburton had repeatedly and recently denied the company would need to raise more money, it was a bad look, and shareholders gave the board a working-over.

"Well, the last two years they've destroyed more than a billion dollars," said Stephen Mayne, who was representing the Australian Shareholders' Association. "The stock price has tanked from, you know, $1.50 to close to 20 cents. They've been doing emergency capital raisings and their ratings are at record lows, so it's been an absolute car crash for two years and there needs to be some director accountability."

Lachlan toughed it out. His lobbying of shareholders paid off and the protest vote was small. He reserved his post-meeting comments for a tribute to his late grandmother, describing her as "the closest person I will ever know to a saint" who had lived "a beautiful life and a very meaningful life and she passed away peacefully, which is all we can ask for."

After the meeting, Mayne wrote a withering critique for *Crikey*, describing Lachlan's performance as "singularly unimpressive . . . he ummed and ahhed his way through the meeting, struggling with the detail and refusing to engage on key issues. I left the meeting more convinced than ever that he is simply not up to the job and should be moved on."

In his opening remarks, Lachlan had blamed poor execution for Ten's woes, widely interpreted as a direct shot at Warburton, whom he pointedly refused to vouch for. But instead of laying the blame at the feet of the chief executive, Mayne attacked the Ten board for allowing the situation to deteriorate:

> This goes to one of the problems of effectively putting Lachlan in charge of Network Ten for the past two years: he simply doesn't have the skills or time to make a good fist of it. The issues within the News Corp board, the Murdoch family and Lachlan's personal investments such as DMG have clearly been very distracting over the past two years. Given the disaster that has unfolded, it is surprising all these billionaires haven't yet called time on Lachlan's tenure. If he wasn't a Murdoch, he'd be long gone.[10]

Fair or unfair, Mayne was saying publicly what plenty of industry people both inside and outside Ten were saying privately.

Lachlan got a kinder reception that night at the Melbourne Press Club, where he delivered a tribute to Sir Keith Murdoch, who had been honored as one of twenty initial inductees to the Victorian Media Hall of Fame. As he took to the lectern, Lachlan told the crowd he had read the speech to Dame Elisabeth on her deathbed. "I think she appreciated it," he said, beginning to choke up, before quickly apologising: "Sorry, but it's a difficult night for my family."

In a heartfelt speech, Lachlan drew deeply from his family's history in his testimonial for the grandfather whose career had inspired him to come to Australia in the first place, "a man whom I feel I know intimately, but who I never met." Lachlan told the well-known story of Sir Keith's career: his lifelong ambition to become a journalist; his struggle against a debilitating stammer; his start as the Malvern correspondent for the Melbourne *Age*; his co-founding of the Australian Journalists Association; and then perhaps what remains the seminal act of journalism for the Murdoch family: the famous "Gallipoli letter," sent back to Australian Prime Minister Andrew Fisher in 1915, after Murdoch was dispatched to visit the troops dug into trenches at Anzac Cove in Turkey's Dardanelle Strait. Sir Keith was horrified at what he saw and penned an 8,000-word letter full of praise for the Aussie "diggers" and condemnation of the British command. The letter was never intended for publication and was a deliberate breach of the censorship restrictions, but it was copied to British prime minister Herbert Asquith and widely circulated inside the government. Within days, the leader of the expeditionary force, Ian Hamilton, was relieved of his command and planning began for the evacuation of Gallipoli, which took place two months later, undoubtedly saving many lives.

Lachlan went on to trace Sir Keith's rise to the editorship of the Melbourne *Herald*, his marriage to Dame Elisabeth, and his drive to expand the Herald and Weekly Times into the first national media chain:

> He was a patriot, who believed in Australia, and for thirty of his sixty-six years, my grandfather was a builder, a maker of newspapers, and of newspapermen. He would turn a modest company producing one daily newspaper and a weekly agricultural journal into an Australia-wide publishing company, transforming its cornerstone—the *Herald* itself—into one of the world's largest evening newspapers. As well as being a successful publisher, he was also a pioneer of commercial radio networks, and a person who at the same time was president of Melbourne's library, museum and gallery, and would sponsor international

exhibitions in the city. But Keith Murdoch, newspaperman, still had an unfulfilled yearning. He wrote: 'The old journalist dies, still stretching out for better English; better cover of actualities; better comments; better taste; more happiness in his paper's pattern.' These are aspirations which we can all still strive for today, no matter by whichever means we choose to deliver the message. Stretch out, that was my grandfather's motto for success, and he did.

The confluence of the tribute to Sir Keith and the death of Dame Elisabeth clearly affected Lachlan, the most deferential of the grandchildren to the Murdoch legacy. A private burial for Dame Elisabeth was held at Cruden Farm, followed by a state memorial service at St Paul's Cathedral. If any of the Murdoch clan could claim to be Australian royalty it was the beloved old dame, admired even by Rupert's many detractors.

Although Wendi was at the state funeral for Dame Elisabeth, by now her marriage with Rupert was on the rocks as he grew suspicious over rumors she was having affairs, in particular with former British prime minister Tony Blair, who was godfather to Grace. As would emerge much later, staff at Carmel had told Murdoch of their suspicions after the supposed girls' weekend in October, when Blair had turned up instead and stayed over. Rupert had spoken to Blair the following week on another subject, and Blair didn't mention having seen Wendi in Carmel. As *Vanity Fair* would eventually reveal, a scrunched-up, lovelorn note handwritten by Wendi was subsequently found in a wastepaper basket. In it, she moaned about missing Blair: "Oh, shit, oh, shit," Wendi wrote to herself. "Whatever why I'm so so missing Tony. Because he is so so charming and his clothes are so good. He has such good body and he has really really good legs Butt . . . And he is slim tall and good skin. Pierce blue eyes which I love. Love his eyes. Also I love his power on the stage . . . and what else and what else and what else . . ."[11] Some insiders say the note was found by Lachlan, although his representatives question why he would ever be alone at his father's place, rummaging through bins.

By the end of 2012, a News Corp spokesman would later confirm, Wendi and Rupert were living "separate lives." The UK's *Mail on Sunday* would later report on a cache of more than 300 pages of messages between Blair and Wendi's newscorp.com email address, containing details of further private meetings in London, at Rupert's apartment, and at an exclusive nightclub. It is not clear how the emails came to light. According to some reports, an email Wendi had intended for Blair but accidentally sent to the wrong person got back to the Murdochs and sent them down a rabbit hole looking for more evidence. Other sources say they were discovered in the wake of the hacking crisis, during an audit of emails sent to and from News Corp in the United States, as the company conducted its own internal review in preparation for the pending lawsuits and federal investigations. Suspicions were soon broader, as it appeared Wendi also had liaisons with Google chief Eric Schmidt and MySpace cofounder Chris DeWolfe (subsequently denied on all sides). However the emails were discovered, in February 2013 Lachlan decided to front Rupert about it, telling his father as gently as possible that people were talking about Wendi's entanglements. When Blair stayed over at Carmel again with Wendi the following April, staff reportedly saw them feeding each other at dinner and him entering the master bedroom.

For Rupert, it was the last straw. Rather than confront Wendi or Blair, he prepared divorce proceedings, which were filed in a New York court two months later. Citing an "irretrievable breakdown" in their marriage, the divorce filing came as a complete shock to Wendi and the kids. Rupert spent that first night in New York with Lachlan and James. He had been increasingly harried by Wendi. There were even reports she'd physically attacked him and a source told *Vanity Fair* the two sons feared for his safety: "Given the fact that there was abuse before, and that [Wendi] was extremely emotional, [they] didn't want her alone with him, much less under the same roof."[12] When it finally became public, the divorce sparked headlines around the world. Blair steadfastly denied any affair, but Rupert would never speak to him again. Lachlan told close contacts that Rupert had long since come to regard his marriage to Wendi as "a mistake."[13]

14

'I Need You to Do This for Me'

TWO DAYS BEFORE Dame Elisabeth died, News Corp announced the details of the spin-off of the so-called "new News Corp," which would house the worldwide newspaper and book publishing businesses, plus an odd set of Australian assets including News' half of Foxtel and its majority stake in the REA digital real estate group. REA was Lachlan's baby and he had fought hard for News to hang on to its stake, even dragging Rupert out of a June board meeting in Milan that was contemplating a sale of the asset pushed by Chase Carey and his brother James. Lachlan persuaded his father and the sale was off. Insiders familiar with Carey's position say that REA, as a latter-day version of a classifieds business, was important to the newspapers but no longer at the strategic center for News or Fox, and if it was fully priced and could be sold for a fortune, it was a good time to take profits. Lachlan believed REA still had an exciting future still ahead of it, and was proved right: the company continued to expand, launching into the US by buying a 2 per cent stake in Move Inc., owner of Realtor.com, and into Asia via websites Myfun.com and PropTiger.com. REA was becoming a global powerhouse, a source of enormous pride to Lachlan.

Likewise, Kim Williams had fought to keep Foxtel on the News Corp side of the ledger. Years later, both decisions would prove essential for the viability of the mastheads globally, as profits from REA and Foxtel helped newspapers make the painful transition to digital. Williams touted the new News as the largest publishing business in the English-speaking world. Rupert would be executive chairman of News Corp and Robert Thomson would become chief executive. There was no mention of a role for Lachlan, either on the board or in management, which was somewhat surprising given the drumbeat of speculation he would run the print side. At the company's annual meeting in LA in October, Rupert had hinted that he'd tried without success to persuade Lachlan to return. Lachlan skipped the meeting and copped the highest "no" vote of any director seeking re-election, including his brother. According to Rupert's biographer Michael Wolff, Murdoch senior had tried to engineer a role at the new News, focused in Australia and concentrating on newspapers, that would be perfect for his oldest son: "so custom-fit, that so surrounds him, and that is so potentially helpless without him that it would become, within the family, an inside joke. Lachlan would have to leave Australia to escape the future his father made for him."

Lachlan, however, was busy with Ten and Illyria and highly sensitive to suggestions he was not his own man. When a business writer in Australia suggested that he was continuing to fly free in the News Corp jet, Lachlan insisted on an apology and launched defamation proceedings. As it happened, it was James who'd been using the private jet, according to company filings. Lachlan successfully forced a donation of $50,000 to the Murdoch Children's Research Institute. The point for Lachlan was to assert his independence and, surprisingly enough, his affidavit pointed out he had not flown in News' plane for seven years.

More financial details of the News Corp split were released on Christmas Eve, 2012, not a time for the closest analysis. In the effort to liberate Fox, and to cauterize the wounds from the phone hacking scandal, the picture painted in the company's regulatory filings was stark. The new News, based on accounts which "backcast" the performance of the assets to be spun out, had lost more than $2 billion in the 2012 fiscal year. Mostly that was to do with a massive $2.7 billion in impairments related to the closure of *News of the World* but also due to the restructuring of the Australian newspaper business, where the mastheads were devalued. Revenues over the past five years had been declining, and the "risk factors" included abundant warnings about the structural decline in print circulation, readership, and advertizing. There was also an eye-catching section under the bold heading: "We face criminal investigations regarding allegations of phone hacking and inappropriate payments to public officials and other related matters and related civil lawsuits." Pages and pages of detail about pending class actions, investigations and government reviews spelt danger and there was no attempt to put a ceiling on the potential liability for the company.

On the plus side, from an investor point of view, the new News would start life with a strong balance sheet. Its asset values had been aggressively written down, and the company had a billion dollars in cash and literally no debt. The new News Corp would also have an indemnity from the parent company, which would be renamed 21st Century Fox, for any future payments from the phone hacking scandal. In a way, it was back to the future for Rupert: apart from its interests in REA and Foxtel in Australia, and with the addition of Dow Jones, the new News Corp was quite like the old print-dominated business he had built in the 1980s, before launching his global push into pay-TV and movies. The new organization would be headquartered in New York and listed on the Nasdaq exchange but would have a secondary listing on the Australian Stock Exchange so that it could continue to attract support from institutional investors from down under.

While the new News Corp was given the best possible start in life financially, it was essentially a collection of undesirable legacy media assets, dragged down reputationally by the phone hacking scandal and facing a highly uncertain long-term future. For many North American investors, News Corp dropped off the radar altogether. Their focus was on 21st Century Fox, listed only in the US, which owned the Fox film and television businesses, plus the Sky satellite television businesses in Europe and Star in Asia. It was perceived to have brighter growth prospects. The Murdoch family, of course, remained in control of both News and 21st

Century Fox, with just under 40 per cent of the voting shares in each. At this stage, even after the hacking crisis, the Murdochs showed no intention of selling, and certainly not at the bottom.

* * *

James Warburton would say years later that he knew the writing was on the wall when Ten directors stopped looking him in the eye. The execution, when it came, was brutal. Warburton was terminated, effective immediately, in mid-February 2013. It was a stunning fall from grace for someone who had, less than two years earlier, been universally regarded as the next chief executive of the country's leading TV network, Seven, and had played the rival media moguls Stokes and Murdoch off against each other.

Lachlan had been quietly sounding out potential candidates, and a fortnight earlier flew to New York to interview someone already working for the Murdochs: Hamish McLennan, the former chair of marketing firm Young & Rubicam, who for the past year had been working in the Office of the Chairman for Rupert. McLennan was also chairman of REA Group, a business close to Lachlan's heart, and an old neighbor of Lachlan's from Lafayette Street in Manhattan. As soon as it was announced by Lachlan, McLennan's appointment sparked a sharp rally in Ten shares as investors assumed it was a prelude to a Murdoch-led buyout of the company.

The prospect of even greater concentration of Australia's media under Murdoch ownership spurred a political backlash. The leader of the Greens, Christine Milne, wrote to the Australian Communications and Media Authority (ACMA), Australia's broadcast regulator, insisting that it investigate whether Lachlan was in breach of the media ownership laws, by virtue of his shareholdings and position on the boards of both Channel Ten and News Corp. Backbench Labor MPs feared the relevant minister, Stephen Conroy, would propose a set of media reforms allowing the Murdochs to add a free-to-air network to their empire of pay-TV and newspapers. Lachlan engaged his familiar lawyer, Gina Cass-Gottlieb from Gilbert & Tobin, who had represented him when he was found in potential breach of the cross-media restrictions in 2010 and had to step down from the board of Prime. ACMA's ruling confirmed that Lachlan did not control the board of News, that he did not act in concert with his father "in relevant deals relating to the relevant media assets," and that "neither were in a position to exert influence over the business dealings of the other."

Conroy's media reforms floundered, and the debacle only hardened the News line against the Gillard government, which by 2013 was sinking in a mire of Labor Party infighting. In May, Rupert Murdoch, still in his tweeting phase, put his views on the record: "Oz polls show nothing can save this miserable govt. Election cannot come soon enough. People decided and tuned out months ago." This was hardly news to his editors: Murdoch had privately endorsed the Liberal opposition leader, Tony Abbott, two years earlier at a company love-in at Carmel. When Rudd took back the prime ministership from Gillard in June, the News Corp animus against Labor only increased.

For his part, Lachlan was already firmly in the Abbott camp and personally donated $22,000 to the Liberal Party that year. According to Kevin Rudd, ahead of the 2013 election, a senior member of Rudd's cabinet had a private meeting with the younger Murdoch in Lachlan's Surry Hills offices to talk about News Corp's position on climate change. Rudd says the minister, whom he won't name, dealt directly with Lachlan and "found him to be infinitely more denialist than even his father. [The minister] came back quite horrified from the discussion about his far-right views on climate denialism, which I think, when you look at how that's permeated through various branches of the News Corporation system over the years, it's a cocktail of both Rupert but increasingly Lachlan, and I would say more stridently, Lachlan." A spokesman for Lachlan declined to comment on the meeting.

* * *

The Murdoch family in London in 1973: Rupert and Anna with (from left) James, Elisabeth and Lachlan. (David Graves/Shutterstock)

Lachlan, James, Anna and Rupert Murdoch attend the Coronet Theater in New York City, December 1987. (Ron Galella/WireImage via Getty Images)

Lachlan Murdoch with rugby league player Willie Carne at the Adelaide Oval in 1996. (Phil Hillyard/Newspix)

The One.Tel team: Brad Keeling, Lachlan Murdoch, James Packer and Jodee Rich. (Jessica Hromas/*The Sydney Morning Herald*)

Lachlan Murdoch in his Sydney office in 1998. (Michael Amendolia/Mitchell Library, State Library of New South Wales)

Lachlan reads the *Hobart Mercury* on deck of Sayonara, after arriving in Hobart following the 1998 Sydney to Hobart yacht race. (James Kerr/Newspix)

Lachlan Murdoch and Sarah O'Hare in November 1998, shortly after announcing their engagement. (Rose Prouser/Reuters)

Sarah and Lachlan Murdoch with Rupert Murdoch and Wendi Deng at the Cannes premiere of Baz Luhrmann's *Moulin Rouge* in 2001. (Paul Smith/ Featureflash/Alamy)

Lachlan and Rupert outside the Surry Hills headquarters of News Ltd, April 2004. (Fairfax/Getty)

Lachlan leaving Rupert's London home during phone hacking scandal, 2011. (Reuters / Andrew Winning)

Lachlan and his family leave Dame Elisabeth Murdoch's funeral, 2012. (Reuters/Mal Fairclough)

Rupert and Lachlan during the annual Allen & Company Sun Valley Conference in Idaho, 2017. (Drew Angerer/Getty Images)

Lachlan and Sarah arrive at the Trump White House for a state dinner in honour of visiting Australian prime minister Scott Morrison, 2019. (Newscom/Alamy)

Lachlan and Sarah aboard their new $30 million yacht, *Istros*, on Sydney Harbour in 2022. (Jayden Seyfarth/ Media Mode)

In July 2013, a secret recording leaked of Rupert Murdoch talking to reporters in the newsroom of the London *Sun* a few months earlier. Unrepentant and angry, Murdoch bemoaned the heavy-handed arrests of his reporters and editors, including Rebekah Brooks, by police officers with Operation Elveden and, when asked whether News would hit back, vowed, "We will." In the 45-minute recording, he said payments for news tips from cops were part of the culture of Fleet Street, "going on a hundred years, absolutely . . . you didn't instigate it.' Rupert promised to support the reporters through their trials and, in the worst-case scenario, imprisonment. When asked who would run News if he was no longer there, he let slip: "It will either be with my son, Lachlan, or with Robert Thomson . . . and you don't have any worries about either of them."[1]

Rupert had no idea the meeting was being recorded, of course, and when the tape was leaked he quickly recanted. Lawyers for "Hacked Off," an activist group campaigning for stricter press regulation, accused him of committing contempt of parliament by giving misleading evidence about his remorse. In May, News and Fox had confirmed the list of board appointees ahead of the pending division of the company, with Lachlan and James serving on both; there was no role for Elisabeth.

At the Sun Valley media conference later that month, Rupert got a chance to sit down and have a proper face-to-face conversation with his two sons. With the empire splitting and the contentious marriage to Wendi behind him, Rupert had gradually come to understand what Lachlan wanted to hear: "I need you to do this for me." Rupert had always bestowed favors upon his children, whether buying out Liz's Shine business, sending Lachlan to run News Ltd. in Australia, or putting James forward to run BSkyB. But that kind of patronage was no longer what Lachlan needed. It was no longer any use saying to Lachlan, "You could come and run Fox." Lachlan was already on a path to running his own media business. And so, in the end, Rupert realized that he needed to say, "I'm asking you as my son . . . to abandon your own plans, which are, I accept, going very well, and instead do something for me." It was an entirely different conversation to any he'd had with his children before.

Lachlan knew that his father had been through the wringer, in business and in his personal life. However, in his own mind—and in this Lachlan saw himself as unlike either Liz or James—Lachlan didn't want or need his father to do him any more favors, financially or professionally, whether that meant creating a job for him or buying his business. It was not that Lachlan believed he could do a better job running News or Fox than his father; he was happy to go on learning from Rupert and to continue his decades-long apprenticeship. He just needed his old man to recognize at last that perhaps, at eighty-two, he could no longer do everything himself. For once Lachlan would be doing something for his dad, not the other way around. When it came to the crunch, Lachlan felt he could not refuse at a time when his father seemed vulnerable.

Once the in-principle decision was made, however, there were plenty of details to sort out. Lachlan took his time deciding what role he could accept, and then took his time deciding whether he should commute from Australia or relocate the whole family back to the US. By mid-2013, Lachlan and Sarah were finally about to start renovating Le Manoir, their 1928 Georgian-style mansion at Bellevue Hill, after renting a beachfront pile in Vaucluse for three years. They'd bought the former French trade commissioner's house for $23 million in 2009, Sydney's biggest sale of the year and a record for the suburb, beating nine underbidders including the actor Russell Crowe. Set on more than an acre, the sprawling six-bedroom mansion had a tennis court, pool, and panoramic views from Sydney Harbour to the Pacific Ocean, but it needed a lot of work. Especially important to Lachlan was an underground cinema, gym, and James Bond-like lift access to a three-car garage for his wheels, which included two Porsche Panamera sedans he'd bought for $300,000 each (he wanted the manual, which wasn't available in right-hand-drive Australia, so he'd had them custom-built). The Porsche equivalent of a family car, the V8s could do 0 to 100 kmh in a bit over five seconds and had a top speed of almost 300 km/h.

Le Manoir wasn't quite big enough, so a year later the Murdochs splashed $2.6 million on an adjacent block. In late 2011, they lodged a development application for an $11.7 million renovation, which went to the Land and Environment Court after neighbors complained about trees being removed, the construction of an overlooking pool house, and the impact on their privacy and views. After spending a year resolving the approvals, work finally started and Le Manoir was a building site for almost three years. The Murdochs had sunk at least $35 million into the property. Their three kids, Kalan, Aidan, and toddler Aerin, had known no other hometown than Sydney. Neither Lachlan nor Sarah was keen to uproot them. In short, the couple were finally about to establish their dream Sydney base and suddenly Lachlan was talking about moving back to America.

Sarah, who had always wanted the kids to have a Sydney upbringing and who was being sounded out for another TV hosting role, this time on breakfast television with Channel Seven, was especially slow to come around to the idea. Lachlan did not have to look far to have the importance of family underlined for him: his old friend James Packer's marriage was in trouble as Packer kept up a relentless pace, developing an $8 billion pipeline of casinos in Sydney, Las Vegas, and Macau, living large in Hollywood and investing hundreds of millions in his RatPac film production company with Brett Ratner.

Meanwhile, at News, it was becoming increasingly clear to Kim Williams that his job was in danger. It did not matter that he'd pulled off News Ltd.'s biggest deals in decades with the acquisition of Austar and Consolidated Media Holdings, perhaps the last the company would ever be able to make in Australia's small market. A backlash against him was building as he pushed hard for a digital transformation that would streamline editorial management, erode personal fiefdoms, and favor online over print. Three top editors in particular were undermining Williams: Chris Mitchell at *The Australian*, Paul Whittaker at *The Daily Telegraph*, and Peter Blunden at *The Herald Sun*. Each had a direct line to Rupert and, Williams knew, each was giving Rupert negative feedback. One former editor says bluntly that Williams was not a journalist and didn't understand the craft of journalism:

Kim was a square peg in a round hole. Some of his intentions were right and a lot of the things he wanted to do are happening now, it's just the way he went about it. Kim regarded editors as like people who made widgets in a factory . . . he didn't understand the role of the editor and the special relationship that editors have. Yes, managing directors report to Rupert, but editors, even though they don't report directly to Rupert, effectively there's a dotted line to Rupert—for the key editors—because he's the proprietor.

Williams's relationship with Lachlan remained under a cloud and it seemed nothing could be done to rebuild the trust between them. It wasn't long before Williams got a shock email from Robert Thomson, leaked almost immediately to the papers, advising that the feared editor-in-chief of the *New York Post*, Col Allan, had been sent out from New York to provide some extra "editorial direction." Williams, perhaps wondering if he was still in charge, enquired politely how long Allan would be in Australia and was given some bland assurances. But the truth was that after almost twenty years at News, and less than two as Australian CEO, Williams' time was up. Allan was there to calm the horses and make sure Williams didn't do anything rash on the way out. Soon after arriving, he took the top News editors out to a two-hour lunch. Lachlan was there, Kim wasn't.

Williams began negotiating a dignified exit with Thomson, Carey, and chief financial officer Bedi Singh. When the announcement was finally drafted, Williams was bundled out the door with less twenty-four hours to clean out his office. After two decades' service to the Murdochs, during which he turned Foxtel from a chronic loss-maker into the profit engine that sustained the entire Australian business, he did not even get a farewell party. He had to pay for his own farewell drinks with his key managers and staff. Lachlan, who had helped engineer his appointment as CEO, was not invited. Williams was replaced by Julian Clarke, the recently retired former managing director of the Herald and Weekly Times, who at sixty-nine was widely viewed as a seat-warmer for Lachlan himself.

With Rupert tweeting up the occasional storm, the News Ltd. cove.
of the Australian federal election campaign in 2013 was controver: ...
from the very first day, when *The Daily Telegraph* blared "KICK THIS
MOB OUT" the morning after the election was called. It was a Col Allan
special: he readily acknowledges today that he considered there was no
point beating about the bush or waiting until the traditional election-eve
editorial to declare a position. Prime Minister Rudd took the unusual
step, for a campaigning politician, of calling out the "blatant bias" of the
Murdoch press, and subsequent analysis would bear out that the headlines
and stories of News Ltd.'s newspapers were overwhelmingly negative
about Labor and favorable to the Liberal–National Coalition.

Tony Abbott stormed into office and moved as quickly as possible
to make Australia the first country in the world to *abolish* a functioning
carbon price. For News Corp, the new government meant the prospect of
some friendly reforms, with communications minister Malcolm Turnbull
cutting public expenditure on the national broadband network (NBN)
to instal cheaper "fibre-to-the-node" technology. One of Turnbull's
first meetings as minister was with Rupert Murdoch and there was soon
speculation that he would ease the path for a News takeover of Ten. At
the same time Turnbull sacked the entire board of the NBN, including
Siobhan McKenna, who had been lobbying to retain the plum post, a
move which would hardly have endeared Turnbull to Lachlan.

At the end of 2013, Lachlan attended what would prove to be his last
annual general meeting as chairman of Channel Ten, using his speech
to call on the Abbott government to review media law "from the ground
up." Arguing there was not a level playing field, that online media was
unregulated while traditional media was heavily regulated, he called for
comprehensive reforms focused on "how to best serve Australia for the
next 100 years, not the past 100 years." Weeks later, Turnbull dismissed
Lachlan's call, saying the industry had been "reviewed to death," which was
true, but the necessary substantive reform had never been implemented
and the manifest problems with Australia's media laws remained
unfixed.

Ten had had another torrid year in 2012–2013, despite the appointment of Hamish McLennan as CEO. The company released a dire set of earnings results: it had eked out an operating profit, but the net loss after tax was $285 million, driven by a $292 million write-down to the value of its TV licenses. Fearing shareholders would not stomach another emergency capital raising, Ten's billionaire owners, except miner Gina Rinehart who was fed up with the mounting losses and had lost interest in media, announced they would guarantee a $200 million loan. A second high-profile foray into breakfast television proved a disaster: Lachlan had personally recruited morning producer Adam Boland, the young whizz who had made Nine's *Today* and then Seven's *Sunrise* unbeatable programs. His touch eluded him on Ten's *Wake Up*, which aired live from a studio in Manly. Ratings were even worse than the breakfast show hosted by Paul Henry and Boland resigned within weeks.

Lachlan admitted Ten's performance was "unacceptable" and strongly backed McLennan as the right person to turn the company around. Like Warburton, McLennan's background was in sales rather than programming, but he had taken on board the live sports imperative, winning broadcast rights to the Big Bash cricket tournament, a T20-style contest which Lachlan knew well from the Rajasthan Royals, as well as the Sochi Winter Olympics, and the V8 Supercars. The November debut of *The Bachelor* had proved a hit, and so did the Big Bash League, played over the Australian summer. Ratings were so good that Ten shares surged, albeit from a very low base.

A bigger groundswell was lifting Lachlan above his woes at Ten, along with the rest of his family. Since the demerger of Fox and News had been announced in mid-2012, and particularly after the split was effected in mid-2013, the value of the combined empire had surged. Something like $10 billion dollars of extra value had been created, and the family's wealth had increased proportionally, by some four billion dollars. The phone hacking crisis of mid-2011 had changed everything, splitting the company, tearing up the family's succession plans, perhaps even wrecking Rupert's marriage, but the Murdochs had weathered all of it.

In March 2014, Lachlan flew to Los Angeles to be with his father on his eighty-third birthday. Rupert was being inducted into the Television Academy Hall of Fame, and he told the gala function that Fox was a "family company." James was there, too, but not Liz, and after the awards, the three of them went back to Rupert's Beverly Hills mansion for a drink. Between them, they hatched the plan that would be taken to the boards of Fox and News and duly endorsed a fortnight later: a muddling solution in which Lachlan would become non-executive co-chairman of both 21st Century Fox and News Corp, allowing him to split his time between Sydney and New York, while James would be elevated to the position of co-chief operating officer at Fox, working alongside Chase Carey rather than reporting to him.

In Australia, the US and the UK, the headlines blared that the announcement marked the return of the "prodigal son." The near-universal assumption among commentators was that Lachlan now had the edge on James. On day two, Rupert tried to correct that impression, describing the new appointments as "a partnership," but there was little doubt among the pundits as to who was favored, notwithstanding Lachlan's so-far patchy track record as an investor. One of Rupert's many biographers, David Folkenflik, wrote that "Lachlan's chief virtue appears to have been his iron-clad alibi amid the hacking and corruption nightmare in the UK—he was literally and emotionally a half-world away."[2] Inside the family, Lachlan may have felt he had nothing left to prove. The rest of the world would need more convincing.

PART 3

Sly Fox

15

Continental Shift

L ACHLAN MURDOCH RETURNED to the US from Australia to a family empire, and a political environment, that was profoundly different than when he'd left a decade earlier. Few could anticipate the wild disruption that was coming. In business, the talk was convergence between media, telcos, and tech companies amid a new wave of mega-deals. The newly separated Fox and News Corporations would soon face a grave choice: get big or get out. In politics, the trend was polarization, as the Obama administration battled a Republican-controlled Congress. Lachlan would have a ringside seat as the US, where he was raised, entered a period of volatility unlike anything in living memory.

Lachlan was tentative rather than elated to be returning to Fox and America, and at first preferred to spend long hours on the company plane commuting back and forth to Australia to see Sarah and the kids, rather than uproot them for what could yet turn out to be a short stint back in the fold. He had returned out of a sense of duty and obligation to his father and the family business, rather than a burning desire to run Fox or News, those close to him say. Lachlan had also been shaped by his decade in Australia, enlivened to the possibilities of a world beyond New York. "He has a deep appreciation of that part of America that is ignored by the coastal liberal elites," says Col Allan, pointedly distinguishing

Lachlan from his brother, James. "I think it is true that Australia and its egalitarianism has had a profound and very positive effect on Lachlan's nature and on his cultural views."

Lachlan's first decision was where to base himself. With Rupert and James in New York, it made sense to live and work in Los Angeles, where the time zone made it easier to keep in touch with Illyria in Sydney, not to mention his family. Lachlan had a few of the family's mansions in west LA to choose from, including the historic Moraga Vineyards in Bel Air, LA's only working vineyard, which Rupert had bought for $29 million at the end of 2013. Lachlan would spend months in the guest rooms at Moraga, and when Sarah and the kids finally came over, they were at first sleeping on blow-up mattresses. It would be more than a year before Lachlan and Sarah settled on their own home: a $12.5 million ranch-style mansion in the trendy Mandeville Canyon, with spectacular views down the coast to Santa Monica.

Previously regarded as the wrong side of western LA's 405 freeway, the Mandeville market hotted up after Gwyneth Paltrow and then husband Chris Martin bought in for $10 million in 2012. Lachlan and Sarah's new five-bedroom spread was on a secluded 2.3 acre block near the top of the Boca de Canon Lane, finishing at walking trails through the Westridge-Canyonback wilderness park. The new home was an ultra-private retreat from the Hollywood madness, with an extensive closed-circuit camera surveillance system, security patrols to repel paparazzi, and neighbors including Harrison Ford and top talent agent Ari Emanuel. But there was only one way in and out, via Mandeville Canyon Road down to Sunset Boulevard, and the Murdochs soon found there were downsides to being surrounded by forest.

Within three months of Lachlan's return to the fold, Fox took advantage of the share price surge after the spin-off of News Corp and launched an $80 billion-plus bid for Time Warner, owner of HBO and arch-rival CNN. The Fox bid was audacious, the biggest deal Rupert Murdoch had ever attempted, and if successful promised the world's most valuable media and entertainment company. Fox's bid came hard on the heels of a bid for the separate Time Warner Cable division by the voracious telecommunications giant Comcast, which had gobbled up NBC Universal a year earlier. That takeover had spurred a wave of consolidation, partly in response to the rise of Netflix, which began streaming in 2010 and had since branched into original productions and was enjoying a hit with AMC's *Breaking Bad*.

The key to competing at scale was to integrate content and distribution. Fox was exposed as the only big provider without its own cable or satellite network in the US. The theory was that if Fox could acquire Time Warner, it would have more leverage in negotiations with these bulked-up distributors.

Speculation about a Fox move on Time Warner ramped up ahead of the Sun Valley retreat in Idaho in July 2014. Lachlan, James, and Chase Carey were all at the conference, alongside Rupert and Time Warner CEO Jeff Bewkes. Comcast chief executive Brian Roberts told the conference he thought television would change more in the next five years than it had changed in the previous fifty. Fox had made a formal bid the previous month, at a one-on-one meeting between Chase Carey and Bewkes, who took the bid to the Time Warner board, which summarily rejected it. When news of Murdoch's bid became public, it sent the target shares soaring immediately, while Fox shares plunged, making the deal much more expensive to complete.

Most commentators expected that Rupert would be back for another try and that he would ultimately prevail, just as he had done after being rebuffed by Dow Jones. The news broke while Rupert and Lachlan were in Sydney, celebrating the fifty-year anniversary of *The Australian* newspaper at a function attended by the prime minister, Tony Abbott, who had once worked on the paper. When they learned of the Time Warner offer later, guests were amazed that neither father nor son had said a word. Fox quickly poured cold water on the prospect of a higher offer, however, announcing that it was not in negotiations with the board of Time Warner. Rupert insisted the company knew what it was doing. Chase Carey, who had led the June negotiations, hammered home the message on the earnings call. "Let me be clear: we are done," he said. For all its strategic logic, analysts regarded the Fox bid for Time Warner as half-hearted.

Fox still needed scale and came out of the unsuccessful bid swimming in cash, including some $21 billion raised by advisers Goldman Sachs to debt-fund the abandoned takeover. Fox was widely expected to revive its bid for the 61 per cent of BSkyB it did not already control, which had been shelved in the wake of the phone hacking scandal and described by James Murdoch as "unfinished business." As former chief executive of BSkyB, James was most keen to complete the transaction and take outright control of the highly profitable machine. A milestone was reached in June 2014, when after a three-year police investigation and eight-month trial, a jury unanimously found former *News of the World* editor Rebekah Brooks not guilty on all charges related to the phone hacking. In an emotional doorstop, Brooks declared she was innocent, thanked the jury, and voiced her support for her former colleagues still facing jail. The Brooks verdict meant that criminal prosecution of anyone higher up the management chain, including James Murdoch, or of News International itself, was now extremely unlikely. A year later, Brooks was reinstalled as chief executive of News UK. A path was opening for a fresh bid for the rest of BSkyB, which was rebranded simply Sky Plc. after it took over Sky Italia and Sky Deutschland.

In the meantime, Lachlan and James had to work out a new modus vivendi and in typical Murdoch fashion their job titles, roles and responsibilities were left deliberately vague for the first year. Rupert was executive chairman at Fox and clearly had the last word, and Carey was the president and chief operating officer trusted by investors to run the company from day to day. Lachlan's "non-executive co-chairman" and James "co-chief operating officer" roles were both made-up jobs. It was opaque to outsiders and insiders alike, except that the underlying intent remained crystal-clear: one or both of the sons would succeed Rupert.

Members of the then 21st Century Fox board, directors hoped that Lachlan and James would work through any confusion about their roles and, given they were brothers, simply come to an understanding. It didn't pan out that way. If anything, the ill-defined roles were a new source of tension between the two men. Lachlan professed not to care about his job title, or about defining his responsibilities on an org chart, because he was a non-executive at 21st Century Fox and partly because he had other responsibilities back in Australia, which had nothing to do with the Murdoch empire: although he had stepped off the board of Channel Ten, he was still chairman of Nova and was running Illyria. James, by contrast, had relinquished directorships of Sotheby's and GlaxoSmithKline when he left the UK in 2012, and was now wholly focussed on his senior executive role at Fox—testing the extent of his authority, attempting to clarify which hires he could make and how much he could spend without the approval of Chase, Rupert, or the board. Lachlan felt Rupert had built the business, had every right to intervene as he saw fit, and that both he and James had decades ahead of them and could still learn a lot from their father. In Lachlan's view, James seemed to think he was a better businessman than Rupert, who was a meddlesome old codger who had to be managed. The brothers' natural rivalry was turning catty.

Lachlan and James clashed over plans for 21st Century Fox and News to build brand-new headquarters at 2 World Trade Center, the last of four towers under construction at Ground Zero. Designed by British architect Norman Foster, the new tower would be exorbitantly expensive, costing Fox and News hundreds of millions of dollars more in rent. Lachlan, based in LA, saw the new building as lavish and counter-cultural for the Murdoch companies. James was spearheading the project, however, and in June 2015 he announced that Fox and News had ditched the Foster scheme, unveiling a splashy new design by boutique Danish architect Bjarke Ingels featuring stacked boxes of open-plan office space on large floorplates. James had directed that he didn't want a conventional office tower, which he saw as more suited to an investment bank than a media company. Six months later, the whole project was axed, with Lachlan and News Corp chief Robert Thomson announcing capital could be better deployed elsewhere.

The tension between the brothers was rather trying for Carey, who was by now in his early sixties. With his employment agreement set to expire, he had a friendly discussion with Rupert about a plan to transition out of the company. He could not retire until Rupert decided which of his sons should lead Fox and Carey had a view on who it should be. While he was proud of his tenure, he told Rupert, twenty years his senior, it was time for Lachlan to step up and come back into the business full-time. Rupert agreed, and at a lunch in Manhattan, Chase and Lachlan told James he would thenceforth be reporting to his older brother. James was so enraged he threatened to quit and flew off to Indonesia for a break.[1]

Fox subsequently struck new four-year contracts with both Lachlan and James and in mid-2015 the new leadership structure was revealed publicly. The brothers were taking over: Lachlan would now become executive co-chairman of Fox, alongside Rupert, while James became CEO, reporting directly to his father, not his brother. If the structure was messy, the salaries were huge—roughly $20 million a year each, including bonuses—and the brothers presented a united front. Lachlan told investors the new roles reflected "a true 50/50 partnership . . . James and I have been working together for many years; I think we know each other better than anybody else knows us. We are both uniquely invested in the success of the company."

Two months later Lachlan and James gave their first joint interview, an hour-long sit-down at the Fox studio lot with *The Hollywood Reporter*'s Matthew Belloni. Lachlan acknowledged a generational transition was underway, but insisted his father was "still the boss," was "still there guarding the company every day," and for good measure threw in a joke at the end: "Rupert's never retiring." He deflected a question about whether his politics were the same as his father's:

> I disagree with some of the premise of the question in that while externally people have combined the company with our father's personal opinions, which are super interesting, or his politics, they're actually not always the same. We have a huge number of creators in this business, on this lot, a huge number of journalists and editors around the world who have nothing to do with his politics or his thoughts. They make entirely their own decisions.

Lachlan and James said they were closer than ever, talking multiple times a day. "Functionally, everyone reports to both of us equally," said Lachlan, adding: "we make the decisions together" Belloni pressed both men on rumors they bickered at board meetings:

> JAMES: No, not true. Actually, I don't think we bicker.
>
> LACHLAN: I don't think we ever disagree.
>
> MATTHEW: Oh, please. You're brothers.
>
> JAMES: From a strategy point of view, on the board-level stuff, I don't think Lachlan and I have ever had any major or, really, any minor disagreements with respect to where the direction of the business needs to be and how we prosecute that. But we're brothers, we used to fight like cats in a bag. But you know, we were young then. (Laughs.)
>
> LACHLAN: I always won, which was good.
>
> JAMES: I'm not so sure.
>
> LACHLAN: I was bigger back then.

Lachlan said Fox had "moved on" from the failed Time Warner bid and James admitted that the focus would soon shift to a full acquisition of BSkyB, conceding that "having 40 per cent of an unconsolidated asset is not an end state that is natural for us." He regretted that Liz had decided not to join the business after selling Shine to News Corp: "She made a choice to go do some new projects, and she's got a bunch of stuff she's doing philanthropically and entrepreneurially and is very happy doing those things . . . and we're very supportive of that. We're a close family, but she's doing other things now." The conversation ended on a mischievous note when Belloni asked James:

> MATTHEW: You quit Harvard, dyed your hair different colors, got some piercings, founded a rap label. Does any of that rebel remain?
>
> JAMES: One hundred and fifty percent of it. (Laughs.) The

nice thing about middle age is that you still think to yourself,
pathetically, that you're still that guy.
LACHLAN: Why do you assume he doesn't have any piercings?

The trauma of the phone hacking scandal was healing, it seemed, with
Lachlan and James in a good place: competitive, sure, but photos showed
the two forty-something brothers beaming and standing close.

One thing buoying the spirits of the Murdoch children was the
romance between their father, by now eighty-four, and former model Jerry
Hall, fifty-nine, the ex-wife of Mick Jagger. The London gossip website
Popbitch first published the rumors under the nasty catchline "Gruesome
Twosome," and it was worldwide news when the couple confirmed their
first public outing would be at the Rugby World Cup final in Twickenham.
Rupert had been introduced to Jerry by his niece Penny Fowler, who
had met Hall when Hall was in Melbourne to promote her upcoming
performance in a stage production of *The Graduate*. Rupert and Jerry
spent Christmas 2015 with Lachlan and Sarah in Sydney, where Hall
was performing in the play.

After a whirlwind romance, Murdoch and Hall announced their
engagement in the classified section of the London *Times* in January and
were married two months later in London. Lachlan was witness, along
with Hall's best friend, Suzanne Acosta, wife of ex-Stones bassist Bill
Wyman. Mick Jagger was said to be seething, given it was Murdoch's
Sun which had reported the affair that caused his break-up with Hall.
The wedding reception was held the next day at the seventeenth-century
St Bride's church in Fleet Street where there's a memorial plaque to
Rupert's father, Sir Keith. About a hundred guests attended, including
Michael Gove and Michael Caine, with Rebekah Brooks in charge of the
list. There were no prime ministers in attendance, but the Murdoch family
was reasserting its place at the heart of the British media establishment.
The *Financial Times* reported the marriage would have "zero impact" on
control of the Murdoch Family Trust or the succession. Jerry and Rupert
appeared primarily interested in keeping each other company.

As the elderly couple headed off for their honeymoon, Rupert sent his last tweet: "No more tweets for ten days or ever! Feel like the luckiest AND happiest man in world." At *The Australian*'s fiftieth anniversary party in Sydney, conservative prime minister Tony Abbott had gushed that Rupert Murdoch's creation was the greatest newspaper in the English-speaking world, which had not only shaped the intellectual life of the country more than any other masthead, but "no think-tank, no institution, no university, has so consistently and so successfully captured and refined the way we think about ourselves." Hundreds of Australia's most powerful political and business leaders were there to celebrate: Rupert, Abbott, and former prime ministers John Howard and Paul Keating were at the head table, while Lachlan chaired an adjoining table with Sarah, James Packer, Kerry Stokes and communications minister Malcolm Turnbull. In Australia at least, Lachlan had reached the very apex of power: his closest friend in politics had the country's top job, and two of his favorite News Corp editors, Chris Mitchell at *The Australian* and Paul Whittaker at *The Daily Telegraph*, both of whom he'd worked with two decades earlier in his first stint in Queensland, were at the peak of their influence, having backed the new coalition government into office with encouragement from the *New York Post*'s Col Allan.

News Corp had already benefited from some early decisions of the Abbott government and by early 2014, Turnbull as communications minister had conceded Lachlan's point on the need for media law reform, writing in an op-ed for *The Australian* that "the media and telecommunications sectors in particular need a thorough re-evaluation of regulatory frameworks, which are still fundamentally grounded in a mid-1990s world of relatively stable technologies and business models."[2] An informal consultation process would culminate in draft legislation and a Senate inquiry that dragged on into 2015.

With the coalition in power, News Corp could expect that any campaign launched by its newspapers would be taken seriously in Canberra. Backed by Lachlan, Whittaker at the *Telegraph* had flexed his muscles with a "Fair Go for the West" campaign for better services and infrastructure in the disadvantaged western half of the city. Lachlan said the fifty-seven-day "Fair Go" campaign, which claimed to have resulted in $17 billion of new government spending, was a great legacy of *The Daily Telegraph*, although Whittaker was embarrassed when Lachlan took Rupert out to Rooty Hill to show him what the Tele was doing in the heartland. Father and son stopped at a takeaway joint to grab a copy of the Tele and found they didn't carry it. Dozens of copies were sent the next morning.

The Murdoch media were at the height of their power, but the close relationship between News Corp and the newly elected coalition government led by Prime Minister Abbott began to strain as News Corp's papers, particularly Mitchell's *Australian*, turned sceptical about the shambolic new government. In an editorial marking a hundred days since the election, the paper warned Abbott was failing to make the transition from opposition. The coalition's first federal budget turned into a policy and public relations disaster, with deeply unpopular austerity measures and a litany of broken pre-election promises. The government had destroyed its fiscal credibility within nine months. Abbott took umbrage at *The Australian*'s worsening coverage and not only called Mitchell but went over his head to Lachlan. Unfailingly polite, Lachlan heard the PM out and then discussed the situation with Mitchell as editor-in-chief. As Mitchell recorded in his memoir, *Making Headlines*, he never backed down or softened the paper's coverage under pressure from the prime minister's office, nor did Lachlan ask him to.

Lachlan himself took issue with the Abbott government's introduction of increasingly draconian national security laws that impinged on freedom of the press. Amid rising international fear about the war on terror, Australian media organizations including News Corp were up in arms and, delivering the 2014 Sir Keith Murdoch oration at the State Library of Victoria, Lachlan launched his own attack on the Abbott government, again harking back to the actions of his grandfather during the First World War. Murdoch slammed the introduction of national security legislation under which journalists could be jailed for up to ten years for disclosing information relating to a "special intelligence operations," an ill-defined concept left to the discretion of the attorney general. "Would the Gallipoli campaign have been a special operation," Lachlan asked? "Would Sir Keith have been arrested? Then he almost channelled Ronald Reagan:

> 'Trust us, we're from the government' seems to be a common theme when attempting to censor the media. But trust is something that should not be a consideration when restricting our fundamental freedoms. Our freedom of speech and freedom of the press are not things we should blindly entrust to anyone. The first amendment of the Constitution of the United States, adopted as part of the Bill of Rights in 1791, reads in part that 'Congress shall make no law abridging the freedom of speech, or of the press'. Australia has no equivalent constitutional protection of freedom of speech or freedom of the press. Already we have literally hundreds of separate laws and regulations that currently govern the working press . . . we certainly do not need further laws to jail journalists who responsibly learn and accurately tell.

Lachlan followed up with Abbott a week later, writing directly to the prime minister to argue that the national security legislation contained:

> provisions that specifically and wrongly curtail freedom of speech and the public's right to know. Can I respectfully suggest that instead of having a situation where professional journalists continue to work in an uncertain environment and risk prosecution and jail at the discretion of the attorney general, it would be better to simply fix the legislation . . . I raise these matters because we are deeply and genuinely concerned to get the balance right between giving security agencies the power they need to do their job, while also preserving media freedoms which are so fundamental to what makes Australia a great nation.

The simmering hostilities erupted again when Abbott, an ardent monarchist, announced the reintroduction of the knights and dames honors system on Australia Day, 2015, beginning by knighting Prince Philip, husband of Queen Elizabeth. The gesture was so out of touch that Abbott was soon fighting to keep his hold on the prime ministership. Even Lachlan told his friend it was a mistake. There was widespread speculation that Malcolm Turnbull would soon challenge Abbott for the top job. When *The Australian* ran a front-page report that Abbott had asked the military brass whether Australia alone could defeat ISIL if it invaded Mosul, Abbott rang Lachlan to complain about his treatment by his alma mater. A smoothing-over dinner was arranged with Lachlan, Abbott, and Mitchell. Ahead of the dinner, Rupert rang Mitchell, worried that Lachlan was too polite with politicians and wishing he would be more muscular. And, in fact, Lachlan did play the role of peace-maker, supporting Mitchell while sometimes also backing the prime minister.

The fate of two Australian heroin smugglers on death row in Bali came up. Abbott talked passionately about his efforts to persuade the Indonesian government to show compassion to the two young men, Andrew Chan and Myuran Sukumaran, who were facing imminent execution. Disagreeing with Abbott, Lachlan argued that the two men deserved exactly what they were about to get. As Mitchell wrote, in a line that would be hung around Lachlan's neck: "As with his views on gun control in the United States, Lachlan's conservatism is more vigorous than any Australian politician, Abbott included, and usually to the right of his father's views."[3] After Mitchell left, Lachlan and Abbott kept drinking.

In early 2015, when it leaked that Turnbull favored dumping the two-out-of-three and reach rules, which barred any proprietor from controlling assets in more than two mass mediums (print, radio and free-to-air TV), and which ensured the biggest games in top sporting codes were broadcast free, Rupert put out a tweet: "Aust! Turnbull's plans to scrap certain rules suit buddies at Nine. Can't oppose dumping all regs but not this. Nice to see how MT plays." Keen to avoid antagonising the Murdochs, the

Abbott government left media reform in the too-hard basket and it would be two more years before the legislation was finally overhauled.

Throughout the second half of 2014, big US private equity firm Providence had been stalking the ailing Channel Ten, which continued to lose money. In October, Providence was joined by Anchorage, and Ten resolved to conduct a strategic review process, effectively putting itself up for sale to the highest bidder. Three of the four billionaires on the register, including Lachlan, were known to be willing sellers. In December, Foxtel partnered with Discovery Communications to offer more than $600 million for the ailing network, holding out the tantalising possibility that Lachlan might recover at least some of Illyria's original investment. Foxtel might have been able to buy Ten outright, but that would have put Lachlan Murdoch, as co-chairman of News Corp, in breach of the two-out-of-three rule, so Foxtel was limited to 15 per cent. The Discovery-Foxtel bid was blocked, however, by Ten director Bruce Gordon, who hoped to launch his own bid. It was a stalemate. Discovery pulled out but Foxtel persevered, paying AUD$77 million for 15 per cent of Ten in mid-2015, hoping the deal would get past the regulators. Later that year, both ACMA and the competition regulator announced that they would not oppose the deal – although it would increase Foxtel's influence over Ten, it would not diminish competition, especially as streaming services took off. ACMA's chair, Chris Chapman, ruled that Lachlan's level of influence fell short of control.

As part of the deal, Ten took a 25 per cent stake in the subsidiary company that sold advertizing for Foxtel, called Multi Channel Network, along with an option to become a 10 per cent shareholder in Presto, a streaming firm jointly owned by Foxtel and the Stokes-controlled Seven conglomerate. Insiders at Ten were astonished that the company would outsource ad sales, which generated more than 95 per cent of the network's revenue. With such close integration of Foxtel and Ten, it was almost universally assumed that the deal was a prelude to a full bid for the network. Sources close to Lachlan say that was never his plan, insisting neither he nor Illyria has ever "sought to profit by selling assets back to

News Corp, or Fox, for that matter." The contrast with Liz or James, who had both sold businesses back to News in the past, barely needs pointing out.

When it came, Malcolm Turnbull's successful challenge to the leadership of Tony Abbott was welcomed across much of the media, including at the News Corp mastheads, as the new prime minister enjoyed a honeymoon with voters. Never popular with the electorate, Abbott had lost the faith of all but his most ardent conservative supporters during his chaotic two years in office. Lachlan had enjoyed unrivalled influence while his friend Tony was in the top job, and he would maintain a close relationship with Abbott. now a humble backbencher. even as his focus shifted increasingly to the United States. After the dust of the Turnbull coup had settled, Lachlan was one of twenty of Abbott's closest friends and allies to gather for an intimate dinner paying tribute to him, including former prime minister John Howard and a bunch of star News Corp heavies, including Paul Whittaker and Andrew Bolt. Meant to be a celebration, the evening felt more like a wake.

16

The Donald and the
Loudest Voice

O N THE AFTERNOON OF Tuesday, June 16, 2015, Donald
Trump and his wife Melania descended the escalator to the
lobby of Trump Tower in Manhattan and declared he would
nominate to be the Republican Party's candidate for president. Trump's
speech was full of populist promises to beat ISIS, stop Iran going nuclear,
fix broken trade deals, bring back manufacturing, and be "the greatest jobs
president that God ever created." He immediately got into hot water by
promising to build a wall along the southern border, paid for by Mexico,
to stop illegal immigrants, many of whom, he said, were "rapists" who
brought in crime and drugs. He would repeal and replace Obamacare,
which he dubbed the "Big Lie." Politicians were all talk, no action, he
said, declaring that only a truly successful person like him could make
the country great again. Claiming a net worth of $8.7 billion, Trump
promised to file details of his assets and liabilities with the government
"right on time." Trump's whole family, campaign staffers, hundreds of
journalists, some fans and some rent-a-crowd onlookers crowded into the
glitzy atrium to witness the unlikely spectacle on what would soon be called
"escalator day." *The Apprentice* star was a rank outsider, and his declaration
was the culmination of years of "Will he or won't he?" speculation.

Trump was well known to Rupert. Donald's daughter Ivanka was on the trust managing the assets of his two children to Wendi, Grace and Chloe, and he was a fixture of the Murdoch media. As a developer, Trump expertly promoted himself as man-about-town through the *New York Post*'s Page Six gossip column. Roger Ailes had glommed onto Trump as he pushed the "birther" conspiracy about Obama and Ailes almost single-handedly turned Trump into a political pundit by giving him a weekly slot on the breakfast show *Fox & Friends*. Debuting on March 28, 2011, the Monday mornings with Trump segment "changed the course of American politics" according to Brian Stelter in his book *Hoax: Fox News and the Dangerous Distortion of Truth*. Although the Donald was usually nearby in Trump Tower, he liked to phone in to *F&F*: it made him seem hard-to-get, and similar calls would later become a feature of his presidency. Trump built his Twitter following into the millions and learned the talking points that would resonate with the Fox audience and ultimately make him the "Fox News president."

Although he received glowing coverage on Fox, Trump was far from a favorite of the Murdoch family, particularly Rupert, who was at first deeply sceptical of his campaign for president. "When is Donald Trump going to stop embarrassing his friends," Rupert tweeted early on, "let alone the whole country?" At the first Republican primary debate between the leading candidates the following month, Fox News prime time host Megyn Kelly opened with a famously tough question to Trump on his misogyny, marking the beginning of a long-running feud between the two. Rupert subsequently backed rival GOP candidates Jeb Bush and Ben Carson, and a *Wall Street Journal* editorial called Trump's campaign a "catastrophe." Ailes himself did not necessarily think Trump would win but could see his appeal to the Fox base and humored his campaign on the network.

Fox News was the part of the Murdoch empire where Lachlan and James had least sway: when they were appointed as co-chair and CEO, Roger Ailes had boasted mischievously that he would continue to report directly to Rupert. Fox quickly and publicly corrected him in a statement saying Ailes would report to the father and his two sons jointly, although his special relationship with Rupert would continue. As a rule, the Murdochs did not directly involve themselves in Ailes' programming decisions.

Asked if he had much of a relationship with the Murdoch sons, Trump told the *Hollywood Reporter*: "A little bit. I like them, they like me. They're good guys. I think they're very worthy and that they'll do well." As to whether they had any influence over Fox News, or whether it was really Ailes' show, Trump equivocated: "I've never known. I could understand why it might be because Roger's done such a good job. But I can't believe that the Murdoch family wouldn't have certain influence, frankly."[1]

Lachlan kept his own counsel as Trump gained momentum, while his brother grew increasingly alarmed. Whereas in the past, James had donated to both Republican and Democratic campaigns, in the 2016 presidential cycle his personal contributions would be all blue and total more than $80,000. After a series of private meetings with the candidate, Rupert was heading the other way: by early 2016, he was calling on the Republicans to unite behind Trump if his nomination became inevitable. The *Post* endorsed Trump in April, he clinched the nomination and Rupert swung firmly behind him in June after touring his eponymous golf course at Aberdeen, not far from the ancestral Murdoch hometown of Rosehearty, Scotland, in June. Britain had just voted in-principle for Brexit, which had been championed by Murdoch's *Sun* and by would-be prime minister Boris Johnson. A populist shift was definitely underway.

On the morning of July 6, 2016, Fox host Gretchen Carlson filed her celebrated lawsuit alleging sexual harassment against Ailes. A fortnight earlier, Ailes had told Carlson her contract would not be renewed and now, suing her former boss personally rather than suing Fox as her employer, she claimed he had punished her for refusing his advances and included detailed conversations between them which she had secretly recorded. In one, Ailes told her: "you and I should have had a sexual relationship a long time ago and then you'd be good and better and I'd be good and better." Both Lachlan and James were at the Allen & Co. media conference at Sun Valley, Idaho, for the first time without their father, who was holidaying on the French Riviera with Jerry.

As *Vanity Fair*'s Sarah Ellison would chronicle months later, Lachlan had just finished a workout at the Ketchum YMCA and at about 10 a.m. checked in with Fox's communications chief, Julia Henderson, back in New York.

"Have you seen the suit?" she asked.

"What suit?" he replied.[2]

Lachlan immediately plunged into crisis mode: there was no doubting the gravity of Carlson's strike against the head of the Fox News profit engine. Lachlan called James, who was hiking in the nearby mountains. The two brothers differed on many things, but they were united in their dislike of Ailes and with their father at that moment in the air en route to the US, it was up to them to decide on a response. On a short conference call with Henderson and Fox general counsel, Gerson Zweifach, Lachlan and James agreed to hire an outside law firm to investigate the extent of the company's exposure to any misconduct by Ailes. Fox put out a statement, expressing full confidence in Ailes, while acknowledging that the allegations were serious and would be the subject of an internal review. Hours later Ailes put out his own statement, denying Carlson's allegations and claiming her legal action was in retaliation for losing her job, a decision he blamed on her poor ratings.

Ailes' future hung in the balance. Fox sources told Ailes' biographer Gabriel Sherman, then reporting for *New York* magazine, that Lachlan and James intended to force the domineering Fox News boss out, saying: "It's a coup."[3] Former company insiders say Lachlan has a talent for vengeance: "Roger Ailes had got him back in 2005 . . . from 2005 to 2016 he festered and waited and waited and he got him." Returning to work, this time Rupert backed his sons over Ailes. Within days, Sherman was reporting there were at least half-a-dozen historical allegations against the Fox News supremo, some dating back decades. Ailes fought back and so did his wife Beth, recruiting Fox TV host (and future Trump adviser) Kimberley Guilfoyle to back her husband. Greta Van Susteren and Jeanine Pirro joined in, the former describing Carlson as a "disgruntled employee."

A dozen other female anchors defended Ailes, as did Sean Hannity, Geraldo Rivera, Neil Cavuto, and Brit Hume.

One Fox host remained conspicuously silent: Megyn Kelly, the cable network's biggest female star. There was a reason. Three days after the Carlson suit was filed, Megyn called Lachlan to explain that she too had been harassed by Ailes. He simply replied: "I'm sorry."[4] Megyn told Lachlan that Roger was blocking the independent investigation by an external law firm. Sources close to Lachlan say his response to Megyn was: "Okay, if he's done that, give us the names of people we can talk to," and then he put down the phone and called Fox general counsel Gershon Zweifach to get the ball rolling on an inquiry. "Lachlan did the right thing and thank God Megyn Kelly picked up the phone and called him." Within a week, Fox appointed top Sixth Avenue law firm Paul, Weiss to conduct the investigation; they interviewed dozens of Fox employees at their own offices. Memories of the phone hacking crisis were still fresh and the Murdochs were acutely aware of the potential for reputational damage to the company to be compounded by a cover-up or stonewalling.

Ailes' attorneys asked Zweifach why Fox was not simply defending the lawsuit, suggesting that's what his predecessor Joel Klein would have done. "Maybe that's why he's my predecessor," Zweifach shot back.[5] At the same time, by confining the investigation to Ailes, the Paul, Weiss review left unexamined the wider questions of how such a deeply ingrained culture of harassment could have taken hold at Fox, how widespread it was, and who knew what, when, and who should be held responsible.

For Fox News, the timing of Carlson's suit was disastrous, coming in the middle of a presidential election year and within days of the Republican National Convention on July 18. James had been pushing for the immediate termination of Ailes but then left for Europe on business. On the first day of the convention, Sherman reported that Lachlan was aligned with Rupert and thought no action should be taken until after the GOP convention.[6] The next day, however, came news that would tip the balance decisively against Ailes: citing two unnamed sources, Sherman reported that Megyn Kelly had told Paul, Weiss that Ailes had sexually harassed her a decade ago when she was a young correspondent: Ailes had tried to kiss her in 2006, and said he wanted to see her in "very sexy bras."[7] Kelly rebuffed him, relocated to the Washington bureau, and somehow established a professional relationship with him, managing to avoid any damaging career repercussions. Coming from one of Fox's most credible anchors, who was nipping at the heels of Bill O'Reilly in the ratings, Kelly's allegations were the last nail in the coffin for Ailes' reputation. The *New York Post* tweeted the next day's front page: "The end is near for Roger Ailes." From the filing of Carlson's lawsuit to the ouster of Ailes took thirteen days. At the age of eighty-six, Rupert rolled up his sleeves and took over as interim chairman of Fox News.

Lachlan was right in the thick of Ailes' downfall. It was Lachlan whom Megyn Kelly called first, and there were other female Fox employees who confided in him. It was Lachlan who accompanied Rupert to the Fox newsroom where the elderly proprietor told his employees that Ailes was gone and he would be taking charge, adding: "I wanted you to hear it from me." And it was Lachlan who turned up to the difficult, final lunch with Ailes, at his father's luxurious East 22nd Street triplex apartment, so that Rupert could acknowledge his service. Lachlan helped smooth things over—one Fox executive described him as "a great therapist"—and Ailes was given a $40 million severance package and kept on as an occasional consultant to Fox. He was soon advising Trump's presidential campaign and in cahoots with Steve Bannon, chairman and founder of the alt-right news site Breitbart.

* * *

Between the downfall of Ailes in July, and the election of President Trump in November, there was an opportunity to remake the Fox News Channel, and signals that a period of "retrograde stupor" may have ended.[8] Ailes had run the network as a personal fiefdom and it reflected his priorities absolutely. He blurred the line between hard news and entertainment and while he made Fox watchable, the flipside was under-investment in newsgathering: national and international bureaus were neglected, thinly staffed newsrooms had threadbare carpet, and studios were held together with duct tape. There was no digital strategy, with Fox News' website languishing well outside the top twenty most popular sites in the country.

James was all for a radical overhaul, pushing for Fox to hire David Rhodes, the former Fox producer who was now the youngest-ever president of CBS News and whose appointment would signal a return to less partisan coverage. Rupert canned the idea, and Lachlan was on the same page as his father, cautious about messing with the formula that had made Fox News so successful. At an investment banking conference in September, Lachlan said there were no plans to change the channel's style. "We don't see any change at all," he said. "It would be foolish of us to copy a failed strategy vs. stick with a winning strategy." For Lachlan, it was just business: Trump was god's gift to the whole media industry, from Fox to CNN to *The New York Times*. Whether he loved Trump or loathed him, for Lachlan there was an overwhelming commercial logic in following the news cycle and creating audiences where there was a gap in the market, on the right.

Some Ailes loyalists were fired, such as CFO Mark Kranz, who had approved many of the payments that had sustained a reign of terror, including millions spent on shadowy political operatives and private investigators who conducted surveillance, opposition research, and negative PR campaigns against targets inside and outside the company. Ailes' infamous "black ops" unit, which operated from an out-of-the-way office on the twelfth floor, was shut down. The skulduggery revealed at Fox News under Ailes was at least as bad as, if not worse than anything that happened at *News of the World*. On the other hand, the Murdochs still had a top-rated cable channel to run and opted for continuity by promoting Ailes' loyal deputy Bill Shine to co-president of Fox News, serving alongside Jack Abernethy and reporting directly to Rupert, while Suzanne Scott was promoted to head of programming and Jay Wallace stayed in charge of hard news. All four executives were key Ailes lieutenants.

In an interview around this time, Fox anchor Shep Smith told *The Huffington Post* he had asked Rupert Murdoch about the direction of the channel post-Ailes and whether the center of gravity was shifting toward news or toward the opinion side. "I'm a newsman. I want to be the best news organization in America," Murdoch told Smith, saying he had big plans. Smith continued:

> He [Murdoch] wants to hire a lot more journalists, he wants to build us a massive new newsroom, he wants to make more commitments to places like this [studio], to hire reporters to work on beats, just enlarge our news gathering. When the biggest boss, who controls everything, comes and says 'That's what I want to do,' that's the greatest news I've heard in years. And he didn't mention one thing about our opinion side.[9]

At the same time, Lachlan and James were trying to overhaul the workplace culture at Fox, pushing something warmer and fuzzier, although not necessarily liberal left. They held town-hall meetings with employees and in the fall of 2016 sent out a memo to company employees introducing additional benefits including more paid vacation and vastly enhanced health insurance coverage, with coverage for women's reproductive treatments and "our transgender colleagues." At this stage, James was the capable, progressive CEO who was trusted by investors while Lachlan remained the unknown quantity who was still to shake off the perception that he was constantly off sailing and mountain climbing. "James has a lot of experience in senior management, and he is capable of running a business," one broking analyst told *The New York Times*. "Lachlan? I don't know. People don't know him as well. He is looked at a bit more skeptically by investors."[10]

Media pundits detected a subtle post-Ailes shift in Fox News' political coverage. Fox was highly critical of Trump after the release of the *Access Hollywood* tapes, which captured him boasting about grabbing women "by the pussy." The company simply had to condemn sexual harassment in the wake of the Ailes scandal. Gabriel Sherman told an October media conference that there had definitely been a change since Ailes was ousted: "Without question . . . they've been more down the middle with Trump than they ever were in the past." Almost nobody, including the Murdochs, thought Donald Trump would win. Already in 2016, there was talk that Trump might launch his own television network after his expected defeat in November, "monetizing" the enormous MAGA support base he had created through his campaign. As the early returns came in on election night, Rupert Murdoch was in the Fox newsroom and texted his daughter-in-law, Kathryn, who'd worked for the Clinton Foundation: "Looks like your girl's going to win."[11]

But Hillary Clinton did not win and the Murdoch patriarch quickly reverted to type: cosying up to Trump, championing pet conservative causes, and seeking political deals favorable to his business. At the annual meeting a week later, Lachlan took Trump's upset win as a validation of Fox's coverage. While much of the American media was "navel-gazing," he said, wondering how it "got it so wrong . . . I think in fact Fox News and the wonderful journalists and producers that we have there really should be given great credit for playing this election down the middle and broadcasting in a fair and balanced way." If Lachlan was hoping some of the credit would rebound on the family, he was mistaken. President-elect Trump's chief strategist Steve Bannon was unsparing, telling Michael Wolff in a triumphant interview that the Murdochs "got it more wrong than anybody. Rupert is a globalist and never understood Trump. To him, Trump is a radical. Now they'll go centrist and build the network around Megyn Kelly."[12]

Bannon was right on that score, although calling Kelly a centrist was a stretch. All three Murdochs agreed she was the future of Fox News. "We need her more than ever," Lachlan told one Fox insider.[13] Kelly's feud with Trump had come at a personal cost. including extreme right-wing trolling and death threats, but had also lifted her profile. Standing up to Trump and Ailes had turned her into something of a feminist icon. Both the Murdoch sons were huge fans and when Kelly decided she wanted to write a book, *New York* magazine reported, it was Lachlan who personally approved her $6 million advance from News Corp's HarperCollins.[14] When her contract came up, Lachlan offered Kelly a staggering $25 million a year for four years to renew, which would have made her the network's top-paid star, perhaps only behind Bill O'Reilly.

But Kelly was interested in more than money: when her book, which came out a week after Trump's shock election victory, included details of her harassment by Ailes, she was appalled to find herself subject to an on-air attack by Fox's own Bill O'Reilly. Kelly could not believe that O'Reilly would be able to get away with such a character assassination. She described it as a "drive-by" shooting and, feeling unsupported, quit the channel altogether, defecting to NBC.

"I wish she'd stayed, genuinely," Lachlan said, but he also conveyed that Fox was unstoppable, with or without her. Some saw the failure of Lachlan and his father to rein in O'Reilly at this point as a "basic lack of leadership."[15] To replace Kelly at 9 pm, Rupert hand-picked Tucker Carlson, the former co-host of CNN's *Crossfire* program and founder of right-wing news and opinion site the *Daily Caller*, who had had a patchy career as a commentator but was enjoying a sudden rebirth at Fox. To celebrate, Rupert took Tucker out to brunch with Jerry Hall. A few months later, Lachlan had lunch with Carlson in Los Angeles and reassured him that management would be hands-off. "I haven't got any notes," Tucker said afterwards. Close in age, with a kind of philosophical bent, the two men saw eye to eye on a lot of things and Lachlan would become one of Carlson's biggest fans.

An unfortunate consequence of Kelly's exit was that it made Fox more dependent on O'Reilly, still the highest-rating anchor across cable news, but behind the scenes another storm was brewing. Gretchen Carlson's lawsuit against Ailes, which Fox settled in September for some $20 million, had opened up the floodgates as more women came forward. Sexual harassment at Fox had not been confined to Ailes and there was speculation that knowledge of the misconduct must have gone to the top. The US Attorney's office commenced a criminal investigation, led by southern New

York southern district attorney Preet Bharara, into whether Fox had failed to inform shareholders about payments to settle sexual harassment claims. To make things worse, another wave of litigation loomed as twenty minority employees filed suits alleging racial discriminatory practices at Fox News. A *New York Times* investigation revealed that O'Reilly had been subject of historic sexual harassment allegations, some of which had been quietly settled by the network in the wake of the Ailes scandal. That did not stop the Murdochs from approving a renewal of O'Reilly's contract, reportedly offering him $100 million over four years, the same amount Lachlan had offered Kelly, which suggested that deep down, Fox had not changed much at all. At the end of the year, after the details of the complaints against O'Reilly were revealed by the *Times* and after the #MeToo reckoning had levelled the media industry with allegations against Harvey Weinstein, Charlie Rose, and others, Lachlan had to account for the difference in his response to allegations against Ailes and O'Reilly.

Welcoming #MeToo as a "cathartic moment" for the industry, he said it took Fox News just thirteen days "from the time we learned of the first allegation about Roger Ailes to the time we walked him out of the building. By historical standards, I think [that] is a pretty good track record." However, Lachlan said the "fact sets" were different with O'Reilly, who had never been subject of an employee complaint to the company and whose private settlements with his accusers prevented Fox from talking to its employees. "Once, however, these claims [about O'Reilly] became public we were able to change his contract, if any allegations came up we could fire him immediately, which is what we did," Murdoch said. Fox paid $90 million to settle the raft of sexual harassment and racial discrimination lawsuits, in which all company directors including Lachlan were named as defendants, and agreed to set up a new in-house council for "Workplace Professionalism and Inclusion" at Fox News.

Fox got some good news in March, when Trump summarily fired forty-six Obama-era federal attorneys, including Bharara. That hardly relieved the pressure, however. When the *Times* reported in April that O'Reilly personally, or Fox as his employer, had paid out at least $13 million to settle five sexual harassment claims, there were more calls for the network to terminate O'Reilly. A new element in the media backlash was an anonymous Twitter account with the handle Sleeping Giants. It began targeting Fox advertizers, making them aware of the damage to their own reputation by advertizing on O'Reilly's program, the single-biggest earner for the news channel. Once again it was James who took the harder line, arguing that it was time to jettison O'Reilly, while Rupert and Lachlan were reluctant to hand the *Times* a win. According to one Fox source at the time, in the end it was Lachlan's wife, Sarah, in the end, who convinced him O'Reilly had to go, moving him from Rupert's camp into James's.[16]

Within a fortnight, the same dynamic would play out again as Bill Shine was named in lawsuits alleging that although he had not directly engaged in sexual harassment, he had enabled it. In May, Rupert Murdoch, loyal to Shine only ten days earlier, sat down to hammer out an exit package. When he read the news, Sean Hannity tweeted at Sherman: "I pray this is NOT true because if it is, that's the total end of the FNC as we know it. Done." The stellar rise of Tucker Carlson continued: he was promoted into O'Reilly's 8 p.m. slot, while panel show *The Five* took over at 9 p.m. and Hannity stayed at 10 p.m. The shifting from a primetime line-up dominated by O'Reilly and Kelly to one dominated by Carlson and Hannity noticeably ratcheted up the level of right-wing trolling and pro-Trump fervor. Ailes died after a fall at home, in May 2017, at the age of seventy-seven.

Brian Stelter would report that there remained for years a degree of nostalgia for the Ailes regime within Fox News and a power vacuum that was never quite filled. Stelter described Lachlan as a "soccer-dad at heart," ensconced in Hollywood, far from the action in the New York newsroom, an almost indifferent owner and manager of Fox who was content to leave daily decision-making about programming and talent to the line executives.[17] Rupert had always been up to his neck in political intrigue and speculation about his direct, personal interventions as a media proprietor had fuelled Murdoch-watchers for decades. Hands-off to a fault, Lachlan was quite unlike his father.

17

Payday

THE ESCALATING CONTROVERSY at Fox News in 2016–2017 was not only costly and demoralising internally, it was also threatening to have major commercial ramifications for the Murdoch empire. In October 2016, AT&T had launched its giant $85 billion bid for Time Warner, taking up where the Murdochs had left off two years earlier. The pressure was on Fox again to either scale up or be left behind. Two months later, Fox took advantage of the devaluation of the British pound post-Brexit to launch a second, lowball bid for the 61 per cent of Sky that it did not already own. The takeover, the largest in British corporate history, would give Fox complete control of Europe's largest pay-TV business and would be a huge personal vindication for James Murdoch, who had been reappointed as chairman of Sky. The family had good grounds to believe the regulatory path would be much easier than in 2011, as Fox was now an entirely separate company from News Corp, which owned *The Sun* and *The Times* and was still dealing with the legacy issues from phone hacking. James thought the deal would be approved within six months.

As it happened, Trump's victory and constant headlines about sexual harassment, racism, and scandal at Fox News had stoked British fears about the role of the Murdochs. Former Labour leader Ed Miliband led a group of senior cross-party MPs calling on the UK's media regulator,

Ofcom, to do a full investigation of the bid. Online activist group Avaaz joined with Media Matters and others to submit a 300,000-strong petition, warning the proposed takeover was a serious threat to democracy and that Sky could become "Foxified." Under pressure, culture secretary Karen Bradley did as expected and referred the bid to Ofcom. Both Lachlan and James flew to London to brief Ofcom's chief executive, Sharon White, giving full details of their response to the sexual harassment claims against Ailes and O'Reilly. Midway through the review, Conservative prime minister Theresa May called a snap election, which put the regulatory process on pause for months and cost her government its majority. Holding onto power by forming a coalition with Northern Ireland's hard-line Democratic Unionist Party, May's fragile government found controversial decisions difficult.

Ofcom finally found Fox was fit and proper to hold a broadcast license, but recommended the bid be referred to the competition regulator for further investigation on media plurality grounds. Avaaz quickly threatened legal proceedings to overturn Ofcom's decision and flew over US lawyer Lisa Bloom, who was representing four women who had filed claims against Fox. "There is an epidemic of sexual harassment and retaliation [at the company]," said Bloom at a press conference. "It's phone hacking part two." To try to smooth the process, the Murdochs pulled the Fox News channel off Sky in the UK, where it had a tiny audience but had generated outrage airing claims that London's Muslim mayor, Sadiq Khan, was rolling out the red carpet for extremists, that parts of the city were already under Sharia law, and that Birmingham was a "no-go" area for non-Muslims. It didn't help. Miliband argued that British media impartiality requirements could not be relied on to keep Sky News balanced, and called for a full inquiry:

> Fox News has played a major role in polluting the well of public conversation in the US, stirring division and hatred. We know also that Rupert Murdoch has mused about making Sky more like Fox . . . The case for referral is overwhelming, based on the record

of Fox News as well as the total failure of corporate governance in the Murdoch empire revealed by what happened at the *News of the World* and at Fox.

Fox found itself in "Westminster purgatory."[1] When James Murdoch agreed to appear with journalist Sarah Sands at the Royal Television Society's biannual conference at Cambridge in September, he was grilled. "I wonder if the message that comes through," Sands asked, "is that you presided over this rotten culture at News International and, again, at Fox News, and that people just don't trust you. Is that what you think the message is?"[2] When Sands asked if he was wounded by questions over Fox's commitment to broadcasting standards, Murdoch replied stiffly: "You're over-personalizing that a little."[3] For James, the new Sky bid was turning into a re-run of his 2011 nightmare. For Lachlan, the backlash confirmed his feeling that James was the wrong public face for Fox's bid for Sky.[4]

Through 2017, the Trump presidency changed Fox and just as it polarized the United States, began to deepen the divide between the Murdoch brothers as they competed to run the company. It started almost straightaway, when the new president banned immigration from seven Muslim-majority countries overnight, causing chaos at airports and triggering immediate legal challenges from human rights activists and a restraining order. Three days later, Lachlan and James issued a statement to Fox's 20,000 employees gently criticising the ban, saying that as a global company:

> ... we deeply value diversity and believe immigration is an essential part of America's strength. Moreover, as a company that is driven by creativity and innovation, we recognize the unique perspective offered by our many people who came to the US in search of the opportunity for unfettered self-expression.

People close to James later told *The New York Times* he had wanted to go much further, to forcefully denounce the policy and reassure Muslim employees, while "Lachlan wanted it to be less confrontational and to not specifically mention Trump or the Muslim ban, which Fox News's opinion hosts were defending night after night." Getting Lachlan's agreement on the watered-down statement ultimately released was "like pulling teeth."[5]

Fox News embarrassed itself three months later, publishing a baseless conspiracy theory that a young Democratic staffer, Seth Rich, had been murdered for giving Wikileaks emails which damaged the Clinton campaign ahead of the 2016 election. Washington police were said to have been pressured to shut down investigation of the unsolved crime, suggesting instead that it was a botched robbery. Appallingly, the story had been cooked up by a Trump donor, Ed Butowsky, as a distraction from the allegations of collusion with Russia bedevilling the president. Butowsky was going between Sean Spicer in the White House and a private investigator he'd hired, Rod Wheeler, an occasional Fox News contributor who was a source for Fox's reporter. Ahead of its publication, Butowsky messaged Wheeler: "The president just read the article. He wants the article out immediately." The story caused a sensation, of course, but Fox had to pull it down within a week, although Sean Hannity continued to lend credibility to the theory. Wheeler sued Fox, claiming the story made allegations he had never made himself. So did the Rich family. Their case was finally settled in November 2020. The terms were confidential but included a curious proviso that the closure of the case could not be made public until after the presidential election.

In their definitive study *Network Propaganda: Manipulation, Disinformation, and Radicalization in American Politics,* academics Yochai Benkler, Robert Faris, and Hal Roberts wrote that "no single case more clearly exhibits the characteristics of a disinformation campaign aimed to divert attention from the President's political woes than Fox News coverage in May of 2017 of the conspiracy theory." They add: "conspiracy theories that germinate in the nether regions of the internet stay there unless they find an amplification vector." That vector, in the Rich case, was Fox News. Benkler, Faris and Roberts concluded that while sites like Breitbart and Trump himself mobilized the support necessary to take over the

Republican Party and win in 2016, *after* the election Fox News reasserted its role at the center of the right-wing media ecosystem on behalf of the embattled president. Quoting Hannity's own observation that "for years we've been telling you, journalism is dead," the authors wrote that their data "warrant the conclusion that Fox shares little but a few visual trappings with the world of professional journalism at the core of the rest of the US media system. It is, across its online and television properties, America's leading propaganda outlet."[6]

Politically, Lachlan and James continued to diverge. When News Corp's senior vice-president Joseph Azam, who happened to be Afghan American, grew tired of Tucker Carlson's immigrant-bashing in mid-2017, he tweeted: "Why does America benefit from having tons of people from failing countries come here? If you come upstairs to where all the executives who run your company sit and find me, I can tell you, Tucker." Azam was given a stern warning and quit News months later.[7] Nobody at News or Fox reached out to support Azam, during the ordeal or afterwards. Carlson kept it up, later making one of his most controversial comments: "We have a moral obligation to admit the world's poor, they tell us, even if it makes our country poorer and dirtier and more divided." Dozens of advertizers bailed after that but Lachlan personally texted Carlson to support him, according to two sources familiar with the texts who confirmed them to *The New York Times*.[8]

By contrast, when a "Unite the Right" rally of neo-Nazis and Klansmen defending a statue of confederate general Robert E. Lee turned deadly in Charlottesville, Virginia, with a car slamming into counter-protesters, killing one and injuring nineteen, James and Kathryn Murdoch announced they would donate $1 million to the Anti-Defamation League. The crowd, revved up by former KKK wizard David Duke, shouted "Jews will not replace us," alluding to the anti-Semitic, white supremacist "Great Replacement" theory. When President Trump said there were "very fine people" on both sides, Kathryn insisted that she and James say something, without consulting with Lachlan or Rupert. "If we're not going to say something about fucking Nazis marching in Virginia, when are we going to say something?" she told James, according to *The New York Times*. In a personal statement to all Fox employees, James said:

> I can't even believe I have to write this: standing up to Nazis is essential; there are no good Nazis. Or Klansmen, or terrorists. Democrats, Republicans, and others must all agree on this, and it compromises nothing for them to do so.[9]

The statement was widely reported, not always uncritically. *Washington Post* media critic Erik Wemple wrote a scathing op-ed, headlined "Hey, James Murdoch: You have no standing to denounce Trump's Charlottesville reaction." Said Wemple: "Your network turned a blind eye to Trump's racism. Period."

On Fox News, there were some commentators who condemned Trump, like Charles Krauthammer, who described Trump's "both sides" comment as a "moral disgrace." But there were plenty of others who jumped in to defend him, like *The Five* co-host Jesse Watters, who said the president was just trying to get "all the facts," while Sean Hannity asked why the media were not focusing on the "alt-left." Tucker Carlson, predictably, went furthest by attacking the left and the anti-fascist protestors at Charlottesville, declining to condemn the neo-Nazi protesters and then doing a bizarre segment on slavery in which he listed good people who had owned slaves, including Plato, the Aztecs, and Thomas Jefferson, using their example as a reason to keep confederate statues standing. Fox's defense of Trump after Charlottesville marked a "tipping point" for some of the channel's more moderate reporters and personalities. Fox Jerusalem correspondent Conor Powell told Brian Stelter that Charlottesville was the last straw for him, although he had to wait until his son could finish the school year. "I didn't get into journalism to have co-workers defend neo-Nazis and white supremacists," he'd told his wife. It was a similar story with *F&F Weekend* co-host Clayton Morris, who decided to terminate his contract when his wife tried to explain Charlottesville to his son and the boy asked her: "Is Daddy a white supremacist?"[10]

By the end of 2017, Fox and Trump were converging. Rupert spoke to the president or his son-in-law, Jared Kushner, weekly, if not daily. Lachlan, by contrast, had never met Trump. In October, CBS calculated that Trump had given Fox News eighteen television interviews since his inauguration, out of a total of twenty-six. A clever Stanford study titled "Bias in Cable News: Persuasion and Polarization" tracked the impact of Fox News viewership on voting patterns and estimated that every extra 2.5 minutes per week watching the channel in a given market increased the Republican vote share by 0.3 percentage points. *Newsweek* reported there had "never been a relationship this close between a sitting president and an American media organization." Shortly before he was fired, Roger Ailes had warned Rupert Murdoch: "Trump gets great ratings, but if you're not careful he's going to end up totally controlling Fox News."[11] After a year of Trump's presidency, there was an incipient debate about whether Fox News was morphing into something like state-run TV.

Lachlan, atop the whole operation as co-executive chairman, dismissed the suggestion Fox had aligned itself with Trump in a frank Q&A at *Business Insider*'s Ignition conference in late 2017. "I don't think any media organization should be behind an individual," Lachlan told Henry Blodget:

> You can be behind ideas or concepts. You can be behind whether you think your viewers want lower taxes or higher employment—there are certain principles that are important to your readers or your viewers, that are important or should be important to the organization, particularly on the opinion side. But you should never get behind an individual, because individuals can be fallible, right?

If that was meant as a signal from the top, it was too subtle for Fox's primetime stars Hannity, Carlson, and Ingraham, who continued to boost and defend President Trump, day in, day out. Trying to remain above the fray, if that is what he was doing, Lachlan was in danger of being ignored.

* * *

All through the first half of 2017, Lachlan had a different disaster on his mind, as Illyria's ill-fated investment in Channel Ten ground towards its inevitable result: failure.

In late 2016, Ten had hired McKinsey to work with chief Paul Anderson on a radical plan to cut expenses and transform the business and for a time it seemed to be working. A key element of the plan was to renegotiate Ten's onerous output deals with US studios CBS and Fox, which had an escalator clause that raised costs each year and a bottom-line impact an order of magnitude bigger than any local programming flops like *The Shire* or *Being Lara Bingle*. Unexpectedly, Illyria hit a roadblock: CBS was prepared to take whatever terms Ten could renegotiate with Fox, but Fox dragged its heels, saying it would be a related-party transaction to do a special deal with Murdoch, given he remained a director of News Corp. While most people would assume that Lachlan's position as co-Chairman of Fox would help with Ten's negotiations, it seemed to present an obstacle.

What happened next took all sides by surprise. Stymied in its transformation plan, Illyria appears to have formulated a plan B, working with the network's largest shareholder Bruce Gordon who, along with James Packer, was also a guarantor of the company's main $200 million loan facility. The idea was to let Ten go broke and then buy it back cheaply out of insolvency. The planets seemed to be aligning in March 2017, when Siobhan McKenna suddenly resigned from the Ten board and took up an executive role as the head of broadcasting at News Corp in Australia, ultimately responsible for Foxtel and its 15 per cent stake in Ten. As Tim Burrowes would later write in *Media Unmade*, three months later Illyria and Gordon dropped a bombshell, writing to inform the Ten board that they would not renew their guarantee of Ten's loan facility when it fell due later in 2017 and warning directors that they would be held personally liable for any expenses incurred from that point on. It was a hardball tactic: Ten's directors had no choice but to put the company into administration.

In Burrowes' account, the delay with the renegotiation of Ten's arrangement with Fox helped Illyria at this point: if Lachlan and Siobhan hoped to buy the network out of administration, the last thing they needed was for Ten to make a major breakthrough in cost reduction. In an apparently grim coincidence, after days of ignoring increasingly desperate emails from Ten management, Fox finally sent an email agreeing to a much cheaper output deal an hour after administrators were appointed. If they thought it was game over, however, Lachlan and Siobhan were about to be blindsided by CBS: as Ten's major creditor, claiming debts worth $844 million, and a partner in Ten's digital channel, Eleven, the US network took a bold gamble and launched its own bid for the busted Australian free-to-air network. Lachlan, Gordon, and Packer had not banked on the ability of the US giant to move so fast and were aghast when administrators Korda Mentha advised creditors that the CBS bid was better their own. A last-ditch court case to stop the takeover failed and Lachlan's whole seven-year saga came to an ignominious end when creditors, including the long-suffering employees, voted overwhelmingly in favor of CBS, which bought Channel Ten for a song. The Murdochs had missed their last opportunity to own one of Australia's free-to-air television networks, and Lachlan's Illyria had lost more than $170 million of equity that he had sunk into Ten through his initial investment and three more capital raisings.

Of Lachlan's oft-mentioned business fails, the collapse of Ten may have hit home the most. Super League was never his idea, and he had been so young. Through the One.Tel saga he had relied on James Packer, who himself accepted the blame. But Lachlan had to accept his share of responsibility for the failure of Ten, where he had rolled up his sleeves, serving as both chairman and reluctant chief executive, and been intimately involved every step of the way. It was an expensive lesson, which hurt all the more because this time it was his own money that went down the drain, rather than the funds of News or Fox Corp shareholders.

* * *

On August 8, 2017, Disney chief executive Bob Iger announced a divorce from Netflix, pulling its films, including classics like *Bambi* and anything by Pixar, Marvelm or Lucasfilm, off the platform so that it could launch its own Disney Plus streaming service in 2019. The next day, Iger turned up at Rupert Murdoch's Bel Air vineyard, Moraga, where he'd been invited for a catch-up. In his memoir, Iger wrote that he and Rupert had met for dinner occasionally since he became CEO in 2005 and that although they were of different generations and had different political views, "I've always been impressed with how he built his media and entertainment empire from scratch."

Iger thought Murdoch was going to ask if he was going be a presidential candidate for the Democrats in 2020, and he did, right up front, but it turned out Rupert also had another agenda. Over chicken salad and a few glasses of chardonnay, Murdoch spent the better part of an hour talking with Iger about the incursion of big tech into media and its threats to Fox. "We don't have scale," he said. "The only company that has scale is you." After sleeping on it, Iger rang Murdoch the next day and said: "If I am reading you right, if I said we are interested in acquiring your company, or most of it, would you be open to it?" Rupert said yes, asking whether Bob was seriously interested in buying Fox, before clarifying: "I would not do anything unless you agree to remain at the company beyond your current retirement date" in June 2019.

Iger was quickly hooked on the idea. Disney, owner of the ABC broadcast network, did not want Murdoch's endlessly controversial Fox News, and as the owner of ESPN would almost certainly be prevented from buying the Fox Sports cable networks. Fox News, Fox Business, and Fox Sports, as well as Fox's local TV stations, would be the heart of a rump company that would remain in Murdoch hands, tentatively called "New Fox." But Disney was a natural acquirer of the historic 20th Century Fox film and television studios in Hollywood, the cable networks FX and National Geographic and rights to series such *The Simpsons*, and the Fox stakes in Sky, Star, and the joint streaming service Hulu. Iger and his team at Disney did the numbers and were convinced the Fox assets would bolster their ambition to compete with the direct-to-consumer digital platforms Netflix and Amazon. The culminating, defining transaction of Rupert Murdoch's life, to sell the bulk of the empire he'd created over sixty-five years into what would become the largest media conglomerate in the world, was underway.

An immediate hurdle for Rupert was the opposition of both his sons, who were blindsided by his initial conversation with Iger and took a dim view of having their inheritance sold out from under them. Iger wrote that Lachlan and James had watched their father build the company since they were kids, "hoping and assuming that one day it would be theirs. Now he was selling it to someone else. It wasn't an easy situation for any of them."

Lachlan was the most fervently opposed to a sale, given he and his family had been coaxed back from Australia to run the whole empire only three years earlier, and he had no desire to take the top job at the much-diminished New Fox. He told friends: "Why the fuck would I want to run this company?" It came to a head at a heated Manhattan dinner in the fall, at which Lachlan reportedly told Rupert, "If you take one more call on this deal, you will not have a son! I will never talk to you again."[12] Lachlan's people deny he would talk that way to his father.

After CNBC broke news of the talks between Disney and Fox a few months later, Lachlan put his scepticism on the record when taking questions from investors. He insisted Fox already had the scale required to "continue to both execute on our growth strategy and deliver increased returns to shareholders," adding: "historically, we've always been asset builders . . . whether it's Sky or Star or Fox News or the Fox network, we operate these businesses to build them and to grow and we will continue to do so."[13] Behind the scenes, however, Lachlan was reconciling himself to the sale and telling Rupert that if the business was going to be put on the block, the family should at least hold an auction to make sure they got a good price, rather than taking the first offer they received.

Meanwhile, Fox management continued to work on the nuts-and-bolts with Disney. A stumbling block emerged in the form of an enormous potential tax liability for shareholders (and particularly the Murdoch

Family Trust). Disney firmed up an offer price of $23 per share. It represented a decent premium to the market price, but both sons were able to convince their father that Disney's bid was inadequate. Murdoch called Iger to reject it.

CNBC's November 6 report of Disney's bid, however, stunned markets and not only dragged Iger back to the table, but flushed out another player. The day the story broke, Comcast's chief Brian Roberts called Rupert Murdoch and made an unsolicited proposal for the same Fox assets. Now there would be some real competitive tension. Fox sent Comcast a confidentiality agreement so that proper due diligence and negotiations could begin. Lachlan met Roberts and NBC Universal's CEO Steve Burke in Bel-Air and heard how NBC was beating Disney's ABC in ratings and Universal's theme parks were growing faster than Disney's much-bigger parks. Lachlan came away impressed and left Roberts and Burke feeling hopeful.[14]

While Lachlan was drumming up interest from Comcast, he was also keen to improve the offer from Disney, which he believed was trying to rip off his family, telling his father and brother, "You're only going to sell the company once."[15] At one meeting with Disney's negotiators he made an intervention that would prove extremely valuable later, insisting that the storied Fox Studios film lot on LA's Pico Boulevard was not for sale. Lachlan loved the history of the Century City lot, which dated back to the golden age of Hollywood. He also had a sentimental attachment to his father's old office, where he worked most days. Fox's bankers, Goldman Sachs, worried that Disney would walk away if the lot was carved out of the transaction, but Lachlan held firm. When Disney's negotiators resisted the transfer of the lot back to the Fox side of the ledger, Lachlan replied: "We can start again if you like." Disney gave up on the lot, which real estate industry observers reckoned could be worth more than $1.5 billion, based on comparable sales.

Helping to focus the minds of Rupert, Lachlan, and James was uncertainty about the future of Prince Al-Waleed bin Talal, the Saudi billionaire who controlled 7 per cent of the voting shares in Fox and whose support had allowed the Murdoch Family Trust to maintain control of the company with only a 39 per cent voting stake for more than a decade. Al-Waleed stood accused of funding Muslim extremists and in early November he was arrested as Mohammed bin Salman took over the Saudi throne and centralized power in his own hands. Instability on the Fox register—specifically, the possibility that a large friendly block of voting shares could turn hostile—provided yet another reason for the family to sell. Michael Wolff wrote there were "two warning flags for the Murdochs and for 21st Century Fox as a public company: that one of the key shareholders and allies might be outed as a terrorism supporter, and that they may lose his key vote."[16]

With Fox now clearly in play and Disney and Comcast in a dogfight, events moved quickly. Disney sweetened its bid to $28 a share and offered to shoulder the bulk of the tax bill that would accrue to Fox shareholders if the deal went through. These were crucial concessions to Fox and amounted to an equity value (not including debt) of $52 billion. Iger was determined he would not go higher. Comcast, on the other hand, had offered more than $34 a share, valuing the Fox assets at roughly $65 billion. A key problem with the Comcast bid for Fox, however, was regulatory uncertainty, which was particularly acute as the Trump administration battled to block another mega-merger, AT&T's bid for Time Warner. When that $85 billion bid was announced in October 2016, then presidential candidate Donald Trump had vowed to oppose it, claiming it would put "too much concentration of power in the hands of too few." The following year, the department of justice sued to block the deal on anti-trust grounds, a remarkable step because AT&T was a distributor of content and Time Warner was a producer of it, meaning they were not direct competitors and the proposed merger was the kind of vertical industry consolidation that is rarely opposed by regulators. AT&T's outraged chief executive, Randall Stephenson, told reporters the department's suit "defies logic, and it's unprecedented." If AT&T's bid for Time Warner went down in court, it was extremely likely that Comcast's bid for Fox would also fail.

James had his own history with Comcast and did not want to sell Fox to what he viewed as a stodgy utility with low-quality service and a poor track record on innovation.[17] James also had another motivation: the possibility of a top job at Disney, which was set to become the largest media company in the world, and perhaps to take over from Iger, whose contract expired in mid-2019. In early December, the *Financial Times* reported that James had been suggested as a potential successor to Iger, although the report quoted one unidentified person saying "no promises have been made." The story also quoted a source close to the family indicating that the sale of Fox would mark the end of James' partnership with Rupert and Lachlan, who would continue to oversee the new Fox, describing it as "a very amiable separation."[18]

The separation would not prove as amiable as everyone hoped. Lachlan suspected James had leaked to the *FT*, one of his go-to newspapers, ahead of the next day's critical Fox board meeting to choose between the Disney and Comcast bids. That morning, the *Wall Street Journal* published a closely briefed feature citing stresses in the relationship between Rupert and the two brothers, claiming James had felt like a CEO in title only and quoting an unnamed executive saying "it's crowded when you have three people making decisions."[19]

Fox's independent directors were entirely comfortable with the prospect that James would emerge with a senior executive role at Disney, and believed it could actually strengthen the deal.

According to Lachlan's camp, Iger called Rupert and told him that James was saying, he could deliver 21st Century Fox to Disney, but only if he would become his successor as CEO. Murdoch told Iger that was not part of the deal. In fact, he hoped his old friend would remain in charge. James' camp reject any suggestion that he tried to make his role at Disney a condition of the deal. Years later, Iger told the *Times*' Maureen Dowd that James was "nothing but a gentleman in the whole process."[20] In Lachlan's eyes, however, what James had done was highly inappropriate, putting his own personal interests ahead of Fox shareholders' by trying to make his own post-merger role at Disney a condition of the sale. It would remain a source of bitterness between the brothers: Lachlan suspected James hoped to wake up one morning as CEO of Disney, the world's largest media company, answerable only to minor shareholders and beyond his father's control. James, according to others, felt this was the moment at which his father and brother left him out in the cold and that Lachlan's camp would not let go of the CEO issue, constantly using it to background journalists against him. The middle ground between the two brothers was rapidly eroding under the pressure of such a major deal, with billions of dollars at stake, and the future of the Murdoch family business—their lifetimes' work—up in the air.

The Fox board, advised by Goldmans, decided Disney's bid was superior even though the offer price was billions lower, because it had better terms and fewer regulatory risks. Rupert called Brian Roberts to suspend talks with Comcast. In truth, Murdoch preferred to sell Fox to Disney, which was more of a content business than a telco, and preferred to emerge as a powerful minority shareholder in Disney. The Murdoch brothers were jockeying for influence at Disney, including potential board seats for Lachlan, James, and even Rupert.[21] Speculation about the Disney–Fox deal was now destabilising both companies. Murdoch asked Iger to extend his contract, a fourth time, until 2021, in order to bed down the merger.

On the same day the Fox board was meeting to consider the Disney bid, a ferocious wildfire threatened the LA homes of both Rupert and Lachlan, as southern California suffered its worst fire season on record. Fanned by the Santa Ana westerly winds gusting up to 80 miles per hour, the enormous Thomas fire had torn into Ventura County two days earlier, burning hundreds of homes and forcing thousands of evacuations as firefighters battled the uncontained blaze. Then, at a homeless camp near Mulholland Drive on the morning of Wednesday, December 6, as the Fox board was meeting in New York, an illegal cooking fire escaped and torched 150 acres at Bel Air, racing down hillsides towards the interstate freeway 405, shutting down a nine-mile stretch for hours. Hellish videos shot by motorists went viral as what would be known as the

Skirball fire directly threatened some of the most expensive real estate in the country, including Rupert's Moraga Estate. Murdoch senior issued a short statement, confirming Moraga had been evacuated and staff were monitoring the situation as closely as possible: "We believe the winery and house are still intact . . . some of our neighbors have suffered heavy losses and our thoughts and prayers are with them at this difficult time."

Mandeville Canyon, where Lachlan and Sarah lived, was not subject to evacuation orders, but authorities urged residents to leave nonetheless. Hollywood celebrities evacuated, including Jay-Z, Beyoncé and Paris Hilton, who posted on Instagram: "This wild fire in LA is terrifying! This literally looks like Hell!"

The Skirball fire was quickly contained and at Moraga the damage was limited to a storage shed and some vines. On the Friday, the vineyard announced it was open for business: "Harvest was completed in mid-October and the vines are dormant so they won't be affected by the smoke." Coverage questioned the contribution of global warming to California's horrendous wildfires and social media pointed up the irony of Rupert Murdoch's close call at Moraga, given he had previously tweeted about the "endless alarmist nonsense" spoken at UN climate talks.

The following week, Rupert Murdoch and Bob Iger finally announced the $52 billion deal, posing for photos atop the *Times* building in London. Having previously sought assurances from Rupert that Fox News would not be sold to Disney, Donald Trump welcomed news of the deal, phoning Murdoch to congratulate him. White House press secretary Sarah Huckabee Sanders said the president thought the deal could be "a great thing for jobs," renewing speculation about political favoritism, especially since Disney and Fox were direct competitors and such a horizontal merger was certain to increase media concentration.

Rupert tackled the doubters head-on. "I know a lot of you are wondering, 'Why are the Murdochs making such a momentous decision? Are we retreating?' Absolutely not . . . we are pivoting at a pivotal moment." Journalists covering the deal immediately clocked the significance of the announcement for the family, with James effectively carved out of the line of succession, and Lachlan remaining as executive heir to the family empire.[22] Iger was non-committal at the press conference, saying only that "James and I have had a lot of conversations about the future of the two companies. He will be integral to us integrating these two companies over the next few months. During that time, he and I will talk about whether there is a role for him here or not."[23]

At the end of 2017, with the Disney deal on track and his succession almost assured, Lachlan and Sarah took Rupert and Jerry sailing in the Caribbean on Lachlan's massive $50 million yacht, *Sarissa*. Shortly after New Year's celebrations, Rupert fell down the stairs on his way to the bathroom and seriously injured his back. The eighty-six-year-old was helicoptered off *Sarissa* and flown to a hospital in LA, where he was diagnosed with broken vertebrae and a spinal hematoma, which increased the risk of paralysis or even death. He was operated upon and *The New York Times* would later report that Jerry called Murdoch's adult children in a panic, urging them to rush to their father's bedside for fear of the worst.[24] Whether or not Rupert's injury was genuinely life-threatening, the accident certainly came as a reminder of the mortality of the company founder and to some extent underlined the wisdom of the Disney sale. On January 12, Rupert emailed his senior management team:

I hope you all are having a great start to 2018. I suspect it has been better than mine. I am writing to tell you that last week I had a sailing accident and suffered a painful back injury. While I am well on the road to recovery, I have to work from home for some weeks. In the meantime, you'll be hearing from me by email, phone and text![25]

In May, 21st Century Fox confirmed what had been widely assumed by the Murdochologists: Lachlan would be chairman and CEO of the New Fox, with Rupert designated co-chairman. Conspicuously missing was any role in the empire for James, although he would remain on the News Corp board as a non-executive director, in terms of a job he was effectively out on his own, and with his prospects at Disney receding. In his announcement, Lachlan crowed that winter had been spent reimagining Fox as "the only media company solely focused on the domestic market; focused on what Americans love best—sports, news and entertainment, built and delivered for a US audience."

Through their family trust, the Murdochs would remain firmly in control of the new, smaller Fox Corporation, keeping Fox News, Fox Sports, and the fabled lot at Century City, which would house a new slimmed-down division called Fox Entertainment, as well as the twenty-nine local stations owned and operated by Fox Television. The Murdochs also remained in control of News, which was unaffected by the deal. The announcement lauded Lachlan's business track record, growing the *New York Post* circulation by 40 per cent, boosting local news coverage at Fox TV stations, turning $1 million into $5 billion through his investment in REA, and trebling earnings at Nova, now Australia's leading network of FM stations. Needless to say, there was no mention of the Super League, One.Tel or Channel Ten debacles.

Through the first half of 2018, as Fox and Disney worked to complete their merger, there was increasing media speculation that Comcast was preparing a counter bid. Then on June 12, federal court judge Richard Leon ruled in favor of AT&T and against the Department of Justice. The main perceived regulatory barrier to Comcast's Fox bid had disappeared. Brian Roberts was ready to go and the next day raised the bid to $35 a share, all in cash, giving the Fox assets an equity value of $65 billion and indicating that Comcast had "highly confident" letters from potential financiers. Comcast also flagged that it was prepared to go hostile, requisitioning details of Fox shareholders in preparation for a proxy war. Lachlan wrote to the Fox board, ensuring the revised Comcast proposal be considered at the next board meeting, scheduled to be held in London on June 20. At Disney, Iger prepared to make what he hoped would be a knock-out bid, lining up banks to outbid Comcast and add a cash component. Playing hardball, Disney also told Fox any improvement in its bid would be conditional on the offer being accepted or rejected at the meeting on June 20. The day before the board was due to meet, Iger again met Murdoch in London and told him the offer price had been lifted to a staggering $38 a share, valuing the Fox assets at $71 billion; not only would the bid be 50:50 stock and cash, but shareholders could choose for themselves, alleviating any tax disadvantages.

When the board of Fox met the next day, the revised Disney offer received overwhelming endorsement, given the offer price was well above that of Comcast. Rupert and Lachlan both recused themselves from the decision of the Fox board, given they stood to be employed by the new Fox, as did independent director Viet Dinh, who was already being lined up for the general counsel's role. Fox and Disney signed on the dotted line, and when the Murdochs' big pay-day was announced it generated headlines worldwide. Moving fast, Fox and Disney set dates in late July to put the deal to shareholders. Lachlan and James got enormous incentive packages, worth more than $27.4 million each, although it was unlikely that James would ever see the full value of his payout, given he was headed for the exit.

Years later, Iger would quip that although Rupert Murdoch was not primarily motivated by the money and genuinely believed the Fox assets would do better combined with those of Disney, "if he was looking for top dollar, in many respects he got it."[26] Having paid some $18 billion more than he had intended for Fox, Iger was soon given an opportunity to recover some of Disney's money. Rupert Murdoch had come to the view that Fox's outstanding bid for the rest of Sky was going nowhere under the May government and was happy to handball the whole problem to Disney. Iger had described Sky as one of the crown jewels of the Fox deal and upped the bid, hoping again to trump Comcast. Roberts was determined not to miss out again and, after an intense one-day auction, emerged victorious with a whopping bid that valued the whole of Sky at $39 billion, a price that analysts feared represented gross overpayment. Disney recouped $15 billion for its 39 per cent stake, meaning it could pay down the huge debts it had incurred acquiring Fox.

For British regulators, the Comcast bid solved an unwanted political problem and the deal sailed through. The Sky sale price was both a vindication and an emotional wrench for Rupert who'd launched Sky in 1989 with a self-described "planeload of pirates" from Australia and literally risked his whole empire in the debt crisis. It was also difficult for James, who had transformed the company as CEO in the 2000s and consolidated the operations in Germany and Italy in preparation for a full takeover.

If Lachlan was proved right about one thing, it was that the first Disney bid had valued Fox far too cheaply. Having opposed the sale initially and then fought to garner interest from a counterbidder, Lachlan could look forward to a spectacular financial windfall, proceeds of the biggest deal of his lifetime. The sale valued the Murdoch Family Trust's 17 per cent stake in the Fox assets at some $12 billion, meaning the six children would get roughly $2 billion each in Disney shares. By mid-2018, with the sale approved by shareholders and well on the way to clearing regulatory approvals in the US, and his brother James now charting his own course beyond Fox and News, Lachlan could claim his place at the top of the business empire built by his father. As the media world buzzed about the first season of a hit new television series based loosely on the Murdoch family story, *Succession*, Lachlan had the comfort of knowing that in real life the battle had already been fought and won. By him.

18

Last Man Standing

UARANTEED THE TOP JOB, Lachlan moved quickly to stamp his authority on what would be left of Fox Corporation after the bulk of the business was sold to Disney. There was no point waiting weeks until 21st Century Fox shareholders approved the sale, much less months while regulators at home and abroad cleared the deal and the transaction finally completed. Lachlan wanted to project confidence and ensure the new Fox would hit the ground running, with himself firmly in command.

The first task was to pick his management team. Lachlan would later say he "literally started with a blank sheet of paper," but many of the appointments emphasized continuity rather than disruption. One appointment was especially significant to Lachlan: Viet Dinh would step off the Fox board and into an executive role as chief legal and policy officer. Lachlan had first met Dinh over a drink with Col Allan at an Aspen Institute conference at the Wye River in Maryland. Allan recalls there were strict rules at the conference, "about where you could go and what you could do so we decided 'to hell with that' [and] so Lachlan and I and Viet went into [Queenstown], outside the resort, into some sort of Honky Tonk bar and we were drinking vodka and playing pool." Dinh had just resigned as assistant attorney general under President George W. Bush, where he had written the *Patriot Act*, and was teaching law at

Georgetown University. Lachlan told Col he was really impressed with Dinh, then put him forward as a director of News Corp. When Lachlan's second son, Aidan, was born, he asked Viet to be the godfather. "It was just interesting that Lachlan identified Viet very quickly as somebody that was intelligent and could be valuable to the business," says Allan. "And he pursued him and you know, fifteen years later, here we are." Starting with a total package worth $24 million, including a $4.5 million sign-on bonus, Dinh was the third-highest-paid executive after Rupert and Lachlan on $42 million each. Dinh would become an increasingly powerful figure inside Fox.

Within days of his own role being confirmed publicly, Lachlan announced perhaps the most important appointment he could make: Suzanne Scott would become the first female chief executive of Fox News, the profit engine which analysts said represented 80 per cent of the value of the whole company. Previously considered one of Roger Ailes' key enforcers and enablers, Scott now represented a break with the heavily sexualized, male-dominated culture of the old Fox regime and her appointment burnished Lachlan's reputation for putting women into leadership roles. Intensely loyal, Scott rarely gave interviews and had kept a low profile as Fox's head of programming, running the opinion side of the news channel and quelling the endless controversies stoked by stars like Sean Hannity and Tucker Carlson. Lachlan credited her with helping to create "some of the most popular and lucrative primetime programs on cable." She would report jointly to Lachlan and Rupert, who remained executive chairman but was gradually stepping back from day-to-day responsibility. Jay Wallace was promoted to president of Fox News and remained executive editor, responsible for the news side. Jack Abernethy, the former Ailes confidant, shifted sideways to work alongside Lachlan in Los Angeles, running the Fox Television stations.

The appointment that overshadowed all these came a few months later when Lachlan hired former Trump aide Hope Hicks to become Fox's chief communications officer. Hicks had been one of the president's closest advisers since the very beginning of his campaign for the

Republican nomination. Having fallen into Trump's orbit doing PR for Ivanka's clothing line, Hicks was regarded as one of the only people who "totally understood" the president. She had quit the White House in February 2018, shortly after a tumultuous period including an awkward nine-hour appearance in closed-door hearings of the Mueller probe into collusion with Russia on the Trump campaign, in which she refused to discuss anything official but admitted telling occasional "white lies" in her job. With an unrivalled knowledge of the Trump administration and continuing close contact with the president and his family, Hicks spent months weighing her options, including flacking in the private sector or even writing a book about her experience in the White House. Not yet thirty, she resisted entreaties to switch to a career in television but agreed to meet with management at Fox's Sixth Avenue headquarters. Hicks had a one-on-one lunch there with Lachlan, who was looking for his own comms chief. Not only were Hicks's political connections impeccable, but she also knew how to handle the dynamic of a wealthy family headed by an unpredictable patriarch. Aware that she had interviewed for the Fox job, Trump lobbied Rupert personally on Hicks' behalf. She got the job, beginning the following year and when the news broke it confirmed the fears of many on the left that there was a "revolving door" between the Trump White House and Fox News. Bill Shine, the ousted former deputy to Ailes at Fox, had gone to work for Trump earlier in the year, joining a steady stream of Fox staffers and contributors who had become a part of the administration. Now, Hicks was headed the other way.

Lachlan's last major hire was finding someone to do the difficult job of running the entertainment side of the new Fox, for the first time without its own TV studio, which was being sold to Disney. That task was made more difficult by distaste in Hollywood for the divisive Fox News, whose primetime hosts remained rock-solid behind Trump even as his administration engendered a humanitarian crisis at the Mexican border, adopting a "zero tolerance" policy toward illegal immigrants that included separating children from their parents and housing them in detention centers. In June 2018, when Laura Ingraham described the child detention centers as "essentially summer camps [or] boarding schools," the co-creator of *Modern Family*, Steve Levitan, tweeted he was "disgusted to work at a company that has anything whatsoever to do with Fox News." *Modern Family* was produced by 20th Century Fox Television, which was being sold to Disney, but Levitan's criticism stung, all the more so because he was adding his voice to that of Seth MacFarlane, creator of the animated series *Family Guy*, which had been a Fox hit for more than a decade and would remain part of its new entertainment division. MacFarlane tweeted he was "embarrassed to work for this company," after Tucker Carlson told his viewers to "always assume the opposite of what they're telling you on the big news stations." MacFarlane wrote: "In other words, don't think critically, don't consult multiple news sources, and in general, don't use your brain. Just blindly obey Fox News. This is fringe s——."

Once again Rupert got personally involved in the delicate recruitment, calling cable network AMC president Charlie Collier, a pioneer of television's new golden age who had overseen production of the hits *Mad Men* and *Breaking Bad*. Over breakfast in Manhattan, Rupert asked Collier: "How would you like to run a start-up company?" Collier asked: "What's it called?" The answer was Fox, of course, and Collier's recruitment was announced in October. Collier would report to Lachlan, whom *The New York Times* reported was relatively unknown in Hollywood, compared with his brother James.[1] No longer tied to Fox's own studios and with a limited schedule of entertainment programming to fill, Collier was given a wide brief, able to green-light shows from anywhere.

Lachlan's core strategy was for the new, slimmed-down Fox to concentrate on the kind of live programming—news and sport—which offered huge audiences to advertizers and was less susceptible to an assault by the streamers. In the fall of 2018, Fox announced a major deal with the NFL to air Thursday night games. With exclusive rights to Major League Baseball and the NBA and traditional NFL games on Sunday, and rights to the FIFA World Cup until 2022, the Fox schedule was pretty much saturated with live sport.

Lachlan had a larger opportunity in mind. In a much-anticipated May ruling, the Supreme Court had overturned the Professional and Amateur Sports Protection Act, a 1992 federal law that banned commercial sports betting in most states. The landmark ruling paved the way for live sports betting to be opened up, state by state. Laws had already passed legislatures in Connecticut, Mississippi, New York, Pennsylvania, and West Virginia, and had been introduced in a dozen other jurisdictions. It was a gold rush and it was clear from the beginning that media companies with broadcast rights stood to gain from the deregulation of sports wagering, opening up a market that analysts estimated could quickly exceed $150 billion in annual revenue. It was generally assumed that dedicated sports channel ESPN would be the prime beneficiary, but Fox was first out of the blocks instead, and it was Lachlan driving the strategy.

News Corp had already made a small investment in an Australian online sports wagering company, PointsBet, through the Scaleup Mediafund. Set up in late 2016, the fund was a 40:20:20:20 partnership between News, Fox Sports, Nova, and Channel Ten and was meant to take minority stakes of less than 10 per cent in new digital ventures in exchange for contra advertizing. It was the kind of deal Lachlan had originally done with REA. News would contribute $1.5 million cash a year to the fund. Although based in Australia, PointsBet was heavily focussed on US sports and was the largest online bookmaker covering the NBA. Australia already had a mature, sophisticated market for live sports betting, with a plethora of domestic and international players, and Canadian giant the Stars Group had just pounced on a majority stake in CrownBet, a joint venture with James Packer's Crown Resorts, hoping to use its online wagering technology in the US. Lachlan's favorite football game, rugby league, featured wall-to-wall gambling ads and he knew in his bones that live sports betting in America could be an order of magnitude bigger. Studies showed bettors watched twice as much sports coverage as non-bettors, as every second of every game of every week turned into a gambling opportunity. One sports lawyer described the phenomenon as the "gamblization of sports."[2] Lachlan was quick to work out that digital sports betting was one of those areas in which Australia happened to be ahead of the US, and he could use his experience down under to give Fox an early-mover advantage in the US, just as he had done with REA and digital real estate, which by now underpinned the worldwide operations of News Corp.

Another precedent was in Lachlan's mind: his own brother's success investing in online gambling in the UK. The Murdochs had made a fortune out of SkyBet, which was the market leader in Britain, and was sold to the Stars Group in 2018 for $4.7 billion, creating the world's largest publicly listed online gambling firm. Lachlan figured Fox should be able to pull off in America what Sky had been able to do in the UK.

In the fall of 2018, Lachlan called the best minds across the Murdoch empire to the Fox Studios in Hollywood to come up with a sports betting strategy. "The goal was unashamedly to mirror the success of SkyBet," says one person who was present. "We spoke to everyone, and everyone wanted to speak with us, but the most logical partner was the owner of SkyBet. Who was that? The Stars Group." Lachlan was "all in" from the beginning, even as the industry struggled to shed its fringe reputation, and other players such as ESPN hesitated, and in doing so he put Fox in a position to jump on what some consider "the single biggest tailwind for legacy media in the last century."

* * *

Back in Australia, Lachlan was soon facing accusations he had helped orchestrate the downfall of Prime Minister Malcolm Turnbull. By mid-2018, the Turnbull government was travelling poorly, behind in the polls and scrambling to retain its one-seat majority after months of by-elections triggered by what was billed as the world's most ridiculous constitutional crisis, with a procession of sitting MPs ruled ineligible because they were found to be dual citizens. More seriously, having abolished a carbon tax in 2014, the coalition government remained bitterly divided over energy and climate change. Commentators across the Murdoch media were squarely behind the conservatives on climate, drumming up speculation about the potential for a leadership challenge from the home affairs minister, Peter Dutton. In his memoir *A Bigger Picture*, Turnbull would later accuse Dutton of "conspiring with News Corporation—a foreign-owned media company."[3]

Lachlan jetted into Sydney on Sunday, August 12, ahead of News Corp's annual journalism awards, a fixture on the calendar for him and his father, who'd arrived two days earlier. On Tuesday night, Lachlan and Sarah hosted drinks at their Bellevue Hill home for a small group of senior managers and staff, mostly from Sky News. As *The New York Times* would later reveal, at one point during the conversation Lachlan asked, "Do you think Malcolm is going to survive?" It could be interpreted as a perfectly innocent question, or as a coded instruction that the Murdochs believed the PM's leadership was terminal. Either way, word of Lachlan's question got back to Turnbull's office, where a former editor of *The Australian*, Clive Mathieson, was chief of staff. *The Times* reported that the PM's office contacted executives at News in an effort to get a meeting with the Murdochs and ward off what seemed to be a concerted campaign against Turnbull, texting they knew "Lachlan had made it clear at the editors' drinks on Tuesday night that he would like MT to get rolled."[4] It would emerge later in disputed accounts that on the Thursday of that week, rival media mogul Kerry Stokes had a private meeting with Lachlan and Rupert at Holt Street. It was mainly to talk business, but according to the well-connected *AFR* columnist Joe Aston, the conversation went as follows:

> RUPERT MURDOCH: Malcolm has got to go.
> KERRY STOKES: That means we get Bill Shorten and the CFMEU.
> RUPERT MURDOCH: They'll only be in for three years— it won't be so bad. I did alright under Labor and the Painters and Dockers; I can make money under Shorten and the CFMEU.[5]

Lachlan later told *The Monthly* magazine that the reported conversation was wrong: "I was the only other person in the meeting and [Rupert

Murdoch] definitely never said 'Malcolm's got to go' or mused on how business would be under a Labor government. His mind doesn't work like that and I have never heard him say anything like it.'" Stokes similarly rejected the characterization and details of the reported conversation, but Turnbull dumped him in it on national television by revealing he had got the account from Stokes firsthand.[6]

Whether the Murdochs were behind it all or not, the knives were out for Turnbull. On the Friday morning, *The Daily Telegraph* splashed a story predicting that Dutton would challenge within weeks. From that point, things unfolded very quickly and by Tuesday morning, as politicians returned to Canberra, Turnbull had thrown open the leadership to a ballot in which he beat Dutton by forty-eight votes to thirty-five, a margin narrow enough that a second challenge was almost certain.

The next day, Turnbull finally got to have his long-awaited conversation with Rupert, by phone, although Rupert was still in the country. According to the verbatim account of the conversation in Turnbull's memoir, the embattled prime minister accused the Murdoch newspapers of firing up the Dutton insurgency, along with *Sky After Dark* hosts, including Peta Credlin, the former chief of staff to Turnbull's nemesis, Tony Abbott:

MALCOLM TURNBULL: This whole exercise is seen as being written and directed by your company. Credlin and Abbott's fingerprints are all over it. This has been a whole process of destabilization, and Bill Shorten, the most left-wing leader since Whitlam, will be the beneficiary. Do you seriously want us to lose, so that Abbott can come back in opposition? It's crazy.

RUPERT MURDOCH: I think Boris [Paul Whittaker, editor of *The Australian*] is the only one who wants to do that. But Abbott would say that's what you did to him.

MALCOLM TURNBULL: Rupert, it's not the same. I went to Abbott, told him that I was going to challenge him, and won the ballot. If I'd lost, I would've gone, and I told him that. This has been a News Corp-backed guerrilla campaign against me.

Paul Kelly would agree with everything I have said to you; that's madness.

RUPERT MURDOCH: We can't have an election now . . . let me talk to Lachlan. I'm retired. I'll talk to Lachlan.[7]

Whether Rupert did speak to Lachlan about his conversation with Turnbull remains unclear, but his deflection to his son was a telling admission to a desperate prime minister. In truth, the coverage from *The Australian* and Sky News was hostile to Turnbull's government before the Murdochs arrived in the country, particularly on climate and energy policy, and it remained so afterwards. If Turnbull had hoped it might let up after he spoke with the ageing proprietor, he was badly mistaken. A then senior editor recalls the ageing mogul was left bemused after the conversation with Turnbull: "He asked me what the hell was going on. He didn't even really know who Peter Dutton was. I think at the time, he hadn't even met him, or maybe he'd met him very briefly, but . . . he wanted to know what his policies were and what he stood for. Rupert knew nothing about him. He was flummoxed by the whole thing. It is rubbish to say there was some agenda."

That same afternoon, after three of his most senior cabinet ministers defected to the Dutton camp, the prime minister knew he was done for. Turnbull and his supporters threw all their effort into backing an alternative to Dutton, Scott Morrison, who won by forty-five votes to forty and became Australia's sixth prime minister in a decade. Turnbull's downfall prompted more global headlines marvelling how the country had become the "coup capital of the democratic world," as BBC correspondent Nick Bryant dubbed it.[8]

In the aftermath, respected ABC political commentator Chris Uhlmann accused News and Sky of going beyond their remit as journalists by campaigning against Turnbull and becoming players in the leadership contest inside the Liberal Party. "If they are making phone calls to people trying to push people over the line, then they're part of the story," Uhlmann told Nine's *Today Show*. "They're among the biggest bullies in the land and it's about time that people called them out for what they are."[9]

Turnbull's memoir, published in 2020, argued that Rupert and Lachlan Murdoch resented his prime ministership because he was not deferential to them. As a successful businessman in his own right, he was personally and financially independent, his "own man."

The ousted PM wrote that News Corp no longer behaved like a media outlet, but "operates now like a political party," joined at the hip with the coalition, just as in the United States, Fox News' relationship with Trump and the GOP was "like that of the state-owned media of an authoritarian government."[10]

19

Wages of Fear

THE STAKES WERE INCREDIBLY HIGH in the 2018 midterm elections in the US and it was obvious to President Trump and his supporters that the loss of a Republican majority in the House of Representatives would likely lead straight to an impeachment trial. The bitter Senate confirmation hearings of Trump Supreme Court pick Brett Kavanaugh, a former member of a dinner club which included Viet Dinh, and whose nomination was announced on Fox by Sean Hannity, took place in the lead-up to the election and generated enormous ratings for the channel.

Fox News went completely overboard in its coverage of a caravan of thousands of Central American migrants en route to the US, embedding a reporter among the throng, known as La Bestia or "The Beast," to cover the supposed "invasion" live. Primetime host Laura Ingraham described the refugees as an "invading horde," and Trump himself tweeted the term "invasion" and ordered 5,000 troops to the border, implying there were terrorists among the crowd. The hysteria was completely unfounded. The caravan was 1,700 miles from the border. An administration official admitted to *The Daily Beast*, "It doesn't matter if it's 100 percent accurate . . . this is the play." Fox would drop the whole caravan story the day after the election.

Meanwhile, the fearmongering continued and some viewers took the hysteria to heart. At the height of the manufactured crisis, pipe bombs were mailed to a dozen prominent Democrats, including Barack Obama, Hillary Clinton, Joe Biden, and Kamala Harris, as well as former national intelligence director James Clapper and Jewish billionaire George Soros, a bogeyman of the far right, constantly vilified by anti-Semites and anti-globalists. The FBI quickly traced the mail bombs to Cesar Sayoc, Jr, a fifty-six-year-old Republican and fervent Trump supporter from Florida, who was a former bankrupt with a criminal history dating back to 1991.

Then, in a particularly sinister episode of *Lou Dobbs Tonight* on Fox Business, a guest, Chris Farrell, director of conservative activist and watchdog group Judicial Watch, suggested the whole caravan was being funded by the "Soros-occupied State Department." Fox News daytime anchor Shep Smith valiantly sought to correct the record, saying: "The president has called it an ASSAULT on the US border. It is absolutely not." On October 27, 2018, a lone shooter entered the Tree of Life synagogue in Pittsburgh and killed eleven worshippers, the country's worst-ever attack on the Jewish community. The alleged shooter, Robert Bowers, a neo-Nazi sympathizer who is still awaiting trial, blamed Jews for the caravan, raged on social media about the Hebrew Immigrant Aid Society, a group that helped resettle refugees, bringing "invaders in that kill our people," and repeatedly posted an image from a Fox News report that showed a truck emblazoned with a Star of David helping to transport asylum seekers to the US border. In the wake of the attack, Fox pulled the Dobbs episode from rotation, banned Farrell from any future appearances, and apologized. Nonetheless, *New York Times* star columnist Paul Krugman wrote, "there's a straight line from Fox News coverage of the caravan to the Tree of Life massacre," while in *The Washington Post*, Jennifer Rubin wrote that the Pittsburgh massacre should cause self-reflection at Fox:

> Unless and until Fox cleans up its act—drop conspiracies made up out of whole cloth, end demonization and hysteria about immigrants, and stop invoking Soros to explain every political

threat (real or imagined)—people of good will should not appear on Fox News, advertize on it or watch it.[1]

Modern Family co-creator Steve Levitan again weighed in, and this time made it personal, tweeting: "I sincerely hope Lachlan Murdoch recognizes the damage this is doing and finally brings sound journalistic ethics and standard to his network before more unhinged people are riled up to send bombs and shoot up churches and synagogues. I'm not going to do anything for the Fox network ever again as long as Fox News remains such a destructive voice in our society."

Five days after the Pittsburgh massacre, Lachlan Murdoch did a wide-ranging Q&A with veteran business journalist Andrew Ross Sorkin at *The New York Times* Dealbook conference and was put on the spot about Levitan's criticisms and Fox News more broadly. Murdoch described Levitan as a "genius story-teller" whom he knew "pretty well," and said he understood exactly where he was coming from. But he continued that Fox's biggest critics were "frankly . . . not watching Fox News," and were instead reacting to controversies on Twitter and elsewhere. He said the straight news coverage on Fox during the day, anchored by Shep Smith, Chris Wallace, and Martha MacCallum, drew 22 million viewers on average, while the opinion programming from *Fox & Friends* in the morning to primetime in the evening, drew just 14 million. Asked if he was upset about the *Lou Dobbs Tonight* segment, Lachlan said, "We wouldn't ban him and apologize if [we] didn't think it was a mistake." Asked about Sayoc, who lived in a van plastered with a huge "CNN Sucks" sticker, Lachlan again pushed back: "I don't take responsibility for a criminal who was a criminal before Fox News even started, right . . . [and] I think it's unfair to make that criticism of me or Fox News or of any other media organization." Lachlan opened up further, describing himself still as a conservative on economic policy and more liberal on social policy:

> . . . so I don't fit neatly into a left–right, Republican–Democrat bucket, right? . . . I think you need to be, particularly running

media organizations, you need to be an independent thinker. What I do find is that when people tell me to think a certain way, or that I should think a certain way, I'm more inclined to think a different way, or certainly examine, 'Why are they telling me that'?

It was as neat a summation of his personal politics and philosophy as Lachlan had ever given publicly. At the end of the session, *New Yorker* journalist and shrewd Murdoch observer Ken Auletta asked Lachlan how he reconciled his more liberal views on social policy with the social conservatism on Fox News, and whether he planned to make any changes.

MURDOCH: I do have strong views on these things [but] I've run newspapers since I was twenty-one or twenty-two years old . . . I don't tell journalists what to say, or what to write. That's not my role. What I do do, running a media organization, is obviously, you know, work closely with the managers of those newsrooms and with the managers of those newspapers, and it's important that they get the positioning and the messaging right. We don't always get it right, and we have to call ourselves out on that when we make a mistake.

AULETTA: I understand that . . . but are you embarrassed by what they do?

MURDOCH: No, I'm not embarrassed by what they do at all. You have to understand that Fox News is the only mass media company in America, in this country, with conservative opinion, with strong conservative opinion in prime time . . . it's not one of a few, it's the only one. And I frankly feel in this country, we all have to be more tolerant of each other's views. And that does for everyone, everyone in this room, everyone in this country, everyone on both coasts, and in the middle. And that's the problem—we've come to this point where we are more and more intolerant of each other and frankly that just has to change.[2]

Such nuanced reflections and debate were a world away from the partisanship and misinformation that was nightly fare on Fox News' primetime programming, however. Perhaps the crowning controversy of Fox's midterm election coverage was a decision by Sean Hannity to join President Trump as a "special guest" at his last official campaign rally, in Cape Girardeau, Missouri. Hannity was scheduled to interview the president live beforehand for his show, but had explicitly denied the claim, made in a Trump campaign press release, that he was himself on the bill. When Trump asked him to come onstage, however, Hannity agreed. Pointing to the rest of the media up the back of the hall, including Fox correspondents, Hannity labelled them all "fake news" and publicly endorsed the president by repeating his re-election slogan: "Promises made, promises kept." Fellow Fox News host Jeanine Pirro did likewise. Hannity later tweeted that he was surprised and honored by Trump's invitation, insisting: "This was NOT planned." Fox News issued a statement saying: "FOX News does not condone any talent participating in campaign events . . . this was an unfortunate distraction and has been addressed." How the flagrant breach had been addressed, if at all, was not clear—there was no apparent punishment for Hannity or Pirro—but the nakedly partisan display would not be forgotten, including by many of the straight news journalists at Fox.

The Democrats regained the House in the midterms and in the wash-up came a new bout of soul-searching about the impact of the Trump presidency on the media and on Fox News in particular. Roger Ailes' biographer Gabriel Sherman decried the absence of leadership at Fox since Ailes' downfall, describing the atmosphere at the network as every man for himself, with no one clearly in charge. Lachlan Murdoch had never been a political junkie like his father, Sherman wrote, and hardly ever attended Fox News morning editorial meetings. If he did, he was polite and tended to ask questions rather than give instructions. Lachlan was content to let the Fox machine run and be "a caretaker rather than an empire builder."[3]

For the first time, the activist group Media Matters for America did some opposition research on Lachlan Murdoch, recognizing he was increasingly calling the shots at Fox. Examining his business and personal relationships in a power-mapping exercise, Media Matters' aim was to identify how Lachlan was different from his father and whether there was a pressure point which could be used to make Fox a less destructive force in American politics. The organization's president, Angelo Carusone, recalls that what they found out about Lachlan was kind of frightening: he had few friends in politics or the media and was purely interested in making more money. If that meant chasing a perceived gap in the market by turning Fox News into MAGA media, so be it. In a way, that tendency to be hands-off editorially and to place profits above all else made Lachlan a bigger threat than Rupert. "It seemed that he just didn't care," says Carusone. "There's nothing tethering him." For Lachlan, Fox was simply "a cash grab . . . he doesn't have a long-term vision for the company." Media Matters gave Lachlan their "Misinformer of the Year" award for 2018, declaring:

> Fox News' transformation into an unchained pro-Trump propaganda outlet that promotes white nationalism came as Lachlan Murdoch's control over the network steadily increased . . . If he wanted the network to operate as a responsible media outlet, he could make that happen. Instead, he suggests that any attempt to rein in his network's stars would constitute unacceptable censorship of their opinions. Whether the media scion, who is reportedly seen as more conservative than his father, is encouraging the network to shift in its direction or simply standing idly by as it moves, he is happy to profit from the forces he continues to unleash. Lachlan Murdoch is gaslighting America about the damage Fox News is doing to the country. For these reasons, he is the Misinformer of the Year.

Lachlan saw this kind of criticism as left-wing bullying and, if anything, it reinforced his determination to stand behind Fox News and its provocative stars. True to his word, he doubled down and made his influence felt across both Fox and News. At the beginning of 2019, Rupert and Lachlan brough the feared former *New York Post* editor Col Allan back as a consultant and News Corp chief Robert Thomson announced that the newspaper's CEO and publisher Jesse Angelo would leave the company after twenty years. Allan was a known Trump supporter—he wore his MAGA hat in the newsroom during the 2016 election. Pundits immediately speculated that the *Post* was being brought into line ahead of the 2020 cycle. Allan insists that he was never asked to stir up support for Trump but says that Rupert and Lachlan were concerned that the *Post* had lost its way since he retired. "The paper had become a little soft in its views," Allan says, and "[Rupert] wanted me to return it to where it was."

* * *

The broader significance of Angelo's ouster from the *Post* was the widening divide between Lachlan and James, whose influence was already being purged from the Murdoch empire. Although Angelo had worked alongside Lachlan at both *The Daily Telegraph* in Sydney and the *New York Post*, he was closest to James: the former roommates had studied together at Harvard and Jesse was best man at James' wedding to Kathryn. With the Murdoch brothers now increasingly at odds, it was getting harder to remain good friends with both of them. While Lachlan did not feel embarrassed by Fox News, James certainly did and with a role at Disney now off the table, he was beginning to chart his own course in preparation for the multi-billion-dollar windfall coming his way when the Disney transaction completed. In September 2018 he had leased a new office in Manhattan's West Village for his venture capital firm Lupa Systems and had begun hiring staff. In a way, James was doing much as his older brother had done with Illyria more than a decade earlier. Asked some months later what involvement he would have in his family's businesses after the Disney sale, James quipped: "Precisely zero."[4] Angelo would re-emerge mid-year as head of news and entertainment at Vice Media, where Lupa was already an investor.

If the "blue wave" marked the beginning of the end of the Trump presidency, the midterms also gave Fox News a gift in the form of "the Squad," four young, hard-left congresswomen who had unseated Democratic incumbents and won election to the House, of whom former waitress Alexandria Ocasio-Cortez from New York was best known. Fox hosts relentlessly derided the Squad, who were mostly supporters of avowed socialist presidential hopeful Bernie Sanders, until Jeanine Pirro overstepped the mark by attacking Minnesota representative Ilhan Omar, a Somali-born Muslim, as "un-American" and asking whether her hijab was "indicative of her adherence to sharia law, which in itself is antithetical to the United States Constitution." Suzanne Scott suspended Pirro over the Islamophobic rant, issuing a statement that: "We strongly condemn Jeanine Pirro's comments about Rep. Ilhan Omar. They do not reflect those of the network, and we have addressed the matter with her directly." The Fox statement did not quote and was not vetted by Lachlan, who was not into virtue-signalling and was happy to let Scott handle it. Trump tweeted his support for his friend Pirro, fretting that Fox was turning liberal and should "stop working soooo hard on being politically correct." Pirro was back on air in a fortnight.

One person seemed almost to be a protected species at Fox: Tucker Carlson, the controversy magnet who was gradually overtaking Sean Hannity as the network's biggest star. There was a dark side to Carlson and as his popularity soared, the scrutiny and pressure ratcheted up. As Lachlan prepared for the new Fox's first pitch to advertizers for the 2019–2020 season, Media Matters published a trove of leaked messages from a far-right chat site in which a white supremacist group Identity Evropa celebrated Carlson for delivering extremist talking points, saying he had "done more for" their cause than they "could ever hope to."[5] A week later, Media Matters dropped a damning collection of cuts from Carlson's weekly appearances on a radio show hosted by Florida shock jock Bubba the Love Sponge. In the unearthed audio, from 2006 to 2011, Carlson had mocked a Miss Teen USA contestant—"so dumb"—and joked about having sex with her, amid a stream of other misogynistic, homophobic and racist remarks, including that Iraq was "a crappy place filled with a bunch of, you know, semiliterate primitive monkeys [who] don't use toilet paper or forks."

Carlson put on a brave face, refusing to apologize on-air that Monday and saying Media Matters was working to kill his show. Promising never to "bow to the mob," he refused to "express the usual ritual contrition" and insisted he had the full support of his network bosses: "Fox News is behind us as they have been since the very first day." It was true, and the management support went right to the top: Lachlan was in Carlson's corner. For Lachlan, it was an issue of free speech, which as the head of a media organization he was obliged to defend. In a landmark ruling that does the rounds at Fox, *New York Times Co. v. United States*, US Supreme Court Justice Hugo Black argued that a free press not only meant holding the government accountable; it also meant supporting "a vibrant marketplace of ideas, a vehicle for ordinary citizens to express themselves and gain exposure to a wide range of information and opinions." A vibrant marketplace of ideas, serving to raise the standard of public debate, must offer a diversity of news and opinion, and if most of the media leaned to the left, then Lachlan felt Fox had a responsibility, even an obligation, to serve up a right-leaning point of view. It was almost as if the cab-rank rule applied to media proprietors: just as the worst criminals have a right to legal representation, so too somebody in the news business had to represent the center-right. A higher purpose was involved, and for better or worse, by virtue of his family history and circumstance, the job of owning, running and defending Fox and News had fallen to Lachlan. In another universe, Lachlan might have been born the proprietor of a small-l liberal media empire, but as things stood, he would go into bat for his side like any barrister and keep his innermost thoughts on his client's guilt or innocence to himself. His closest advisers say a belief in free speech, in all its diversity, is Lachlan's "north star." At Fox Corporation, notwithstanding Lachlan's frequent dismissal of corporate governance "box-ticking," they point to their corporate social responsibility report, which states:

We zealously guard and defend our journalists in their search for the truth. Indeed, we believe so strongly in these core values that we have often come to the defense of our competitors, recognizing that a free press benefits all of us and requires the support of each and every one of us.

What part misogyny, homophobia or racism played in the "search for truth" was, and is, unclear, and Tucker Carlson would test the outer limits of Lachlan's commitment to free speech repeatedly over the next few years. Media Matters organized a "Drop Fox" protest outside the company's 6th Avenue headquarters to remind advertizers of the potential brand damage from an association with Fox News. *Business Insider* tallied thirty-three advertizers that had dumped Carlson's program since December, although Fox insisted overall ad revenue was up 6 per cent during the quarter. Fox adopted a new marketing slogan: "America is watching," intended to highlight the channel's news operations rather than its opinion programming. It was a favored theme of Lachlan's, playing down the significance of the nightly outrages on Fox News by reminding critics of the many hours of straight programming outside primetime. From now on, Lachlan would be held increasingly responsible for everything that went to air on the network, and with his own reputation on the line would be constantly doing damage control.

20

The Power of Now

AFTER MONTHS OF PREPARATION and a lifetime's apprenticeship, by early 2019 Lachlan was fully focussed on the looming spin-off of the new Fox Corporation, set down for March 19. The thumping price fetched for the family business had helped reconcile him to the diminution of the empire. His friend Chris Silbermann, founding partner at talent and literary agency ICM Partners, compared the situation to Rupert Murdoch inheriting two Adelaide newspapers in 1952 and building them into a global media juggernaut. "Lachlan is looking at it in a similar way," said Silbermann.[1]

A day before the transaction completed, Fox announced the appointment of new directors, notably including the former House speaker Paul Ryan, an establishment Republican who had announced his retirement at the midterms. "The spin" of Fox, as it would come to be known inside the company, was the first step in a complex $71 billion transaction that unfolded hour-by-hour over two days of trade: first 21st Century Fox shareholders hived off the businesses which would be retained (principally Fox News, Fox Sports and Fox Broadcasting) and exchanged them for shares in a new listed entity, Fox Corporation; second, the businesses that were being sold to Disney (principally the 20th Century Fox film and television studios) were exchanged for either cash or Disney shares, depending on the preference of individual shareholders; finally, the old 21st Century Fox ceased to exist.

Early on, it had been assumed that the Murdoch Family Trust, as the most substantial shareholder, would be certain to take Disney shares to avoid any capital gains tax liability. If they were united, personally and financially, the Murdoch family could have become Disney's largest shareholders with a combined stake of more than 5 per cent and a seat on the board. In the weeks before the sale completed, however, the Bloomberg Billionaires Index reported that the Murdochs had declined an offer of board representation and that the cash and Disney shares worth $12 billion would be distributed among Rupert's children.

Given none of the Murdochs would hold more than 5 per cent of Disney, the threshold above which reporting became mandatory under US corporate law, the details of individual holdings remained undisclosed. Assuming, however, like most observers, that Lachlan took Disney shares rather than cash, he would have gained 17 million, worth $1.9 billion at the time of the merger. It was a stunning inheritance in itself, not to mention that it came on top of the separate stakes in the new Fox and News, which Lachlan retained through the Murdoch family trust and were valued at roughly $675 million and $160 million at the time of the Disney deal, making a fortune of at least $2.7 billion. Quite apart from all that, of course, Lachlan had his private vehicle Illyria, with major asset Nova in Australia, and a portfolio of prestige properties, including mansions in LA, Aspen, and Sydney. According to the 2019 rich list in the *Australian Financial Review*, Lachlan Murdoch was now worth at AUD$3.6billion, less any debt—and that figure looked conservative

In theory at least, Lachlan was now rich enough to buy his siblings out of the family business for good. In a scintillating three-part investigation of the Murdoch empire, "Planet Fox," published straight after completion of the Disney deal, *The New York Times*' Jonathan Mahler and Jim Rutenberg revealed that the previous year, James, Elisabeth, and Prudence had enthusiastically supported the idea of selling out to Lachlan, leaving their brother and Rupert to own and manage the empire together. Rupert, the *Times* reported:

. . . was excited about the idea, seeing it as an opportunity to rid the company of an in-house critic. He urged Lachlan to do it: the two of them, father and son, would own the company together. The documents were drawn up, but in late 2018, given the chance to have the company to himself, Lachlan balked. (Through a spokesman, Lachlan said that buying out his siblings wasn't financially feasible.)[2]

Nobody has revealed the asking price, but in round figures the three siblings' one-sixth stakes in the Murdoch Family Trust's 40 per cent holdings in the voting shares of Fox and News Corporation were worth at least $5 billion combined at the time, which would have been a stretch for Lachlan, but not impossible with Rupert's backing and the right financial structure. Lachlan came to the view, however, that he had nothing to gain from a buyout: he was already in control of the family business, so it wouldn't give him any more or less than he already had. Sources close to other members of the Murdoch family now say the three siblings' share of the trust is no longer for sale: "There was a window where that was a possibility, and Lachlan wasn't able to secure the funds."

The Disney transaction was the occasion for a $123 million corporate splurge designed to compensate the top people at Fox for the lost opportunity to take severance payments from 21st Century Fox as a result of the sale—a kiss-off from the old company. Of the overall amount, $51 million went to four executives named in the proxy filings, Rupert, Lachlan, John Nallen and Steve Tomsic, while another $60 million went to unnamed senior executives. Just $2 million was left for the bulk of the new Fox's 7,000-odd employees. Lachlan's own filings with the Securities and Exchange Commission show that in the week leading up to the merger, he liquidated more than $15 million worth of stock in 21st Century Fox. The rest of his holding appears to have gone straight into the LKM Family Trust. All told, in the five years since his return to the fold, Lachlan had received compensation from Fox and News worth at least $148 million. It was part of a staggering haul by the Murdoch men of an estimated $932 million in nominal compensation over the previous twenty years at both Fox and News. Lachlan's share of that haul was smallest (bearing in mind he was out of the business as an executive for almost a decade) but was still at least $172 million. To celebrate their newfound wealth, Lachlan and Sarah started hunting in earnest for a bigger and better home in LA. As he had done at a few key financial milestones in his life, Lachlan had already begun obsessing about buying a bigger yacht—*much* bigger.

The day after the Disney sale completed, Lachlan held his first town hall meeting for employees at the Fox lot in Hollywood. Lachlan liked to turn up to work in a big brown RAM 1500 pickup truck, roomy enough so he could drop the kids off to school on the way, and he had the entrance to the lot emblazoned with a banner reading "Welcome to Fox," just to make it clear to staff who still owned the physical space following the Disney sale. At the town hall meeting, Lachlan announced an employee share scheme, declaring: "You're all owners . . . each and every one of you has a voice and we want it to be heard." Under the scheme, Fox employees with under ten years' service received $1,000 in stock, while those with ten to twenty years received $2,000, and those with twenty years' service received $3,000. Meant to ensure employee loyalty to Fox, the share scheme also provided a contrast to the new Disney, where thousands of workers were expected to be laid off.

Within days, Lachlan had jetted back to Sydney with Sarah and the kids to celebrate a significant milestone: the couple's twentieth wedding anniversary. Beginning with a Friday-night knees-up on the top floor of the swanky Bondi Icebergs club, directly overlooking the beach, the lavish partying would go on for three days. Family and friends flew in from across Australia and around the world and were greeted by a hungry gaggle of journalists waiting to pap them on their way in. Anna was at the Icebergs party, as were Lachlan's Sydney-based half-sister Prue and her husband Alasdair MacLeod, but there was no sign of either of his full siblings. A handful of executives were there from inside the Murdoch empire, including his right-hand at Illyria, Siobhan McKenna, Cathy O'Connor from Nova, Brian Walsh from Foxtel, and News UK stalwart Rebekah

Brooks, out from London. Of their invited friends, there was Collette Dinnigan, who'd originally introduced the couple, *Vogue* editor Edwina McCann, and a bevy of billionaire mates including James Packer and his former wife, Erica (and her new boyfriend), mining mogul Andrew Forrest, rival media scion Ryan Stokes. Lachlan and Sarah's political bestie, Tony Abbott, was there along with his former treasurer, Joe Hockey, who was now US ambassador. Asked the secret to his long marriage, Lachlan told *Sydney Morning Herald* gossip columnist Andrew Hornery the answer was simple: "Sarah is an amazing wife."

The next day, Lachlan and family drove off down the highway to Cavan for a Saturday night party hosted by Rupert and Jerry. If the anniversary celebrations were a peek at the Australian elite, it was also fascinating who had not been invited, including the groomsman, Joe Cross, and his old sparring partner from the nineties, Ian Roberts. Plenty of others who had been left behind. The Lachlan caravan rolled on without them. For many who were previously close to the Murdochs, friends and employees of Rupert and his children alike, it felt strange to find yourself on the outs, often without reason and certainly without explanation, not bitter so much as puzzled over what went wrong.

* * *

Lachlan returned to LA refreshed and thoroughly incentivized by a new three-year contract at Fox that would reap him at least $60 million over the years to mid-2022, and possibly as much as $72 million. The contract allowed Lachlan to terminate his employment for "good reason" (unless within twelve months of a change of control of Fox), which harked back to his 2005 decision to leave News Corp when he believed he was being blocked. Lachlan's contract was announced at the end of April 2019 and investors barely raised an eyebrow. He spent most of the month closing a deal with Rafi Ashkenazi, CEO of the Canadian gaming giant Stars Group, to launch the new Fox Bet app. Fox would provide the sports content and the audience while Stars would do the odds and handle the technology side. Fox was not a licensed bookmaker and did not intend to become one. The deal included a $236 million investment by Fox, which would take 5 per cent of Stars, as well as a clause which gave Fox an option to take a half-stake in Stars' sports betting business in the US. The options were a critical part of the deal, giving Fox significant leverage to the economic upside of Fox Bet with minimal upfront outlay and without having to get a bookmaker's license. The Fox Bet deal was timed to perfection, coming out the morning of the company's first investor day, held on May 9 at Credit Suisse's offices in New York. The quarterly figures provided a baseline snapshot of the company Lachlan was now running: revenue was up to almost $12 billion a year with $2 billion in profits.

* * *

Rupert welcomed investors, reminding them that the new company's journey had "started, really, with a little newspaper many years ago in Australia." He commended Lachlan's "proven leadership" and quickly handed over to his son, the chief executive. Just seven weeks after "the spin," Lachlan was pumped. Paying tribute to his father, Lachlan said the roots of the company began in 1985, when News bought "a relatively tired movie studio that was short on cash and lacking ambition" and saw an opportunity to create a media company around the Fox brand, creating the Fox Network, Fox stations, Fox Sports and ultimately Fox News—the core businesses of the new Fox Corp. Describing Fox as "the best brand you could ever want," Lachlan stressed that with the exception of the Fox stations, those businesses were "all built from the ground up." Lachlan promised to be disciplined with acquisitions. It was unsaid, but the inference was clear that he would not launch overpriced takeover bids like his father, and in the face of commentary that Fox was going in the opposite direction to its peers, who were all seeking to up-scale, he reiterated that he saw "no logic" in reversing the 2013 separation of Fox and News Corp. "We will not reunite," he insisted. Lachlan said he wanted the new Fox to have a start-up culture and described the structure of the diminished company, now wholly focused on the US, as "insanely simple: half of our revenue is from contracted, growing affiliate relationships, and half is from advertizing, of which about 70 per cent comes from live news and sport." In a prize bit of management-speak, Lachlan called this focus on live content the "power of now," and the theme was hammered home by the execs who followed. In the Q&A afterwards, one broker asked whether the de-platforming of conservative voices by Facebook and Twitter might present an opportunity for Fox. "That's not a controversial question at all," Lachlan responded, and his answer was revealing:

> . . . we see our audience as not a linear TV audience . . . we see our future as not being just two revenue streams where you have affiliate revenue and you have advertizing revenue. And absolutely we think in both of those streams we can grow and grow aggressively. But the ability to tap into that audience and tap into the passion around those brands to create new businesses— new technologies and new business models—we think is incredibly exciting. And Fox News is a great example of that because the strength of that brand and what it means to middle Americans— many, many Americans—is remarkable. I always use the example of when our Fox News hosts write books, and they are books from history books to political books to cookbooks, they shoot to the top of *The New York Times* best seller lists. And so clearly, our audience is engaged with us not just around the breaking news of the day or the opinion in prime time, but really about . . . they have an emotional engagement to the Fox brand in a much richer and more important way. And that's an engagement we can do much more with . . . [and] monetize more efficiently.

It was a succinct encapsulation of Lachlan Murdoch's philosophy: to extract more and more profit from the particular passions and loyalty aroused by Fox content. At the end of the day's trade, Fox shares were up a few per cent, nothing to crow about, but better than a thumbs down from investors after Lachlan's first big outing as CEO.

Lachlan would soon demonstrate the kind of new businesses he had in mind, to "monetize more efficiently" the eyeballs on Fox News, Fox Business, Fox Sports, and Fox Entertainment. In August, Fox acquired a $265 million two-thirds stake in San Francisco-based, Australian-listed Credible Labs, which had developed a personal finance app that compared loans and matched borrowers and lenders, a challenger to US-based LendingTree. It was Fox's first move into the booming fintech sector and the deal was generous. Credible was losing money yet the bid was priced at a 30 per cent premium to the prevailing share price. The 35-year-old, Queensland-born founder, Stephen Dash, would continue to run Credible in partnership with Fox. He likened the deal to Lachlan's investment in REA Group, saying, "There's a lot of similarities in the potential." One shrewd columnist observed that Credible seemed far outside Fox's core competency, and that the acquisition sent a signal that Lachlan might rebuild the slimmed-down empire he'd inherited "in ways you might not expect of a Rupert scion."[3] Credible would be one of a string of modestly sized, bolt-on acquisitions Lachlan would unveil as Fox chief over the next few years.

There is no doubt that taking on the top job at Fox Corp gave Lachlan more clout. A demonstration came during the annual Australia–US Ministerial Consultations (AUSMIN), bilateral security talks that in 2019 were held down under in early August and were dominated by discussions of Iran, China, and North Korea. US Secretary of State Mike Pompeo and Defense Secretary Mark Esper both touched down in Sydney on the Saturday ahead of talks with their Australian counterparts the next day and an official dinner at Kirribilli House, Prime Minister Scott Morrison's Sydney residence. Unknown to the public, and unreported until now, Pompeo spent the Saturday night at a private dinner and drinks at Lachlan and Sarah's home in Bellevue Hill, attended by News Corp's top editors, Paul Whittaker and Christopher Dore, executives Siobhan McKenna and Michael Miller, and former prime minister Tony Abbott. Pompeo's

arrival was hardly low-key: he travelled straight to Le Manoir
airport in a huge motorcade of police motorbikes and vans flash
lights, accompanied by an armored vehicle and two ambulances to protect
the fourth in line to the presidency. The motorbikes blocked off sleepy
Victoria Road until Pompeo's limo had disappeared down the Murdochs'
long driveway.

Once Pompeo and his wife Susan were inside, the pomp and ceremony
fell away: guests were casually dressed and ate home-made pizza topped
with fresh lobster caught by Lachlan's old friend Ian 'Pucko' Puckeridge,
a multi-time Australian spear-fishing champion who worked on the
wharves at Botany Bay and joined the feast. As one guest remembers,
"This is a pretty interesting guy, who is there at the table with the secretary
of state and the most down-to-earth, easy-going bloke you could ever
meet . . . Lachlan had him there as if he was just as important as any
member of the cabinet. Lachlan has kept firm with those people—he has
an eclectic group of friends." Whatever was discussed remains private.

In September, Lachlan and Sarah were invited to an opulent state
dinner in the White House Rose Garden in honor of visiting Australian
prime minister Scott Morrison. Morrison had won a surprise May election
victory and President Trump was keen to reinforce the alliance and to
secure stable supplies of rare-earth minerals as US relations with China
deteriorated. It was only the second state visit Trump had hosted, after
French president Emmanuel Macron, and the guest list featured famous
Australian expats such as golfer Greg Norman and Australian billionaires
Anthony Pratt, Andrew 'Twiggy' Forrest, and Gina Rinehart. The First
Lady was host and Melania saw to the arrangements personally: violins
serenaded the guests from the White House balcony, and the tables on the
lawn were decked out with thousands of roses from California and wattles
from Australia. The menu featured sunchoke ravioli entrees and Dover
sole for mains, served with Napa Valley sauvignon blanc. Rupert was a
late scratch, but Lachlan represented the family. It was his first chance to
meet Trump in person, along with Sarah. Among the 180 guests were
Fox hosts Maria Bartiromo and Lou Dobbs, whose suspension for on-air

anti-Semitic comments earlier in the year had clearly not damaged his standing in the eyes of the White House. Lachlan and Sarah were at the head table with the president, next to Ginni Thomas, the conservative activist and wife of the Supreme Court judge Clarence Thomas. Lachlan and Sarah had reached a social pinnacle of sorts, part of the American and Australian elite at a time of huge division in both countries.

Even as the guests partied through an enchanted evening in the Rose Garden, Trump's presidency was spiralling towards impeachment. *The New York Times* would soon publish details of a complaint by an unnamed intelligence officer turned whistle-blower about a phone call between Trump and Ukrainian President Volodymyr Zelenskyy on July 25, transcribed by the White House Situation Room. Trump had frozen US military aid to Ukraine without explanation and pressured Zelensky to investigate the Bidens. The bombshell revelations led directly to the impeachment of the president by the House.

On Fox, the news caused turmoil and division, as anchors including Tucker Carlson sought to defend the president. In one segment on Carlson's show, a guest dismissed veteran Fox News legal analyst Andrew Napolitano as a "fool" for saying Trump's behavior was criminal. The next day, chief news anchor Shep Smith declared it was "repugnant" that a guest would insult a Fox News colleague and go "unchallenged" by Carlson. The next night, Carlson shot back at Smith: "Unlike maybe some dayside hosts, I'm not very partisan." As the *Times* reported, such an extended on-air feud between Fox anchors represented a deterioration of the discipline imposed under Roger Ailes. There were other on-air flare-ups: on *The Five*, after liberal pundit Juan Williams said that "asking a foreign government to investigate a political rival is illegal," his co-host Greg Gutfeld retorted: "You get that from Media Matters, Juan?"

Paradoxically, the on-air sniping and resignations did not do any damage to Fox News' ratings. In fact, the opposite was true. As usual, Fox shareholders were doing very nicely out of the discord, and none more so than the Murdochs. The turmoil at Fox News culminated in the shock resignation of Shep Smith, a mainstay of Fox News' daytime, straight-news coverage who had been with the network for more than two decades, since it was founded in 1996. He had reportedly been asked by Suzanne Scott and president Jay Wallace to refrain from attacking Carlson. Smith's departure was especially unusual because his contract had only been renewed in 2018, and his resignation went all the way up the chain to Rupert's desk. According to Brian Stelter's book *Hoax*, Rupert let Smith go, saying, "If he doesn't want to work here, he shouldn't work here" and "We'll replace him and get better ratings." Smith was followed by other senior reporters, including Catherine Herridge and Ellison Barber. Smith was replaced in the afternoon slot by morning host Bill Hemmer, an avowed conservative who golfed with Rudy Giuliani, in what Stelter described as "yet another turn to the right"[4]. After a break, Smith announced he would join CNBC, and in a PBS interview the following year summed up his feelings about Fox:

> I don't know how some people sleep at night because I know there are a lot of people who have propagated the lies and pushed them forward over and over again who are smart enough and educated enough to know better. And I hope that at some point, those who have done us harm as a nation—and, I might add, as a world—will look around and realize what they've done. But I'm not holding my breath.

At the same time, Lachlan found the ground shifting when the Stars Group announced that, unbeknownst to its new partners at Fox, it had been negotiating a friendly merger with another of the world's top four online gambling groups, Flutter Entertainment. The proposed merger, which would create an $11 billion giant, made it less likely that the Fox Bet venture would get the management focus needed to win the US market, the so-called "favored child" problem, with Flutter preferencing its own FanDuel app, it also made Fox's equity options more valuable. Lachlan threw an anodyne line into the joint statement by Flutter and Stars, welcoming news of the merger, but behind the scenes he began negotiating hard to protect Fox's position and as part of Fox consenting to the merger, struck a deal under which Fox got an additional 18.6 per cent option in FanDuel. Compounding the difficulty, by late 2019 Fox's share price was down 25 per cent, trading at around $30 and stubbornly refusing to recover. Investors remained concerned about Fox's over-investment in linear TV and were scratching their heads at how the Credible finance app fit into the picture. "Fox's early life as a new company has been nothing short of disappointing," wrote media analyst Michael Nathanson. "Earnings estimates have been cut twice since mid-March [. . .] and the company's acquisition of Credible Labs has not been seen as . . . well, credible."[5] The new Fox's first annual general meeting in mid-November, opened by Rupert and chaired by Lachlan, was over and done with in nineteen minutes.

* * *

As Fox Corp management tried to bed down the company strategy, and the Trump impeachment scandal worsened, Lachlan had a much more personal decision on his mind: he and Sarah were about to buy the most expensive house in Los Angeles. The *Beverly Hillbillies* mansion, setting for the 1960s sitcom featuring the hapless oil baron Jed Clampett, occupied a full ten acres in Bel Air, right near both Rupert's and James's Hollywood piles, but far bigger than either. Known as Chartwell, the estate had been put on the market in mid-2017, after the death of owner Jerry Perenchio, the billionaire founder of Spanish-language TV network Univision, with an asking price of $350 million. Built in the 1930s by celebrated LA architect Sumner Spaulding, Chartwell was bought by Perenchio in 1986, and he had gradually expanded the estate, buying neighboring properties, including the former home of Ronald and Nancy Reagan, which was now part of the sale as a separate, five-bedroom guest house. At 875 Nimes Road, Chartwell had eleven bedrooms, eighteen bathrooms, a tennis court, a motor court for forty cars, and a 12,000-bottle wine cellar connected by tunnels to the seveny-five-foot pool and pool house. There was a morning room, garden room, billiard room, and a ballroom for entertaining with motorized screens that opened to reveal a grand piano on stage for private performances for up to a hundred guests. Landscaping included a private Redwood grove and perfectly sculpted gumdrop trees lining the perimeter. The interiors were by French designer Henri Samuel and the dining room had seats for eighteen and eighteenth-century panelled walls, imported from Europe.

Putting a price on this unique property was almost an arbitrary exercise, but the market for mega-mansions in LA took off in the middle of the decade, fuelled by near-zero interest rates in the wake of the recession. The $100 million sale of Hugh Hefner's Playboy Mansion in 2016, with him still living in it, meant Hollywood vendors and developers alike were now fixated on the nine-figure price tag. But as 2017 and then 2018 passed, it became clear that the original hoped-for sale price for Chartwell was profoundly unrealistic. It was lowered first to $295 million, then $245 million, then $195 million, but still it languished on the market. In mid-2019, the *Wall Street Journal* reported that with more than a hundred homes for sale for more than $20 million and fifty ultra-high-end homes under construction in the area from Beverly Hills to Bel Air to Brentwood, there was a glut of mansions on the market in LA and not enough buyers. "We have this enormous oversupply of white boxes," mourned one broker. "There's years of inventory out there."

For Lachlan and Sarah, Chartwell offered some relief from the fire danger at Mandeville Canyon. California had suffered a bad wildfire season in 2018 and by November was in the middle of another. In early December 2019, the couple pounced, settling for $150 million, the most ever paid for a home in LA. Friends in Australia who knew Lachlan back in the nineties could not reconcile that he would buy such an outlandish, extravagant home. Within two months, however, Amazon's Jeff Bezos, who had also inspected Chartwell, passed Lachlan for the LA record, buying the fabled Warner Estate for $165 million. Pundits noted that the two properties had something in common: a sense of history, which was more appealing than the glitziest features of the newer mega-mansions with their candy rooms, helipads, bowling alleys, and marijuana-growing rooms. In any event, Chartwell appeared to have been a bargain.

Six months later the Murdochs followed through, as they had done in Sydney, by paying $14 million for the adjacent property owned by former model Cheryl Tiegs, adding another 1.5 acres, meaning their estate now occupied almost the entire block. Walking around the outside of the property takes the better part of an hour, although nobody walks there, of course. There are no pavements in sight. Guards patrol in golf buggies and every entrance bristles with cameras and signs threatening an armed response to any intrusion. Like many wealthy enclaves, the 'hood is a permanent construction site, with cranes towering over mansions under refurbishment or development and trucks and utility vehicles coming and going constantly. The bustle and the high fences remind you that here is some of the most desirable real estate in the world.

Lachlan and Sarah flew home to Sydney for Christmas and an Australian summer that was soon dubbed "Black Summer." The first lives had already been lost in an unprecedented fire season that would eventually burn 24 million hectares. Sydney and other cities choked in bushfire smoke, registering some of the worst air quality in the world and triggering hundreds more premature deaths. Lachlan's first order of business was to attend the annual News Corp awards for company journalists. The ceremony was notable for a standing ovation for Grace Tame, a survivor of sexual abuse by her high school teacher. The "Let Her Speak" campaign had been supported by News' Hobart *Mercury* and Lachlan described it as a reminder that "the purpose of journalism is not to give journalists a voice but to give people like you a voice, to give truth a voice." Tame gave a speech that left many in tears. She would go on to become Australian of the Year.

Next, Lachlan and Sarah hosted their annual Christmas drinks, which sparked controversy later when it was revealed that the prime minister, Scott Morrison, and treasurer, Josh Frydenberg, had billed taxpayers almost $5,000 for their private flight from Canberra to Sydney, as though it were official business. Bellevue Hill suffered the smoke like everywhere else. It was a harbinger of worse to come. Over Christmas and the New Year, terrifying scenes unfolded through south-eastern Australia and the mounting toll of death and destruction was front-page news globally, with a smoke plume circling the southern hemisphere. New South Wales bore the brunt of the fires, including the loss of twenty-five of thirty-three lives nationwide.

At the annual general meeting in November, in answer to a question about News Corp's climate coverage, Rupert Murdoch had insisted, "There are no climate change deniers around, I assure you." But as the bushfires worsened, with the navy effecting the largest peacetime evacuation in Australia's history as the coast town of Mallacoota was surrounded by inferno, *The Australian* published a highly misleading story blaming the crisis on arsonists. The article was shared in conservative media around the world, the hashtag #arsonemergency took off, and top commentators on the Murdoch-controlled Sky News channel, including Andrew Bolt, Alan Jones, Peta Credlin, and Chris Kenny, went out of their way to talk about a lack of hazard-reduction burning and to attack climate "hysteria." In early January, it became too much for one News Corp finance manager, Emily Townsend, who resigned in an email that went to the whole company and was quickly leaked to *The Guardian*:

I have been severely impacted by the coverage of News Corp publications in relation to the fires, in particular the misinformation campaign that has tried to divert attention away from the real issue which is climate change to rather focus on arson (including misrepresenting facts). I find it unconscionable to continue working for this company, knowing I am contributing to the spread of climate change denial and lies. The reporting I have witnessed in *The Australian*, the *Daily Telegraph* and the *Herald Sun* is not only irresponsible, but dangerous and damaging to our communities and beautiful planet that needs us more than ever now to acknowledge the destruction we have caused and start doing something about it.[6]

The Daily Beast editor-at-large Lachlan Cartwright, back in his native Australia for summer holidays, knew some of the Murdoch siblings had strong views on climate that were at odds with the News Corp coverage, started calling and hit the jackpot. James sent a statement through his PR representative:

> Kathryn and James's views on climate are well-established and their frustration with some of the News Corp and Fox coverage of the topic is also well-known. They are particularly disappointed with the ongoing denial among the news outlets in Australia given obvious evidence to the contrary.[7]

The public rebuke, from a serving director of the News Corp board, generated more embarrassing headlines for the company and drove the wedge deeper between James and Kathryn on the one hand and his father and brother on the other. Lachlan and Sarah responded, pledging $2 million to rural relief and recovery efforts, and soon Rupert and Jerry followed suit, announcing they would donate $2 million themselves, while News Corp gave another $5 million to bushfire relief. Across Fox and News, in Australia and the US, if not the UK, the misleading climate coverage continued regardless.

21

Contagion and Crisis

ON JANUARY 30, 2020, the World Health Organization declared a new coronavirus which had broken out in the Chinese mainland city of Wuhan to be a "Public Health Emergency of International Concern," stopping short of describing it as a pandemic. Lachlan and Sarah were back in America and the first case in the US had already been reported by the Centers for Disease Control. As Bob Woodward would later reveal in his second Trump book, *Rage*, the president had already been briefed in late January that the coronavirus was transmissible by air, from human to human, with or without symptoms. The outbreak could be as bad as the Spanish influenza pandemic of 1918, he was warned, and "the biggest national security threat you face in your presidency."

But Trump wanted to pretend it was not a problem for America. After announcing inbound travel restrictions, he told Fox News' Sean Hannity in a sit-down interview the day before the Superbowl, "we pretty much shut it down coming in from China." In his State of the Union address on February 4, the president again played down the threat, saying only that the US was "coordinating with the Chinese government and working closely together on the coronavirus outbreak in China. My administration will take all necessary steps to safeguard our citizens from this threat." Trump's effort to play down the coronavirus would get more pronounced.

The president spoke blithely through February about how it would "disappear" in spring and many Fox News anchors on the opinion side would follow suit.

Tucker Carlson was something of an exception, quick to appreciate the significance of the outbreak, saying in January that coronavirus "seems like an emergency" and a "serious, serious threat" and keeping up the coverage most nights. Carlson's coverage had a slant, of course, seeming overly interested in what the coronavirus said about the "repulsive" Chinese habit of eating dogs and bats and koalas from "wet markets." Still, Carlson could not be accused of downplaying the outbreak. He even travelled to Mar-a-Lago to urge Trump to take the pandemic more seriously.

Fox Corp raked in the cash at the 54th Superbowl, or Superbowl LIV, pulling an audience of 150 million and selling ads worth $600 million in what Lachlan called the "largest revenue day in TV history." In the December quarter earnings call a few days later, Lachlan crowed that Fox News had achieved double the ratings, for the previous night's State of the Union address, of CNN and MSNBC combined. He said how exciting it was for Fox "to be the home of the two events that command the attention of the entire country in the same year. We started calendar 2020 with the first event, the broadcast of Superbowl LIV on Fox. We now set our focus on the second event—the news equivalent of the Superbowl—the presidential election." In a call lasting three quarters of an hour, the coronavirus was not mentioned once. Fox shares climbed back above $38, the level set in the sale to Disney, but the resurgence would be short-lived.

The Senate acquitted President Trump the same day, bringing the impeachment crisis to an end. A week later, Hope Hicks quit Fox to return to the White House as counsellor to the president, as Trump's re-election campaign got underway in earnest. COVID-19, as the WHO designated the new coronavirus in mid-February, now loomed as the most serious threat to Trump's re-election. Investors began to weigh the economic implications and by late February sharemarkets were plunging. Fox and News Corp shares dropped 15 per cent in a week.

The president name-checked Lachlan during a signing ceremony for an $8.3 billion coronavirus rescue package. Spotting News Corp chief Robert Thomson standing among the press corps, Trump acknowledged "the most powerful man in all of media!" and kept up with the flattery:

> He has a little something to do with the *Wall Street Journal*. I don't know if you know. It's his real power, right? [Points at press pool] You used to do what they did, right? [Thomson: Yes] . . . and he did it so well that he's the boss at News Corp. Of course, Rupert has something to say with that, I guess, right? And Lachlan. They treat me very nicely, the media, right? Except the *Wall Street Journal*, but that's OK.

While Trump was buttering up the press, media companies worldwide were scrambling to figure out how to remain on-air and online 24/7 without spreading COVID. Fox News was no exception: by late February, chief Suzanne Scott had deep-cleaned and disinfected the newsrooms and offices and installed hand sanitizers. Fox News soon sent non-production staff home to work, introduced social distancing protocols and mask mandates, and announced it would pay employees' health insurance premiums.

On the programming side, however, a very different public health message was getting out to viewers. Laura Ingraham found the Democrats' politicization of the virus, and attacks on Trump, "more unsettling" than the virus itself. Jerry Falwell, Jr., on *Fox & Friends*, nodded to a conspiracy theory that the virus was man-made, a plot by China and North Korea. Sean Hannity, on March 9, warned of liberal efforts to "bludgeon Trump with this new hoax," echoing the president himself. On March 13, two days after the WHO had declared a pandemic and on the same day that Fox News was holding its first coronavirus town hall broadcast, a low-profile Fox Business host Trish Regan opened her show with a segment called "coronavirus impeachment scam," calling COVID "another attempt to impeach the president." Finally, Fox News clamped down and Regan was dismissed, although primetime stars like Hannity and Ingraham were not sanctioned.

A week later, Fox announced it would make Fox News and Fox TV freely available as a public service. Fox followed up with a COVID-19 benefit special, which raised more than $15 million, and did a second coronavirus town hall with Facebook in which both companies donated a million dollars each to Feeding America. "Our highest duty as a company is to provide the individuals and communities we serve with information and analysis to help educate and protect them during dangerous times," Lachlan said in a statement. At the Fox lot, which was empty as most people were working from home, instead of shutting down the canteen Lachlan got foodservice workers to keep cooking and some 80,000 meals were loaded onto trucks and given to charity.

It was all seen as too little, too late. At the end of March, a damning piece by *The New York Times'* influential media writer Ben Smith described Lachlan's appointment as Fox CEO as a "dangerous mistake." Smith wrote that Lachlan was a "laid-back executive" who had delegated much of the running of the company to Viet Dinh and was seldom seen at Fox News. He did not even watch the channel much, being "sometimes surprised to learn of a controversy it had generated." As a result, Smith wrote, Lachlan had misread criticism of Fox's COVID coverage as partisan noise. Smith quoted a Harvard public health expert confirming that people would die as a result of the misinformation on Fox in those early weeks. Fox News' communications chief, Irena Briganti, told *The New York Times* that "cherry picking of clips from our opinion programs is the definition of politicizing this serious threat."[1]

With the US officially becoming the country worst-hit by the pandemic in late March, the president's handling of COVID was going from lame to inane. After pretending for weeks that everything was under control, then tweeting about the "Chinese virus," which he repeatedly said would simply go away, by April he was musing about injecting disinfectants and whether sunlight might cure COVID. Trump and Fox were caught up in a deadly embrace. Early that month, a group of seventy-four professors of journalism and journalists signed an open letter to Rupert and Lachlan, calling Fox News' coronavirus coverage a danger to public health and to the health of its viewers, whose average age was sixty-five. "Inexcusably, Fox News has violated elementary canons of journalism. In so doing, it has contributed to the spread of a grave pandemic."

Lachlan bore ultimate responsibility for all Fox content, but whether he should have taken the *The New York Times*' advice and spent more time watching the news channel each day was debatable: he had a capable CEO in Scott and complete confidence in her. Whether in print or broadcast, Lachlan had never really been the kind of all-seeing, interventionist editor-in-chief that his father had been throughout his career. Instead, Lachlan's mind through March was on a corporate takeover deal that would come to define his leadership of Fox: the $440 million acquisition of Tubi, a free streaming service supported by ads (known as "advertizing video on demand," or AVOD), rather than subscriptions ("subscription video on demand" or SVOD). Fox had sold its film and entertainment businesses in the belief that they could compete more strongly with Netflix and Amazon if they were under the Disney umbrella. After the sale, Fox was hardly about to do a 180-degree turn and try to scale up in SVOD, entering a content arms race it could not win. (Fox Nation, a streaming service sold to Fox News superfans, was so niche the company refused to release subscriber numbers.) Moreover, the streaming industry broadly remained unprofitable and the impact of the pandemic uncertain, although shelter-in-place viewing was undoubtedly boosting audience figures. Disney+ and NBCUniversal's Peacock had just launched and HBO Max was launching within weeks.

Believing consumer willingness to pay for multiple different streaming services would soon max out, Lachlan decided to zig while most of the industry zagged. Fox would target the bottom end of the streaming market with Tubi, which had a library of 20,000 titles totalling 56,000 hours of movies and episodic TV, and 25 million active users a month, who skewed younger. Lachlan was not going out on a limb. Comcast had recently bought another free streaming service, Xumo, and Viacom had bought Pluto TV the year before, and the cash outlay was comparatively small. Most of the money came from the sale of Fox's 5 per cent of the streaming app Roku, raising $340 million, which was less than half its $809 million book value at the end of 2019 but well up on the $40 million Fox had originally paid for its stake. (As it turned out, Roku shares went through the roof in 2020 and the Fox stake would have been worth $2.5 billion by the end of the year, posing the question of whether Lachlan had backed the wrong horse, or should have funded the Tubi deal some other way.)

Analysts were initially perplexed about the Tubi deal. It was hardly the main game, and not a convincing digital strategy for Fox which was focused on producing live news and sport rather than serving up cheap programming from a library. Fox's acquisitions under Lachlan's leadership—the Stars Group, Credible, Tubi—seemed idiosyncratic so far. For anyone following his career closely, it was like a repeat of the early deals done by Illyria, investments in Quickflix, Funtastic, the Rajasthan Royals, which left pundits questioning the overall strategy.

Although Fox shares ticked up on the day of the Tubi announcement, they were soon crashing again and within a week were trading below $20. The following month, Lachlan announced he would forego his $3 million base salary until September, along with Fox's other top five executives, as well as imposing staggered temporary pay cuts for 700 managers and employees in an austerity drive. Still, the combination of an election year plus the pandemic propelled Fox News to its largest audience in history, Lachlan told investors at a quarterly earnings call in May. "We are living through extraordinary times," he said. "Since we last all spoke together, who would have imagined our lives could have all been turned so upside down?" Despite the turmoil from COVID, Lachlan reiterated that Fox was confident it could hit the targets set out a year earlier, although he said it did "feel like ten years ago. I'm sure we all have a few more gray hairs."

* * *

The murder of George Floyd by Minneapolis police officer Derek Chauvin on May 25, captured on video, turned Black Lives Matter into the biggest protest movement in the history of the United States, with more than 15 million people turning out to demonstrations, some of them violent, in 550 towns and cities across the country. Fox News had a history of antipathetic coverage of BLM, which took off after the police killing of an eighteen-year-old black man, Michael Brown, in Ferguson, Missouri in 2014. Former primetime host Megyn Kelly subverted the narrative, asserting that Michael Brown's reported last words, "Hands up, don't shoot," were a lie, and that Brown was the aggressor. Twenty-six-year-old Fox Nation host Tomi Lahren describing Black Lives Matter as "the new KKK." Fox commentators had also defended police and rejected claims of systemic racial injustice in America. Nevertheless, the public reaction to Floyd's murder was on a completely different scale to earlier protests, and it took place amid swirling speculation that Trump would declare martial law. On the Monday morning, Lachlan Murdoch tried to set a conciliatory tone in an internal statement, urging Fox employees to "come together in their grief, work to heal, and coalesce to address injustice and inequity in our country." After the tragic death of George Floyd, Murdoch continued:

> It is essential that we grieve with the Floyd family, closely listen to the voices of peaceful protest and fundamentally understand that Black Lives matter. The FOX culture embraces and fosters diversity and inclusion. Often we speak of the 'FOX Family,' and never has the need to depend on and care for that family been more important. We support our Black colleagues and the Black community, as we all unite to seek equality and understanding . . . This is an ongoing conversation, and no one has all the answers in this moment.

Some of Fox's highest-profile commentators seemed to miss Lachlan's memo. That same night, Tucker Carlson bemoaned the protests. "The nation went up in flames this weekend," he opined. "No one in charge stood up to save America. Our leaders dithered and they cowered, and they openly sided with the destroyers, and in many cases, they egged them on . . . The worst people in our society have taken control." Laura Ingraham blamed Antifa and "other radical elements" and said the death of Floyd had nothing to do with the violence, which was "part of a coordinated effort to eventually overthrow the United States government." Days later, Fox News had to apologize after an episode of *Special Report with Bret Baier* aired a chart showing how the stock market had rallied in the days immediately following the assassination of Martin Luther King, Jr. in 1968, the bashing of Rodney King in 1991, and the more recent killings of Michael Brown and George Floyd. Fox acknowledged the chart was insensitive and Baier apologized for a "major screw-up." There followed an internal phone hook-up with many of its black staffers, led by Scott, to discuss the network's racist and hostile rhetoric towards the BLM protests. The open forum was unprecedented, but Lachlan wasn't there and it resolved little.

As the protests dragged on, Carlson only grew more strident, attacking the president for failing to re-establish law and order, calling BLM a "terror organization" and Minneapolis "our Wuhan." In early July, CNN discovered that Carlson's chief writer, Blake Neff, had for years been using a pseudonym to post a stream of bigoted remarks denigrating African Americans, Asian Americans, and women on an online forum, AutoAdmit, that was a hotbed for racist, sexist, and other offensive content. Fox accepted Neff's resignation within hours of CNN's inquiry and Suzanne Scott and Jay Wallace condemned his "horrific racist, misogynistic and homophobic behavior," saying neither the show nor the network had known of the forum and there was zero tolerance for such behavior "at any time in any part of our workforce."

More mainstream advertizers abandoned Carlson and Lachlan personally approved the comments Tucker made about Neff's resignation in his next show. Carlson refused management requests to pre-tape the comments and struck a defiant tone, suggesting he knew he had Lachlan's full backing. Dissociating himself from Neff's posts, Tucker added "we should also point out to the ghouls beating their chests in triumph of the destruction of a young man that self-righteousness also has its cost . . . when we pose as blameless in order to hurt other people, we are committing the gravest sin of all, and we will be punished for it, there's no question." Tucker announced he was going on a week's vacation, effective immediately, which he insisted was "long planned." One staffer told *The Daily Beast* off the record that Fox News had "created a white supremacist cell inside the top cable network in America, the one that directly influences the president . . . this is rank racism excused by Murdoch."

It was all too much for James Murdoch, who had been negotiating an exit for some months, hoping to sever his connection to the family business. At the end of July, James sent a two-line letter of resignation to the board of News Corp, effective that day, with only the briefest explanation: "My resignation is due to disagreements over certain editorial content published by the Company's news outlets and certain other strategic decisions." In a bland joint statement, Rupert and Lachlan thanked James for his service and wished him well.

James continued, of course, as beneficiary of a one-sixth share of the Murdoch Family Trust, which ultimately controlled both Fox and News Corp. In a sit-down interview with *The New York Times* a few months later, James told Maureen Dowd that he felt he could have little influence as a non-executive director, wanted a cleaner slate and "pulled the ripcord" because:

> I reached the conclusion that you can venerate a contest of ideas, if you will, and we all do and that's important. But it shouldn't be in a way that hides agendas. A contest of ideas shouldn't be used to legitimize disinformation. And I think it's often taken advantage of. And I think at great news organizations, the mission really should be to introduce fact to disperse doubt—not to sow doubt, to obscure fact, if you will.

It was a direct shot at Lachlan, whose mantra was to defend free speech, even that of commentators he did not agree with from time to time, and apparently regardless of whether the speaker was spreading disinformation.

Dowd canvassed a scenario which was doubtless briefed by James and which could give Lachlan nightmares. Despite appearances, she wrote, the succession game may not truly be over: "Murdoch watchers across media say James is aligned with his sister Elisabeth and his half-sister, Prudence, even as he is estranged from his father and brother."[2] It was true that there had been a thawing of the relationship between James and Elisabeth, which had come apart during the hacking crisis. When James bought Tribeca Enterprises, which ran the famous New York Film Festival, Liz soon joined the board. The implied threat from the Dowd piece was clear: once their father was gone, when control of the empire passed to the four elder siblings, each with an equal vote on the Murdoch Family Trust, Lachlan could find himself getting rolled by James, Liz, and Prue, who were generally more liberal than Rupert. In a plausible scenario, after Rupert has passed and his shares are dispersed among the four adult children, the three on the other side of Lachlan could choose to manifest control over all of the Murdoch businesses, and to do it in a way that enhances democracies around the world rather than undermining them. In this scenario, the role of Fox News has become so controversial inside the family that control of the trust is no longer just about profit and loss at the Murdoch properties. In one view that has currency among at least some of the Murdoch children, it is in the long-term interests for democracies around the world for there to be four shareholders in the family trust who are active owners in the business. Just such a scenario is freely canvassed by investors: a Wall Street analyst who has covered the Murdoch business for decades and is completely au fait with the breakdown in the relationship between the brothers, volunteers off the record that it would be "fair to assume Lachlan gets fired the day Rupert dies." It is a formula for instability and intra-family feuds that must weigh on the minds of directors of both Fox and News Corporation as they contemplate the mortality of the 91-year-old founder, although they deny it. A source close to members of the Murdoch family questions the extent of succession planning by the boards of Fox or News Corporation and whether discussions among the directors can be genuinely independent, as corporate governance experts would like. "Rupert has total control over all the companies as long as he is alive," the source says. "It's an unrealistic expectation that the boards of those companies are going to use their voices to manifest independence. What is their succession plan? What if something happens to Lachlan? Do they put Viet in charge?"

At the same time James announced his resignation from the News Corp board, he and Kathryn were ploughing millions into the defeat of Trump, climate activism, and other political causes. The couple had invested $100 million worth of Disney shares into their foundation, Quadrivium, and through 2020 were heavy backers of mostly Democrat-leaning outfits, including $1.2 million to the Biden Victory Fund and a handful of anti-Trump Republican organizations such as Defending Democracy Together, led by Bill Kristol. That was only *some* of the couple's total political funding. A year later, CNBC obtained a Quadrivium tax return showing donations of $38 million toward election organizations, including those dedicated to protecting voting rights.

Lachlan's personal political donations through the 2020 cycle were much smaller and were overwhelmingly directed towards the GOP, according to Federal Election Commission records. The politician he favored most was Senate Majority Leader Mitch McConnell, an establishment Republican who made a calculated decision to become Trump's "enabler-in-chief" and was married to Trump's transportation secretary, Taiwanese-born Elaine Chao, a former director of News Corp. Lachlan contributed $31,000 in four donations in March, including to the Bluegrass Committee for Kentucky Republicans. Ten days after the November election, Lachlan made a much bigger personal donation, of a million dollars, to the Senate Leadership Fund, which had one goal: protecting the Republican Senate majority. Lachlan did make one small donation on the Democrat side in the 2020 cycle, after he attended a fundraiser for Democratic candidate Pete Buttigieg, the gay ex-mayor of South Bend, Indiana, pledging $1500 to his campaign. Realizing the potential for embarrassment, he asked for it back and was duly refunded.

Fox's profitability fell by more than two-thirds in the June quarter, which would later prove to be the low point of the pandemic, as sports leagues went dark and general ad revenue collapsed. Fox News was the only bright spot, accounting for 90 per cent of operating profit, despite advertizer boycotts of *Tucker Carlson Tonight*, as the 2020 presidential election campaign intensified.

Three weeks out from polling day, on October 14, the *New York Post* broke a story which might have influenced the outcome of the 2020 election. It had obtained a trove of messages, documents, photos and videos "purportedly" recovered from a laptop belonging to Hunter Biden, son of the Democratic presidential candidate, which had been taken to a Delaware computer shop for repair in 2019 and never picked up. The computer shop owner was a Trump supporter and handed the water-damaged laptop to the FBI, but also sent a copy of the hard-drive to Rudy Giuliani, who had long sought to tarnish Joe Biden with conflict-of-interest allegations concerning his son's involvement with Ukrainian oil and gas company Burisma. The *Post* story zeroed in on a "smoking gun" email sent to Hunter in 2015 by Vadym Pozharskyi, an adviser to Burisma. The email read: "Dear Hunter, thank you for inviting me to DC and giving an opportunity to meet your father and spent [sic] some time together."

According to the *Post*, the email gave the lie to Joe Biden's claim that he had "never spoken to my son about his overseas business dealings." However, it was not clear whether Pozharskyi had in fact ever met with Biden, who as vice president had handled the Ukraine portfolio for President Obama, and the Biden campaign explicitly denied it, after going back over his official schedule.[3]

However irresistible the story was to the *Post* and its warhorse editor Col Allan, the rest of the mainstream media was exceedingly wary. The *Post* would not provide a copy of the laptop or hard drive to allow other media to verify the contents. The timing was transparently intended to damage the Biden campaign and memories remained fresh of the FBI's momentous decision to investigate Hillary Clinton in the final days of the 2016 election campaign, after emails stolen by Russian operatives were dumped online by Wikileaks. Twitter and Facebook intervened dramatically to stop circulation of the *Post* story. Twitter even temporarily locked White House press secretary Kayleigh McEnany's account, as well as that of the *Post* itself. More than fifty intelligence experts signed an open letter stating that the story "has all the classic earmarks of a Russian information operation." The *Times* reported that at least two *Post* journalists had refused to put their by-line on the laptop story, while the lead reporter, Emma-Jo Morris, had not had a previous by-line with the paper. Furthermore, News Corp stablemate the *Wall Street Journal* had been offered much the same story before the *Post* but concluded the central claims could not be proved. The whole story failed to gain much traction beyond the *Post*, Fox News, and avowedly right-wing media like Breitbart.

Post-election, Hunter Biden would reveal that he was under federal investigation for tax offenses and over the following year-and-a-half, the industrial scale of his influence-peddling became clearer, including potential breaches of the *Foreign Agents Registration Act*, the same legislation that Trump's 2016 campaign manager, Paul Manafort, had pled guilty to violating. In mid-2021, the *Post* revealed that Joe Biden had indeed met Pozharskyi in 2015, and in early 2022, both *The New York Times* and *The Washington Post* reported that independent experts had examined the files which purported to be from Hunter Biden's laptop and they appeared genuine. That did not prove Hunter Biden was guilty of anything, of course, only that the laptop was his. But for his part, Lachlan believed that an important news story about the Bidens had been deliberately suppressed by the tech companies and a liberal-leaning media, saying much later:

> . . . had the laptop belonged to another candidate's son, it would certainly have been the only story you would have heard in the final weeks of the election. But lies were concocted: 'the laptop was

hacked, or stolen;' it was not. Or 'it was Russian disinformation;' it was not, and the story was completely suppressed. It was censored by EVERYONE.[4]

The scene was set for one of the most contentious presidential elections in American history.

22

The Decision Desk

ELECTION DAY FOR LACHLAN began with the September quarter earnings call, and he was filled with excitement on such a "big day" for Fox:

> . . . not just because we get to brag about our strong financial performance, continued operating momentum and burgeoning digital assets such as Fox Bet and Tubi, but because every four years we have the privilege and responsibility of reporting on a US presidential election.

The studios were lit for a long day and night ahead, and news anchors Bret Baier and Martha MacCallum would be live in a few hours. Fox News had been the most watched network in all of television from Memorial Day through to election day, Lachlan boasted, and political advertizing had shattered the record set at the 2018 midterms. In the second half of 2020, Fox would push close to $300 million in political ad revenue, the company forecast, of which roughly two-thirds would be at the local level and a third would be national, surprisingly high for a presidential election.

Lachlan rammed home the appeal of Fox News to independent and Democratic voters, refuting the criticism that Fox was "Trump TV" for a Republican base. Fox, he said, had a share of cable equal to CNN and MSNBC combined in swing states and key blue states (he did not specify which). It had the broadest audience of the cable network, he claimed, and it was relied on by 38 per cent of registered independents and likely voters which "speaks directly to the quality of our journalism and the balance of our reporting."

Asked if Fox ratings would suffer depending on the election outcome, and whether he feared Trump might launch a rival conservative news network if he lost, Lachlan insisted Fox loved competition and would maintain its leading position in cable market share regardless of the result. "As we enter a more normal news cycle, which has to happen eventually, that appetite for news will shift back to appetite for the great American pastimes of watching football and watching baseball and watching *The Masked Singer* . . . and we look forward to that shift."

Fox had invested heavily in its election coverage under the "Democracy 2020" banner, and was particularly proud of its fabled decision desk, led by polling consultant Arnon Mishkin since 2008. Mishkin was a registered Democrat but checked his politics at the door when running Fox News Voting Analysis. He shared University of Chicago data with the Associated Press and stood apart from the other media in the National Election Pool, which relied on data from Edison Research. Mishkin and the voting analysis team had a solid record of being first to make accurate calls, including the Democrats taking the House in the 2018 midterms and Obama taking Ohio in 2012.

The historic turnout in 2020 smashed all records, with 158 million votes cast, representing two-thirds of eligible voters in America. As the count progressed, the Trump campaign was buoyed early by re-taking the battleground state of Florida, which had ushered in victory in the previous election. It came as a shock at 11.20 p.m. when the Fox News decision desk was first to call Arizona, a purple state that Trump had held in 2016, for Biden. Fox's Bill Hemmer, live in front of the giant touch screen, noticed Arizona change color and said aloud: "What is this happening here? Why is Arizona blue? Did we just call it? Did we just make a call in Arizona?" Anchors Baier and MacCallum grasped the significance immediately. As has been well documented, the president's team went into overdrive, tweeting that the call was premature with a million votes yet to count in Arizona and ringing Fox News in an attempt to get the call reversed. Jared Kushner even called Rupert Murdoch himself. Bret Baier interviewed Mishkin an hour later, at 12.30 a.m., confessing, "Arnon, we're getting a lot of incoming here, and we need you to answer some questions."

Under pressure, Mishkin stood by his call, insisting there was no way Trump could still take Arizona: "I'm sorry, the president is not going to be able to take over and win enough votes. We're not wrong in this particular case." Associated Press, which had its own decision desk, followed suit and as his prospects crumbled, Trump soon gave the infamous press conference in which he refused to concede defeat, insisting instead that, "Frankly, we did win this election." It was the beginning of the "Big Lie."

It was months before the role Lachlan had played on election night was even discussed. The first inkling came in Michael Wolff's book *Landslide*, the last of his Trump trilogy, which contained a brief but apparently verbatim conversation between Lachlan and his father ahead of the Arizona call. Wolff, who did not cite his sources, claimed that the decision desk was simply cover to "bypass the news desk and be directly answerable to the Murdochs." According to Wolff, given no other network had called Arizona, the decision desk felt the Murdochs might want to delay the call, and so had notified Lachlan.

Wolff wrote: "Lachlan got his father on the phone to ask if he wanted to make the early call. His father, with signature grunt, assented, adding: 'Fuck him.'" This account triggered headlines worldwide, as though Rupert had brought Trump down himself, which was ridiculous: the voters had brought down Trump, and nobody else.

The next day, in a statement, Fox News said Wolff's account was "completely false. Arnon Mishkin who leads the Fox News Decision Desk made the Arizona call on election night and Fox News Media President Jay Wallace was then called in the control room. Any other version of the story is wildly inaccurate." Those carefully chosen words did not in fact deny Wolff's account of the conversation between the Murdoch men. Wolff, who'd already told *Der Spiegel* that Rupert no longer talks to him, came in for a lot of criticism and clashed with CNN's Brian Stelter on air. Fox political editor Chris Stirewalt, who was on air on election night providing analysis and commentary, later said in a podcast that Wolff "did not get this right":

> . . . it couldn't have been the case . . . the team made the call, and my boss Bill Sammon clicked the box that clicked the box. If you want to know how false the Michael Wolff claim is, you can find the clip on-air, when our on-air colleagues reported our call. They are genuinely surprised . . . the decision desk has to operate autonomously, because it's the only time that the news organization really gets to make news itself. We spend a lot of time [and] a lot of money in being able to make these forecasts in elections, and when you're ready to do it, the whole goal is to beat the competition . . . we got a lot of resources to do it, and you can't wait around, to make your calls until other news executives at the network feel good about it. It is one of those things you've just got to go do . . . they could've stopped it—they could have quit putting it on television after we made it—but no, he [Rupert Murdoch] did not make the call and I'm very proud to have been part of making the call, and part of best decision desk in the business, for a long time.[1]

Lachlan was indeed notified by Jay Wallace on election night that the decision desk was about to call Arizona for Biden and given the reasons why. Lachlan understood the background to the decision desk's call, and the significance of Arizona, and thanked Wallace for letting him know. The decision was made, and Lachlan's advisers will not comment on whether he then called his father.

When it mattered most, Fox News called the 2020 election straight, confounding years of criticism that the network had turned into "Trump TV" or "MAGA media." To their credit, neither Lachlan nor Rupert

Murdoch tried to meddle in the election night coverage. What followed over the next two months, however, as Trump and his supporters rounded on Fox, was the most determined attack on American democracy in living memory, and here the company's role was much less honorable, and even dangerous. Lachlan's hands-off approach to the management of Fox's stable of right-wing provocateurs, it would turn out, carried grave risks both for the company and the country.

The backlash against Fox on the right was visceral and immediate. Outraged conservatives on social media targeted the Murdochs, sometimes confusing Lachlan with his more liberal brother James or, at least, suspecting that both sons were left of their father and unreliable.

Fox itself was divided. Some on-air talent were trying to stick to the facts: when the Trump campaign announced a slew of legal challenges to "Stop the Steal," national political editor Chris Stirewalt was frankly dismissive, saying, "Lawsuits, schmawsuits. We haven't seen any evidence yet that there's anything wrong." Likewise, anchor Neil Cavuto made headlines when he cut away from White House press secretary Kayleigh McEnany's briefing mid-sentence, saying: "Whoa, whoa, whoa—I just think we have to be very clear. She's charging the other side as welcoming fraud and welcoming illegal voting. Unless she has more details to back that up, I can't in good countenance continue to show you this." Tucker Carlson, to his credit, lambasted Sidney Powell for failing to provide any evidence to back up her fraud claims. And when CNN anchor Jake Tapper said on air that "the Murdochs and the people at Fox have an obligation to put their country above their profits . . . it is very important that people make it very clear that there is no credible evidence of widespread fraud," Kathryn Murdoch tweeted: "I agree with this."

On the other hand, Fox was desperate to hang on to the Trump base: in the two weeks after it called the election for Biden on November 7, Fox News cast doubt on the results of the election at least 774 times, according to watchdog Media Matters.[2] CNN obtained internal memos from Fox News directing anchors and other staff not to call Joe Biden the "president-elect," even after the election was called.

On her *Sunday Morning Futures* Fox show, Maria Bartiromo interviewed Trump lawyer Sidney Powell, who declared there had been a "massive and coordinated effort to steal this election . . . to delegitimize and destroy votes for Donald Trump, to manufacture votes for Joe Biden." Bartiromo asked about apparent irregularities with the software used by a little-known company, Dominion Voting Systems, which supplied voting machines in twenty-eight states. "That is where the fraud took place," said Powell, "where they were flipping votes in the computer system or adding votes that did not exist . . . that's when they had to stop the vote count and go in and replace votes for Biden and take away Trump votes." A few days later, Giuliani tweeted: "Did you know a foreign company, DOMINION, was counting our vote in Michigan, Arizona, and Georgia and other states. But it was a front for SMARTMATIC, who was really doing the computing. Look up SMARTMATIC and tweet me what you think? It will all come out." Lou Dobbs shared it and got Giuliani back on the show.

The claims of Powell and Giuliani were utterly baseless but were quickly worked up into a full-blown conspiracy theory that the election had been stolen by vote-flipping algorithms in Dominion machines created in Venezuela by parent company Smartmatic to rig elections for Hugo Chavez. It was demonstrably false on every particular, but it got major airtime on Fox News, even after Dominion sent out releases headlined "SETTING THE RECORD STRAIGHT," which were emailed to the channel's ninety most senior executives, producers, hosts, and reporters.

Trump kept piling on the pressure, attacking Fox, pumping up rivals Newsmax and One America News Network, and fuelling speculation he might launch his own MAGA media channel. On November 12, Trump unleashed a barrage of anti-Fox tweets, about how daytime ratings had collapsed: "Very sad to watch this happen, but they forgot what made them successful, what got them there. They forgot the Golden Goose. The biggest difference between the 2016 Election, and 2020, was @FoxNews!" That happened to be the day of Fox's annual meeting at the Century City lot in LA. Lachlan chaired the meeting, held under strict social distancing rules with Rupert attending by phone from England. It was all wrapped up in eighteen minutes. Lachlan said nothing about the election or Trump, except to praise Fox staff and Fox News after a record-breaking year.

Dominion Voting Systems, which by now was being bombarded with death threats from Trump supporters, directly approached Fox News chief Suzanne Scott and president Jay Wallace and had a detailed conversation with the latter. The attacks on Dominion continued, particularly on Lou Dobbs' Fox Business program. On November 20, Dominion's lawyers sent a letter of demand directly to Fox general counsel Lily Fu Claffee, listing some of the many false and defamatory allegations made on Fox News, setting out the facts, and expressing the hope that the news channel was "committed to truth, will correct the most outlandish of the false allegations it has helped perpetuate, and will also ensure that future reporting about Dominion is both fair and accurate."

If Lachlan was not personally aware of the serious legal risk at this point, he certainly should have been, and the risk only escalated as Trump's electoral lawsuits collapsed and Trump-appointed officials, including Chris Krebs, director of the Cybersecurity and Infrastructure Security Agency, and attorney general Bill Barr publicly denied there was evidence of fraud involving electronic voting machines. Trump fired Krebs and branded Barr a "traitor," while rewarding Fox and Bartiromo with his first sit-down interview since the election. In early December, Smartmatic sent its own blistering legal letter accusing Fox of running a "disinformation campaign" against it. Smartmatic, in fact, had no ties to Dominion and had only supplied voting machines in Los Angeles County, where 71 per cent of votes were for Joe Biden.

After receiving the legal threat, Fox News produced a strange segment with voting technology expert Eddie Perez, in which he debunked claims of election fraud against Smartmatic but not Dominion. The interview was conducted by an unidentified Fox staffer who remained off-camera. The segment went to air on the shows of Dobbs, Bartiromo, and Pirro in mid-December, without any comment from the hosts. The tactic raised eyebrows and suggested Fox knew it was in trouble. Three days before Christmas, Dominion sent a second letter of demand to Fu Claffee:

Unfortunately, *after* Dominion had provided Fox with the facts and requested a retraction and even *after* Mr. Carlson's realization Ms. Powell was playing Fox's viewers and had no evidence to back up her inherently improbable claims, Lou Dobbs and Sean Hannity repeatedly featured Ms. Powell—and Jeanine Pirro featured Ms. Powell's former client, convicted felon Michael Flynn—and they, along with Maria Baritoromo, repeated demonstrably false accusations against Dominion.

Dominion quoted verbatim from some of the terrifying death threats received by its employees by voicemail and text. The letter warned that defamation complaints were being drafted against Powell and Giuliani and that they would prefer not to add Fox News, Fox Business, or its journalists. Fox did not respond to the letter and the news channel's smears against Dominion continued and, if anything, became less restrained. In early December, Fox tweeted an official promo for an upcoming episode of the *Lou Dobbs Tonight* show, saying "The 2020 Election is a cyber Pearl Harbor: The left-wing establishment have aligned their forces to overthrow the United States government" and attaching a type-written document without references or letterhead accusing Dominion, Smartmatic, and two other companies of trying to "overthrow the US system" and execute an "electoral 9-11" in cooperation and collusion with the Democrats and China, adding: "We have technical presentations that prove there is an embedded controller in every Dominion machine." It was not so much inaccurate as unhinged and, by citing Pearl Harbor and 9/11, undoubtedly inflammatory.

At the same time, Nielsen data for the month after the election showed Fox had been knocked off by CNN as the top-rating cable channel, for the first time since 9/11. Upstart rival Newsmax was surging ahead. Its primetime host, Greg Kelly, beat Fox's Martha MacCallum one night. So as year-end approached, Lachlan was juggling Fox News' plunging ratings and a beleaguered Fox Corp share price down by a quarter since the start of the pandemic, all while trying to cultivate the growth opportunity presented by his signature digital investments, particularly Fox Bet and Tubi. In early December, Lachlan took a call from Flutter chief Peter Jackson, who let him know the company would be raising $2 billion cash to buy out one of the minority partners in market leader FanDuel, lifting its own stake to 95 per cent. FanDuel, valued at $11 billion under the deal, was certainly beginning to look like the favored child, while Fox Bet languished. Jackson was playing hardball. Lachlan kept quiet about his intentions while talking up Fox's long-term commitment to Flutter.

The electoral college, meanwhile, met to affirm Biden's victory and Trump was running out of options. In mid-December, the White House issued a report on the stolen election by trade adviser Peter Navarro, titled "The Immaculate Deception." It repeated the Dominion fraud allegations. *The Washington Post* called it the most embarrassing document ever produced by a White House staffer.[3] Trump tweeted: "A great report by Peter. Statistically impossible to have lost the 2020 Election. Big protest in D.C. on January 6th. Be there, will be wild!"

It was the first indication of what was in the president's mind. As Jonathan Swan reported in a ground-breaking series for *Axios*, the anti-Trump PAC Lincoln Project had cut a 38-second commercial, airing on Fox News, intended to rattle the president and including the script: "The end is coming, Donald . . . On January 6, Mike Pence will put the nail in your political coffin." The ads, designed to goad Trump about the looming certification of the electoral college votes, worked too well.

Almost immediately after the presidential election, political focus had shifted to the January 5 runoff elections in Georgia, where two Senate seats were still up for grabs. If Democrats won both, they could use vice president Kamala Harris' casting vote to break a 50:50 tie. If the Republicans won either race, Mitch McConnell could remain Senate Majority Leader and stymie the Biden agenda. This is when both Lachlan and Rupert Murdoch contributed $1 million to the Senate Leadership Fund, intended to protect the Republican majority. More than $830 million was spent by both sides, making the two Georgia Senate contests the most expensive congressional races in US history.

While control of the Senate hung in the balance on January 6, a Trump-fuelled insurrection was unfolding in Washington. As would emerge in the Congressional inquiry almost a year later, Sean Hannity, Lara Ingraham, and *Fox & Friends* host Brian Kilmeade all separately texted White House chief of staff Mark Meadows, urging the president to come out and stop the riot.

Hannity texted: "Can he make a statement? Ask people to leave the Capitol."

"Mark, the president needs to tell people in the Capitol to go home," wrote Ingraham. "This is hurting all of us. He is destroying his legacy."

Kilmeade texted: "Please, get him on TV. Destroying everything you have accomplished."

These messages were starkly at odds with the messages they put to air on Fox in the immediate aftermath of the attack. Hannity cast doubt on the political affiliations of the mob: "I don't care if the radical left, radical right—I don't know who they are. They're not people I would support." Ingraham suggested that "antifa sympathizers may have been sprinkled throughout the crowd." Kilmeade simply expressed disbelief: "I do not know Trump supporters that have ever demonstrated violence that I know of in a big situation." On the news side, Fox's coverage was directionless, veering from celebrating the protest to grimly acknowledging the unprecedented assault on American democracy that was taking place, as it became clear that people were dead or injured, including security guards and law enforcement. The coverage morphed into whataboutism, contrasting the protests with the BLM demonstrations of the previous summer. Trump spiralled into his second impeachment.

While Lachlan kept his head down after January 6, his brother James did not hold back. In an interview with the *Financial Times* ten days after the attack, he castigated the US media (without naming Fox News), saying proprietors were as culpable as politicians who "know the truth but choose instead to propagate lies":

The sacking of the Capitol is proof positive that what we thought was dangerous is indeed very, very much so. Those outlets that propagate lies to their audience have unleashed insidious and uncontrollable forces that will be with us for years. I hope that those people who didn't think it was that dangerous now understand, and that they stop.[4]

Fox's ratings slide continued through January as the network slumped beneath both CNN and MSNBC, culminating in a major overhaul of the weekday line-up: Martha MacCallum was dropped from her "straight news" show at 5 p.m. and shifted to afternoons, to be replaced with more conservative opinion programming.

"This is the Murdochs," a Fox source told *The Daily Beast*. "The world changed for Fox the day they called Arizona and the question that remains is, will the audience ever forgive the news people for doing it?" A week later, Fox fired political editor Chris Stirewalt, who had vigorously defended the decision desk's call in Arizona but had not been seen on-air since mid-November. Fox also confirmed that veteran DC bureau chief Bill Sammon would retire at the end of the month. Fox flacks insisted that Stirewalt's dismissal had nothing to do with Arizona and was instead related to underperformance, while Sammon's retirement was long-coming. But the moves certainly looked like a sop to the Trump base, purging anyone less-than-fervently pro-Trump from the news side. Fox was in a degree of turmoil, brought to a head when *The Daily Beast* reported that CEO Suzanne Scott and president Jay Wallace were both fighting for their jobs. Pressed for a statement of support for Scott, Lachlan did not respond to the *Beast*'s Lachlan Cartwright. Rupert, who had arrived in the US after getting his second COVID vaccination at home in England, was now taking a much more hands-on role at Fox to address the ratings slide. Cartwright quoted one company insider saying: "Fox News has been absent a leader with the exception of Viet Dinh running the operation between the network and the White House. Rupert re-taking the reins is a sign of the gross mismanagement to date."[5]

Smartmatic filed a stunning $2.7 billion-plus defamation and punitive damages claim against Fox News in the New York State Court on February 4, and also named Lou Dobbs, Maria Bartiromo, Jeanine Pirro, and Trump's lawyers, Giuliani and Powell. "Fox News engaged in a conspiracy to spread disinformation about Smartmatic," said the company's attorney, Erik Connolly. "They lied, and they did so knowingly and intentionally. Smartmatic seeks to hold them accountable for those lies." Connolly had authority: *The New York Times* reported he had previously won the largest ever defamation settlement in American media, more than $177 million, for a beef producer whose "lean finely textured beef" was described by ABC News as "pink slime." The next day, Fox News cancelled the *Lou Dobbs Tonight* show. Although Dobbs was kept on contract, he was kept off air.

Two days later, Lachlan announced that Suzanne Scott had been renewed on a multi-year contract. He lavished high praise upon her and endorsed her programming shake-up. Media industry pundits were confused. *The Daily Beast* was reliable and its January story suggesting Scott was on her way out had appeared extremely well sourced, but the Murdochs had managed to keep a lid on any ructions at the top and were now stonewalling. Lachlan told investors that Fox had finished 2020 with the highest average primetime ratings in the history of cable TV, but conceded that ratings had dropped by about 13 per cent in the months after the election. He said that ratings drop was exactly what he'd predicted three months earlier and was smack in the middle of the range experienced at Liberal-leaning CNN and MSNBC, 17 and 10 per cent respectively, immediately after Trump won the 2016 election. Lachlan predicted that Fox would rebound. In fact, he said the recovery had already begun.

Asked about the implications of the Democrats' victory for Fox in the longer-term, Lachlan said there would be no change to the strategy. "We believe where we're targeted, to the center right, is exactly where we should be targeted," he said. "We don't need to go further right. We don't believe America is further right, and we're obviously not going to pivot left." A few weeks later, at Morgan Stanley's annual media industry conference, Lachlan sat down for a lengthy Q&A and was asked whether he was anxious about Fox News' leadership position. In reply, he noted:

> If history is any lesson, the main beneficiary of the Trump administration, from a ratings point of view, was MSNBC . . . and that's because they're in loyal opposition, right? They called out the president when he needed to be called out. That's what our job is now with the Biden administration. And you'll see our ratings really improve from here, and we'll do so for at least the next four years.

Lachlan's "loyal opposition" comment was taken as an admission and confirmation of Fox News' deliberate partisan bias and sparked headlines round the world. From a ratings point of view, it would gradually become clear that he was dead right. Ratings, however, are not everything.

At the end of March, Dominion filed its own $1.6 billion defamation lawsuit against Fox News. The 139-page affidavit, which laid out all the baseless claims, Dominion's attempts to set the record straight, the continued repetitions regardless, and the damage to Dominion and its employees, was devastating. Even other Murdoch-controlled outlets, such as the *Wall Street Journal*, had rejected the allegations against Dominion as baseless. Yet the allegations were repeated, the claim read, as part of a manufactured storyline about election fraud which cast Dominion as the villain, turning the little-known company into a household name in a concerted effort to lure back Trump supporters, "to serve its own commercial purposes." Towards the end, the claim concluded:

> Fox acted with actual malice through the people—agents of Fox—who had responsibility for airing these broadcasts and publishing these defamatory statements. They include—but are not limited to—the hosts of the relevant programs: Maria Bartiromo, Tucker Carlson, Lou Dobbs, Sean Hannity, and Jeanine Pirro; the producers and editors of those programs; the

Fox executives responsible for airing each of those broadcasts, including but not limited to Suzanne Scott, Jay Wallace, Tom Lowell, Meade Cooper, John Fiedler, Lauren Petterson; and the Fox executives responsible for overseeing Fox, including but not limited to Rupert Murdoch and Lachlan Murdoch.

Once again, just as he had been in Australia through the sagas of Super League and the endless litigation over One.Tel, Lachlan was embroiled in a major lawsuit. At least he could draw some comfort from the confidence of his chief counsel, Viet Dinh, who boasted to a legal blogger that the US constitution protected news organizations covering elections, and said he was not losing sleep over the Smartmatic or Dominion cases:

Obviously, the biggest story in Washington, in America, and in the world at the time was the post-election challenge to the election results. When a presidential contender challenges the fairness of the election, when his campaign and his attorneys are litigating the results of the election, and when that contender is the sitting president of the United States, that is a newsworthy event to the third order. The newsworthy nature of the contested presidential election deserved full and fair coverage from all journalists, Fox News did its job, and this is what the First Amendment protects. I'm not at all concerned about such lawsuits, real or imagined. The job of our news reporters is to cover the news fully and fairly. The job of our opinion hosts is to entertain guests who can voice their own opinions. The opinion hosts also speak very clearly, and at times passionately, about the views they hold themselves. Both aspects are important to the enduring appeal and relevance of Fox News. We have a world-class news operation, and we have opinion hosts who attract very good guests. Not only do I have no regrets, but I think they are serving in the proudest tradition of American journalism.[6]

Dinh's confidence would prove misplaced.

23

Keep Winning

WITH AMERICA RACKED BY COVID and tearing itself apart in race, religion, and culture wars stoked at least partly by Fox News, Lachlan and Sarah made the decision to move back to Sydney. Australia had come through the pandemic much better than America, measured in COVID cases and deaths, and although the couple could, of course, afford the best care in the US, they believed Australia was a healthier place to raise teenagers. On March 11 2021, they celebrated Rupert's ninetieth birthday at his Bel Air vineyard, strictly a family affair, as a much bigger party was planned for later in the year, and the next day boarded their Gulfstream 650 and jetted off to Sydney, hoping to make a stealthy arrival. The corporate aviation terminal at Mascot airport is closely watched, however, and inevitably word got out. *The Sydney Morning Herald*'s gossip columnist Andrew Hornery, well sourced on the Murdochs, got the scoop, reporting that the family would be living in Sydney for "years, not months." Kalan, Aidan, and Aerin were enrolled in private schools, and after two weeks' self-isolation at Cavan, they all moved into the enormous Bellevue Hill mansion they had renovated at huge expense but had so far hardly lived in since leaving five years ago.

Hornery suggested that Lachlan and Sarah were sick of the opprobrium coming their way in liberal Hollywood, even suggesting the kids had been targeted. "I heard things got pretty rough, especially for the kids at school," an anonymous source in Los Angeles source told Hornery. "The school communities here are very close knit, and it extends into the wider families and the circles and parties they all go to. That Hollywood set is very pro-Democratic. They are mostly big fundraisers for Biden, so you can imagine how well it went down when one of their classmates' dads is at the helm of the biggest anti-Biden machine in the country."

Lachlan's spokesman flatly denied those reports but would not provide any more detail than to say the move was for family reasons. It was certainly true that criticism of Fox News had a sharper edge after the Capitol insurrection. "They own this," wrote the influential Washington Post media columnist Margaret Sullivan, about the pro-Trump media, led by Fox News.[1] *Wolverine* director James Mangold called on Hollywood to boycott Fox and made it personal, tweeting: "The Murdochs have inflicted so much racism, sexism, virulent lies & damage to our nation. Fellow content makers, we must cancel appearances on Fox & use our power to keep ads 4 our shows off Fox." *Knocked Up* director Judd Apatow tweeted: "Sure people in the administration will quit. Who will show some honor and quit working for @FoxNews? Who will stop working for Lachlan Murdoch and the people who monetize division, racism, corruption, bad covid information which kills and treason? They helped create all of this."

Two days before he left Los Angeles, Lachlan had sent a company-wide email deferring a physical return-to-work from April until September. Arguably it made little difference where Lachlan was, and he supposedly turned nocturnal, working through the Sydney nights to keep normal business hours in Los Angeles and New York. Nonetheless, Lachlan's move to Australia raised eyebrows, reinforcing perceptions that Viet Dinh, rather than Lachlan, was really in charge at Fox, as *The New York Times* reported in April. Dinh tried hard to pour cold water on the chatter, professing his loyalty to Lachlan in a *Variety* piece,[2] and Lachlan declared he'd return to the US in September. To show he could run the joint from down under, Lachlan did a rare interview with *Business Insider*'s chief media correspondent Claire Atkinson at 2 a.m., Sydney time, 10 a.m. her time, telling her how he went to bed at 8 p.m. every evening and only slept four hours, and then pulled all-nighters. According to the article's headline, it was all to "prove he is a worthy successor to his father."

Waking up at midnight and taking a strong coffee, just one, on advice from his friend Pucko, who did nightshifts on the wharves, Lachlan would then join Zoom meetings stateside, including a daily conference call with Suzanne Scott. He listened, mostly, only weighing in when it came to the big talent, or hirings and firings. Atkinson reported that an unnamed source close to the Murdoch family blamed James for the critique in *The New York Times*, saying the younger brother was "running a whisper campaign that Lachlan is not good at his job and doesn't deserve it." Lachlan opened up a little on the polarization of America, arguing it was not the fault of Fox News, but of social media, which "algorithmically drives people into echo chambers. If Facebook or Twitter and others ultimately become a bias filter for the facts that we take as truth in the world, I think that's really dangerous and a sort of scary world to live in." He also pointed up the vociferous criticism directed at Fox from conservatives, from Trump down. "In a strange way, if you've got the left and the right criticizing you, you're doing something right. You really are in the middle." Lachlan downplayed speculation that Fox would be recombined with News, or taken private, and insisted he was in the job for the long haul: "It's a terrific job," he said. "It's one I look forward to for decades and decades into the future."[3] Just like his father, Lachlan was proposing that he'd still be in the job in his nineties. Given his track record of ambivalence about working inside the family company, it was hard to picture.

* * *

The Australian political environment was not as welcoming to the Murdochs as Lachlan might have hoped. At the end of 2020, former Labor prime minister Kevin Rudd had launched an online petition to the federal parliament calling for a Royal Commission into the Murdoch media's abuse of its effective monopoly in Australia. Dubbing it the #MurdochRoyalCommission, Rudd explained in a punchy two-minute video that:

Murdoch has become a cancer, an arrogant cancer, on our democracy. Number one, it's the sheer concentration of Murdoch's media ownership. Seventy per cent of our print readership is owned by Murdoch. In my state of Queensland, which swings so many federal election outcomes, Murdoch owns virtually each and every one of the newspapers up here. Number two, over the last decade, in eighteen out of the last eighteen federal and state elections, Murdoch has viciously campaigned in support of one side of politics, the Liberal National Party, and viciously campaigned against the Australian Labor Party. There's no such thing as a level playing field anymore. Number three, why does he do it? Murdoch, in fact, has loss-making newspapers, but he keeps them, and buys more of them, with a single purpose in mind, which is to maximize his political power in the country, in defense of his ideological interests, like climate change denial, as well as to prosecute his commercial interests as we've seen with the national broadband network. And the final reason we need this Royal Commission is the sheer arrogance and swagger and bullying behavior by Murdoch and his editors against anybody— anybody—who stands up against him or has a different point of view.

The petition crashed the parliament's website, attracting more than 38,000 signatures within twenty-four hours, and would go on to become the largest e-petition ever submitted, with more than half a million signatures. Rudd's one-time political enemy Malcolm Turnbull signed as well, although he doubted there would be a Royal Commission and pointed out the Murdoch print monopoly dated back to 1987. Sure enough, the Morrison government ruled out a Royal Commission as soon as the petition was lodged, but the Senate backed a Greens motion for an inquiry into media diversity in Australia. Hearings got underway in Canberra in February, and Rudd was the first witness. He told senators:

... the uncomfortable truth in this building is that everyone is frightened of Murdoch—they really are. There's a culture of fear across the country, and the fear is rationally based. They've seen many cases of individual political leaders and others who have had their characters assassinated through a systematic campaign by the Murdoch media ... it's not in your personal political interests ever to go after Rupert Murdoch or Lachlan Murdoch, because they will get you. Therefore, if we in 2021 have to deal with such a culture of fear in this building and across the nation, where the Murdoch media monopoly is the monopoly which dare not speak its name—we can't mention the 'M' world because we know it invites retribution—that's just dead wrong for any democracy.

In a parting shot, knowing that News Corp's local chairman Michael Miller and corporate affairs manager Campbell Reid were about to give evidence, Rudd suggested that perhaps the committee should call Rupert or Lachlan Murdoch to appear, given they ran the show. "That would be a great exercise in transparency," he said. "Tough, but I leave that little challenge with you."

Turnbull, when it was his turn to appear in April, told the committee that the fundamental problem was that "the most powerful political actor in Australia is not the Liberal Party or the National Party or the Labor Party. It is News Corp. And it's utterly unaccountable. It's controlled by an American family and their interests are no longer, if they ever were, coextensive with our own." Coming from two former prime ministers, the testimony was damning. The inquiry hearings dragged on through the year. Lachlan had no intention of appearing.

A more positive development for the Murdoch media in Australia was the introduction of the federal government's long-awaited legislation to compel digital platforms such as Facebook and Google to come to an agreement with traditional media companies to pay for the news content they distributed. The laws were bitterly opposed by the tech industry. Facebook at one point blocked its news feeds in Australia, in protest. But the Morrison government had a history of taking on the platforms and the reforms were supported by Labor, the Greens, and most of the media industry, which stood to gain a new revenue stream to offset the loss of advertizing. Through February and March 2020, News chief Robert Thomson, who had been a key player in the development of the Code, holding meetings with the ACCC commissioner Rod Sims during the design phase, announced multi-year deals with both Google and Facebook. In a statement littered with his trademark alliteration, Thomson said the deals "simply would not have been possible without the fervent, unstinting support of Rupert and Lachlan Murdoch, and the News Corp board. For many years, we were accused of tilting at tech windmills, but what was a solitary campaign, a quixotic quest, has become a movement, and both journalism and society will be enhanced. While others in our industry were silent or supine as digital dysfunctionality threatened to turn journalism into a mendicant order."

It was big news, not only in Australia, but around the world, as legacy media hunted for more sustainable business models in the digital era. Brokers estimated that the deals with News were worth north of $50 million a year. The US Congress took note of the legislation and the *Columbia Journalism Review* speculated that America might go next, while noting criticisms of the opacity of the code regime, inequity about how the money was shared around, and a lack of detail about whether the money would be invested in journalism or not.[4] Small Australian media outlets such as *Crikey* at first thought the code regime smacked of political favoritism—the latest in a long line of handouts from the coalition government to News Corp—but were soon sharing the benefits as millions of dollars poured into the coffers of recognized publishers across the industry.[5] A year later, however, the *Wall Street Journal* reported Facebook was re-examining its commitments to pay for news. While Facebook had paid more than $10 million to the *Washington Post*, $15 million to *The New York Times*, and over $20 million to the *Wall Street Journal* itself, the social media giant had provided no indication it would renew its partnerships and the story suggested it may prove the end of a détente between big tech and legacy media.[6] If newspaper and television companies round the world had been counting on rivers of gold from digital platforms flowing endlessly, they were once again on notice.

* * *

Lachlan Murdoch's observation that Fox News would be the loyal opposition to the Biden administration dropped out of the news cycle quickly, but it did not take long for the next controversy to erupt. When Suzanne Scott switched the 7 p.m. weeknight slot from news over to opinion after the Biden inauguration, trying out a rotating panel of hosts for a new show, *Fox News Primetime*, the balance of programming shifted a little more towards conservative opinion. Fox's former longstanding political correspondent Carl Cameron told *The Washington Post* that the network hoped to restore their conservative base. "Conservatives are going to want to hear what's wrong with Joe Biden," said Cameron. "It's easier for Fox to beat Newsmax and everybody else back into the woods than it is for them to try to compete with the real journalism networks."[7] One of the slated fill-in hosts of *Fox News Primetime* was Canadian author and commentator Mark Steyn. On a Thursday in early April, he did an interview with Tucker Carlson that went quickly off the rails. Winding himself up on one of his favorite topics, immigration, Carlson told Steyn:

> Now, I know that the left and all the little gatekeepers on Twitter become literally hysterical if you use the term "replacement," if you suggest that the Democratic Party is trying to replace the current electorate, the voters now casting ballots, with new people, more obedient voters from the Third World. But they become hysterical because that's what's happening actually. Let's just say it: That's true . . . If you change the population, you dilute the political power of the people who live there. So every time they import a new voter, I become disenfranchised as a current voter.

So I don't understand what we don't understand cause, I mean, everyone wants to make a racial issue out of it. Oh, you know, the white replacement theory? No, no, no. This is a voting right question. I have less political power because they are importing a brand new electorate. Why should I sit back and take that? The power that I have as an American guaranteed at birth is one man, one vote, and they are diluting it. No, they are not allowed to do it. Why are we putting up with this?[8]

Carlson appeared to be explicitly endorsing the deeply racist and anti-Semitic Great Replacement Theory, which had surfaced in the mainstream in the 2017 Unite the Right rally in Charlottesville where neo-Nazis had chanted "Jews will not replace us!" The theory had been cited by far-right murderers in the 2018 Tree of Life synagogue shootings in Pittsburgh, and the Christchurch, New Zealand, and El Paso, Texas, massacres in 2019, which targeted Muslims and Hispanics respectively. The theory, which has roots in European anti-semitism going back to before World War II, was popularized in a 2011 book *Le Grand Remplacement* by French nationalist writer Renaud Camus, who argued that a globalist elite was engineering a replacement of the white population using non-white immigration, particularly of Muslims, and demographic change driven by a lower white birth rate (in turn often blamed on abortion, homosexuality, and feminists).

It was far from the first time Carlson had touched on this theme, but it was the first time it captured widespread attention. The Anti-Defamation League immediately condemned Carlson, with CEO Jonathan Greenblatt pointing out in an open letter to Suzanne Scott that it was not a first offense, citing Carlson's numerous attacks on diversity and people of color, his full-throated defense of the antisemitic QAnon conspiracy, and his denial that white supremacy was a problem in America. Greenblatt concluded that Carlson's embrace of the replacement theory was a bridge too far and given his "long record of race-baiting, we believe it is time for Carlson to go." Greenblatt followed up with an interview on Brian

Stelter's *Reliable Sources* program, accusing Carlson of introducing the Great Replacement Theory to his millions of viewers and "serving as a gateway to one of the most damaging and dangerous conspiracy theories out there." Stelter pressed Greenblatt on the likely dismissive response from Fox and Greenblatt zeroed in on the role of the Murdochs, and Lachlan in particular:

> . . . the Murdochs have given up on it, they think Tucker is in charge. You know, someone needs to remind the Murdochs, they pay Tucker. Tucker is their employee. They're allowed to sanction him. They're allowed to, you know, give him some guidance. But it doesn't seem to ever happen. There is a lack of leadership that is emphasized by the fact that Lachlan Murdoch is basically living in Sydney, Australia . . . now, what is that? Fifteen time zones away from Fox News' headquarters in New York.

Stung into action, instead of allowing Scott to respond to the ADL, Lachlan wrote to Greenblatt himself that day in a letter that was quickly shared with CNN:

> Fox Corporation shares your values and abhors anti-semitism, white supremacy, and racism of any kind. In fact, I remember fondly the ADL honoring my father with your International Leadership Award, and we continue to support your mission. Concerning the segment of 'Tucker Carlson Tonight' on April 8th, however, we respectfully disagree. A full review of the guest interview indicates that Mr. Carlson decried and rejected replacement theory. As Mr. Carlson himself stated during the guest interview: 'White replacement theory? No, no, this is a voting rights question.'

With such a rare, public defense from the very top of the company, according to Media Matters' president Angelo Carusone, Lachlan gave

Carlson a "green light" to continue to perpetuate the theory. It would come back to haunt him. Greenblatt rejected the Fox response out of hand in a letter replying directly to Lachlan, insisting that Carlson had given an underhanded endorsement of a white supremacist trope. He again brought the argument back to the responsibility of the Murdochs:

> Although I appreciate the sentiment that you and your father continue to support ADL's mission, supporting Mr. Carlson's embrace of the 'great replacement theory' stands in direct contrast to that mission. As you noted in your letter, ADL honored your father over a decade ago, but let me be clear that we would not do so today, and it does not absolve you, him, the network, or its board from the moral failure of not taking action against Mr. Carlson.

Harking back to the ADL's recognition of Rupert underlined how far the Murdoch empire had shifted to the right, and that Lachlan had now gone further right than his father. For his part, Tucker Carlson revelled in in the criticism the following week, replaying his comments and describing it as "provably true" that "demographic change is the key to the Democratic Party's political ambitions," telling his audience their goal is "to make you irrelevant." Carlson was clearly not going to be fired and Greenblatt used a speech to the World Federation of Advertisers to call for a boycott of Fox News, in an extension of ADL's broader "Stop Hate for Profit" campaign against social media giants like Facebook. The ADL was backed by a coalition of more than forty non-government and activist groups who wrote an open letter to advertizers:

> Media buyers who aren't watching Fox News daily are an easy target to get duped by the network's empty promises of feel-good and fact-based reporting . . . More and more, we have seen major corporations and brands publicly state that they cannot simply sit idly by and do or say nothing as political extremists attack our

democratic institutions, undermine our public health response to the COVID-19 and climate crises, spew misogynistic beliefs, and stoke racial, anti-LGBTQ and xenophobic violence.

In response, a Fox spokesperson told *The Wrap* that the company was "about to close out its fourth consecutive year delivering new records in advertizing revenue, so clearly Media Matters' predictable ongoing partisan attacks have zero impact outside of their irrelevant echo chamber on social media."

Activist groups Media Matters and Sleeping Giants soon signalled a shift in tactics, targeting the cable providers who underpinned the news channel with lucrative affiliate revenues, rather than advertizers, with an #unfoxmycablebox campaign pointing out that consumers were propping up Fox News whether they watched it or not, by paying for those hidden affiliate fees that were two and three times higher than those paid to CNN or MSNBC. There was little impact. Fox enjoyed ad pricing gains of 20 per cent in "unprecedented" upfronts mid-year, including a tripling in revenue for streaming service Tubi, and cable affiliate renewal deals surged. A few months later, after a live cross to a Fox reporter in Del Rio about the "flood" of Haitian immigrants being released into the US by border officials, Tucker Carlson returned to the replacement theory again, and this time left no room for doubt. He played an edited 2015 clip of then Vice President Biden describing the "unrelenting stream of immigration" that would leave white Americans in the minority as "a source of our strength." Then Carlson went on:

> . . . there's a reason Biden said it. In political terms, this policy is called the great replacement, the replacement of legacy Americans with more obedient people from far away countries. They brag about it all the time, but if you dare to say it is happening, they will scream at you with maximum hysteria. And here you have Joe Biden confirming his motive on tape with a smile on his face.

Again the Anti-Defamation League called for Carlson to be fired but this time, neither Fox nor Lachlan bothered to respond. Carlson was backed up by Florida Republican Rep. Matt Gaetz, who tweeted he was "CORRECT" about the Great Replacement and that the ADL was itself a "racist organization." Former Fox anchor Megyn Kelly, who had launched her own podcast on Sirius XM after leaving NBC, had Carlson on as a guest and asked him about the ADL. "Fuck them," said Carlson, denying the replacement theory was racist and attacking Greenblatt, a former Obama administration official, as a Democratic apparatchik.

* * *

A furore about Tucker Carlson and white supremacy. appealing as it was to a section of the MAGA base. was an unwelcome distraction for Lachlan Murdoch in the first half of 2021 as he tried to breathe life into Fox Bet. Online sports gambling was in a "land grab" phase in the US. Flutter's majority-owned FanDuel was already the clear market leader, well ahead of DraftKings and third-ranked BetMGM. Flutter chief Peter Jackson said that while the power of Fox was important, Fox Bet itself was "not a great product and they didn't come to market with an enormous set of customers on their database."[9] Despite forecasting it would bring in $20 billion in revenue by 2025, Flutter shares were undervalued. The company flagged the possible float of a stake in Fanduel to trigger a re-rate of the stock by investors. In April, Lachlan responded in kind to Jackson's hardball tactics, suing in New York's Judicial Arbitration and Mediation tribunal to force the exercise of Fox's option to buy 18.6 per cent of FanDuel at the same effective price that Flutter had paid in December. Flutter refused, arguing Fox would have to pay fair market value as of July, when the option would be exercised, and vowing to defend itself "vigorously." The difference was significant. Analysts reckoned the price would be a billion pounds higher if Fox's suit failed and the whole case was set down for compulsory and confidential arbitration which was unresolved at the time of writing.

Lachlan was conciliatory in public, constantly reiterating t looked forward to a long partnership with Flutter, but the stakes grew higher as Fox Bet languished in the US market while FanDuel grew and grew. By March 2022, Lachlan was admitting he was "disappointed" that Fox Bet was only available in four states, although gaming by then was legal in thirty. Although analysts described Fox as "the best-positioned media company to benefit from sports betting," and anyone could see the potential upside. more than three years after the Stars Group deal, the promise remained unfulfilled.

The legal battle over its FanDuel option came as Lachlan approved a series of acquisitions at both Fox and News. None was earth-shattering individually, but combined they added up to some $7 billion worth of investment across twenty different deals since the Disney sale in 2019, according to a tally by the *Financial Times*. "Lachlan appears to have taken his cue from Rupert, who was known for constant dealmaking," wrote the *FT*, noting that Lachlan had pushed Fox into sports betting, streaming, and even blockchain, with an unspecified investment in non-fungible token company Eluvio in the second half of 2021. Fox continued to invest in content, too, buying sports site Outkick in May, gossip website TMZ in September, and launching a new streaming service, Fox Weather, to compete with The Weather Channel. There was immediate speculation about how Fox News Media, which broadcast so much climate denial, could be trusted to report on the weather in the era of climate change, but Suzanne Scott believed weather reporting was overdue for an overhaul. Over at News Corp, Lachlan as co-chair, greenlighted the $1.2 billion acquisition of financial data provider the Oil Price Investment Service, to be merged with Dow Jones, as well *Investor's Business Daily*, and book publisher Houghton Mifflin Harcourt for $349 million, while REA group expanded into Singapore's digital real estate market by buying *PropertyGuru*. Again, none of these acquisitions really transformed News Corp, and there was more head-scratching about Lachlan's strategy, except to note that all were small-to-middling in size. Unlike Rupert, Lachlan refused to overpay.

Whatever the strategy, by August it seemed to be working: Fox Corp unveiled profit results that showed the company bouncing back from the pandemic in rude health, doubling its net income to $2.2 billion. At the investor briefing, Lachlan crowed that revenue and profits at Fox had "exceeded even our own bullish expectations" even without the Superbowl that year. The results were driven partly by record political advertizing through the 2020 presidential campaign. The most important driver, by far, was Fox News, which had recovered from its ratings wobble after the defeat of Trump and notched its seventy-eighth straight quarter as the leading cable news channel in total viewers. Total view time at Tubi was up by half on a year earlier and Lachlan talked up Tubi's new original content as well as its library, while stressing that Fox's strategy was very different to streaming. "We have no interest or plans to invest in high-cost programming to drive subscriber acquisition, as we are not in the subscriber business," he said. "We are focused on delivering programming that drives total viewing time and hence monetization in very short order . . . measured in weeks, not years." A good chunk of the Fox earnings were reinvested in the business, including a state-of-the-art multi-platform advertizing, distribution, and streaming data and technology center in Arizona. Lachlan again talked up the potential of Fox Nation, without releasing figures, and of squeezing more money out of Fox through "new verticals of content . . . around real estate, around cooking, around some engaging games and crosswords and things as we drive the Fox News brand into more lifestyle categories."

The criticisms of Fox News' editorial decisions, however, kept coming. At the end of August, the flagship current affairs program of Australia's ABC TV, *Four Corners*, aired a two-part investigation, "Fox and the Big Lie," in which former staffers including Gretchen Carlson and Chris Stirewalt criticized the Murdochs for letting Trump dictate Fox News' coverage and purveying misinformation that led to the January 6 insurrection. Carlson said that for all his faults, her old boss Roger Ailes had genuinely believed Fox was "fair and balanced," and suggested he would never have indulged the Big Lie, even if it did come from the president. "I don't believe he would have allowed it to get to this point," said Carlson. "He would have called up Trump and, you know, said knock it off, right? And he did in the past." Carlson, who had to decline to answer questions about the Fox News culture due to the strict non-disclosure agreement she had signed when she settled her claim against the company for $20 million, said it was "up to the morality of news operations to provide factual information." If they didn't, she said, no doubt choosing her words carefully, "I believe that it's proof that opinion television has gone in a completely, you know, far right direction." For his part, Chris Stirewalt became visibly upset when he talked about his dismissal from Fox News, and said he was disappointed that instead of being proud of the Arizona call, the network had repeatedly given voice to people claiming the election had been stolen. After the downfall of Ailes, Stirewalt said, he had been under the "false belief" that the Murdochs would "elevate the value of news . . . [but] they were not there to make Fox more mainstream. Quite the opposite." The program concluded with a searing quote from Stirewalt:

> If we don't find in the United States a healthier way to run the news business, we're going to fall apart. This is killing us. We saw the consequences on January 6th. We are rapidly, radically eroding public confidence in institutions for the most rotten of reasons, which is profit and power.[10]

The *Four Corners* program was met with a furious volley of articles in News Corp papers—forty-five in two days—criticising it and attacking the ABC. Fox followed up with written complaints of bias to the public broadcaster, the federal government, and the Australian Communications and Media Authority. The full-court press contributed to impressions that Lachlan, who already had defamation actions underway against Australian journalists Neil Chenoweth (for revealing the 2004 buyer of Lachlan's Lafayette Street apartment) and Steven Mayne (over a disparaging reference to his track record at Channel Ten), was not as thick-skinned as his father, who had never sued another journalist.

At the same time, Fox News was coming under scrutiny over the Big Lie, its Australian cousin Sky News, wholly owned by News Corp, was under attack over its pandemic coverage, culminating in Google banning the channel from YouTube for a week in August, citing alleged breaches of its COVID misinformation policies. The furore came at a sensitive time for Sky, which had just done a deal with broadcaster Southern Cross Austereo to play Sky News as a free-to-air multichannel 24/7 in more than a million homes in rural and regional Australia. Sky News boss Paul Whittaker, a former newspaper editor who reported to News Corp's Australian broadcast chief, Siobhan McKenna, and who was personally close to Lachlan, was charged with reining in some of the excesses on Sky. One host, former conservative radio star Alan Jones, had had his column in *The Daily Telegraph* cancelled after he called the chief health officer of New South Wales a "village idiot." He was soon struggling to get his television contract renewed.

Sky was the biggest Australian news channel on YouTube, with a huge number of its clips watched by people in the US. The social media platform generated significant revenue for News Corp. When Whittaker was called in to appear at the Senate Media Diversity inquiry, he argued that the Google ban was ridiculous and that when it came to the crunch, YouTube had been unable to identify any breaches of its COVID misinformation policies. The inquiry also heard again from Kevin Rudd, who ripped into Lachlan personally for his "no-show":

> . . . when you've requested Mr Lachlan Murdoch to attend this inquiry, it's not just a matter of color and movement and interesting journalism and reportage; it goes to the essential nature of the power within the Murdoch media operation and who calls the shots and dictates the editorial direction of Sky News. I regard Mr Lachlan Murdoch's non-attendance today as not only deeply disappointing but, frankly, utterly spineless, given the power which he wields within the operation. And Mr Whittaker knows that Mr Murdoch wields that power.

The committee also examined Robert Thomson, the News Corp chief executive, over reports that he had met in New York with prime minister Scott Morrison, Australian ambassador Arthur Sinodinos, and former consul-general Nick Greiner. It was suspected that the prime minister wanted supportive coverage for the government's adoption of a "net zero emissions by 2050" target ahead of the UN climate talks in Glasgow. Coincidentally or otherwise, in a stunning about-face given years of downplaying or outright denying climate change, News Corp had indeed announced an Australian campaign supporting the net zero target on the day of the committee hearings, which duly ran in a burst of pre-Glasgow reporting. Both Whittaker and Thomson downplayed the internal politics behind News' decision to support the campaign.

Lachlan might have looked like he was dodging parliamentary scrutiny, but he had flown back to the US for a reason: the previous March, Fox had deferred the date for News staff to return to the office to no earlier than September 7, the Tuesday after Labor Day. He wanted to be on site. As it happened, that was also the day before Lachlan's fiftieth birthday. With his family back in Sydney, it was a subdued affair. *Crikey* wished Lachlan "many happy returns," running an article by Christopher Warren, the former long-time federal secretary of the Media, Entertainment & Arts Alliance (the union co-founded by Sir Keith) and past president of the International Federation of Journalists. Warren contrasted Lachlan's achievements at fifty with those of his father and grandfather at the same age, describing the uber-privileged successor as still under Rupert, waiting in the wings:

He's never demonstrated the older Murdochs' taste for the play of politics, nor their deep passion for journalism. It's not even clear what he thinks about the big issues of the moment or, more importantly, what the family's media should do about them . . . Sometimes it seems Lachlan's major achievement is, like Prince Charles, simply surviving as heir-apparent in his parents' court. It seems to have taught a withdrawn caution. Maybe that's the skill News Corp needs as its industry declines.[11]

It was an unkind assessment from afar, which showed that even after decades in the media, and in Australia, a small pond where the Murdochs exerted maximum influence, many journalists still did not know what to make of Lachlan.

After reopening the Fox offices, Lachlan flew to England for his father's much-delayed ninetieth birthday party, which had been in planning for over a year. It was hosted by Jerry Hall at Holmwood, the £11 million, eleven-bedroom Georgian manor in the Chilterns west of London, the couple's temporary home while they finished a £30 million renovation of their palace in the Cotswolds, which was nearer both to Elisabeth Murdoch and to Rebekah Brooks and her family.

As it happened, his birthday party coincided with a significant deal for Rupert: after getting bored watching British TV through the pandemic, and after the spectacular failure of the mismanaged online news channel GB News, the ageing mogul hatched a plan to launch a Fox News-like digital channel, TalkTV, anchored by former *News of the World* editor Piers Morgan. Brooks was reportedly not sold on the commercial prospects of TalkTV, but both Rupert and Lachlan were in favor, and soon Morgan had a staggering £50 million, three-year deal to do a nightly show that would appear on TalkTV in the UK, Fox Nation in the US, and Sky News in Australia. He would also host a true-crime series, write his next book for HarperCollins, and pen tabloid columns for *The Sun* and *New York Post*. It was possibly the first talent deal that tied together properties across both Fox and News corporations, and Morgan tweeted that he was coming "home" to the Murdoch empire after an absence of nearly two decades. The news added a bit of sizzle to Rupert's birthday party. A ninety-minute homage had been in preparation for ages. Requests for footage had gone to Australia's National Film and Sound Archive over a year earlier. Pulled together by Liz Murdoch and David Hill, the film opened cheekily with the *Succession* theme song and featured tributes from Lachlan, British prime minister Boris Johnson, former Australian prime ministers John Howard and Tony Abbott, all of from the political right, of course. There were few high-profile politicians in the 150-strong guest list, but the most remarkable

absentee was Rupert's son, James, who had been invited but chose
attend. It was a very public sign of the depth of division within the family.
Six weeks later, another birthday party would be held in New York, in a
tent next to the famous Tavern on the Green restaurant in Central Park.
The same tribute was played to 130 guests including political and business
leaders Henry Kissinger, Mike Pompeo, Mike Bloomberg, Jeff Shell, Henry
Kravis, Roger Goodell, distinguished former Murdoch executives from
Barry Diller to Peter Chernin, and the top brass from Fox and News. Once
again, James was invited but did not turn up.

In between the two parties, Lachlan celebrated a milestone that had
more significance for the cultural fabric of America: the twenty-fifth
anniversary of the launch of Fox News on October 7, 1996. A special
ceremony was held to coincide with the opening of Fox's brand-new,
all-digital bureau in Washington DC. Lachlan and Suzanne Scott cut
the ribbon with a pair of giant Fox scissors, and the pair went on to
host a town hall meeting in New York, relaying messages from the 136
employees who had been there since the beginning. The Empire State
Building was floodlit in red, white, and blue to mark the occasion, and on
the Sunday ahead of the anniversary, the Fox News Channel produced a
special one-hour show drawing heavily on the network archives; forty of
the network's top stars appeared in one-minute promo videos explaining
what Fox meant to them, alongside tribute clips from Donald Trump,
George W. Bush, and dozens more. In one interview, breaking news
correspondent Trace Gallagher marvelled at the incredible loyalty of
the Fox audience: "I have been in so many homes, I kid you not, [where
the] Fox News Channel emblem on the bottom of the screen is burned
into the television. It is on 24 hours a day. They feel you are their family."

On the day of the anniversary, anchor Greg Gutfeld pondered how
Fox News had come to dominate cable television in a chat on panel show
The Five, and summed up the outsider mentality at Fox perfectly:

How did this happen? First, it was necessary, it had to happen.
The mainstream news not only refused to serve most Americans,

they felt they didn't have to. They controlled the narratives, and you had little choice but to take it. They abused your trust, they lied to you, thought you were stupid, they shared the same brain. So the industry devolved into a corrupt insular machine out to stoke division, to make money. Then Fox came along. We were different. We knew this monolithic media was derelict in its duty, so Fox provided the balance that was missing. It did so fearlessly, knowing that it would paint targets on all of our backs, but its popularity grew, and why? Because we're people! We weren't perfect, we were human. You could relate to us. It wasn't a network, it was a relationship. Oh, you could get mad at us and turn us off, but you also knew that we had your best interests at heart, so you stuck with us through all the great stuff and the not-so-great stuff. Fox didn't speak down to you like the pompous gas bags at other networks. We spoke directly to you. We assumed you were as smart as us, if not smarter. We did not see family or religion as a joke. We celebrated the American idea, we relished providing a voice for the unheard.

Amid all the on-air tributes at Fox, mostly to Rupert or to Roger Ailes, or in the acres of critical commentary in other media, noting how Fox News had changed America, there was very little mention of what Lachlan had contributed to the network or what role he would play in the future. Lachlan did not do much publicity himself, preferring to keep Suzanne Scott front and center as head of Fox News Media. Intensely private, Scott did one of her only interviews, with *The Hollywood Reporter*, which portrayed her as much less of a GOP kingmaker than her predecessor Ailes had been, suggesting she was more motivated by brand success than political influence and was eager to reposition the network for the post-Trump era. Scott praised Lachlan's deal-making ability, downplayed the endless controversy surrounding primetime, which she described as "one little piece of real estate," and shared a revealing anecdote:

Five years ago, I remember going to Rupert's office and talking about the future and he just said, "We have a lot to do, ignore the noise." And that's been my mantra, really. If I wasted any time reading stories about myself or social media posts or what have you, I wouldn't be able to get my job done . . . and you know what I always say? I sleep well at night.[12]

The twenty-fifth anniversary celebrations concluded at the end of October with the renaming of Fox News' biggest studio where panel shows *Fox & Friends* and *The Five* were shot, as well as the network's election coverage. It was dubbed Studio M, in honor of Rupert. An awkward plaque-unveiling went to air, in which Rupert and Lachlan stood arm-in-arm and stumbled over each other's words in a mix of affection and embarrassment at the self-congratulation:

> LACHLAN: We are inspired . . .
> RUPERT: You too . . .
> LACHLAN: . . . by your passion for journalism and for news, and it's inspired us for the last twenty-five years at Fox News and for the next twenty-five years . . .
> RUPERT: . . . thank you . . .
> LACHLAN: . . . and many, many years to come. Congratulations . . .
> RUPERT: Thank you very much! I'm sure it'll go for a long time . . .
> LACHLAN: . . . alright, Dad . . .
> RUPERT: Keep winning!

24

Patriot Scourge

STRAIGHT AFTER THE ANNIVERSARY came a fresh reminder of why a celebration of Fox News could only ever be defensive or combative, rather than happy. Fox Nation dropped an incendiary trailer promoting a new "Tucker Carlson Original" series called *Patriot Purge*. Opening with a grim military drum roll and introducing itself as "The true story behind 1/6: War on Terror 2.0 and the plot against the people," the trailer showed army helicopters circling Congress, cut through with footage of the shooting of Capitol stormer Ashli Babbitt, Osama bin Laden, Trump, FBI agents crashing through doors, waterboarding and, of course, the protesters outside the Capitol, with a script that could not have been more alarmist:

> VOICE: The domestic war on terror is here, it's coming after . . . half of the country!
>
> TUCKER: The helicopters have left Afghanistan, and now they've landed here at home . . .
>
> VOICE: The left is hunting the right. Sticking them in Guantanamo Bay, who are American citizens, leaving them there to rot . . .
>
> BIDEN: . . . terrorism from white supremacy is the most lethal threat we face . . .

TUCKER: . . . they've begun to fight a new enemy, in a new war
on terror . . .

BIDEN: . . . not Al Qaeda, white supremacy . . .

VOICE: . . . false flags have happened in this country, one of
which may have been January 6th.

It was crazy stuff, amping up a baseless conspiracy theory that the FBI
had orchestrated the January 6 protests to ensnare Trump supporters.
Carlson's three-part series did not quite live up to the promise of the
terrifying trailer, but as an attention-grabber it worked brilliantly. There
was an immediate backlash across the mainstream media: a well-sourced
story by the fact-checking project PolitiFact labelled the whole premise of
the series "false," finding that it presented no credible evidence because,
of course, there was none.[1] Spokespeople for Fox News stressed that *Patriot
Purge* was only streaming on Fox Nation, the paid service for superfans,
and not Fox News. There was turmoil inside the company, nonetheless:
Geraldo Rivera joined the chorus of criticism of Tucker, telling *The
New York Times* he wondered "how much is done to provoke, rather than
illuminate."[2] Others such as Bret Baier and Chris Wallace reportedly
raised concerns internally, but two Fox contributors, Stephen Hayes and
Jonah Goldberg, who were launching their own website, *The Dispatch*, quit
Fox over the program, writing a stinging open letter.

Lachlan kept his head down, concentrating on delivering another
strong set of profit figures for the September quarter and slogging
through a November annual meeting at the Fox lot in Hollywood,
which was closed to the media and the public. Outside, two black trucks
organized by Media Matters' "Drop Fox" campaign circled the lot for
almost an hour with huge screens displaying grim signs phrased like health
warnings:

FOX'S COVID COVERAGE IS
KILLING ITS VIEWERS

FOX NEWS AND ITS SHAREHOLDERS ARE
KILLING PEOPLE

THE MURDOCHS HAVE BLOOD ON
THEIR HANDS

Inside, Lachlan and the rest of the directors and executives almost certainly saw none of it, but the bunker mentality could be forgiven, as attacks seemed to be coming from all directions. In early December, a Delaware judge threw out Fox's motion to dismiss the Dominion Voting Systems lawsuit on First Amendment grounds, an ominous verdict given Dinh's earlier assertions that the case had no merit. Another ruling six months later allowed the case to go to discovery, raising the prospect that internal emails and other documents implicating Fox or its employees, including Lachlan, could be made public. Expectations for a settlement began to increase. Days later came the shock resignation of Chris Wallace, an eighteen-year Fox veteran who was jumping ship to host his own show on CNN+, the streaming service set for launch in early 2022. Wallace said that when he joined Fox News, executives promised him that they would not interfere with his work and they had "kept that promise," but the departure of the determinedly non-partisan anchor was another sign of the rightwards drift at Fox.

In an ever-so-subtle acknowledgement that Fox had an image problem at the very least, a week later another closely briefed piece by Sarah Ellison appeared in *The Washington Post*, reporting that Lachlan was said to be "troubled" by the trailer for *Patriot Purge*. The piece included a substantiating quote from Lachlan's spokesman at Fox, Brian Nick: "When Lachlan has a concern, he addresses it internally with the team, not through the media."[3] But the story did not change the perception that Tucker Carlson, now being talked about as a potential 2024 presidential candidate for the GOP, was untouchable.

By early December, Lachlan was back in Australia with his family, preparing for the annual Christmas party he and Sarah hosted at Le Manoir in Bellevue Hills. The day before the party, the Senate's media diversity inquiry released its final report, including the key recommendation for a judicial inquiry into media diversity, ownership, and regulation with the same powers as the royal commission called for by Kevin Rudd's petition. Without specifically identifying News Corp, the committee wrote that the regulatory system for news media was no longer fit-for-purpose, observing that "large media organizations have become so powerful and unchecked that they have developed corporate cultures that consider themselves beyond the existing accountability framework." But the key recommendation was not unanimous. Conservative members of the inquiry produced dissenting reports and the opposition communications spokeswoman, Michelle Rowland, immediately ruled out Labor support for a judicial inquiry. Less than six months out from a federal election, the opposition was hardly about to pick a fight with the owner of two-thirds of the country's newspapers.

Sensing that the Senate inquiry would prove a disappointment, Rudd had established a new organization, Australians for a Murdoch Royal Commission, which would campaign at the grassroots level to turn the energy generated by his petition into a popular movement for change. Activist and author Sally Rugg, a veteran of successful campaigns on marriage equality and the rights of asylum seekers, was recruited as national director. "It's essential that Rupert and Lachlan Murdoch front up to an inquiry and answer questions," she says, adding that they must "come up and face the music":

> That's the thing about a Royal Commission—it's independent.
> It won't be Labor or Greens politicians asking the questions, it'll
> be an independent commissioner [with the authority to make
> recommendations]. Once the Murdochs are compelled to give
> evidence in a Royal Commission, we can't see how the Parliament
> won't take action to curb their monopoly and create regulatory
> frameworks that are fit for purpose.

One senior News Corp executive argues that any inquiry should be into the whole media, not one company, and sounds an ominous warning for the two former prime ministers campaigning against the Murdochs:

"If there was a royal commission, let's just say that Rudd had a lot of contact with a lot of journalists at News Corp and editors over many years, and those conversations would probably be regarded as off the record, unless of course Rudd and Turnbull were asked to give a release of any confidentiality that was carried with those conversations, and I don't think Kevin would come out of it too well."

Lachlan was not about to lose sleep over the prospect of another inquiry, however. The following evening, rainy and hot as Sydney's summer felt increasingly like a tropical wet season, he and Sarah had the top execs and talent from News Corp and Illyria over for drinks. Guests were papped on the way in, as always, and the list included former *Post* editor Col Allan and Sky News boss Paul Whittaker, investigative journalist Sharri Markson, Fitzy and Wippa from Nova, and a string of business leaders. Federal politicians were thin on the ground, except local Liberal member Dave Sharma and the state health minister, Brad Hazzard. A few days after the party, Lachlan, Sarah and the kids flew back to the US on the private jet to spend Christmas at their lodge in Aspen, recently refurbished and complete with a saltwater swimming pool.

* * *

The working year at Fox kicked off with remembrances of January 6, and in a sign of things to come, Tucker Carlson marked the occasion by downplaying the significance of "Insurrection Day" in a segment comparing it with previous watersheds like the attacks on Pearl Harbor and 9/11. Carlson then attacked MAGA firebrand Republican senator Ted Cruz for repeating the Democrats' talking points when he described January 6 as "a violent terrorist attack on the Capitol." Cruz texted Carlson immediately after the segment, begging to come on the program to explain, and the next night he did, apologising for his "mistake," which he put down to "sloppy phrasing." He copped another tongue-lashing from Carlson. The chyron read "CRUZ'ING FOR A BRUISING," making it very clear where the power lay.

The year also began with informed speculation that even at ninety-one, Rupert had one last big deal in him. News Corp was being shunned by investors who thought it a fading newspaper company, but it housed the digital growth engine Dow Jones, which was trading at a huge discount relative to the comparable *New York Times*. Did Rupert have a plan to unlock this hidden value? The speculation centered on a break-up of News, which had an unwieldy conglomerate structure dominated by the 61 per cent holding in digital real estate giant REA, but also including valuable businesses in Dow Jones, HarperCollins, and Australia's pay-TV monopolist, Foxtel, as well as the collection of venerable mastheads from the *New York Post* to *The Sun* and *The Times* in the UK, plus the Australian newspapers, which were all of negligible value, described by analysts as "the stub."

An influential column in *The Australian Financial Review* speculated that, if consensus emerged among the members of the Murdoch Family Trust, an external private equity partner could join with them to take Dow Jones out of News Corp, and that third parties could also easily be found for REA and HarperCollins.[4] Foxtel was trickier: for most of the second half of 2021, News and 33 per cent owner Telstra had been softening up investors for a potential float of the pay-TV arm, which had pushed successfully into live sports streaming with its Kayo app and was diversifying into news and entertainment. Although Foxtel had been losing subscribers before the pandemic, lockdowns had boosted audiences so much that a full or partial selldown of the business looked possible. Foxtel had never been the most logical fit inside News Corp, but it had been structured in 2012 to hold all of the Australian businesses in one company, potentially as a vehicle for Lachlan to run or own himself. Now, with Lachlan back in the family fold and chairman of both Fox and News, it could fall to him to break up the company and the Foxtel float was key to unlocking the potential for a deal. Unfortunately for News, analysts and investors remained sceptical that Foxtel's audience boost would prove sustainable, especially since the pending merger of Discovery and Warner Media meant that the HBO contract was unlikely to be renewed beyond 2023. They also doubted that the new streaming apps would generate anywhere near the earnings of the legacy pay-TV business.

In early February, News put out its most profitable set of earnings figures since the company had split with Fox: record revenues and almost a billion dollars' profit in the last six months of 2021, up 30 per cent on the year before. Its licensing deals with Facebook and Google had substantially boosted the company's revenue. News boasted that Foxtel's subscribers were up by two-thirds, with Kayo and its entertainment equivalent Binge each now reaching more than a million Australians. Profits were up at REA, Dow Jones, book publishing, and even newspapers. Foxtel was the exceptional division: it shrank, although it still made money.

Late February, as it happened, was the anniversary of Sky News Australia, which had been scheduled for August but delayed by six months. Lachlan flew in from LA on the private jet with Piers Morgan, who shared a cheery selfie on the tarmac with garland and Mai Tai from a stopover in Hawaii. With a federal election approaching in May, there was no shortage of politicians on hand to mark the occasion, held at the prestigious Bennelong restaurant at the Sydney Opera House, including prime minister Scott Morrison and opposition leader Anthony Albanese, as well as News Corp bosses Siobhan McKenna and Michael Miller. Morgan spoke, vowing that when his new show launched within weeks he would call out "extremists from all sides, not just in Australia but anywhere— and especially those who think cancel culture's a great idea and want to compel us all to lead their own dreary, joyless lifestyles." (Morgan's debut, when it came, was an interview with Trump that flopped; in the UK, Morgan's ratings fell 80 per cent within a week and a ratings agency reported other TalkTV slots had "zero viewers.")

The shine was taken off Sky's celebrations by Russia's invasion of Ukraine, unfolding on the very same day. Financial markets tumbled worldwide as the impact on oil and food prices, fuelling rising interest rates and inflation, rattled investors. By April, the Foxtel float was deferred amid market uncertainty and with it, the possibility of a near-term break-up or restructure of News.

Many of Fox News' primetime hosts, who like Trump had been pro-Putin, were thrown by Russia's invasion of Ukraine, none more so than Tucker Carlson. On the eve of the invasion, Carlson asked why "permanent Washington" opposed Putin and, in a racially barbed clip watched millions of times, posed a string of questions laced with venom:

> Why do I hate Putin so much? Has Putin ever called me a racist? Has he threatened to get me fired for disagreeing with him? Has he shipped every middle-class job in my town to Russia? Did he manufacture a worldwide pandemic that wrecked my business and kept me indoors for two years? Is he teaching my children to embrace racial discrimination? Is he making Fentanyl? Is he trying to snuff out Christianity? Does he eat dogs? These are fair questions, and the answer to all of them is, no. Vladimir Putin didn't do any of that.

Carlson's reference to dog-eating seemed blatantly Sinophobic and those close to Lachlan say it is absurd to imagine that a man with two Asian-American sisters, Grace and Chloe, would ever support racism. Carlson's pro-Putin contrarianism flew in the face of American sentiment, which was overwhelmingly sympathetic to Ukraine. It was widely denounced in the US but went down very well in Russia, where the Kremlin told state-run TV to rebroadcast clips from Carlson's show.

At the end of March, ahead of the launch of his new show on CNN, Chris Wallace sat down with *The New York Times* and dumped on his old network, admitting he'd spent much of 2021 looking for a new job after the network shifted right in the wake of Trump's defeat. "I just no longer felt comfortable with the programming at Fox," Wallace told the *Times*. "I'm fine with opinion: conservative opinion, liberal opinion. But when people start to question the truth—Who won the 2020 election? Was Jan. 6 an insurrection?—I found that unsustainable." Fox retaliated immediately, briefing reporters the network was glad to be rid of him.[5]

Through most of the controversy surrounding Fox News, Lachlan refrained from going on the record. He preferred to keep his thoughts to himself and to avoid sending signals to the editors and talent round the world which might be perceived as attempts to stifle diversity of opinion at Fox and News. At the end of March, however, Lachlan gave a half-hour speech in Sydney in which he nailed his colors to the mast, launching a new "Centre for the Australian Way of Life," conceived by Tony Abbott and John Roskam, director of the Institute of Public Affairs, an influential Australian think tank that Keith Murdoch had co-founded seventy years earlier. The new center was a conservative-leaning project intended to fight a long rear-guard action in defense of Christianity and capitalism as part of the never-ending culture war.

The launch was held at Sydney's Museum of Contemporary Art, which Lachlan had long patronized and whose network had introduced him to Sydney's elite. But now, Lachlan was there to launch a broadside at those elites, as though an outsider. As *The Washington Post*'s Sarah Ellison observed, his monologue "could have fit in seamlessly with the lineup of right-wing commentary served up every night by Fox News's prime-time opinion hosts."[6] For an Australian audience, in the lead-up to a federal election dominated by post-pandemic recovery and inflation, integrity in politics, equal treatment of women and climate change, the speech was oddly American. Lachlan lobbed the traditional Murdoch grenades at the rest of the media, mentioning the suppression of the Hunter Biden laptop story, *The New York Times*' 1619 project, Sharri Markson's book on the Chinese origins of COVID, *What Really Happened in Wuhan*, and the fringe anti-lockdown and anti-vax protests in Canberra, which played to an American idea that Australia, which at the time had a COVID death rate far lower than the US, had turned into some kind of dictatorship during the pandemic. Lachlan warned that Australia's core values were under attack. But at root his speech was an unexceptional and unobjectionable call for freedom:

> An Australian way of life is something that by definition must allow
> us to be Australian. It can't be that our way of life would disallow

any of the traits that make up our unique Australian identity. Rather, the unifying characteristics that make us Australian must be allowed to flourish under our way of life. That is why freedom is not only a core value of our way of life, it is essential to it. As Australians we are free to practise our 'rugged optimism'; we are free to be 'authentic', free to be 'egalitarian', and free to aspire to a 'fair go'. We are free to practise our religions, and be Christian, or Muslim, or Hindu. We are free to be gay, or straight, or trans. We are free to make our own health choices about our own bodies. We are free to travel and to explore. As Australians we are free to have our own opinions. Free to be Labor or Liberal. We are free to be left, and we are free to be right. We are free to disagree. We are free to choose what we read and what we watch. We are free to make our own minds up about things. These freedoms are UNIFYING. And such freedom is at the core of who we are.

Who could disagree? Plenty, as it turned out. Lachlan was mocked as a foreign billionaire on left-Twitter, and influential *Crikey* reporter Guy Rundle counter-argued that Australia, a convict colony on stolen Aboriginal land, was hardly built on freedom at all; if anything, the country's way of life was collectivist.[7] After Lachlan, Abbott gave his own speech, announcing he would write a patriotic new Australian history:

> Our school students deserve better than politically correct brainwashing, with every subject taught from an indigenous, sustainability and Asian perspective. All of us deserve better than being treated like irresponsible children, as we have [been] for much of the past two lost years, locked up in our homes and behind our borders and scolded by officials lest we not take a virus seriously enough.

Naturally, both speeches were republished and celebrated across News Corp's Australian mastheads and on Sky News, as if the real war in Ukraine underlined the importance of the confected culture wars at home.

* * *

Between the invasion of Ukraine in late February and early May, when the company reported its March quarter earnings, Fox Corp shares fell 20 per cent, a worse slump than the rest of the market, with the NASDAQ dropping 13 per cent. Continuing uncertainty over the FanDuel arbitration, compounded perhaps by fears about the progress of the multi-billion-dollar Dominion and Smartmatic lawsuits, no doubt played a part.

More importantly, the media sector was in turmoil amid a huge reversal in the streaming wars. Netflix chief Reed Hastings had warned in January that intense competition from newer subscription services such as HBO Max and Disney+ was eating into its growth prospects in North America. Netflix shares plunged more than 20 per cent in a day and kept falling as it downgraded earnings. By early May, the company was 60 per cent off its 2021 peak. The long-anticipated merger of AT&T's Warner Media with Discovery, Inc. in April added to the fallout: new chief David Zaslav cancelled CNN+ a month after its launch. "We've been very happily on the sidelines watching this sort of bloodbath which is going on in the SVOD [streaming] market," Lachlan confessed at an industry conference in New York, "and what that's meant is we haven't had to spend billions of dollars propping up an SVOD service." One of Lachlan's key strategic decisions as Fox Corp CEO to sit out the expensive streaming wars and adopt an AVOD strategy with Tubi, was thoroughly vindicated. "Lachlan has done a good job of avoiding the black hole of everyone chasing Netflix," says Rich Greenfield, long-time media analyst at Lightshed Ventures, who was there at Fox's Investor Day in 2019. "Is Tubi the next Netflix? No. It's not the savior of the industry, but you can look at Tubi as a measured, calculated, reasonable bet."

Fox Corp's own earnings figures for the first three months of 2022 were solid rather than spectacular. One analyst described it as a "blah" quarter for the company, another described Fox as "shelter from the storm." But the results carried special significance for Lachlan, marking three full years since he took the helm. They had been tumultuous years. From a Fox investor's point of view, the report card was mixed: quarterly revenues. grown by 25 per cent to $3.5 billion, but profits had fallen by almost half, to $283 million. The comparison was somewhat arbitrary, and the Fox figures suffered from up-front losses on Tubi, which would probably generate returns down the track and certainly paled next to the losses in SVOD. Still, from the debut share price after the spin above $41, Fox's non-voting shares had been on a roller-coaster ride over three years, falling below $20 at the depth of the pandemic and hitting a high of almost $45 in February 2022. By the end of March 2022, however, Fox shareholders were below where they'd started, with the stock trading just above $39. Over the same three-year period, the Nasdaq and S&P indexes jumped an impressive 85 and 60 per cent respectively. From Lachlan's perspective, he had delivered on the promises Fox made three years earlier at the investor day. With record advertizing spending expected through the midterm election cycle, and the World Cup and Superbowl LVI around the corner, Fox was set for another record year in 2023. For investors, however, the jury was still out. "Fox still feels like the media company most likely to be sold," says Rich Greenfield, who at the beginning of 2022 had tipped a Fox News merger with News Corp sooner rather than later, "especially with Lachlan being in Australia."

Three years after he took charge of Fox Corp, and almost three decades after his career began in Brisbane, Lachlan remained an unknown quantity as a businessman. and that was how he liked it. Never the rock-star CEO doing mega-deals, Lachlan preferred Fox and News to stick to their strategies and grow organically or through targeted acquisitions; he liked to keep his public appearances as limited and as controlled as possible. Around him were advisers, like his most trusted partner, Siobhan McKenna, who contrasted the endless commentary about the ill-fated investment in Channel Ten with the general disregard for his runaway success at Nova and put it down to the difference between public and private markets. Having been in the trenches together through the Illyria years, Lachlan and Siobhan much preferred the latter. Running publicly listed companies came with investor and media scrutiny and corporate governance restrictions which Lachlan tended to view as box-ticking, contrary to the swashbuckling Murdoch culture.

Illyria, perhaps more than any other part of the empire, gave Lachlan the confidence that he has what it takes. In his own mind, he is the only one of Rupert's children who has become a billionaire in his own right. Founding Illyria in 2005 with inherited cash of $100 million, Lachlan had patiently built a collection of assets that analysts reckoned would have a market value of more than $1 billion (although who can say for sure, as there are no public figures), before returning to the family fold at his father's request in 2015. Whatever happened to Fox and News now, Illyria will be his own family's enduring source of wealth, and separate trusts for his three children were set up five years earlier. In his heart of hearts, and quite unlike his father, Lachlan sees himself as an investor rather than an operator of assets. He takes a portfolio approach: Illyria owns all of Nova, an enormously valuable parcel of Disney shares (his single biggest asset), and small stakes in two structurally challenged listed companies, the Fox and News corporations, which represent his day job for now, at the whim and behest of his unpredictable father and siblings. In Lachlan's mind, he has nothing left to prove, to his family, or anyone else, and as far the day job goes, he could take it or leave it.

* * *

In early May 2022, *Politico* obtained an unprecedented leak of a draft ruling by US Supreme Court judge Samuel Alito that would overturn *Roe v Wade* as an unconstitutional infringement of states' rights and so abolish the national right to abortion. The leak caused a furore, as it appeared Christian fundamentalists were poised to achieve what they had spent decades campaigning for. Among the campaigners was Republican Senate leader Mitch McConnell, who considered the engineering of a conservative Supreme Court majority—by denying President Obama a confirmation hearing in 2016—his most important legacy. The draft ruling, which was confirmed as genuine by the court, cast in a new light

Lachlan Murdoch's personal donations to McConnell, by far his largest political gifts, and called into question how he could possibly describe himself as "socially more liberal" any longer.

Ten days later, eighteen-year-old Payton Gendron drove 200 miles to the Tops supermarket in Buffalo, New York, which he had cased out for its many black customers, and livestreamed his murder of ten people and injury of another three. A self-described white nationalist, Gendron cited the Great Replacement Theory in a 180-page manifesto. He appeared to have been inspired by previous racist mass shootings, including the Christchurch massacre, which had also been live-streamed. Fairly or unfairly, fingers again pointed at Fox News and Tucker Carlson for amplifying the replacement theory. A defensive Carlson pointed out on air that the supposed "manifesto" had criticized Fox News; he conceded nothing. But Senate majority leader Chuck Schumer took the unprecedented step of writing directly to Rupert and Lachlan Murdoch, as well as to Suzanne Scott and Jay Wallace (copying in Carlson), urging Fox News to "immediately cease the reckless amplification of the so-called 'Great Replacement' theory on your network's broadcasts." Schumer's letter cited the previous massacres in Pittsburgh and El Paso, as well as a *New York Times* investigation which analysed every episode of *Tucker Carlson Tonight* and found he had amplified the theory more than 400 times. Schumer welcomed the *Wall Street Journal* editorial board's condemnation of replacement theory but said it did not go far enough. "I implore you to immediately cease all dissemination of false white nationalist, far-right conspiracy theories on your network," he concluded. Former Democratic presidential aspirant Howard Dean went further in an interview on MSNBC, calling for Rupert Murdoch to be deported:

> I see the brand of Fox being hate, anger, dishonesty and now murder. That's the brand, that's the brand that the Murdochs have chosen to be their flagship. [Rupert Murdoch] has harmed this country more than any other human being in my lifetime, and he and his family should never have been given citizenship.

The one thing I would change about our immigration policy is to send Murdoch back to Australia and keep him there with the whole family. If you cause that much trouble, you spread lies and hate and anger and tear the United States apart with your crappy TV shows, simply to make money, you do not belong, you do not deserve American citizenship.

A fortnight later, in a sit-down interview with *Axios* at Fox's Sixth Avenue offices in New York, Lachlan pushed back on the criticism, pointing out that the Buffalo murderer's manifesto had also targeted Rupert Murdoch for his support of Israel. "When you're in the news business, and you're number one," Lachlan said, "you get a lot of heat." He was equally dismissive of Schumer's letter, saying "it comes with the territory . . . you've got to kind of realize what it is and how some of it is very organized kind of attacks, very coordinated, but it is what it is." He went on to expand on Fox's push into lifestyle content, emphasising verticals like outdoors content, documentaries, food, and home, all ways of further monetising the brand.

At the end of May, Lachlan Murdoch flew home to Sydney. If anywhere could be called home for the London-born, New York-raised billionaire, Sydney was it. Australia had just elected a new prime minister, Anthony Albanese, who would form a majority Labor government, along with a record number of Greens and independents in a decisive rejection of the culture wars, climate denial, and pork-barrelling that had wracked the hard-right governments of Tony Abbott, Malcolm Turnbull, and Scott Morrison governments over the previous decade. During the election campaign, News Corp papers had overwhelmingly favored the conservative Morrison government. All five major metropolitan mastheads, plus *The Australian*, backed his campaign for re-election, making this the twenty-fourth consecutive state or federal election in which the Murdochs had backed the conservative side of politics. Media analysts and commentators, tracking the unbalanced coverage, pondered whether the election result was a sign of the diminishing influence of

News Corp even in Australia, where the family's power was most heavily concentrated.

The Labor victory made little difference to Lachlan, who had a good personal relationship with the new prime minister; both loved rugby league (Lachlan's Broncos were currently thumping Albo's beloved Rabbitohs). On the day he got home to Sydney, the *Australian Financial Review*'s annual rich list estimated Lachlan's personal wealth at $3.95 billion, down half a billion since the year before, but still making him Australia's twenty-eighth richest person. The same list showed his older half-sister Prudence, who had not worked a day for their father's business and had mostly escaped the Murdoch spotlight, ranked forty-third, with a fortune of $2.58 billion. Both Lachlan and Prue were fabulously rich and could afford whatever they wanted. The numbers raised the question: had Lachlan's thirty years of work and scrutiny been worth it?

* * *

At 8 p.m. on Thursday, June 9, the House Committee investigating the attack on the Capitol held its first public hearings, beamed live into American homes through every major broadcast and cable network in the country, except Fox News Channel. The committee had hired a former ABC news president, James Goldston, to make sure the hearings were not the usual worthy-but-dull congressional fare, but would have maximum impact on a mass audience ahead of the midterm elections. Nothing else, it seemed, would lift the polls for President Biden, stuck in the mire as inflation worsened through 2022 and the threat of recession loomed large. Pro-Trump Republicans had been denied membership of the committee, leaving only two members who weren't Democrats: Wyoming Rep. Liz Cheney and Illinois Rep. Adam Kinzinger, who had already broken with their party over the Big Lie and the insurrection.

With the investigation in danger of being perceived as a partisan exercise, and other networks committed to carrying the hearings live, just as the Watergate congressional hearings had been broadcast live fifty years earlier, garnering huge national audiences, Fox took a gamble. It opted to stick with its usual primetime programming about the hearings from its usual roster of primetime anchors: Tucker Carlson, Sean Hannity, and Laura Ingraham. A live feed from the hearings, interspersed with commentary from news-side hosts Bret Baier and Martha MacCallum, would be shunted over to the little-watched Fox Business, instead. Fox's decision, which was approved by Lachlan personally, staggered the media, once again calling into question whether the channel was really in the news business at all. The contrast between the amount of airtime given to the wild and false claims of a rigged election by Rudy Giuliani and Sidney Powell and the airtime given to the true and verifiable evidence patiently assembled by Congress over the course of an eighteen-month investigation was patently obvious.

The hearings, when they began, were devastating to Trump and his minions, particularly chief of staff Mark Meadows. Committee chair Bennie Thompson, a black Democratic representative from Mississippi, opened with a frank observation: "I'm from a part of the country where people justify the actions of slavery, Ku Klux Klan, and lynching. I'm reminded of that dark history as I hear voices today try and justify the actions of the insurrectionists of January 6, 2021."

Rep. Cheney delivered a withering, fact-driven opening statement, interspersed with President Trump's tweets and taped evidence from former attorney general Bill Barr, testifying that the claims of a rigged election were untrue. Even Ivanka Trump testified that she believed Barr. Over the ensuing days, a string of Republican officials who had served in the Trump administration testified to the president's departure from reality in the wake of the 2020 election, and his reliance on the unconstitutional advice of law professor John Eastman, who told him Vice President Pence could set aside the election results, even though he knew it was illegal.

To watch Fox News that night, while such historic hearings were underway, was a bizarre experience. Tucker Carlson defended Fox's decision not to carry what he described as the "Nancy Pelosi feed." Sean Hannity pretended to be conducting his own investigation, arguing the

Committee had missed the *real* story of January 6th. Laura Ingraham described the hearings as a "show trial" and "political theatre" and a "snooze-fest" bound to flop in the ratings, and smeared Cheney and Kinzinger as Democratic "poodles." As concerning as the florid attacks on the hearings from the opinion hosts, however, was the thrust of the coverage from the straight news anchors Baier and Macallum, when they finally made it to air at 11 p.m., for a two-hour Fox News special broadcast. There was barely any reference to the fresh evidence presented that evening, aside from acknowledgement that some of the testimony from Edwards was powerful. But the rest was about sowing doubt and trying to move on. Mainly, like the opinion hosts, they questioned why the Democrats weren't covering the real problems in the country: gas prices at $5 a gallon; inflation; fentanyl; a crime wave; chaos on the border (again). Fox viewers on the main news channel did not see the powerful testimony for themselves, only snippets interspersed with the takes of Fox anchors.

If Lachlan had a commitment to the search for truth, here was a shining example of his own television network airing precisely the opposite. Many of the most loyal Fox viewers, off whom he made the most money, would be none the wiser. Heading into another polarized election cycle, with Republicans threatening another wracking impeachment scandal, fearing more violence, and even a 2024 presidential election marred by lies about the count, the stakes could not have been higher.

While Fox News was downplaying the January 6 committee hearing, the *Wall Street Journal* and *New York Post* registered its significance right away, denouncing Trump in no uncertain terms. News Corp was more Rupert's domain—he was executive co-chairman there, while Lachlan was non-executive co-chairman, whereas at Fox Corp those titles were reversed—and at the last annual meeting in November the elderly mogul said conservatives had to move on from the 2020 election if they were to play a part in the political debate: "that will not happen if President Trump stays focused on the past. The past is the past, and the country is now in a contest to define the future."[8] News chief Robert Thomson—a favored Rupert confidante—was still a journalist at heart, who knew when a story was moving. Now the *WSJ* editorial board wrote that Trump "betrayed his supporters by conning them on January 6, and he is still doing it," while the *Post* wrote that the former president had become a prisoner of his own ego and "won't stop insisting that 2020 was 'stolen' even though he's offered no proof that it's true".[9] The contrast between the editorial line at Fox and News gave credence to the idea that Lachlan's politics were to the right of his father's. Lachlan rejected the assumption that what went to air on Fox News represented his own thinking, and often sought to downplay his responsibility for the content. But if Lachlan wanted Fox News to draw the line at Trump's attempt to subvert the 2020 election, and to stand up for American democracy, he could do it with a single phone call to Suzanne Scott. There was no sign of that happening—indeed, quite the opposite: Fox News doubled down on its criticism of the January 6 committee, even as the evidence piled up against Trump and his cronies.

Over the next six weeks it seemed that just about everything that could go wrong for Lachlan, did go wrong. His push into live sports betting in the US stalled, as arbitration of the dispute with Flutter over the value of FanDuel—meant to have been resolved by June—ground on and on. Likewise in Australia, a $220 million bid to take over the local division of PointsBet was rejected out of hand. The opportunity remained huge, and Lachlan had seen it early, but execution was proving much harder than expected.

Worse was to come later that month. Delaware judge Eric Davis denied Fox's motion to dismiss the $1.6 billion Dominion Voting Systems lawsuit, which alleged Rupert and Lachlan Murdoch and others made a business calculation to spread former President Trump's false narrative about rigged voting machines on Fox News, in a show of "actual malice" towards the company. Davis ruled Dominion's lawyers had "adequately pleaded" the case, sufficient to allow it to move to discovery of evidence—which meant the plaintiffs could get access to Fox internal correspondence and documents, potentially including the Murdochs' own communications, which would no doubt cause a sensation if they were to come out in court. Fox appointed a new "superlawyer," veteran attorney Dan Webb, to defend the case on free-speech grounds, in a sign it was likely to go to trial. Fox handed over internal evidence to the court in time to meet a deadline of July 1, setting the scene for a potentially explosive trial. Similar litigation by rival vote-machine manufacturer Smartmatic remained on foot. If there was a silver lining for Fox, it lay in speculation that related lawsuits by Dominion and Smartmatic against smaller rivals on the right, One America News Network and Newsmax, which had also aired the baseless claims, could impose penalties severe enough to wipe them out.

Running in Fox's favor was the conservative supermajority on the Supreme Court, which might be presumed sympathetic to a defense pleaded on First Amendment grounds, if potential adverse rulings in the Dominion or Smartmatic cases were appealed all the way to the top. In late June the Supreme Court released a volley of rulings that would fundamentally alter the American political landscape: overturning *Roe v. Wade*, as had been leaked earlier in the year, but also nobbling the ability of the federal government to regulate carbon dioxide emissions that cause climate change, and striking down a longstanding New York law restricting the concealed carry of firearms. The trio of extreme rulings shocked the world, as the six conservative judges—including three appointed by Trump: Neil Gorsuch, Brett Kavanaugh and Amy Coney Barrett—were just getting started and would preside for many years to come. As the northern hemisphere suffered through unprecedented heatwaves and wildfires, and pro-coal West Virginia senator Joe Manchin continued to block climate action in Congress, Joe Biden was now facing an almost impossible task to limit carbon pollution by the world's largest historical emitter. In London, climate activists smashed the windows at News UK's headquarters and plastered posters claiming *The Sun* owner had chosen to publish pictures of women in bikinis and happy toddlers rather than warning of the "increased risks from such heatwaves as the climate crisis intensifies."

A glimmer of hope that bipartisanship was still possible came when Congress passed its first gun control laws in thirty years, after a shooter with an assault rifle murdered nineteen kids and two teachers at the Robb

Elementary School in Uvalde, Texas. Meanwhile, as the reality of post-Roe America settled in, nightmarish scenarios turned real, including the shocking case of a ten-year-old rape victim from Ohio who had to go to Indiana to get an abortion. Fox News host Jesse Waters targeted the Indiana doctor who performed the abortion, Dr Caitlin Bernard, putting her picture on screen and interviewing the state's Republican attorney general, Todd Rokita, who called her an "abortion activist acting as a doctor." Dr Bernard sued for defamation. Amid fears the GOP would seek a national abortion ban, polls began to indicate that November's midterm elections could be tighter than expected.

Even within the Murdoch family, there was new strain in June, as Lachlan's father split with his wife of six years, Jerry Hall. The first public sign of a falling-out came in London at Rupert's annual summer party at the Serpentine Gallery, one of the highlights of the social calendar, attended by then prime minister Boris Johnson. Lachlan was there, but Hall was a notable absentee, as were her family and friends. Two days later, *The New York Times* reported that Rupert and Jerry were divorcing, stunning friends and colleagues of both who had thought their relationship was robust. Within days, Jerry filed for divorce in the LA County Court, citing "irreconcilable differences." As for what went wrong, theories abounded. Celebrity gossip site *PopBitch* wrote that Jerry could not stand Murdoch's youngest children, Grace and Chloe. A friend of Hall's told Britain's *Daily Mail* that Hall blamed Murdoch's children, saying they believed she was trying to use COVID to cut off their contact with their father. The *Mail* also reported discussions in which Hall spoke with the wider Murdoch family about her financial status and what she might get when Murdoch died, but was told that no further provision should be made "at this time." As I reported for *The Saturday Paper* in Australia, a well-placed source told me that money was at the heart of the problem, and that the issue had been simmering for some time:

> When the Disney payday came around, there was a view that
> Jerry should have been given something as Rupert's custodian,

which didn't happen. I think you'll find that's what was at the center of the issue. She's saying she was wrong-footed by it—she probably was—but there's no question Rupert looks at things in a very different way and money is at the center of it. Jerry was constantly trying to work out ways to channel some of Rupert's hard-earned through to her children with Mick. He turned the ATM off.[10]

Lachlan played a crucial role, advising Rupert to pull the pin on the marriage and playing a key part in the legal and PR strategies around the divorce.[11] Immediately there was speculation that Rupert, alone and with time on his hands, would get more active across the family business—potentially making life more complicated for Lachlan. At ninety-one, Rupert was still more than a decade younger than Dame Elisabeth when she died, and he expected to outlive her.

While Rupert's legacy had been debated for decades, Lachlan's legacy was a work-in-progress. In the years since Lachlan had taken over as Fox Corporation CEO, Fox News had become more profitable, but also more extreme. There was no better marker than the ideological drift of his favorite star, Tucker Carlson, whose nightly program had become the most-watched show in cable television history but also more one-sided. A ground-breaking *New York Times* investigation, which analysed more than 1100 episodes of *Tucker Carlson Tonight*, found that the number of appearances of guests who disagreed with Tucker's opinions was decreasing, while his monologues were doubling and tripling in length until they were often running for fifteen or twenty minutes. His favorite topics? America's ruling class, the destruction of society, the decline of masculinity, anti-white racism and immigration, immigration, immigration—the data showed Tucker had amplified the racist replacement theory more than 400 times.[12] And he would keep on doing it, with impunity. In July, after a long-winded rant against the Democrats, stretching right back to the 1965 *Immigration Act* passed by LBJ, he concluded: "The great replacement . . . it's not a conspiracy theory. It's their electoral strategy."

The legacy of Fox News' increasingly unbalanced programming was not only felt in a few-point increase in voter support for the Republican party, but in the lives of ordinary Americans. Perhaps the defining issue of Lachlan's first years at the helm had been COVID, and a poignant example was the story of Washington state trooper Robert Lamay. Lamay was celebrated on Fox after he posted a video that went viral, telling state governor Jay Inslee to "kiss my ass" after twenty-two years' service, in protest against a COVID vaccine mandate. After quitting in October 2021, Lamay soon contracted COVID, was hospitalized, and tragically died in January 2022. Rival news outlets reported that Lamay's passing had gone unmentioned on Fox. When America passed the milestone of a million COVID deaths, research showed the partisan divide between those refusing to be vaccinated: six in ten were Republican voters. And while a majority of Democrats trusted a range of mainstream news sources for information about COVID, the only source trusted by nearly half of Republicans was Fox News, which had repeatedly aired baseless claims that COVID vaccines were ineffective or harmful. Katie Lane, a college student at Washington State University, lost her father Patrick to COVID and told PBS he'd refused to get the vaccine. "He watched some YouTubers. FOX News was an occasional YouTube clip channel he watched, stuff like that, [and] for some reason, with this vaccine, people were telling you not to get it. For some reason, that stuck with my dad. And that's ultimately why he didn't choose to." Lane felt there was nothing more she could have done to change his mind and wished her dad was around, even as she acknowledged America's grim milestone. "That one million is a huge deal," she said. "But that one in that one million is—it's been worth more to me than the other 999,000."[13]

Contrary to the prognostications of Fox News' primetime anchors, piece by piece and hearing by hearing, the January 6 committee began to build a compelling case against former president Trump. When an aide to White House chief of staff Mark Meadows, Cassidy Hutchinson, delivered bombshell evidence in an unscheduled hearing, saying that Trump knew his supporters were armed but wanted the magnetometers turned off to boost the crowd he intended to join in an attack on the Capitol, Fox News' daytime anchor Bret Baier acknowledged that her evidence, given under oath, was far more credible than the furious denials the former president was issuing on 'Truth Social', the only digital platform he could still access. Fox News broadcast the hearings during daytime hours, although ratings figures showed its base was thoroughly uninterested and switched off in droves whenever they came on.

The evidence against the former president continued to build, however, and by the time the committee delivered its "season finale" hearing in primetime in late July, Florida governor Ron de Santis was increasingly seen to be the future of the MAGA movement, most likely challenger to Trump in 2024. Alt-right strategist Steve Bannon was found guilty of contempt of Congress, and it seemed the Trump cabal was unravelling. In forensic detail—tracking the attack on the Capitol minute-by-minute, interspersed with distressing footage, radio grabs and chat logs between members of the secret service guarding former vice president Mike Pence and fearing for their lives—the January 6 committee showed how the president did nothing to stop the violence. The *Wall Street Journal* condemned his inaction, writing that while Pence had passed the test of character, Trump had "utterly failed" his own. So did the *New York Post*, writing that Trump's only focus that day, to his "eternal shame," was to block the peaceful transfer of power by any means. "There is no other explanation, just as there is no defense, for his refusal to stop the violence . . . Trump has proven himself unworthy to be this country's chief executive again."[14]

Most damning was that for more than three hours, as the Capitol was under assault, Trump ignored the advisers urging him to condemn the violence and send the rioters home, instead sitting in his private dining room next to the Oval Office, sending inflammatory tweets and calling his lawyer Rudy Giuliani and Republican allies in the hope he could still stop Vice-President Pence from certifying the election results on the floor of the Senate. And for all those wasted hours—in what the *Wall Street Journal* called the "most horrifying" evidence from the committee to date— America's most dangerous president was watching one television channel, his favorite, the channel that had made and defended him more than any other: Fox News. In a feedback loop from hell, as this evidence emerged from the January 6 committee hearing, Fox News' audience remained oblivious to Trump's gross dereliction of his duty as commander in chief that day. Because the network that Lachlan Murdoch controlled, in a decision he was no doubt personally involved in, refused to show a single primetime minute of it live.

EPILOGUE

Chartwell

FIVE MONTHS EARLIER, on Wednesday, February 9 2022, Lachlan Murdoch had woken up at 4 a.m. at his Chartwell mansion in Los Angeles and psyched himself up to deliver the December quarter profit results for Fox Corporation. Sarah and the kids were back in Sydney already, so he had the whole place to himself, but not for long. He was about to host an unprecedented meeting of the directors and most senior executives of both the Murdoch companies, Fox and News Corporation, from all over the world.

Lachlan swung into the Fox lot at 5 a.m., meeting Viet Dinh, John Nallen, and Steve Tomsic to rattle through the 45-minute webcast presentation before the stock exchange opened in New York, and to field some carefully chosen questions from a handful of analysts well known to the company. They were a decent set of numbers and Fox shares jumped as soon as trading commenced. Afterwards, the three Fox lieutenants joined Lachlan back at Chartwell to greet his guests at 7.30 a.m. sharp. The occasion was a long-planned strategy day, "MegaTrends 2022." Nothing quite like it had ever happened in the Murdoch empire before.

The scene was worthy of *Succession*, as some guests joked to one other. A convoy of luxury black minivans collected the Fox and News bigwigs from three nearby hotels before snaking up Bel Air Road and disgorging them at the mansion. Given Rupert, now ninety years old, was attending, the vigilance against coronavirus was high: everyone had to be fully vaccinated and tested on the way in. Lachlan had already distributed a 124-page dossier of clippings, articles, and links to podcasts, transcripts and corporate announcements, with a glossary in the back for the less geeky. It raised some challenging questions for the century-old empire of influence that Lachlan and his guests controlled, most crucially how a combination of structurally challenged newspaper and cable television businesses would survive "Web 3.0," the next iteration of the internet, a trust-less and permissionless "creator economy" in which content was globally and instantaneously distributed, disintermediated, and tokenized, and barriers to entry were obliterated. Blockchain, crypto, the metaverse—all were on the agenda. It was heady stuff.

The timing was fortuitous, as the guests had barely seen one another in person through two long years of COVID. And it was fun: for most guests, it was a first look at Chartwell, which Lachlan had bought for $150 million just before the pandemic struck. Turning into the driveway, leading to the forty-car motor court, guests walked through the eighteenth-century French replica interiors and downstairs to the cinema, which opened out through big double doors onto a huge terrace with sweeping views over the gardens and Los Angeles. After coffee and breakfast, everyone came back inside and sat in rows, wherever they liked. Lachlan stepped onto the stage, which was set up with a podium and sofas in front of two big projection screens. After welcoming everybody to Chartwell, he gave a short speech before proceedings got underway. Nobody knew what to expect. Apparently, you could have heard a pin drop. Rupert, seated in the front row next to Nallen and Jacques Nasser, said nothing. This was Lachlan's show, in Lachlan's home, following an agenda he had worked out with his chief technology officer. COVID had made both companies stronger, Lachlan said, adding that while in the past both Fox and News had tried to respond to an externally changing environment, "we are now strong enough to shape that environment." That was the point of the strategy day: to make sure the leaders of both businesses had a clear understanding of the forces unfolding in the media industry, so that together the two companies could shape what the future would bring.

Everything about that day at Chartwell was different. Firstly, Rupert had not brought the Fox and News leadership teams together since they had demerged a decade earlier, in the wake of the phone hacking crisis. The ageing mogul had always pitted his top executives against each other, giving them separate P&Ls and letting their businesses compete. Lachlan was more concerned to find synergies between TV, print, radio and other assets, and to foster cooperation among them. It was a theme that had run through his career, right back to the 1998 speech at Sun Valley, Idaho, when he had called for an unofficial system to share information across the Murdoch empire, horizontally, as it were. There were all kinds of pre- and post-meetings between the News and Fox leadership, and the presence of both under one roof invited speculation that a merger of the two companies, ruled out by Lachlan at the investor day three years earlier, was again under consideration.

Secondly, the meeting was about strategy, not about short-term tactics or operations. The last time News Corp's senior executives had all met together, at Rupert's Carmel ranch, was three years ago; at that meeting, there had been much preening about which division had the fastest-loading websites. The day at Chartwell was much more far-sighted. In Lachlan's view, media companies had panicked at the advent of Web 1.0, and only belatedly realized that Web 2.0 meant Google, Facebook, and the rest were going to soak up the advertizing dollars. This time around, with Web 3.0, Lachlan was determined that both Fox and News would be active, working together and even alongside other media companies to confront yet another potentially existential threat. If Web 1.0 undermined revenue from consumers, and Web 2.0 took the advertizing revenue, Web 3.0 could undermine the very relationship between a broadcaster such as Fox or a publisher such as News and their most critical resource: employees. Legacy media businesses were ripe for disruption in the creator economy, warned the pre-read, which would enable individual creatives to build a business around themselves. Once again, this harked back to Lachlan's first big speech at Sun Valley, when he had said he hoped News would become the greatest creative company in the world.

Thirdly, the meeting was all about business. It was not an editorial meeting. Unlike the company gatherings under Rupert, there were no politicians, secretaries of state, or military brass to gladhand over a drink. Editors, journalists, or on-air talent were not invited. No Tucker Carlson or Sean Hannity to throw their weight around; no Miranda Devine or Gerry Baker to lob sceptical questions. And because there were no gossipy journalists there, not a word leaked to the media. "Journalists are going to get time to meet with politicians," said one participant, but meeting with politicians "is not going to help you run your business better. This is for the leadership of these two companies, and it's going to be about our business. That's Lachlan's point: he's setting the bar high and saying 'I need high-calibre executives.' Being able to make chit-chat with politicians is fantastic if you're a journalist, and that's a really important part of our business. But I need strategic people who know what the future is and who are going to help shape that."

After Lachlan stepped down from the stage, it was the invited speakers' turn. There were sessions on the metaverse, gaming, non-fungible tokens, and the awesome, enduring power of live sports content. Shopify founder Tobi Lütke, who'd recently joined the board of crypto exchange Coinbase, talked through the implications of Web 3.0 for Fox and News, although with his own share price tanking, there were a few sceptics. Silicon Valley-based investor Ben Horowitz talked about the changing role of venture capital, which could provide the kind of high-risk, patient funding that had fuelled many of the technological innovations of the previous two decades. That caught some attention, especially among those in the room who knew Lachlan's history of off-again, on-again efforts to take part or all of News Corp private. Was privatization back on the agenda?

By the time the session broke for morning tea, the guests were remarking to each other on the most noteworthy aspect of the whole thing: "Lachlan's in charge." The invited speakers were there because they had a relationship with Lachlan, not his father. Rupert was saying nothing or. if he did, it was to ask questions about Web 3.0 that showed he wasn't up to speed, and he made no speech, either at the meeting or at the dinner and drinks that followed, to which Jerry Hall turned up—one of the last occasions they would be seen together before their divorce shocked the world. The whole mood was different: instead of jokey, beery, and matey, the vibe was serious. There was a lot of talk about Russia's expected invasion of Ukraine, which would occur only two weeks later. One attendee reckoned the whole day at Chartwell was about an explicit transfer of power, from father to son: "It was just a massive turning point. The baton had very obviously been passed and the rest of us, as a group, we all went, 'Okay, we missed the point that the baton got passed, but it's been passed.'"

* * *

Rupert famously had the ability to see around corners and over the course of a seventy-year career he had built the first truly global media empire in News Corporation. From 1922 until 2022, the company had survived and prospered through rapid technological change: from newsprint to wireless, movies to television, pay-TV to the internet, digital real estate to live sports betting. All the way, the Murdochs were challenging and building, buying and selling, ducking and weaving, crashing and burning. The ideas bandied about that day at Chartwell would soon be tested, as a meltdown in crypto and tokens raised new questions about whether any of these digital assets had value. But who was to say now that Fox and News, together or apart, would not survive another century of disruption? As the notes circulated at Chartwell pointed out, technology might change the playing field, but so often it's the same old industry stalwarts who play out the game.

There would never be another Rupert. Everyone agreed on this, especially his family. But here now was Lachlan staring earnestly, furiously, into the future so the next generation of Murdochs, his kids, and maybe theirs after them, might stay on top of the pile, pulling strings, making a fortune, for better or worse.

Outside the walls of Chartwell, debate flared about the polarization of America and the impact of Fox News and, on the other side of the world, Sarah and the kids were surrounded by growing anger at the concentration of power in the hands of News Corp and its biased political coverage. But inside Chartwell, Lachlan's agenda was simple: it was not about right or left; Republican or Democrat; gender, race or class; war or peace. It was just business.

Acknowledgements

I T WAS NOT MY IDEA to write an unauthorized biography of Lachlan Murdoch. Credit must go to Morry Schwartz, founder and proprietor of my Australian publishing house Black Inc., but as soon as it was suggested it was immediately obvious to me that this project was both timely and of enormous public interest. I am grateful to Morry, my publisher Chris Feik and all at Black Inc. for having confidence in me to write it and the patience to wait for it through the disruptions of the pandemic. Lachlan considers himself an Australian at heart, and I believe it is fitting that his biography is written by an Australian journalist.

US President Joe Biden has described Rupert Murdoch as the most dangerous man in the world. Whatever that says about Rupert's eldest son, it is certainly true that many people in America and Australia are afraid to talk, even off the record, about Lachlan Murdoch, serving executive chairman and chief executive of Fox Corporation, and co-chairman of News Corporation. Which speaks to the courage of the sixty-odd people in the US, UK, and Australia who did agree to be interviewed for this book, on or off the record, and sometimes only in correspondence, since I began working on it part-time in mid-2020. What was supposed to be a one-year project turned into a two-year project and (to be honest) could easily have taken up more time. It was slow-going reaching people through COVID, which often prevented meetings face-to-face, limited my travel plans, and created a general gloom. Heartfelt thanks to all those people who returned my calls, answered my emails, met me on Zoom, often at odd hours given the time-zone constraints, and provided invaluable contacts, leads, quotes and insights. Even more heartfelt thanks to those who did agree to go on the record. Either way, off-record or on it, I could not have written the book without your help.

By way of disclosure, I got my start in the mainstream media in 2004 on the business desk of the Murdochs' flagship newspaper down under, *The Australian*, and will be forever grateful to the editors who hired me and promoted me, and the colleagues who trained me up. I remain proud of the journalism we did on the business desk in those years. I only met Lachlan once in my time at News, inadvertently, when I watched him ride a jaw-dropping motorbike into the open-air carpark across from the Holt Street headquarters. "What's *that*?" I called out, as my head followed the hot-read weapon through the boom gate. He turned and told me, very pleasantly, through his helmet visor: "MV Augusta." "Oh, Lachlan," I shrank away, realizing I'd just yelled at the proprietor. I left "the Oz" on good terms, and although I have subsequently written or reported critical pieces on their climate change coverage, for example, I have also been published there since and do not bear any grudge whatsoever towards the masthead, the company, Lachlan, or any of the Murdochs. Although this biography was always going to be unauthorized, warts and all, I spent many months asking and hoping for an interview with Lachlan himself, although I was told all along my chances were slim.

Succession aside, the Murdochs have been arguably the best story in media for more than half a century, attracting the best journalists and writers in the trade. I would particularly like to acknowledge the following reporters and authors whose work I have relied and drawn upon extensively, and who if they read this may feel some (hopefully slight) extra weight on their shoulders: Ken Auletta, Paul Barry, Matthew Belloni, Tim Burrowes, Lachlan Cartwright, Neil Chenoweth, Richard Cooke, Nick Davies, Sarah Ellison, Richard Hack, Nicole Hemmer, David Leser, David McKnight, Peter Maass, Jonathan Mahler, Roy Masters, Jane Mayer, Stephen Mayne, Tom Roberts, Jim Rutenberg, William Shawcross, Gabriel Sherman, Margaret Sullivan, Brian Stelter, Erik Wemple, Christopher

Williams, Pamela Williams, and Michael Wolff. I am especially grateful to Ken Auletta and Neil Chenoweth, who read drafts of the manuscript at short notice. So did others who can't be named, as well as fiercely independent journalist, author, film-maker and friend Antony Loewenstein, who provided constructive criticism and was a constant source of inspiration, encouragement and links to clips from *Tucker Carlson Tonight*. Peter Maass provided background material to his masterful profile of Lachlan for *The Intercept*, including copies of photos from high school yearbooks. Joe Aston, Ken Auletta, Tim Burrowes, Lachlan Cartwright, Neil Chenoweth, Richard Cooke, Rachael Profiloski, Jim Rutenberg, and others who can't be named were especially helpful in various ways.

At Black Inc. I would like to thank Chris Feik for his patience, faith in me, and general brilliance; copy editor Denise O'Dea for staying flexible and focussed through a punishing, piecemeal delivery of the manuscript, along with Julian Welch, Tristan Main, Kate Nash, Iryna Byelyayeva, and former publisher Julia Carlomagno, who was in the trenches with me for the first year. Thanks also to Erin Sandiford and Sophy Williams for representing the book so well overseas. At my North American publishers, Canadian independent Sutherland House, thanks to Ken Whyte for the excellent read-through and edit for an American audience, and thanks also to Serina Mercier and Sarah Miniaci for promoting the title stateside. As always, thanks to my über-professional agent, Tara Wynne at Curtis Brown.

I have recently embarked on a doctorate in media history to mark the first hundred years of Murdoch media, thesis title "A Century of News Corporation in Australia," in the Department of Media, Communications, Creative Arts, Language and Literature at Macquarie University, Sydney. I would like to thank my esteemed supervisor, Professor Bridget Griffen-Foley, director of research and innovation, for her patience while I have been somewhat distracted by this biography, as well as my associate supervisor, senior lecturer Dr Willa McDonald, and research training director Stefan Solomon. Thank you for sharing my hope and confidence that this biography will ultimately inform and advance my research.

Finally, thanks to my family for their encouragement, love, and support through my long absences as a son, brother, husband and father: Peter Manning and Carole Lawson, Maria Manning and Henry Maas, sisters Megan, Thea and Cailin, my darling wife, Melinda, and two fine young men who happen to be my sons, Jude and Milo. Love youse all and can't wait to see you more.

Notes

PROLOGUE: *ISTROS*

1 Nicholas Confessore, "How Tucker Carlson Stoked White Fear to Conquer Cable," *The New York Times*, April 30, 2022.
2 Nicole Wallace, interview with Tim O'Brien, *Media Matters for America*, June 10, 2022.

PART 1: LACHIE

1. A SON IS BORN

1 Susan Adams, "Darker Than Any *Succession* Plot: The Murdoch Kidnap Tragedy," *Forbes*, September 13, 2019.
2 Julie Browning, *Dynasties: Myer, Durack, Macarthur, Murdoch, Downer* (Sydney: ABC Books, 2002), pp. 198–9.
3 Lois Romano, "EXTRA!! Publisher's Wife Pens Novel," *The Washington Post*, October 23, 1985.
4 Browning, *Dynasties*, pp. 196–8.
5 William Shawcross, *Murdoch* (New York: Simon & Schuster, 1993), p. 330.
6 Steve Fishman, "The Boy Who Wouldn't Be King," *New York Magazine*, September 9, 2005.
7 Geraldine Brooks, "Murdoch," *The New York Times Magazine*, July 19, 1998.
8 Browning, *Dynasties*, p. 206
9 Robert Milliken, "Lachlan Murdoch: Heir to *The Sun* and Sky," *Independent on Sunday*, May 7, 1995.
10 ABC TV, "Fox and the Big Lie," *Four Corners*, August 23, 2021.
11 Browning, *Dynasties*, p. 196.
12 Paolo Totaro, "The Reluctant Son," *The Monthly*, March 2012.
13 Ken Auletta, "The Pirate," *The New Yorker*, November 5, 1995.
14 Thomas Kiernan, *Citizen Murdoch: The Unexpurgated Story of Rupert Murdoch* (New York: Dodd, Mead, 1986), pp. 283–4.
15 Neil Chenoweth, *Virtual Murdoch: Reality Wars on the Information Highway* (London: Secker & Warburg, 2001), p. 114.
16 Ken Aluetta, "The Heiress," *The New Yorker*, December 2, 2012.
17 I am indebted to Peter Maas for sharing a scanned image of the Trinity yearbook.
18 Julie Aronovitz, "Martial Arts Club: Mind Over Matter," *The Phillippian*, June 5, 1988.

19 Browning, *Dynasties*, p. 201.
20 Aluetta, "The Heiress."
21 Andrew Cornell, "Rear Window," *The Australian Financial Review*, July 4, 1996.
22 Lachlan Murdoch, Andrew Olle Media Lecture, October 18, 2002.
23 Miliken, "Lachlan Murdoch: Heir to *The Sun* and Sky."
24 Raymond Snoddy, "Murdoch Faces Up to Mortality," *Financial Times*, April 5, 1993.
25 Browning, *Dynasties*, p. 200.
26 Lachlan Murdoch, foreword to Lincoln Hall, *Dead Lucky: Life After Death on Mount Everest* (Sydney: Random House, 2007).
27 Lachlan Murdoch, "A Study of Freedom and Morality in Kant's Practical Philosophy," AB thesis, Princeton University, 1994.
28 Peter Maas, "Power Transfer," *The Intercept*, March 31, 2019.

2. WHY NOT

1 Chris Mitchell, *Making Headlines* (Melbourne: Melbourne University Press, 2016), p. 98.
2 Brooks, "Murdoch."
3 Fishman, "The Boy Who Wouldn't Be King."
4 Browning, p. 201; Diane Mermigas, "News Corp: The Next Generation," *Electronic Media*, January 22, 2001.
5 Mark Westfield, *The Gatekeepers* (Sydney: Pluto Press, 2000), p .247.
6 Ben Potter, "Young Blood," *The Age*, January 27, 1996.
7 Ali Cromie, "The Murdoch Succession," *Financial Review*, October 17, 1994.
8 Potter, "Young Blood."
9 Potter, "Young Blood."
10 Paul Barry, *Rich Kids* (Milsons Point, NSW: Bantam Books, 2003), p. 336.
11 Potter, "Young Blood."
12 Cromie, "The Murdoch Succession."
13 Potter, "Young Blood."

3. THE BIG LEAGUE

1 Mike Colman, *Super League: The Inside Story* (Sydney: Ironbark, 1996), pp. 87, 102.
2 Nick Davies, *Hack Attack: How the Truth Caught Up with Rupert Murdoch* (London: Chatto & Windus, 2014). See also Jane Mayer, "The Making of the Fox News White House," *The New Yorker*, March 4, 2019.
3 Roy Masters, "Leagues of Their Own," *The Sydney Morning Herald*, September 23, 1995.
4 Roy Masters, *Inside Out: Ruby League Under Scrutiny* (Chippendale, NSW: Ironbark, 1997), p. 222.
5 Colman, *Super League*, pp. 124–5.
6 Jonathan Chancellor, "Title Deeds," *The Sydney Morning Herald*, September 2, 1995.
7 Daphne Guinness, "Kate's Big Night, and Lachlan Will Do It His Way," *The Sydney Morning Herald*, June 1, 1996.
8 Pamela Williams, "Murdoch and Me," *The Australian Financial Review*, September 6, 1997.

9 Westfield, *The Gatekeepers*, p. 334.
10 Williams, "Murdoch and Me."
11 Lawrence Money, "Nudge Nudge, Don't Mention Denton," *The Age*, October 9, 2010.

4. FIRST AMONG EQUALS

1 Sally Jackson et al., "1996 in Review," *The Australian*, December 30, 1996.
2 John Gapper, "Inside Track: A Chip Off the Old Block," *Financial Times*, October 5, 1998.
3 Eliot Taylor, "A Letter from the Editor, *The Australian*, March 23, 2000; Jane Schulze, "Heart Is Still Set on Media: Murdoch," *The Australian*, March 23, 2009.
4 Paul Sheehan, "Inside the Lew Lair,' *SMH*, April 19, 1997
5 Ali Cromie, "Memo Lachlan: You Have Mail," *BRW*, November 26, 1999.
6 Stephen Mayne (ed.), "Rear Window: A Sharp Take on Business," *The Australian Financial Review*, August 27, 1999.
7 Michael Sharp (ed.), "Kookaburra," *The Sydney Morning Herald*, November 25, 1995; Stephen Brook, "Lachlan Murdoch: Back to Sydney, *The Guardian*, July 29, 2005.
8 Kim Wilson, "*Star Wars* Coup," *The Herald Sun*, November 5, 1998.
9 "Winners Thought Only of Survival," *The Hobart Mercury*," December 23, 2018.
10 Simon Beavis, "Murdoch Sets Up Son as Heir," *The Guardian*, November 10, 1997.
11 Bernard Hickey, "Lachlan Murdoch Emerges with His Own Style," Reuters News, December 30, 1997.
12 John Gapper, "Inside Track: A Chip Off the Old Block."
13 Ali Cromie, "Must Try Harder," *BRW*, November 26, 1999.
14 Anges Cusack, "Murdoch Jr Warns Howard Over Republic Outcome," *AM*, ABC Radio, September 22, 1999.
15 "Lachlan Murdoch Sees No Internet Threat to Papers," Reuters News, October 13, 1998.
16 "Murdoch's Future for Newspapers," *Herald Sun*, June 3, 1998.
17 Terry McCrann, "Murdoch Hatchet Job Ignored," *Sunday Mail*, December 5, 1999.

5. "THE BEST DEAL EVER'

1 "Lachlan Murdoch's Fiancee Tells How It Happened," Australian Associated Press, November 17, 1998.
2 Neil Chenoweth, "Lachlan the Heir Apparent," *Financial Review*, February 10, 1999
3 Jonathan Mahler and Jim Rutenberg, "Imperial Reach," *The New York Times*, April 3, 2019.
4 Carola Hoyos, "The Grooming of Lachlan Murdoch," *Financial Times*, October 6, 2000.
5 Kate McClymont, "Sauce," *The Sydney Morning Herald*, September 27, 2003.
6 Luke Collins, "News Ltd Facing a Repair Job," *The Australian Financial Review*, January 4, 2000.
7 Kate Kelly and Carmela Ciurary, "The Little Ex That Could: Pat Duff Gets Co-op Without Perelman," *The New York Observer*, December 27, 1999.
8 Diane Mermigas, "News Corp: The Next Generation," *Electronic Media*, January 22, 2001.

6. . . . AND THE WORST

1 Anthony Stavrinos, "Media Heir's Wife O'Hare Turns Out for Debut Film Premiere," *Australian Associated Press*, May 27, 2001.
2 Sally Bothroyd, "Head Over Toilet Bowl," *Sunday Territorian*, June 3, 2001.
3 Susannah Moran and Andrew Main, "Murdoch: The Day Packer Wept Over One. Tel," *The Australian Financial Review*, November 2, 2005.
4 Caroline Overington, "The Fall of the Fabulous Brat Pack Boys," *The Sunday Age*, June 3, 2001.
5 Paul Barry, *Rich Kids* (Milsons Point, NSW: Bantam Books, 2003), pp. 280–81.
6 Jeni Porter, "Joke That Came Back to Haunt One.Tel Founders," *The Sydney Morning Herald*, June 15, 2001.
7 Barry, *Rich Kids*, pp. 287–8.
8 Barry, *Rich Kids*, pp. 340, 333–4.
9 Barry, *Rich Kids*, p. 335.
10 Kate Askew, "Last days of Pompeii," *The Sydney Morning Herald*, August 8, 2002.
11 Neil Chenoweth, "Lachlan Murdoch's $13.3m Payout," *Trust the Toffs*, April 17, 2014.
12 Damon Kitney, *The Price of Fortune: The Untold Story of Being James Packer* (Sydney: HarperCollins, 2018), p. 73.

7. HIS OWN MAN

1 Dan Barry, "The Post Reinvents Itself Again in the War of the Tabloids," *The New York Times*, July 8, 2001.
2 Erin McClam, "Former *Post* Editor Files $8 Million Discrimination Suit," *Associated Press*, April 2, 2003.
3 Sharon Krum, "Girl Gotham," *Australian Women's Weekly*, September 1, 2002.
4 Gabriel Sherman, *The Loudest Voice in the Room: How the Brilliant, Bombastic Roger Ailes Built Fox News – and Divided a Country* (New York: Random House, 2018), p. 265.

8. THE WALK-OUT

1 Diane Mermigas, "The Push for Retransmission Fees," *Television Week*, August 18, 2003.
2 Steve Fishman, "The Boy Who Wouldn't Be King."
3 Sharon Krum, "Girl Gotham."
4 Terry McCrann, "Murdoch Spells Out News' View of Crucial Future Still Call Australia Home," *The Herald Sun*, August 19, 2004.
5 Paul Syvret, "It Was the Deal That Had to Be Done," *The Courier-Mail*, September 4, 2004.
6 Neil Chenoweth, "Heir Apparent Chalks Up String of Losses," *The Australian Financial Review*, September 18, 2004.
7 Neil Chenoweth, "Murdoch Struggles to Sell the Good News," *The Australian Financial Review*, August 21, 2004.
8 Trevor Sykes, "Murdoch Bows Out . . . but He'll Still Visit," *The Australian Financial Review*, October 27, 2004.
9 Phillip Koch, "Sarah's 'Little Miracle,'" *The Sunday Mail*, November 14, 2004.

10 Annette Sharp, "Kalan's First Photo Call," *The Sun Herald*, November 14, 2004.
11 Michael Wolff, *The Man Who Owns the News: Inside the Secret World of Rupert Murdoch* (London: Vintage Books, 2010), pp. 41–5, 51–2.
12 Sherman, *The Loudest Voice in the Room*, p. 304.
13 Fishman, "The Boy Who Wouldn't Be King."

PART 2: ILLYRIA

9. ILLYRIA

1 Emiliya Mychasuk and Aline van Duyn, "Murdoch Children Consider Sharing the Wealth," *Financial Times*, August 4, 2005.
2 Andrew Hornery, "Weekend Spike," *The Sydney Morning Herald*, October 8, 2005.
3 Steve Marshall, "Thorpe and Murdoch Join PNG's AIDS Fight," *PM*, ABC Radio, February 1, 2007.
4 Charlie Rose, "Rupert Murdoch," 20 July 2006, charlierose.com.

10. DEAL OR NO DEAL

1 James Chessell, "Lachlan Back with a Bang," *The Australian Financial Review*, January 22, 2008.
2 Wolff, *The Man Who Owns the News*, p. 376.
3 Fleur Leyden, "Murdoch in $3.3b Bid with Packer – It's Game on as Lachlan Returns to His Old Playground," *The Courier-Mail*, January 22, 2008.
4 Andrew Edgecliffe-Johnson, "Lachlan Murdoch Confident on CMH Bid," *Financial Times*, January 23, 2008.
5 Ingrid Mansell and Karen Maley, "Lachlan Murdoch and the Retreat of Empire," *The Australian Financial Review*, March 8, 2008.
6 Sourish Bhattacharyya, "Meet the Foursome Who Run the Rajasthan Royals Team," *Mail Today*, April 28, 2010.
7 Roger Blitz and James Fontanella-Khan, "Supreme Court to Rule Whether Rajasthan Royals Can Return to the Crease," *Financial Times*, November 27, 2010.
8 Nick Tabakoff, "Illyria Takes a $15m Stake in Prime," *The Australian*, April 30, 2009.

11. TROUBLE BREWING

1 Davies, *Hack Attack*, p. 93.
2 Davies, *Hack Attack*, p. 156.
3 Davies, *Hack Attack*, p. 159.
4 Nick Davies, "Murdoch Papers Paid £1m to Gag Phone-hacking Victims," *The Guardian*, July 9, 2009.
5 Jonathan Mahler and Jim Rutenberg, "Imperial Reach," *The New York Times*, April 3, 2019.
6 Mahler and Rutenberg, "Imperial Reach."

7 Sarah Ellison, "The Rules of Succession," *Vanity Fair*, December 2011.

8 Rick Feneley and Emily Dunn, "Mad Monk Bags a Model for Book Launch," *The Sydney Morning Herald*, July 29, 2009.

9 James Chessell, "Not Just a Board Seat but an Ethos at Stake," *The Australian Financial Review*, February 1, 2012.

10 Sharri Markson, "Mischief and Mayhem in TV Land," *The Australian*, October 10, 2014.

11 Tim Arango, "The Murdoch in Waiting," *The New York Times*, February 19, 2011.

12. THE HUMBLEST DAY

1 Ellison, "The Rules of Succession."

2 Neil Tweedle and Matthew Holehouse, "Murdoch's Empire Implodes," *The Daily Telegraph*, July 16, 2011.

3 Pip Bulbeck, "Lachlan Murdoch Named Chairman of Ten Holdings," *The Hollywood Reporter*, February 10, 2012.

13. A DIFFICULT NIGHT

1 Tim Burrowes, *Media Unmade* (Melbourne: Hardie Grant, 2021), pp. 189–90.

2 Neil Chenoweth, *Murdoch's Pirates* (Crows Nest, NSW: Allen & Unwin, 2012), pp. 355, 382.

3 Kamal Ahmed and Richard Blackden, "Unfinished Business," *The Sunday Telegraph*, April 8, 2012.

4 Pip Bulbeck, "News Corp Makes $1.9 Billion Takeover Offer for Australia's Consolidated Media," *The Hollywood Reporter*, June 19, 2012.

5 Burrowes, *Media Unmade*, p. 194.

6 Burrowes, *Media Unmade*, p. 194.

7 Roy Masters, "Inside AFL's $2.5 Billion TV Deal," *The Sydney Morning Herald*, August 9, 2015.

8 Tony Boyd, "Chanticleer's Chook Roast," *The Australian Financial Review*, October 11, 2013.

9 Auletta, "The Heiress."

10 Stephen Mayne, "If Lachlan Wasn't a Murdoch, He'd Be Gone from Ten," *Crikey*, December 7, 2012.

11 Mark Seal, "Seduced and Abandoned," *Vanity Fair*, March 2014.

12 Seal, "Seduced and Abandoned."

13 David Randall, "Rupert Murdoch and Wendi Deng Hire His 'n' Hers Legal Teams," *Independent Online*, June 15, 2013.

14. I NEED YOU TO DO THIS FOR ME

1 Andy Davies, "Revealed: The Rupert Murdoch Tape," *4 News*, July 3, 2013.

2 Neil Chenoweth, "Perspective: Inside a Dynasty," *The Australian Financial Review*, March 29, 2014.

PART 3: SLY FOX

15. CONTINENTAL SHIFT

1 Mahler and Rutenberg, "Imperial Reach."
2 Malcolm Turnbull, "Reach Rule Changes Won't Affect Regional Content," *The Australian*, March 12, 2014.
3 Chris Mitchell, *Making Headlines* (Melbourne: Melbourne University Press, 2016).

16. THE DONALD AND THE LOUDEST VOICE

1 Janice Min, "The Donald Trump Conversation: Murdoch, Ailes, NBC and the Rush of Being TV's 'Ratings Machine,'" *The Hollywood Reporter*, August 19, 2015.
2 Sarah Ellison, "Roger, Over and Out!," *Vanity Fair*, November 1, 2016.
3 Gabriel Sherman, "Has the Clock Run Out on Roger Ailes," *New York Magazine*, July 7, 2016.
4 Brian Stelter, *Hoax: Donald Trump, Fox News and the Dangerous Distortion of Truth* (New York: Simon & Schuster, 2021), p. 68.
5 Ellison, "Roger, Over and Out."
6 Gabriel Sherman, "Murdochs Have Decided to Remove Roger Ailes," *New York Magazine*, July 18, 2016.
7 Debra Birnbaum, "Creepy Details of Roger Ailes, Donald Trump Dealings Emerge in Megyn Kelly's Book," *Variety*, November 10, 2016.
8 Sarah Ellison, "After Ailes, Fox News Has a New Crisis: Can It Keep Megyn Kelly?," *Vanity Fair*, August 25, 2016.
9 Ryan Grim, "Is Shep Smith the Future of Fox News?," *HuffPost*, October 17, 2016.
10 Brooks Barnes and Sydney Ember, "Sons Steer Murdoch Empire Away from Its Past," *The New York Times*, April 23, 2017.
11 Mahler and Rutenberg, "Imperial Reach."
12 Michael Wolff, "Ringside with Steve Bannon at Trump Tower," *The Hollywood Reporter*, November 18, 2016.
13 Stelter, *Hoax*, p. 90.
14 Gabriel Sherman, "The Revenge of Roger's Angels," *New York Magazine*, September 2, 2016.
15 Stelter, *Hoax*, pp. 87–91.
16 Gabriel Sherman, "Fox News Has Decided Bill O'Reilly Has to Go," *New York Magazine*, April 19, 2017. 1
17 Stelter, *Hoax*, p. 291.

17. PAYDAY

1 Christopher Williams, *The Battle for Sky* (London: Bloomsbury, 2019), p. 186.
2 Mahler and Rutenberg, "Imperial Reach."
3 Williams, *The Battle for Sky*, pp. xv–xvii.
4 Mahler and Rutenberg, "Imperial Reach."
5 Mahler and Rutenberg, "Imperial Reach."

6 Yochai Benkler, Robert Faris and Hal Roberts, *Network Propaganda: Manipulation, Disinformation and Radicalization in American Politics* (Oxford: Oxford University Press, 2018), pp. 145–7, 159–66.
7 Stelter, *Hoax*.
8 Jonathan Mahler and Jim Rutenberg, "The New Fox Weapon," *The New York Times*, April 3, 2019.
9 "Text of James Murdoch's Email Condemning Trump's Response to Charlottesville," *The New York Times*, August 17, 2017.
10 Stelter, *Hoax*, pp. 169–71.
11 Gabriel Sherman, "No One Is in Charge," *Vanity Fair*, October 2018.
12 Jonathan Mahler and Jim Rutenberg, "Internal Divisions," *The New York Times*, April 3, 2019.
13 Anousha Sakoui, "Fox Is in Good Shape, Lachlan Murdoch Says Amid Deal Speculation," *Bloomberg*, November 9, 2017.
14 Shalini Ramachandran, "Standing Between Comcast and Fox: Media Titans' Rocky Relationship," *Dow Jones Institutional News*, June 21, 2018.
15 Sarah Ellison, "Lachlan Murdoch Takes Control of Fox Corp, but How Will He Deal with President Trump?," *The Washington Post*, March 20, 2019.
16 Michael Wolff, "What's Behind the Murdochs' Sudden Sale Talks with Disney," *The Hollywood Reporter*, November 7, 2017.
17 Williams, *The Battle for Sky*, pp. 209–10, 214.
18 Matthew Garrahan, Arash Massoudi and James Fontanella-Khan, "James Murdoch Tipped for Disney Role in Fox Deal," *Financial Times*, December 6, 2017.
19 Amol Sharma, Joe Flint and Keach Hagey, "Behind the Murdochs' Sale Talks: Scale, Price and Family Dynamics," the *Wall Street Journal*, December 6, 2017.
20 Maureen Dowd, "James Murdoch, Rebellious Scion," *The New York Times*, October 10, 2020.
21 Paul Bond, "Murdoch vs Iger: How Much Power Could Rupert and Sons Wield at Disney?," *The Hollywood Reporter*, 7 December 2017.
22 Mark Sweney, "Rupert Murdoch Reshapes Media Empire with $66bn Disney Deal," *The Guardian*, December 14, 2017.
23 Neil Chenoweth, "Splitting Heirs," *The Australian Financial Review*, December 16, 2017.
24 Mahler and Rutenberg, "Imperial Reach."
25 Gabriel Sherman, "Rupert Murdoch Hospitalized with Serious Back Injury," *Vanity Fair*, January 17, 2018.
26 David Faber, "Disney's Bob Iger on Fox deal and business with Rupert Murdoch," CNBC, December 22, 2021.

18. LAST MAN STANDING

1 John Koblin, "New Executive of Slimmed-down Fox Network Faces First Big Test," *The New York Times*, May 12, 2019. 1
2 Adam Liptak and Kevin Draper, "Supreme Court Ruling Favors Sports Betting," *The New York Times*, May 14, 2018.
3 Malcolm Turnbull, *A Bigger Picture* (Richmond, Vic.: Hardie Grant Books, 2020), pp. 620–21.
4 Mahler and Rutenberg, "The New Fox Weapon."

5 Joe Aston, "Rupert Murdoch to Kerry Stokes: 'Malcolm Has to Go,'" *The Australian Financial Review*, September 17, 2018.
6 Pamela Williams, "The War on Malcolm," *The Monthly*, February 2019.
7 Turnbull, *A Bigger Picture*, pp. 626–7.
8 https://www.afr.com/policy/how-coup-capital-status-is-hurting-australia-20180824-h14f6u
9 Amanda Meade, "News Corp Bites Back after Uhlmann's Spray on Liberal Leadership," *The Guardian*, August 24, 2018.
10 Turnbull, *A Bigger Picture*, pp. 481–2.

19. WAGES OF FEAR

1 Paul Krugman, "Hate Is on the Ballot Next Week," *The New York Times*, October 30, 2018; Jennifer Rubin, "Enough Platitudes: Let's Name Names," *The Washington Post*, October 29, 2018.
2 John Whitehouse, "Lachlan Murdoch Wants Empathy for Fox Hosts Who Push Propaganda and Racism," *Media Matters for America*, November 1, 2018.
3 Gabriel Sherman, "Believe Me, Donald Trump Is the Best Cable News President in History," *Vanity Fair*, December 1, 2018.
4 Christopher Williams, "James to Take 'Zero' interest in Murdoch Firms after Split," *The Telegraph*, May 26, 2019.
5 Cristina Lopez G., "Leaked Chat Messages Show Members of White Supremacist Group Identity Evropa Are Obsessed with Tucker Carlson," *Media Matters for America*, March 8, 2019.

20. THE POWER OF NOW

1 Ellison, "Lachlan Murdoch Takes Control of Fox Corp."
2 Mahler and Rutenberg, "The New Fox Weapon."
3 Andrew Wallenstein, "Quick Take: Credible Labs Investment Hints at a Refocused Fox Corp," *Variety*, August 5, 2019.
4 Stelter, *Hoax*, pp. 269–76.
5 Nicholas Jasinski, "Fox Stock Is Way Down Since the Disney Deal. Here's Why It Can Come Back," *Barron's Online*, October 9, 2019.
6 Christopher Knaus, "News Corp Employee Lashes Climate 'Misinformation' in Bushfire Coverage with Blistering Email," *The Guardian*, January 10, 2020.
7 Lachlan Cartwright, "James Murdoch Slams Fox News and News Corp Over Climate-Change Denial," *The Daily Beast*, January 14, 2020.

21. CONTAGION AND CRISIS

1 Ben Smith, "Rupert Murdoch Put His Son in Charge of Fox. It Was a Dangerous Mistake," *The New York Times*, March 23, 2020.

2 Dowd, "James Murdoch, Rebellious Scion."
3 Emma Jo Morris and Gabrielle Fonrouge, "Smoking Gun Email Reveals How Hunter Biden Introduced Ukranian Businessman to VP Dad," *New York Post*, October 14, 2020.
4 Lachlan Murdoch, "We Must Protect the Australian Way of Life," address to the Institute of Public Affairs, March 30, 2022, ipa.org.au.

22. THE DECISION DESK

1 Chris Stirewalt and Eliana Johnson, "Says Who," *Ink Stained Wretches* (podcast), July 16, 2021.
2 Lis Power, "In Two Weeks After It Called the Election, Fox News Cast Doubt on the Results Nearly 800 Times," *Media Matters for America*, January 14, 2021.
3 Phillip Bump, "This Might Be the Most Embarrassing Document Created by a White House Staffer," *The Washington Post*, December 18, 2020.
4 Alex Barker, "James Murdoch Blasts US Media for Unleashing 'Insidious Force,'" *Financial Times*, January 16, 2021.
5 Lachlan Cartwright, "Fox News CEO Suzanne Scott's Job Is in Jeopardy, Insiders Say," *The Daily Beast*, January 15, 2021.
6 David Lat, "Is Viet Dinh the Most Powerful Lawyer in America?," *Original Jurisdiction*, March 18, 2021.

23. KEEP WINNING

1 Margaret Sullivan, "The Pro-Trump Media World Peddled the Lies that Fueled the Capitol Mob. Fox News Led the Way," *The Washington Post*, January 7, 2021.
2 Brian Steinberg, "Fox Corp Exec Viet Dinh Plays Down Speculation He's Making Big Decisions at Company," *Variety*, March 17, 2021.
3 Claire Atkinson, "Exclusive: Fox CEO Lachlan Murdoch Talks about His Dad, Tucker Carlson, Trump and Why He Plans to Stick Around," *Business Insider*, May 19, 2021.
4 Bill Grueskin, "Australia Pressured Google and Facebook to Pay for Journalism: Is America Next?," *Columbia Journalism Review*, March 9, 2022.
5 Bernard Keane and Glenn Dyer, "Mates Looking After Mates," *Crikey*, November 26, 2020.
6 Alexandra Bruell and Keach Hagey, "Facebook Rethinks News Deals, and Publishers Stand to Lose Millions in Payments," the *Wall Street Journal*, June 9, 2022.
7 Jeremy Barr, "At Fox News, a Post-election Shake-up Brings More Opinion at the Expense of News," *The Washington Post*, January 19, 2021.
8 Nikki McCann Ramirez, "Tucker Carlson, the Face of Fox News, Just Gave His Full Endorsement to the White Nationalist Conspiracy Theory That Has Motivated Mass Shootings," *Media Matters for America*, April 9, 2021.
9 Oliver Gill, "Murdoch Set to Wager on Flutter's US Boom," *The Daily Telegraph*, March 3, 2021.
10 "Fox and the Big Lie," *Four Corners*, ABC TV, August 23, 2021.
11 Christopher Warren, "Many Happy Returns, Lachlan. The Biggest Office Awaits," *Crikey*, September 8, 2021.

12 Marisa Guthrie, "'I Sleep Well at Night': Suzanne Scott on Running Fox News," *The Hollywood Reporter*, October 7, 2021.

24. "PATRIOT' SCOURGE

1 "Tucker Carlson," Politifact.com, November 4, 2021.

2 Michael M. Grynbaum, "Geraldo Rivera Criticizes His Fox News Colleague Tucker Carlson," *The New York Times*, October 28, 2021.

3 Sarah Ellison, "A Year Ago, Fox News Considered a Breakup with Trump. 2021 Changed Those Plans," *The Washington Post*, December 23, 2021.

4 Tony Boyd, "It's Deal Time for Rupert Murdoch," *The Australian Financial Review*, January 6, 2022.

5 Michael M. Grynbaum, "Chris Wallace Says Life at Fox News Became 'Unsustainable,'" *The New York Times*, March 27, 2022.

6 Sarah Ellison and Josh Dawsey, "Lachlan Murdoch, Once the Ambivalent Fox Heir, Makes His Views Clear," *The Washington Post*, April 9, 2022.

7 Guy Rundle, "The Australian Way of Life is Collectivist. Lachlan's 'Freedom' Cry is a US Import," *Crikey*, March 31, 2022.

8 Dominic Rushe and Amanda Meade, "Rupert Murdoch says Trump should stop focusing "on the past' in rare rebuke," *The Guardian*, November 18, 2021.

9 Mark Joella, "Sam Donaldson: Fox News didn't air 1/6 hearing because Fox 'learned its lesson' on election night 2020," *Forbes* June 12, 2022.

10 Paddy Manning, "Jerry canned: new details in Murdoch divorce," *The Saturday Paper*, July 16, 2022.

11 Lachlan Cartwright, "Lachlan Murdoch helped daddy Rupert divorce Jerry Hall," *The Daily Beast*, July 11, 2022.

12 Nicholas Confessore, "How Tucker Carlson stoked white fear to conquer cable," *The New York Times*, April 30, 2022.

13 PBS Newshour, "How misinformation and the partisan divide drove a surge in US COVID deaths," May 11, 2022.

14 "The president who stood still on Jan. 6" (editorial), the *Wall Street Journal*, July 22, 2022; "Trump's silence on Jan. 6 is damning" (editorial), *New York Post*, July 22, 2022.